MW01015065

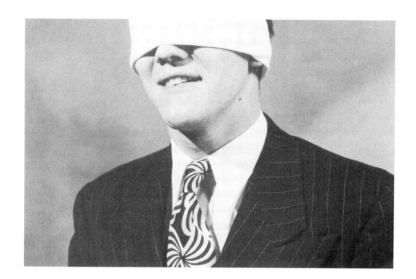

## The DevelopMentor Series
Don Box, Editor

Addison-Wesley has joined forces with DevelopMentor, a premiere developer resources company, to produce a series of technical books written by developers for developers. DevelopMentor boasts a prestigious technical staff that includes some of the world's best-known computer science professionals.

*"Works in **The DevelopMentor Series** will be practical and informative sources on the tools and techniques for applying component-based technologies to real-world, large-scale distributed systems."*
—Don Box

### Titles in the Series:

Essential COM
Don Box
0-201-63446-5

Essential XML
*Beyond Markup*
Don Box, Aaron Skonnard, and John Lam
0-201-70914-7

Programming Windows Security
Keith Brown
0-201-60442-6

Advanced Visual Basic 6
*Power Techniques for Everyday Programs*
Matthew Curland
0-201-70712-8

Transactional COM+
*Building Scalable Applications*
Tim Ewald
0-201-61594-0

ASP Internals
Jon Flanders
0-201-61618-1

Essential IDL
*Interface Design for COM*
Martin Gudgin
0-201-61595-9

Effective Visual Basic
*How to Improve Your VB/COM+ Applications*
Joe Hummel
0-201-70476-5

Debugging Windows Programs
*Strategies, Tools, and Techniques for Visual C++ Programmers*
Everett N. McKay and Mike Woodring
0-201-70238-X

**Watch for future titles in The DevelopMentor Series.**

# Transactional COM+

## Building Scalable Applications

Tim Ewald

**Addison-Wesley**

Boston • San Francisco • New York • Toronto • Montreal
London • Munich • Paris • Madrid
Capetown • Sydney • Tokyo • Singapore • Mexico City

The publisher offers discounts on this book when ordered in quantity for special sales. For more
information, please contact:

Pearson Education Corporate Sales Division
One Lake Street
Upper Saddle River, NJ 07458
(800) 382-3419
corpsales@pearsontechgroup.com

Visit us on the Web at www.awl.com/cseng/

*Library of Congress Cataloging-in-Publication Data*
Ewald, Tim
    Transactional COM+ : building scalable appllications / Tim Ewald.
        p. cm. — (The developMentor series)
        ISBN 0-201-61594-0
    1. Client/server computing 2. COM (Computer architecture) 3.
Microsoft Transaction server. I. Title. II. Series.
    QA76.9.C55 E95 2001
    005.2'76—cs21                                        2001018182

ISBN 0-201-61594-0

Text printed on recycled paper.
1 2 3 4 5 6 7 8 9 – MA – 05 04 03 02 01
*First printing, March 2001*

*For Sarah Shor, who insisted that I finish this project alone and was willing to wait while I did, and for Barbara Shor, a consummate wordsmith who provided endless support, but could not stay to see how it all turned out.*

# Contents

# Foreword

The American president and Civil War general Ulysses S. Grant was no musician. "I know only two tunes," said Grant. "One of them is 'Yankee Doodle' and the other one isn't."

Grant's binary approach to melody isn't really all that different from the problem of building a scalable application: An app is either scalable enough or it isn't. There's not much middle ground.

Yet the truly problematic thing about application scalability is that it's a design-time issue. If an application is designed incorrectly, it will never scale. You need to make the right decisions up front—fixing them later can be very, very painful. The hard part is figuring out what those decisions should be. What are the rules for building scalable multitier applications in the Microsoft environment? More precisely, what are the rules for building those applications using COM+, the core technology Microsoft has given us to help create these kinds of apps?

*Transactional COM+* answers those questions. In these pages, Tim Ewald starts with a quick review of the basics, making sure we're all up to speed on the fundamentals of the problem. Because building first-rate enterprise applications isn't simple, the book ultimately goes into substantial detail, providing what you need to know to create scalable applications using COM+. Best of all, that information is summarized in a series of memorable and easy-to-understand rules.

Tim is uniquely qualified to produce this guide. He has a hands-on understanding of the subject gained through lots of study, teaching, and practical experience. He communicates his knowledge well, and he's an all-around smart guy. He also doesn't shy away from expressing the opinions he's developed through his experience. Not everyone will agree with his views, but it's refreshing to see someone who's so direct.

As Microsoft has grown from a desktop-focused company into its current enterprise orientation, its software has become increasingly complicated. This is mostly a good thing. Because the applications we're trying to build using that software have also become more complicated, we need the services Microsoft gives us. Still, understanding this complexity is a challenging undertaking. Books like this one are an essential part of the process.

Squeezing the most out of COM+ means grasping how it works in a deep way. *Transactional COM+* is the most direct path I've seen between what you know today and what you need to know to build scalable COM+ applications.

David Chappell
www.chappellassoc.com
October 2000

# Preface

I am (metaphorically speaking) the man on the cover of this book. Or at least I was four years ago. That's when I first encountered the Microsoft Transaction Server (MTS), the precursor to COM+, and knew that my life as a COM developer had changed forever. I very rapidly discovered that the traditional COM object models I was used to did not work in the MTS environment. That annoyed and fascinated me, so I set out to understand why. At first I was blind in my belief that the MTS team had things all wrong—that its creators did not understand distributed objects at all. Over time, however, I came to see why MTS worked the way it did. The answer, quite simply, was scalability.

MTS was designed to simplify the development of scalable distributed applications, and everything it did was in service of that goal. Viewed in that light, the things MTS did with objects (e.g., not sharing them between clients and deactivating them when their transactions ended) finally made sense to me. While all of this was happening, I was spending a lot of time writing and teaching classes about MTS. I met a number of developers who were struggling the same way I had and who needed help. Like me, they wanted to know how MTS worked, why it worked that way, and, most important, how to design systems that used it. It became clear to me that I had a story to tell and that I had to write this book.

It took a long time. In fact, the writing process took so long that this book isn't about MTS at all, but its descendant, COM+.

## What Is COM+?

COM+ is a runtime environment that provides services to instances of classes that declare their desire to use the services. For example, if a class declares that it needs causality-based call synchronization, the COM+ runtime makes sure that only one logical thread of action invokes an instance's methods at a time.

Or, if a class declares that it needs a distributed transaction, the COM+ runtime makes sure that one is available. COM+-based systems can be written in C++, Visual Basic 6, or any other COM-friendly language today; and the systems in C#, Visual Basic 7, or any other Common Language Runtime–friendly language tomorrow. (For more information, see Appendix A, "Toward .NET".) The COM+ runtime serves as the foundation for many higher-level technologies, including Internet Information Server (IIS), Active Server Pages (ASP), Site Server, Application Center 2000, and Biztalk Server 2000.

COM+ is the cornerstone of a framework of technologies designed to support the development of large-scale distributed applications on the Windows platform. The current, shipping version of the framework is called Windows DNA. The next version is called .NET. Both versions have similar overall architectures that are based on three assumptions about the needs of scalable systems:

1. They must be accessible by multiple users on internal networks' machines and the Internet, running both browser-based and custom client applications.
2. They must use multiple server machines to handle a high volume of client requests concurrently.
3. They must be robust in the face of failure.

From these assumptions, both frameworks derive three basic principles:

1. *System logic is consolidated on servers, not on clients or in backend databases.* Servers can share resources (e.g., database connections), encapsulate database schemas and data access technologies, and offer a tightly controlled security environment.
2. *Transactions are at the center of the programming model.* They provide a standard model for protecting distributed system state in the face of both concurrent access and system failure. The majority of system state must be kept under transactional control (e.g., in a database).
3. *The components in a system communicate using a variety of protocols.* Clients typically communicate with servers using HTTP and, increasingly, Simple Object Access Protocol (SOAP); DCOM and Microsoft Message Queue (MSMQ) also are sometimes used. Servers typically communicate with one another using DCOM, MSMQ, and database-specific data access protocols; in addition, sometimes HTTP and SOAP are used.

COM+ is designed to make it easier to develop systems that adhere to these principles. It first assumed this position in the Windows DNA framework, and it retains it as we move forward into the .NET arena.

## What This Book Is About

*Transactional COM+: Building Scalable Applications* is about how and why COM+ works and how to build COM+-based applications. You cannot write software to solve a problem unless you understand the problem's essential nature and general solution, as well as the full details of the technology you are using. To that end, in the abstract, this book is about the design of scalable systems. In the concrete, it is about the mechanics of the COM+ runtime, including its use of processes, contexts, causalities, threads, objects, transactions, and communication protocols.

### What to Expect

Here is a brief description of each chapter in the book.

Chapter 1, Scalability, describes the basic problem of scalability, explains why scalable systems use transactions, and why they do not use traditional object models. It evolves the basic object model used in COM+-based systems.

Chapter 2, Atoms, describes context and causality, the two basic constructs on top of which all of the COM+ runtime services are built. It explains how both constructs relate to objects and how objects can interact with them.

Chapter 3, Mechanics, examines the relationship between contexts and objects, including the context relativity of interface pointers and the overhead that contexts represent in both time and space.

Chapter 4, Threads, introduces apartments and activities, the two higher-level constructs COM+ uses to regulate an object's degree of thread affinity and synchronization, respectively.

Chapter 5, Objects, focuses on object pooling and just-in-time activation (JITA) and how these services change the lifecycle of an object in order to use resources more efficiently. Special attention is paid to deconstructing the myths about the scalability benefits that JITA provides.

Chapter 6, Transactions, explores the mechanics of local and distributed transactions and introduces transaction streams, the higher-level construct COM+ uses to associate objects with distributed transactions.

Chapter 7, Isolation, discusses the basic techniques databases use to stop transactions from interfering with one another while at the same time maximizing concurrency and therefore throughput. Cross-transaction application-level locking schemes are also covered.

Chapter 8, Protocols, examines the integration between the Internet Information Server and COM+, including how ISAPI DLLs and ASP pages relate to contexts, apartments, activities, and transaction streams. In addition, SOAP and MSMQ are covered.

Chapter 9, Design, provides general advice on the design of COM+-based systems. Topics include implementing client tasks using one or more transactions; efficient data access; middle-tier, shared-state, and per-client conversation state management; and the inherent tension between scalability and reusability.

There are also four appendices. Appendix A, Toward .NET, covers the shift to .NET and explains how CLR classes take advantage of COM+. Appendix B, Building a Better Connection Pool, shows how to use object pooling to build a database connection pool that is more flexible than the one provided by OLE DB (and used by ADO). Appendix C, Debugging, provides useful information that makes debugging COM+ code easier. Appendix D, Catalog Attributes and Component Services Explorer Property Pages contains diagrams that map catalog attributes to the user interface elements on Component Services Explorer property pages.

**What Not to Expect**

This book is intended for developers who are designing and implementing COM+-based systems. It assumes that you know how to implement COM classes and how to write a simple ASP page. It also assumes that you know how to use the COM+ and IIS administration tools, the Component Services Explorer (CSE), and the Internet Services Manager, respectively.

There are three COM+ topics that I did not include in this book. First, while this book mentions COM+ role-based security at a couple of points in the narrative where it becomes relevant, it does not include a complete treatment of the topic because it has already been covered in detail in Keith Brown's excellent book, *Programming Windows Security*.

Second, I chose to ignore the two ancillary COM+ services—Queued Components (QCs) and Loosely Coupled Events (LCEs)—because both mechanisms have significant limitations that render them useless in the general case. Specifically, although QCs can be used to send messages asynchronously into a COM+ server process, they cannot be used to send messages to other processes, that is, back to a client process. Although LCEs make it possible for a publisher to send an event to multiple subscribers without having to know who they are, the default delivery mechanism is a synchronous, blocking method call. You can make LCEs asynchronous by using them with QCs, but then events can only be fired into COM+ server processes. These problems make both services essentially useless for bidirectional client-server communication (they may in some circumstances be useful for server-server communication). In general, I discard both QCs and LCEs in favor of the Microsoft Message Queue, which makes it easy to build equivalent functionality without these unfortunate limitations.

Third, I did not include Compensating Resource Managers (CRMs) because of a lack of both time and space.

### Rules

This is not a COM+ cookbook. However, I have done my best to provide as much concrete advice as possible to help you understand how to design and implement COM+-based systems. Specific pieces of advice are identified as "Rules," which are highlighted in the text in the manner shown below.

 **P.1** _____

Pay attention to the rules.

_____

There are fewer rules in later chapters, a simple reflection of the fact that as topics get more complex there are fewer concrete guidelines on how to do things. The final chapter compensates for this by offering general advice on system design that follows the rules defined earlier.

## A Note about Source Code

Like COM+, this book is programming language–neutral. It speaks in generic terms whenever possible, but covers language-specific issues when necessary. Most of the sample source code in this book is written in C++, although there are some examples in Visual Basic and JavaScript . I chose C++ partly because it is the only language that allows you to explore all the dark corners of COM+ and partly because it is my personal language of choice (or it was until C# came along). Also, most of the sample code in this book is written in a style I picked up from my friend Chris Sells. It makes heavy use of ATL smart types (e.g., `CComPtr`, `CComBSTR`, etc.) and poor-man's exception handling, that is, returning from the middle of functions. Neither my language nor my style should be seen as significant in any way; you should write your COM+ classes in whatever language and style you desire.

## More Information and Errata

This book includes a Web site, which features sample code and other resources. The URL is *http://www.develop.com/books/txcom*.

I have done my best to ensure that this book is free of errors. However, given the scope of the work, especially spelunking through the dark corners of the COM+ runtime, there are bound to be some issues. If you find a bug, please post it to the book's Web site, where I'll maintain an up-to-date list of fixes.

## Acknowledgments

First and foremost, I would like to thank Sarah Shor for sharing her life with me. Never doubt that you come before all technology. Thank you also to the rest of my family for letting me ignore you for so long. And a special thank you to Alan Ewald for always being willing to share his experiences and insights about the design of distributed systems.

Thank you to all of my technical colleagues at DevelopMentor, the incredibly special community in which I am privileged enough to work. By participating in seemingly endless conversations about how COM+ works, you have influenced this work more than you know. A special thank you to Craig Andera, Dan Sullivan, Martin Gudgin, Jon Flanders, Bob Beauchamin, Stu Halloway, Simon Horrell, Keith Brown, and Chris Sells for believing that I had an interesting story to tell. And an incredibly special thank you to Don Box for knowing I had a song in my heart that I needed to sing and for helping me live a rich and fulfilling technical life. Thank you to everyone else at DevelopMentor, too. You have all been very patient with me while I finished this project. Thanks especially to Mike Abercrombie for understanding that my technical work had to come first.

Thank you to Simon Horrell, Dan Sullivan, Bob Beauchamin, Stu Halloway, Martin Gudgin, Alan Ewald, and Mary Kirtland of Microsoft for reviewing chapters and providing feedback. Thank you to all the students, conference attendees, and mailing list participants who have provided feedback about different parts of this story too. Thank you to Joe Long of Microsoft for answering questions about the mechanics of various COM+ runtime services and to Jonathan Hawkins of Microsoft for explaining the relationship between .NET and COM+.

Thank you to David Chappell for writing my foreword and for dressing so well. You give us all something to aspire too.

Thank you to everyone at Addison-Wesley who helped produce this book, including Marilyn Rash for speeding production despite my endless delays; John Wait for explaining some of the inner workings of the technical publishing industry; Carter Shanklin for signing my contract (before leaving Addison-Wesley to pursue other aims); and, most importantly, my editor Kristin Erickson for suffering through this with me and for still being willing to accept my phone calls.

And finally, thank you to Microsoft for creating the technologies that have kept me occupied for the past ten years. COM+ was quite a puzzle; keep them coming.

Tim Ewald
Nashua, NH
January 2001
http://staff.develop.com/ewald

# Chapter 1

# Scalability

You are striving to build a three-tier distributed system that can service many client requests concurrently. Your system may be for internal use, or it may be for external use by your company's customers and business partners, who want to access it over the Internet. You want your system to have a scalable architecture, but what does that really mean? The architectures of distributed systems are often evaluated in terms of their *throughput,* their ability to complete a given number of logical operations in a specific period of time. The goal is an architecture that ensures throughput high enough to satisfy client demand even at peak load times without sacrificing reasonable response times for individual requests. A scalable architecture can increase throughput as client demand grows, *without redesign,* simply by taking advantage of additional hardware. My goal in writing this book is to help you understand how to design scalable architectures based on COM+, which uses objects to model the specifics of a problem domain. COM+ design style requires a significant departure from the traditional object-oriented models used in stand-alone and small distributed COM-based systems. Before I explain why, let's review some basic concepts about scalability.

## Scalability Basics

An architecture's ability to scale is typically assessed in terms of the eventual maximum height of throughput growth it offers. Consider the graph in Figure 1-1. It measures throughput against hardware resources for a hypothetical design. Note that this graph shows nonlinear throughput growth. In other words, the rate of throughput growth slows and eventually plateaus. The plateau represents the maximum throughput for the architecture regardless of how many new hardware resources become available.

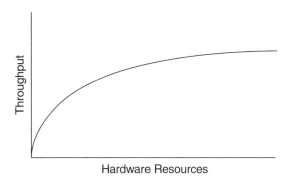

**Figure 1-1  Throughput compared to hardware resources**

The factor that determines how high throughput ultimately climbs is the degree of *contention* for resources at runtime. Contention arises when multiple concurrent operations try to gain exclusive access to a shared resource. Because only one can access the resource at a time, all other operations block and wait until the resource is available or until they decide to—or are forced to—give up. As contention for a resource increases, a bottleneck grows. In this situation, increasing concurrency offers no additional benefit; in fact, it is likely to make things worse. An operation that is waiting for a resource it requires to complete its work may have already acquired *other* resources that *other* operations need to complete their work. Those other operations have to block, too. The resulting ripple effect slows operations dramatically, and it may introduce deadlocks as well. Once this process begins, starting more operations just ties things into tighter knots.

You can take two steps to reduce contention for a given resource. First, you can make sure resources are used only when absolutely necessary and then as quickly as possible. In other words, make code that uses a precious resource as efficiently as possible. Unfortunately, tuning for efficiency simply postpones the time when access to a resource becomes a bottleneck. The most efficient code in the world will not help if concurrency continues to increase. Eventually, enough operations will require access to the resource that a second step will be necessary. The resource will have to be replicated.

Hardware is a contended resource. Servers need access to hardware resources (e.g., CPU cycles, network bandwidth, and disks) to process client requests. If a server accepts enough concurrent client requests, contention for its hardware resources will cause a bottleneck. Once that occurs, accepting more requests is a mistake and produces rapidly diminishing returns. Upgrading the resources and optimizing the code that uses them to service requests can postpone the point at which a bottleneck develops. Once upgrade options are exhausted, or just too expensive, and the code is as efficient as it is going to get, the final step is to replicate the resources—add a server.

Information is also a contended resource. Most client requests need access to data of some kind. In many distributed systems, each piece of data is maintained in one place, that is, in a particular process on a particular server machine, where it can be manipulated using some form of interprocess communication (IPC). Because a piece of data lives on one machine, all the concerns about efficient use of its hardware resources are relevant. But there is another issue. If multiple concurrent client requests need sole access to the same piece of information, their work must be synchronized using an exclusive lock. If a server accepts enough concurrent client requests that need access to the same pieces of data, contention for locks will cause a bottleneck. Depending on the operations being performed and the sophistication of the locking strategy, this may or may not occur before contention for hardware resources becomes a problem. Optimizing the code that uses some data to service requests can postpone the point at which locks become bottlenecks. Once the code is as efficient as it is going to get, the final step is to replicate the resource—make a copy of the data.

Unfortunately, replicating data may not be easy. Data that does not change, such as read-only reference data, is not a problem. You can copy it as many times and to as many places as necessary. But data that changes presents a problem. If data is replicated, you need some scheme to keep all the copies synchronized. This significantly increases the complexity of a design. Efficiency concerns and distributed failure modes make it impossible to keep copies of data on multiple machines synchronized all the time. Instead, the copies are synchronized only periodically, which means there's latency in the propagation of changes from one copy of the data to another. If replicated data is used to respond to client requests, the answer a client gets may depend on which copy of the data was used to respond to its query. Whether replication of data is necessary or acceptable depends on the sort of system you are building. For very large systems, though, it will inevitably be required. (You may be able to resolve some bottlenecks by partitioning data before you replicate it. However, eventually, each contention for data in each partition will force replication.)

Clearly, the degree of contention for shared hardware and information resources constrains the height of an architecture's scalability. The ultimate goal of a scalable design is to eliminate contention, but this is impossible. In every system there is a bottleneck that, when encountered, causes throughput to plateau as shown in Figure 1-1. Throughput improves as each bottleneck is removed, but because some other obstacle always looms on the horizon, you cannot get continued linear throughput growth; there is always a plateau. How many bottlenecks you have to remove from a system depends on how much throughput you need. Removing *just enough* bottlenecks to meet your needs is the essence of scalable system design.

Designing a scalable system—making the right decisions about how to manage resources—is difficult. Designing a scalable system using objects is especially challenging, even when you use COM+. Many traditional object-oriented designs fostered in stand-alone single-process applications have been passed on to distributed object applications. Unfortunately, the tendency of these designs to map each abstract entity in a problem domain to a single object somewhere in memory inhibits scalability. The crux of the problem is that objects themselves, when used as shared resources, represent a source of contention. To understand why requires a firm grasp of the concept of object identity. This is the necessary first step toward an object model that supports scalability, which is the goal of COM+-based systems.

## Identity

Most developers agree that objects are a combination of state and behavior, but there is also a critical third factor, *identity*. Identity is the unique aspect of an object that controls how its class's behavior gets mapped onto its state. In modern programming languages, such as C++, Visual Basic (VB), and Java, that aspect is the location of the object in memory. In other words, identity is defined in terms of an address.

Consider a simple class that describes a person defined in C++.

```
class Person
{
   long m_nAge;
public:
   void AgeGracefully(long nYears){ m_nAge += nYears; }
};
```

This `Person` class tracks age using the data member `m_nAge`. The method `AgeGracefully` adjusts `m_nAge` by `nYears`.

Any process that uses the `Person` class has a single copy of its code in memory at runtime. With that one copy present, any number of `Person` objects can be instantiated and manipulated. For example, you could create three people and ask them to age by 17, 29, and 50 years, respectively.

```
Person p1, p2, p3;
p1.AgeGracefully(17);
p2.AgeGracefully(29);
p3.AgeGracefully(50);
```

This example leads to an interesting question: If there is only one copy of the code for the `AgeGracefully` method in memory, how does it know which object's state it is supposed to affect?

The answer is identity. Every method of every class takes an extra, implicit first parameter, a reference to the state of the object to which the behavior is to be applied. This is hidden from the caller; it gets pushed onto the stack along with the other arguments and the return address. From the callee's point of view, however, the reference is available as a member variable, the `this` pointer in C++, the `Me` reference in Visual Basic, or the `this` reference in Java. The `AgeGracefully` method could be re-implemented to use the reference explicitly.

```
void AgeGracefully(long nYears)
{
   this->m_nAge += nYears;
}
```

Although this might be considered more precise, methods usually aren't implemented this way. Instead, each method relies on the compiler to use the reference implicitly when it refers to data members or other methods of its class.

## Identity in COM

Identity in COM is also based on address, but the mechanics are a bit different. COM deals with pointers to interfaces, not pointers to objects as a whole, and it defines identity in terms of the one interface all COM classes are guaranteed to implement, IUnknown. The COM specification mandates that an object must always return the same physical pointer value when asked for IUnknown via a call to QueryInterface. How COM's notion of identity maps to an underlying implementation language's notion of identity is an implementation detail. In C++ it is usually a side effect of multiple inheritance; in Visual Basic and Java it is managed by the virtual machine. Although identity in COM is very similar to—and maps to—identity in C++, Visual Basic, and Java, it offers one additional feature that language-level identity does not provide. COM identity can be maintained in the face of distribution, even when the code invoking a method on an object and the object itself live in separate processes on different machines on a network.

The COM remoting architecture supports this behavior by using proxy objects. Whenever code executing in one context needs to call a method of a COM object living in another context, perhaps in another process on another machine, the invocation is made through a proxy.[1] A *proxy* is a stand-in for a real object that knows how to package method calls and forward them to the real object, wherever it happens to be. A *stub*, an object running in the real object's context, intercepts the forwarded invocations and converts them back into standard calls.

Proxies and stubs are created automatically as needed when interface pointers are passed to and returned from interface methods and system APIs. The COM plumbing makes sure that an object is associated with at most one stub in its own context and at most one proxy in any other context, as shown in Figure 1-2. In this figure, one object, identified by a unique IUnknown pointer value, exists in context C. One proxy, also identified by a unique IUnknown pointer value, represents the original object in each of the two foreign contexts A and B. These guarantees allow COM's notion of identity to be preserved across contexts. Each stub is linked to a particular IUnknown pointer value and

---

[1] A *context* is an environment within a process that provides runtime services to objects. Contexts are described in detail in Chapter 2, Atoms.

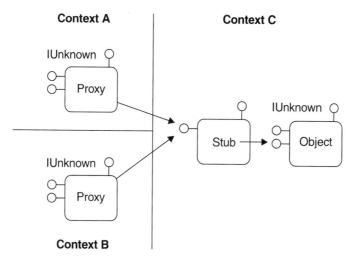

**Figure 1-2 Cross-context identity**

each proxy is linked to a particular stub. Each proxy is a COM object in its own right and is identified by a unique IUnknown pointer value. In other words, in its own context a COM object is uniquely identified by the value of its IUnknown pointer. In any other context, a COM object is uniquely identified by the value of its proxy's IUnknown pointer. This architecture makes it possible for any number of clients to access the same COM object.

## Sharing Identities

One basic tenet of traditional object-oriented design is that an abstract problem domain entity should be mapped to a single object somewhere in memory. This idea has been carried over to the design of distributed COM applications, where it is very often inappropriate. Perhaps the most extreme example of this style is the *singleton* technique. A singleton is an object that is the one and only instance of its class. Clients acquire a reference to a singleton object through some well-known access point. Singletons are often used to encapsulate shared state such as with global variables. An implementation technique that is closely related to the singleton is the *named object*. Like singletons, named objects can be accessed by multiple clients. Unlike singletons, however, multiple named objects—each one representing a different problem domain entity—may be instances of the same class.

### Implementing Named Objects

Returning to the `Person` example, imagine a distributed system that allows multiple clients to access any number of `Person` objects, identifying each one by name. Implementing this scheme using distributed COM is reasonably straightforward; you just need a way to return a reference to one object to each client that asks for that object by name. Then you can sit back and let the COM plumbing work its magic. The easiest way to set this up is to funnel each client request through an intermediate object, a "finder."

Consider this version of the `Person` class modeled as a COM interface called `IPerson`.

```
interface IPerson : IUnknown
{
  [propput] HRESULT Age([in] long nAge);
  [propget] HRESULT Age([out, retval] long *pnAge);
  HRESULT AgeGracefully([in] long nYears);
}
```

This interface can be implemented this way.

```
class Person : public IPerson,
                … // Other details left out for clarity
{
  long m_nAge;
public:
  Person() : m_nAge(0) {}
  STDMETHODIMP put_Age(long nAge)
  {
    m_nAge = nAge;
    return S_OK;
  }
  STDMETHODIMP get_Age(long *pnAge)
  {
    *pnAge = m_nAge;
    return S_OK;
  }
  STDMETHODIMP AgeGracefully(long nYears)
  {
    m_nAge += nYears;
    return S_OK;
  }
  … // Other details left out for clarity
};
```

If a server wants to expose multiple, named `Person` objects, it needs an intermediate object that exposes a helper interface. `INamedFinder` is an example.

```
interface INamedFinder : IUnknown
{
   HRESULT GetNamedPerson([in] BSTR bstrName,
                          [out, retval] IPerson **ppPerson);
}
```

The `GetNamedPerson` method takes a string as input and returns an `IPerson` reference. Here is an implementation of this new interface.

```
Person g_Bob;
Person g_Jane;
class NamedFinder : public INamedFinder,
                    ... // Other details left out for clarity
{
public:
   HRESULT GetNamedPerson(BSTR bstr, IPerson **ppPerson)
   {
     // if name is Bob or Jane, return reference to object
     if (wcscmp(bstr, OLESTR("Bob")) == 0)
       return g_Bob.QueryInterface(IID_IPerson, (void**)ppPerson);
     else if (wcscmp(bstr, OLESTR("Jane")) == 0)
       return g_Jane.QueryInterface(IID_IPerson, (void**)ppPerson);
     else return E_INVALIDARG; // name is unknown
   }
   ... // Other details left out for clarity
};
```

Any number of clients can use their own `NamedFinder`, call `GetNamed Person`, and retrieve a reference to a particular shared `Person`, in this case either Bob or Jane. If a single client retrieves two references to the same remote `Person`, the COM plumbing will ensure that the same proxy is always returned.

```
' create two named fers
Dim f1, f2 As INamedFinder
Set f1 = New NamedFinder
Set f2 = New NamedFinder
' get two person references
Dim p1, p2 As IP
Set p1 = f1.GetNamedPerson("Jane")
Set p2 = f2.GetNamedPerson("Jane")
```

```
' compare references
If (p1 Is p2) Then
  MsgBox "There is only one person named Jane!"
End If
p1.AgeGracefully 32
MsgBox "Jane is " & p2.Age & " years old"
```

It doesn't matter whether `p1` or `p2` is used to manipulate the `Person`; they always refer to the same object. Figure 1-3 illustrates. In this example, the set of available named objects is fixed. But nothing would stop the collection from being dynamic. In fact, if you extended this model so that clients could add named objects to the collection themselves, your `NamedFinder` class would form the basis for the much sought-after COM name service.

### The Problem with Sharing COM Objects

Sharing COM objects as named objects, or in any other way, is perfectly natural and intuitive. It is the legacy of years of experience using objects to build stand-alone, single-process Windows applications. Unfortunately, in terms of scalabil-

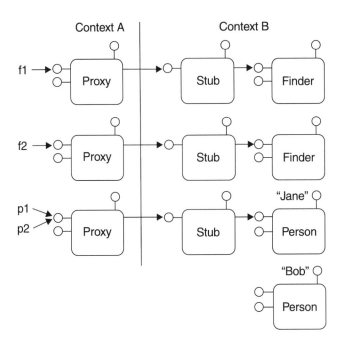

**Figure 1-3   Named objects and finders**

ity, it is also extremely limiting. The beauty and power of the COM plumbing is its ability to make a single object, as uniquely identified by an `IUnknown` pointer value, accessible from any code executing in any context, even another process on another machine. But the implicit communication this entails—the automatic forwarding of method invocations to the object's execution context—is problematic because it binds the object's behavior to a particular machine. *In other words, COM identity is not just a mapping of behavior to state, but to hardware as well.* Remember that every machine has a maximum capacity for doing work. If an object's behavior is bound to a single server, the object's throughput is constrained as well. As more and more clients invoke methods on the object, contention for the underlying hardware resources rises until a bottleneck develops. This leads to this simple observation: Scalable access to a single shared COM—or C++, VB, or Java—object is impossible.

## Identity Revisited

The mechanics of identity restrict the throughput of a single COM object. As long as you translate a single abstract problem domain entity to a *single shared* COM object in one process on one machine, you cannot build a system that scales. This one-to-one mapping is standard practice in classic object orientation, but it must be discarded in favor of something less intuitive but far more flexible. Instead, you need to map one abstract problem domain entity to *multiple* COM objects. This technique allows the objects to be spread across multiple machines, eliminating the hardware bottleneck inherent in sharing a single COM identity. To explain how this approach works, I have to revisit the notion of identity. If multiple COM objects on different servers are going to represent the same abstract problem domain entity, their behavior must be applied to the same state. COM's notion of identity doesn't help. It ties behavior to hardware as well as state, and the whole purpose of using multiple COM objects is to get away from that.

Remember that identity provides a mapping of behavior to state. Pointer addresses are one way to define this mapping, but there are others. One alternative is to define identity in terms of *type,* with all objects of the same class implicitly referencing the same state. Another alternative is to define identity in terms of a *key,* with all objects that hold the same key explicitly referencing the same state. This latter approach parallels the world of databases, where state is referenced by primary key. Both techniques are useful because they enable the development of singleton and named object-style solutions without the same-style scalability problems that arise when a single shared COM object is used. I use the term *logical identity* to refer to these approaches in order to differentiate them from the conventional *physical identity* provided by pointer addresses.

## Implementing Named Objects with Key-Based Logical Identity

The named-object server exposing Bob and Jane can be reimplemented using key-based logical identity. Consider a new interface, IPersonIdentity.

```
interface IPersonIdentity : IUnknown
{
  [propput] HRESULT Name([in] BSTR bstr);
  [propget] HRESULT Name([out, retval] BSTR *pbstr);
}
```

This interface defines a single property, Name, which can be used to associate a COM object with some Person state. The new version of the Person class exposes this new interface in addition to the IPerson interface it supported before. IPersonIdentity can be implemented this way.

```
long g_rgnAges[] = { 0, 0 };
class Person : public IPersonIdentity,
               public IPerson,
               … // Other details left out for clarity
{
  CComBSTR m_bstrKey;
public:
  STDMETHODIMP put_Name(BSTR bstr)
  {
    if ((wcscmp(bstr, OLESTR("Bob")) != 0) &&
        (wcscmp(bstr, OLESTR("Jane")) != 0))
      return E_INVALIDARG;
    m_bstrKey = bstr;
    return S_OK;
  }
  STDMETHODIMP get_Name(BSTR *pbstr)
  {
    return m_bstrKey.CopyTo(pbstr);
  }
```

```
STDMETHODIMP put_Age(long nAge)
{
  if (!m_bstrKey.Length()) return E_UNEXPECTED;
  g_rgnAges[KeyToIndex()] = nAge;
  return S_OK;
}
STDMETHODIMP get_Age(long *pnAge)
{
  if (!m_bstrKey.Length()) return E_UNEXPECTED;
  *pnAge = g_rgnAges[KeyToIndex()];
  return S_OK;
}
STDMETHODIMP AgeGracefully(long nYears)
{
  if (!m_bstrKey.Length()) return E_UNEXPECTED;
  g_rgnAges[KeyToIndex()] += nYears;
  return S_OK;
}
… // Other details left out for clarity
private:
  long KeyToIndex(void)
  {
    if (wcscmp(m_bstrKey, OLESTR("Bob")) == 0)
      return 0;
    else
      return 1;
  }
};
```

Notice that `Person` now stores a key, represented as a string, instead of an age. The ages of the named objects are stored in a global array of longs. When a `Person`'s name is set via the `IPersonIdentity::Name` property, the parameter is validated—only "Bob" and "Jane" are allowed—and then stored. Whenever an operation needs to manipulate the state of a `Person` (e.g., his or her age), the key is used to index into the shared array. The function `KeyToIndex` implements the translation.

Once this code is in place, clients no longer need to use a `Finder` object to access the same `Person`. Instead, each client instantiates its own `Person` object, initializes it with same `Name` property, either "Bob" or "Jane" in this example, and then calls whatever methods it likes. Because two different COM objects are created, the COM plumbing ensures that two different proxies are always returned. As a result, the only way to determine whether two references to `Person` objects are equivalent is to compare their identifying characteristic, in this case their `Name`.

```
' create two people
Dim p1, p2 As IP
Set p1 = New P
Set p2 = New P
' set names
Dim id1, id2 As IPIdentity
Set id1 = p1
Set id2 = p2
id1.SetPName "Jane"
id2.SetPName "Jane"
' compare references by name
If (id1.Name = id2.Name) Then
   MsgBox "There is still only one person named Jane!"
End If
p1.AgeGracefully 29
MsgBox "Jane is " & p2.Age & " years old"
```

Despite the fact that `p1` and `p2` refer to different COM objects, it doesn't matter which reference is used to manipulate the `Person` because the two references have been given the same name and therefore refer to the same underlying state. Figure 1-4 shows the new approach.

This leads to an interesting question: How many objects does this new client code manipulate? Physically, there are two COM objects, each with a unique `IUnknown` pointer, a reference count, and a key value. However,

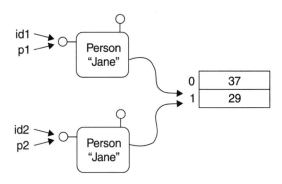

**Figure 1-4   Key-based identity**

because all the interesting methods of the class (discounting the methods that get and set the key, which I don't find interesting) operate on the shared state stored in the global array, in a logical sense there is only one object, with a unique name "Jane" and state, her age. So the answer to the question, How many objects? is two *physical* and one *logical*, as shown in Figure 1-5.

This idea may strike you as very strange, perhaps because there is no obvious way to express this concept using a single, simple programming language construct. But this idea turns out to be very flexible and powerful. It is exactly the change that's necessary to overcome the throughput problems inherent in sharing a single COM object. Because each client talks to a different *physical* instance of `Person`, the requirement that a given logical `Person`'s behavior always execute on the same machine, which causes a bottleneck, is removed.

### Implementing Named Objects on Top of a Database

Fully realizing our goal actually requires one more modification to our named-object server. The current implementation stores the shared state of Bob and Jane in a global array that can be accessed only from a single process. If clients create named `Person` objects on different middle-tier machines, they will not be dealing with the same state; each server process will have its own copy of Bob and Jane. You can solve this problem by moving the objects' state into a

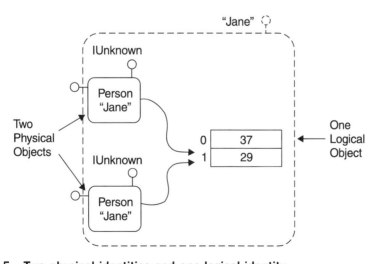

**Figure 1-5  Two physical identities and one logical identity**

repository that can be accessed from multiple middle-tier servers, a back-end database.

Converting the `Person` class to access a database is easy. The implementation can still store a key as a string, but instead of using it to index into a global array, it will use it to index into a database table. The table, called `persons`, is defined in SQL (structured query language) this way.

```
create table persons
(
  name varchar(10) identity not null,
  age integer
)
```

Based on this definition, the implementation of `Person` can be rewritten this way.

```
extern OLECHAR *g_wszConnectString;
class Person : public IPersonIdentity,
               public IPerson,
               … // Other details left out for clarity
{
  CComBSTR m_bstrKey;
public:
  STDMETHODIMP put_Name(BSTR bstr)
  {
    m_bstrKey = bstr;
    return S_OK;
  }
  STDMETHODIMP get_Name(BSTR *pbstr)
  {
    return m_bstrKey.CopyTo(pbstr);
  }
  STDMETHODIMP put_Age(long nAge)
  {
    // make sure key has been set
    if (!m_bstrKey.Length()) return E_UNEXPECTED;
    // build and exec SQL statement
    OLECHAR wsz[64];
    wsprintfW(wsz,
              L"update persons set age = %d where name = \'%s\'",
              nAge, m_bstrKey);
    return ExecSQL(wsz, 0);
  }
```

```cpp
STDMETHODIMP get_Age(long *pnAge)
{
  // make sure key has been set
  if (!m_bstrKey.Length()) return E_UNEXPECTED;
  // build and exec SQL statement
  OLECHAR wsz[64];
  wsprintfW(wsz,
            L"select age from persons where name = \'%s\'",
            m_bstrKey);
  CAccessorRowset<CDynamicAccessor, CRowset> car;
  HRESULT hr = ExecSQL(wsz, &car.m_spRowset);
  if (FAILED(hr)) return hr;
  // extract age from rowset
  hr = car.Bind();
  if (FAILED(hr)) return hr;
  hr = car.MoveFirst();
  if (FAILED(hr)) return hr;
  *pnAge = (long)cmd.GetValue(1);
  return hr;
}
STDMETHODIMP AgeGracefully(long nYears)
{
  // make sure key has been set
  if (!m_bstrKey.Length()) return E_UNEXPECTED;
  // build and exec SQL statement
  OLECHAR wsz[64];
  wsprintfW(wsz,
            L"update persons set age = age + %d where name = \'%s\'",
            nYears, m_bstrKey);
  return ExecSQL(wsz, 0);
}
… // Other details left out for clarity
private:
  HRESULT ExecSQL(OLECHAR *pwszCmd, IRowset **pprs)
  {
    // load and initialize OLE DB provider
    CDataSource dataSrc;
    hr = dataSrc.OpenFromInitializationString(g_wszConnectString);
    if (FAILED(hr)) return hr;
    // acquire session
    CSession session;
    hr = session.Open(dataSrc);
    if (FAILED(hr)) return hr;
    CCommand<CDynamicAccessor, CRowset> cmd;
```

```
      // create and execute command
      LONG cRows;
      hr = cmd.Open(session, pwszCmd, 0, &cRows, DBGUID_DEFAULT, false);
      if (FAILED(hr)) return hr;
      // return any results
      if (pprs) (*pprs = cmd.m_spRowset)->AddRef();
      return hr;
   }
};
```

The interesting methods of the class (again discounting the methods that get and set the key) now perform operations on the state of a `Person` by executing SQL statements. `ExecSQL` has replaced `KeyToIndex` as a helper method to facilitate this. `ExecSQL` simply connects to the database (the connection string is stored in the global variable `g_wszConnectString`) and invokes the desired command, `pwszCmd`. If the calling code passed a valid pointer for the output parameter `pprs`, `ExecSQL` returns the command's resulting OLE DB Rowset.

With each logical `Person`'s state stored in the `Person`'s table of a shared database, a client's code can be rewritten to instantiate physical `Person` objects on whatever server it likes.

```
' create two people on two servers
Dim p1, p2 As IPerson
Set p1 = CreateObject("PersonSrv.Person", "Server1")
Set p2 = CreateObject("PersonSrv.Person", "Server2")
' set names
Dim id1, id2 As IPersonIdentity
Set id1 = p1
Set id2 = p2
id1.SetPersonName "Jane"
id2.SetPersonName "Jane"
' compare references by name
If (id1.Name = id2.Name) Then
  MsgBox "There is still only one person named Jane!"
End If
p1.AgeGracefully 29
MsgBox "Jane is " & p2.Age & " years old"
```

Despite the fact that `p1` and `p2` refer to different objects *on different machines*, it does not matter which reference is used to manipulate the `Person`; because

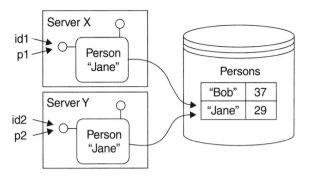

**Figure 1-6  Spreading one logical identity across servers**

the two references have been given the same name, they always refer to the same underlying state maintained in the database. Figure 1-6 depicts this new technique.

### What Has Been Gained?

If clients create their physical `Person` objects on different servers, a logical person's *behavior* no longer represents a bottleneck. But there is always another one. In this case it is the database that stores each `Person`'s *state*. So what, if anything, has been gained?

The answer is simple: This approach gives you a place to implement logic without burdening your database with extra work and without having to deploy code on every front-end client machine. The `Person` example doesn't demonstrate this benefit fully because I kept it simple to highlight the architecture. Up to now, the `Person` class's methods have done nothing more than fetch, store, and change a `Person`'s state. Realistically, however, additional processing needs to be done. Consider a new implementation of the `AgeGracefully` method.

```
STDMETHODIMP Person::AgeGracefully(long nYears)
{
  // check security
  if (!CallerIsFatherTime()) return E_ACCESSDENIED;
  // check initialization
  if (!m_bstrKey.Length()) return E_UNEXPECTED;
  // check input
  if (nYears < 0 || nYears > 5) return E_INVALIDARG;
```

```
    // build and execute SQL statement
    OLECHAR wsz[64];
    wsprintfW(wsz,
            L"update persons set age = age + %d where name = \'%s\'",
            nYears, m_bstrKey);
    return ExecSQL(wsz, 0);
}
```

This version checks to ensure that the caller has permission to ask a person to age and validates the input parameter, `nYears`, to see if it is between 0 and 5, the range of values that can reasonably be accepted.[2] Only if these various checks are passed is a call made to the database to manipulate the `Person's` state.

By implementing this kind of logic on a middle-tier server you keep it off client machines, providing two significant benefits. Clients do not have to be configured to reach the database directly, and you can change the logic without having to update all the client boxes. You may still have to stop servers and force clients to release their connections when you make changes, but you won't have to touch every client machine—a configuration management nightmare.

Putting this logic on a middle-tier server also keeps it out of the back-end database, where it would be an additional, unnecessary load. In general, it makes sense to do work that does not need access to information stored in a back-end database on a middle-tier server. The first half of the `Age Gracefully` method, which checks security privileges and validates input, provides a good example of this sort of task. It also makes sense to do work that can use a cached copy of read-only (or write-seldom) data on a middle-tier server. Work should be done in a back-end database only when it cannot be done without accessing the information stored there.

Off-loading extraneous work from a database will not stop a bottleneck if workload continues to increase. But, by doing as much as you can on your middle-tier servers and going to the database only when necessary, you might get high enough throughput to meet your needs. If not, additional steps (e.g., upgrading the database server machine and caching, partitioning, and replicating data) will be necessary. Whether you have to take one or more of these steps

---

[2] Negative values are not the secret of eternal youth.

depends entirely on how much throughput your system has to provide. Remember, the process of removing just enough of the bottlenecks in a system to meet your throughput needs is the essence of scalable system design.

## The Object-per-Client Model

The previous section explains how each client can create its own COM object with a unique physical identity and map it to a common state based on some form of logical identity. It is easy to see that using multiple COM objects enables scalability by providing a way to spread work across multiple server machines. However, the scalability requirement alone does not explain why each client should use its own object. Why not create a single COM object to represent a particular logical identity on a given server and have clients share it?

As shown in Figure 1-7, this approach provides the same scalability benefits. Work is spread across multiple servers, each with its own COM object representing the same logical identity, Jane. All the clients accessing Jane's state through the same middle-tier server use the same physical identity. It would not be hard to implement this. You could use a combination of the `NamedFinder` class described above and key-based logical identity. Given a name via the `INamedFinder` interface, the `NamedFinder` implementation would simply return the appropriate `IPerson` pointer to all clients, instantiating a new

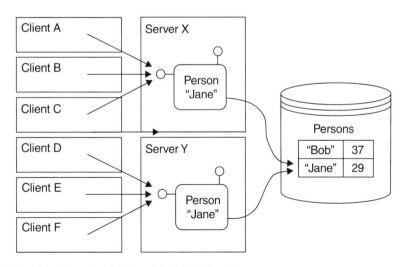

**Figure 1-7   Sharing physical and logical identities**

`Person` object when it receives a name it has not seen before. Each `Person` object would save its name as its key data member and use it to access the shared state in the database.

This is, in fact, a perfectly reasonable approach, but it does present a number of issues. First and foremost, if clients are going to share the same COM object, performance dictates that their calls be processed concurrently. If their method invocations are serialized and only one client request can be serviced at a time, scalability suffers. Executing concurrent work against a single COM object implies that multiple threads can access the object simultaneously. This isn't possible if classes are implemented using Visual Basic 6; the language's runtime does not support it. Concurrent access to objects is possible for classes written in C++ or Java, but the developer must make each class thread-safe by synchronizing access to an instance's state. This synchronization has to be efficient too. Having clients share an object that naïvely locks its entire state on each method call simply creates a new bottleneck. Writing code that is both thread-safe and efficient is far from impossible, but it does represent a heavy burden, especially for developers who do not have a lot of experience with threads. This is the other reason—beyond scalability—that it is beneficial to have each client create an object of its own.

Figure 1-8 illustrates the object-per-client model. Once you adopt the object-per-client model, making classes thread-safe is no longer a concern. If objects are never shared, you can implement your classes without worrying about concurrent access to an instance's data members. Clients' method invocations can still run concurrently—which is necessary for performance and scalability—and development is significantly simpler. It is important to note, however, that this model does not alleviate all concurrency concerns. Access to any shared state in a middle-tier process has to be synchronized using traditional Win32 techniques (e.g., critical sections and mutexes).

The object-per-client model provides benefits beyond simplifying development by reducing concerns about threading. If each client uses its own object, the count of objects reflects the number of clients currently using the system. This information is useful because it provides a way to track and possibly limit concurrency on a particular server. If clients shared a single COM object, ascertaining the number of clients using it would be difficult. You might think the

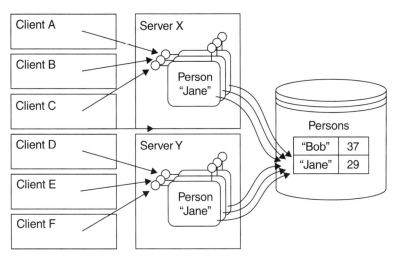

**Figure 1-8** The object-per-client model

object's reference count would tell you how many clients were using it, but that is not the case. The proxy/stub plumbing caches reference counting calls to avoid the overhead of roundtrips whenever possible; the result is that an object never knows how many clients it really has.

More important, if each client uses its own object, per-client state can be tracked on a per-object basis. This would also be impossible with a shared COM object because there is no way for an object with multiple clients to know which client is making which invocation. One way to solve this problem would be for each client to pass some sort of identifier—a cookie—as a parameter with each call. This is certainly possible, but not elegant. If, on the other hand, each client creates its own object, each object reference is effectively a cookie, and each object can be used to store per-client state.

You may see an immediate use for these two side effects of the object-per-client model, or you may not. However, if you plan to use the services the COM+ runtime offers (synchronization, declarative transactions, just-in-time activation, etc.), be aware that many of them assume you are using the object-per-client model and rely on that fact to work correctly. If you reject this approach and try to use some services anyway, you might restrict concurrency or create deadlocks or worse. Which bad things actually happen depends on which services you try to use. I will point out particular trouble spots later on. For now, suffice it to say that violating this architecture and trying to leverage COM+ runtime services are not good ideas. Because it simplifies development by allowing you to implement largely thread-unaware classes and because the runtime services expect it, COM+ architectures should embrace the object-per-client model. This is Rule 1.1.

 **1.1**

COM+ clients do not share physical COM objects; they only share state stored in middle-tier processes and back-end databases. This is the object-per-client model.

## Transactions

Clients manipulate shared state using objects running on middle-tier servers. They use multiple COM objects so that work can be spread across multiple servers. They each use their own COM objects for the reasons outlined previously. Consider the first of those reasons—to simplify development by eliminating concurrent access to objects. The object-per-client model protects state stored in objects' data members implicitly.[3] This makes COM+ classes easier to implement, but it does not alleviate all concurrency concerns. In addition to accessing their own data members, each client's objects may also access shared state. Shared state stored in memory in a process on a middle-tier server can be protected from concurrent access using traditional Win32 techniques (e.g., mutexes and critical sections). But how do you coordinate concurrent access to shared state stored in a back-end database? This is where transactions come in.

Transactions are a standard mechanism for managing changes to state in a distributed system. Transactions provide a model for controlling concurrent access to data and for handling the bizarre failure modes inherent in distributed computing. Without transactions, letting objects' work progress concurrently would result in complete chaos.[4]

---

[3] Object state is generally protected explicitly by an activity as well, as described in Chapter 4, Threads.

[4] This section introduces transactions at a high level. The details of transactions are covered in Chapter 6, Transactions, and Chapter 7, Isolation.

## Enter Transactions

A *transaction* is generally defined as a unit of work done on behalf of a single client. Each transaction may encompass multiple operations performed on data spread across one or more processes on one or more machines. Each transaction does its part to protect the integrity of a system's state by providing four basic guarantees: atomicity, consistency, isolation, and durability. These are known as the ACID properties.

Each transaction's work represents an *atomic* change to a system. All the changes a client makes within a given transaction will succeed or fail *en masse.* In other words, a client using a transaction can count on the fact that, when its transaction ends, a system is either in the desired new state—all the client's changes have been made, the transaction has *committed*—or in its original state—none of the client's changes were made, the transaction has *aborted.* This implies that clients have to expect complete failure in addition to complete success. This is good because it frees you from having to write client code that deals with partial failures, in which some changes have taken effect and others have not. These problems are very hard to track down and repair.

Each transaction's work is guaranteed to leave a system in a *consistent* state. A client may make several changes to a system's state within the scope of a single transaction. While a client is doing its work, the system may be in an invalid state temporarily. For instance, placing an order may entail adding an entry to an order table and then adding several corresponding entries to a line item table. The logic of the order system may dictate that line item records be inserted after their order record has been inserted in order to satisfy a foreign key constraint encoded in the database schema. At the same time, the logic of the order system may dictate that an order record cannot exist without at least one associated line item record. Because a client has to insert the order record and then add the line item record(s), for a moment in time the state of the database is inconsistent—at least one of the order system's logical constraints has not been met. This inconsistency is okay within the scope of a single transaction. When a transaction ends, however, whether it commits or aborts, it must be the case that all logical constraints have been met. There can be no dangling references or incomplete results, and referential integrity must not be compromised. This requirement allows clients to make reasonable assumptions about the pre- and postconditions of a system before and after each atomic operation.

Each transaction's work is done in *isolation* from other transactions. Although transactions are guaranteed to complete atomically, they are not guaranteed to succeed. If a client modifies system state within the scope of a transaction and the transaction is aborted, the client's work is rolled back. If one transaction were allowed to see the changes to system state being made by a second transaction that is still in progress, it might see partial changes or changes that are eventually rolled back, or both. Allowing the first transaction to make decisions based on what it saw could easily lead to consistency violations (e.g., seeing an order record before its corresponding line items have been inserted). To avoid these sorts of logic problems, transactions are allowed to work only in isolation. Without isolation, atomicity and consistency would be meaningless.

Finally, each transaction's work is *durable.* A transaction succeeds or fails atomically without sacrificing either consistency or isolation, even in the face of a catastrophic system failure. The parties involved in a transaction keep as much information as necessary stored on disk to make sure that the transaction can be completed one way or another, even if one of the processes or machines participating in the transaction crashes. When the process or machine restarts, the transaction's work will be finished, either by allowing its client's changes to remain or by undoing them. Durability is necessary if atomicity, consistency, and isolation are to have any meaning in a potentially unstable environment (i.e., the typical distributed system).

To summarize, you can count on transactions to guarantee that changes to the state of a system are applied *atomically,* leave the system *consistent,* are *isolated* from one another while in progress, and will be *durable* even in the face of a catastrophic failure.[5]

### Clients and TMs and RMs, Oh My!

There are at least three parties involved in every transaction. First, every transaction has a client. Clients start transactions, do work within their scope, and

---

[5] For more information about the ACID properties, see *Principles of Transaction Processing* by Bernstein and Newcomer or *Transaction Processing Fundamentals* by Gray and Reuter.

then either commit or abort them as they see fit. Second, every transaction has a transaction manager (TM). Transaction managers create transactions for clients and take care of the details of committing or aborting them. Third, every transaction involves one or more resource managers (RMs) that coordinate changes to durable state on a per-transaction basis (databases are RMs).

Each of these participants plays a role in guaranteeing that the ACID properties hold true. Transaction managers guarantee atomicity when a transaction ends by making sure that the RMs involved in the transaction either keep or undo the client's changes. Clients and RMs guarantee consistency. Only a transaction's client knows when it has made all the changes necessary to leave the system in its new, consistent state, so only the client can commit a transaction. When a client attempts to commit a transaction, each participating RM has the option of aborting it instead. This allows an RM to abandon a transaction in the face of a critical failure, like running out of disk space. RMs do not usually abort transactions in the face of an invalid request (e.g., when a SQL statement fails). Instead they report the error to the client and let it decide whether the transaction should be aborted. RMs are responsible for guaranteeing isolation by tracking which transaction altered which pieces of state. RMs use a combination of locking and versioning techniques to make sure that a transaction's changes are hidden from all other transactions while it is in progress. Finally, TMs and RMs implement durability by logging to disk information about all ongoing transactions. If a process or a machine crashes, the log can be consulted when it restarts and ongoing transactional work can be completed one way or another.[6]

## Local Transactions and Distributed Transactions

If a client wants to change state managed by a single RM, it can protect its work by using a *local* transaction. With local transactions, the RM is the transaction manager. Figure 1-9 illustrates the local transaction architecture.

A client acquires a local transaction simply by asking the RM (acting as the TM) to start one. Some RMs can be configured to start a local transaction automatically when a client request arrives. The RM treats all the work submitted

---

[6] Again, for more information, see *Principles of Transaction Processing* by Bernstein and Newcomer or *Transaction Processing Fundamentals* by Gray and Reuter.

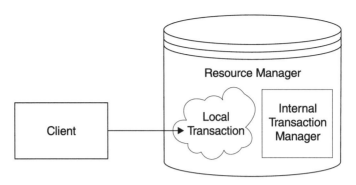

**Figure 1-9  Local transaction architecture**

through the client's connection as part of the ongoing transaction. The RM protects the data the client changed while the transaction is in progress. When the client is done, it ends the transaction by asking the RM (again acting as the TM) to either commit or abort it. The RM either keeps or undoes the client's changes. While all this is happening, the RM keeps information about the transaction recorded durably on disk so it can recover if its process crashes. This is exactly what happens when a client uses a raw SQL transaction—BEGIN TRANS ACTION, COMMIT/ROLLBACK—in SQL Server, Oracle, or any other database.

If a client wants to change state managed by multiple resource managers, it can protect its work with a *distributed* transaction. Because distributed transactions are not specific to any RM, an external transaction manager is necessary. Windows 2000 includes an external TM called the Distributed Transaction Coordinator (DTC). Figure 1-10 illustrates the distributed transaction architecture.

A client acquires a distributed transaction simply by asking an external TM to start one. The client presents its distributed transaction to each RM it wants to work with. This process is called *enlistment* (this is implicit with local transactions; an RM automatically enlists the connection that starts the transaction). Each RM treats all the work submitted through an enlisted connection as a part of the ongoing distributed transaction. As with a local transaction, each RM protects the data the client changed while the transaction is in progress. When the client is done, it ends the transaction by asking the TM to commit or abort it. Ending a distributed transaction is more complicated than ending a local trans-

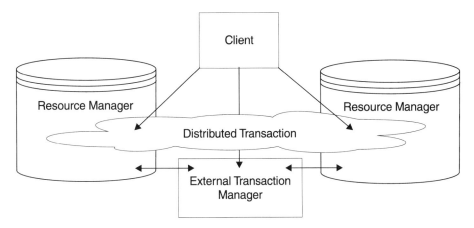

**Figure 1-10  Distributed transaction architecture**

action. When a client ends a local transaction, there is only one RM involved. If the client asks the RM to commit a local transaction that it does not want to commit, it can simply abort the transaction and return a failure code. This simple protocol does not work for distributed transactions if more than one RM is involved. Instead, distributed transactions have to use a more sophisticated two-phase commit protocol.

Distributed transactions provide another, more esoteric functionality. Distributed transactions allow multiple client processes, in addition to multiple RMs, to participate in a single transaction. Once a client has a reference to a distributed transaction, it can pass it to another process. That process can then use the transaction to protect its changes to RM managed state. From the RM's perspective there is no difference between the two client processes; they are both simply "the client." Most RMs don't support this functionality for local transactions.[7]

## The Transactions and Scalability Paradox

Transactions and scalability have a paradoxical relationship. On the one hand, transactions provide a model for coordinating work across process and machine boundaries in a safe and sane manner, enabling scalability. On the other hand,

---

[7] SQL Server 7.0 does support this functionality for local transactions, primarily as a means for allowing extended stored procedures implemented in DLLs to access data within the same transaction as their callers. See the documentation for `sp_bindsession` for more information.

when poorly applied transactions can create major bottlenecks in a system, killing scalability.

Remember that it is the job of each RM to isolate transactions while they are in progress. I already mentioned that RMs implement isolation using a combination of locking and versioning techniques. The locks that RMs use to protect state on a transaction's behalf are a potential source of contention. If lots of transactions are trying to update the same state, they have to acquire the same mutually exclusive lock before they can access the data, and all but one transaction's work will be blocked. An RM typically holds a transaction's locks until the transaction ends.

All this locking is a good thing. It is required for isolation. If RMs did not lock data, atomicity and consistency would not be guaranteed, and chaos would ensue. But all this locking can also be a bad thing, if you are not very careful. If transactions lock data other transactions need access to and hold the locks for a long time, the locks can create a bottleneck. This is an example of contention for information. As is always the case with contention, the first step in solving the problem is to use RM locks as efficiently as possible. Mathematical analysis of transactional locking supports the general conclusion that throughput for an RM is roughly inversely proportional to the scope of locking in time and space.[8] This observation about locking is so important that I made it Rule 1.2.

 **RULE** 1.2

To maximize throughput, lock as little data as possible for as short a time as possible.

If you ignore this issue, you run the risk of designing an architecture that hamstrings your databases and does not scale. Your only recourse would be to replicate the data and the associated locks, in an effort to lower contention by making more resources available. As I mentioned earlier, replication is always necessary at some point if throughput is to continue to grow. It is far preferable,

---

[8] Once more, I recommend *Principles of Transaction Processing* by Bernstein and Newcomer or *Transaction Processing Fundamentals* by Gray and Reuter.

however, to be forced into replication because of the physical limitations of your back-end server hardware than to be driven to it because of inefficient locking. In the latter case, you are wasting your investment in a fast database machine, and you are being forced to introduce replication before it is necessary.

Some of you may be wondering if efficient lock management is really something middle-tier enterprise application developers have to think about. The answer is yes, if they want their systems to scale. Later chapters explain how transaction isolation works and what it implies about how you write your code. Transactions are an incredibly powerful tool. They enable scalability. But you have to treat them with respect if you do not want your system tied up in knots. That means having to understand how they really work.

## Integrating Objects and Transactions

With transactions in hand, I can now return to the earlier problem. There are multiple clients, each with their own object running in some process on a middle-tier machine. The object-per-client model protects the objects' state implicitly. The objects can synchronize access to shared state within their own processes using traditional Win32 techniques. Now, the objects can synchronize access to shared state in back-end databases using transactions. But how should objects and transactions be mixed?

### Using Transactions Explicitly

One approach to mixing these two technologies is to implement objects that use transactions explicitly. In other words, an object simply asks an RM to start a local transaction or an external TM to start a distributed transaction. If the object is using a local transaction, its RM connection is automatically enlisted against the transaction. If the object is using a distributed transaction, it has to enlist its RM connections manually. After completing work with its RM(s), the object commits or aborts its transaction as it sees fit. In essence, the object becomes a traditional transactional client. The advantage of this approach is that objects have direct control over every aspect of their transactions. The disadvantage is that objects are responsible for managing all the details of their transactions by hand.

## Using Transactions Implicitly

COM+ offers an alternative approach in the form of *declarative transactions*. A declarative transaction is a distributed transaction that is made available for an object to use implicitly. The COM+ runtime makes sure that a distributed transaction is simply part of the object's environment whenever a method that needs a transaction is executing. When the object connects to an RM, the plumbing detects the object's transaction and enlists the connection. After completing its work, the object simply finishes its method call and leaves it to the plumbing to commit or abort the transaction. The object can of course influence its transaction's outcome, but it does so indirectly. The advantage of this approach is that objects are not responsible for managing the details of their transactions by hand. The disadvantage of this approach is that objects have little direct control over any aspect of their transactions.

Objects that leverage declarative transactions always use distributed transactions. If an object talks to only one RM, using a distributed transaction is less efficient than using a local transaction because of the extra interprocess communication involved, even considering that the two-phase commit protocol can be optimized in the single RM case. This is one of the prices you pay for hiding the details of transaction management.

## Applying Transactions

Consider the last iteration of the simple `Person` class. Its methods used the `ExecSQL` helper function to manipulate state stored in the `persons` table of a back-end database. As it sits now, the current implementation of the `Person` class does not actually need transactions at all. Each method that affects back-end state executes a single SQL statement that operates on a single record identified by the person's name, as shown in Table 1-1. The SQL specification mandates that statements like these must execute atomically in their own right.

However, if the `AgeGracefully` method were extended to write to an audit log in addition to updating a person's age, a transaction would be necessary to guarantee that either both writes occur or neither write occurs. Here is a new implementation.

```
STDMETHODIMP Person::AgeGracefully(long nYears)
{
    // check security
    if (!CallerIsFatherTime()) return E_ACCESSDENIED;
    // check initialization
    if (!m_bstrKey.Length()) return E_UNEXPECTED;
    // check input
    if (nYears < 0 || nYears > 5) return E_INVALIDARG;
    // build and execute batch SQL statement
    OLECHAR wsz[128];
    wsprintfW(wsz,
            L"update persons set age = age + %d where name
                                      = \'%s\'\n \
              insert into auditlog (name, age_change)
                                      values(\'%s\', %d)"
            nYears, m_bstrKey, m_bstrKey, nYears);
    return ExecSQL(wsz, 0);
}
```

This new implementation updates a person's age and records the fact that the person's age was incremented by a specific amount, nYears, by inserting a record into another table called auditlog in the same database. These two SQL statements are combined into a single batch statement that is sent to the database in one call. They could also be encapsulated in a stored procedure.

This new version of AgeGracefully needs to use a transaction if it wants to maintain atomicity. Because only one RM is involved, AgeGracefully could use either a local transaction or a distributed transaction explicitly. It could also use a COM+-managed declarative transaction. To make this latter approach work, the Person class has to declare its intent to rely on the COM+ transaction service when it is registered at component installation time.

**Table 1-1   Person methods and SQL statements**

| Method | SQL Statement |
| --- | --- |
| put_Age | update persons set age = n where name = 'string' |
| get_Age | select age from persons where name = 'string' |
| AgeGracefully | update persons set age = age + n where name = 'string' |

Beyond that, the only difference in the code is extended error handling for the `cmd.Open` statement in the `ExecSQL` method in order to check the status of each SQL statement in a batch.

```
HRESULT Person::ExecSQL(char *pszCmd, IRowset **pprs)
{
  // load and initialize OLE DB provider
  CDataSource dataSrc;
  hr = dataSrc.OpenFromInitializationString(g_wszConnectString);
  if (FAILED(hr)) return hr;
  // acquire session
  CSession session;
  hr = session.Open(dataSrc);
  if (FAILED(hr)) return hr;
  // create and execute command
  CCommand<CDynamicAccessor, CRowset, CMultipleResults> cmd;
  LONG cRows;
  hr = cmd.Open(session, pszCmd, 0, &cRows, DBGUID_DEFAULT, false);
  // process results
  while (hr != DB_S_NORESULT)
  {
    if (FAILED(hr)) return hr;
    hr = cmd.GetNextResult(&cRows, false);
  }
  // return any results from last statement in batch
  if (pprs) (*pprs = cmd.m_spRowset)->AddRef();
  return hr;
}
```

This modified implementation scans through all the results that `cmd.Open` returns until it encounters either a failed HRESULT or the well-known return code `DB_S_NORESULT` indicating that there are no more results to process. This version of `ExecSQL` will still work fine when it is called by `get_Age` and `put_Age`.

Assuming it is registered correctly, the `Person` class can rely on COM+ to take care of all the details of transaction management. The COM+ plumbing will start a distributed transaction, make sure any database connections the object uses are enlisted on the transaction, and commit or abort the transaction when the object's work is done. However, there still needs to be a way to affect the declarative transaction's outcome. Again assuming the `Person` class is registered the right way, this can be done implicitly as well. The transaction's outcome can be determined by the HRESULT `Age Gracefully` returns. If `AgeGracefully` returns a success code, the transaction is committed; if `AgeGracefully` returns a failure code, the transaction is aborted. The last thing `AgeGracefully` does is return whatever HRESULT `ExecSQL` returns, so if there is any problem updating the database the transaction will be aborted. Figure 1-11 shows how this works.

This figure is a UML sequence diagram. The rectangles arranged horizontally across the top represent the participants in this sequence of operations. The vertical axis represents time, which progresses down from the top. The horizontal arrows represent requests (COM method invocations, SQL statements, etc.) sent from one participant to another. This sequence diagram shows the steps involved in invoking `AgeGracefully` under the protection of a declarative transaction. The client issues a call through a proxy to a `Person` object in a server process on a middle-tier server. The COM+ plumbing knows that the `Person` class uses declarative transactions based on the way it was registered when it was installed on the system. The plumbing will not start a distributed transaction for the object until one is really needed. In the case of the `Person` class, a transaction is not necessary until `AgeGracefully` calls the `ExecSQL` method, which attempts to connect to the database. When that happens, COM+ will start a distributed transaction and automatically enlist the new connection against it. When `ExecSQL` uses its connection, it will use the trans-

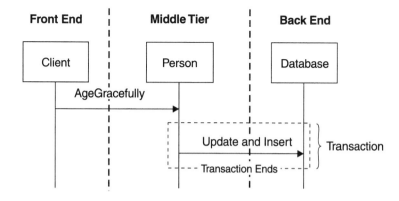

**Figure 1-11   How AgeGracefully works**

action implicitly. The transaction will end when the method the client called, `AgeGracefully`, completes. The plumbing will commit or abort the transaction based on the method's outcome.

I should mention that declarative transactions are not the most efficient option in this situation. Two of the `Person` methods do not need a transaction at all, and the third one could use a local transaction. If the `Person` class uses declarative transactions, the COM+ plumbing will provide a distributed transaction for each method, even though lighter-weight solutions are possible. This chapter focuses on declarative transactions for simplicity's sake.[9]

### Thinking about Roundtrips

You may wonder why I chose to implement `AgeGracefully` the way I did. From the point of view of encapsulating the details of data access, you could argue that it would be better to have `AgeGracefully` call the `get_Age` and `put_Age` methods to modify a person's age. That way, if the details of the `persons` schema ever change, there would be only two simple accessor methods to fix. Here's an example.

```
STDMETHODIMP Person::AgeGracefully(long nYears)
{
  if (!CallerIsFatherTime()) return E_ACCESSDENIED; // check security
  if (!m_bstrKey.Length()) return E_UNEXPECTED; // check initialization
  if (nYears < 0 || nYears > 5) return E_INVALIDARG; // check input
  long nAge;
  HRESULT hr = get_Age(&nAge);
  if (FAILED(hr)) return hr;
  hr = put_Age(nAge + nYears);
  if (FAILED(hr)) return hr;
  OLECHAR wsz[64];
  wsprintfW(wsz,
            L"insert into auditlog (name, age_change) values(\'%s\', %d)"
            m_bstrKey, nYears);
  return ExecSQL(wsz, 0);
}
```

---

[9] The details of explicit transaction management are explained in Chapter 6, Transactions.

At first this may seem like better engineering, but there is a large hidden cost. The previous version of `AgeGracefully` made one call to the database to update a person's age and add an auditing record. This implementation does the same work in three roundtrips; one in `get_Age`, one in `put_Age`, and one at the end of `AgeGracefully`. The COM+ declarative transaction mechanism will still protect the entire operation; however, overall performance will suffer because the database locks these operations acquire will be held longer, a violation of Rule 1.2. The sequence diagram in Figure 1-12 shows the steps involved in invoking this new version of `AgeGracefully` under the protection of a declarative transaction. The difference between this sequence and the previous sequence diagram is the addition of calls from the middle tier to the database.

Many developers ignore this issue, especially when the client's request is being sent over the Internet. The crux of their argument is that the network roundtrip from the front end to the middle tier is so slow that the incremental cost of additional calls from the middle tier to the back end is irrelevant. In other words, the user is waiting for a response for so long anyway, it really doesn't matter that the wait is a little bit longer. That may be true, but it ignores an important aspect of the problem. A single user may not care that her work has been imperceptibly slowed by inefficient middle-tier code, but *other* users' work

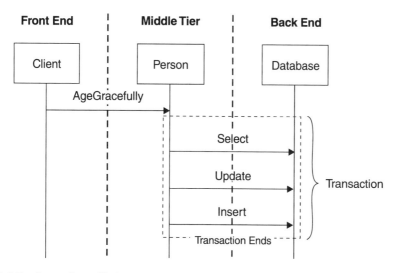

**Figure 1-12  Lowering efficiency in the name of encapsulation**

is also slowed, and the aggregate effect can be quite large. In this example, any locks the declarative transaction acquires in the course of an operation have to be held across three network roundtrips from the middle-tier to the database. Even with databases as fast as they are today, calls across the network take time. If other transactional operations need access to the same state (e.g., the ages of Bob, Jane, or Tazwell), they have to wait longer than they should. As contention for this information rises, a bottleneck will inevitably form; but with this implementation, it will form sooner. Using a batch statement, as I did in the previous version of `AgeGracefully`, makes more sense. As I mentioned before, the two operations could also be implemented as a stored procedure. If the goal is to encapsulate changes to the definition of the `persons` table, this is the better way to go.

## A Complex Problem

The first piece of client code at the beginning of this chapter asks three `Person` objects to `AgeGracefully` by 17, 29, and 50 years, respectively. That example uses instances of a C++ class created on the stack. It is worth considering how you would implement this same client logic using the latest COM-based version of the `Person` class. Consider this example.

```
' define three people
Dim p1, p2, p3 As IPerson
Set p1 = New Person
Set p2 = New Person
Set p3 = New Person
' set their identities
Dim id As IPersonIdentity
Set id = p1
id.SetPersonName "Jane"
Set id = p2
id.SetPersonName "Bob"
Set id = p3
id.SetPersonName "Tazwell"
' age them 17, 29 and 50 years
p1.AgeGracefully 17
p2.AgeGracefully 29
p3.AgeGracefully 50
```

This client creates three `Person` objects, assigns each one a key, and asks each one to age. Figure 1-13 illustrates this complex operation and brings an interesting problem to light.

There is an obvious issue with this sequence of operations. Each `Person` object uses a transaction to protect its work, but each transaction ends when each call to `AgeGracefully` completes (recall Figure 1-11). This results in three transactions, each protecting changes to a single piece of state. If that's what the client wants, this solution is fine. But if the client really wants to change all three peoples' ages as a single atomic operation, this solution will not do.

If the client wants to change all three peoples' ages in a single atomic operation, it needs to do the work in one transaction. But the client is not in charge of transactions; the `Person` objects are. Remember that a transaction relies on its client to enforce consistency because only the client knows the combination of changes that leaves the system in a consistent state. In this case, the objects are the transactional clients. Unfortunately, the objects do not know anything about their client and the overall task it is trying to accomplish. They do not know about each other either, or that they are all being used

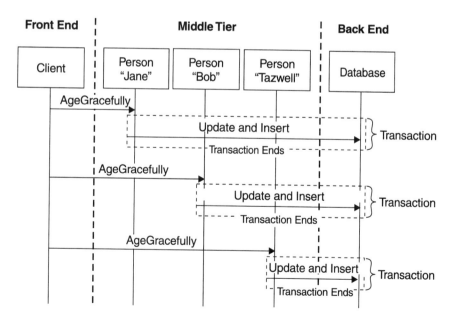

**Figure 1-13   A complex problem**

together in pursuit of one goal, so no one of them can share its transaction with the others. In the absence of this larger worldview, the objects are left to decide on their own when their transactions will end. This is not a weakness of the COM+ declarative transaction model for integrating transactions and objects implicitly. If the objects were using transactions explicitly, they would have the same problem. In this circumstance, the end of the `AgeGracefully` method is as good a place as any for each transaction to complete. But this does not help the client.

The only thread that ties the three `Person` objects together is the fact that they share the same client. This is both the essence of the problem and the key to its solution. The code that controls the transaction has to see things from the client's perspective. It has to understand the entirety of what the client is trying to accomplish as a single atomic change.

## A Possible Solution

One possible solution is to have the client take charge of the transaction. The client could start a new distributed transaction explicitly and pass it to the middle-tier server process as an argument to each call. It would have to be a distributed transaction because only a distributed transaction can be used from multiple "client" processes. This assumes, however, that the client has access to an external transaction manager. This is a big assumption. In most companies, client boxes are not set up to access an external TM. If the client is somewhere out on the Internet, you have no idea what operating system it is running, let alone what transaction management services it has access to. This approach also assumes that the middle-tier object the client is calling accepts a reference to a distributed transaction as an input parameter. The current version of `AgeGracefully` does not, but this could be fixed. Finally, this approach leaves the transaction's lifetime in the client's hands. The transaction will not commit or abort until the client says so. Ultimately, that means the client controls how long any RM locks that the transaction has acquired are held.

In this example, the locks would be held across all three calls the client makes to the `Person` objects on the middle-tier server and the three calls those objects make to the back-end database. Carrying this idea to its worst extreme, if the client ties the life of a transaction to an interactive user interface (e.g.,

"Press OK to commit or Cancel to abort"), you can kiss scalability good-bye. As my good friend Stu Halloway likes to say, "As soon as you put a transaction in a user's hands, they go to lunch." Having the client take charge of the transaction is not a good idea.

## A Much Better Solution

A much better solution is to move the client logic that is driving the transaction to the middle-tier server. There it can make use of either local or distributed transactions. In the latter case, it can use the server's external TM, which you can guarantee will be available. The transaction will start and end on the middle tier, so RM locks will not be held across multiple roundtrips from the client to the server. The client will not even know transactions are being used, let alone control their lifetimes. This scheme is easy to implement: All you need to do is define a new class that encapsulates the task the client wants to accomplish in a single transaction, in this case asking multiple people to age gracefully. Like the `Person` class, you can register this new class as using the COM+ transaction service. The plumbing will make sure each instance has a declarative transaction. The plumbing will still assume the system is in a consistent state and the transaction should end when a client's call completes, but this is no longer a problem. The job of this new class is to implement the atomic change the client wants to make. The system will be consistent at the end of the client's call, or the request will have failed. Either way, the transaction is finished.

Consider a new interface, `IPersonMgr`, which models the change the client wants to accomplish in a single transaction.

```
interface IPersonMgr : IUnknown
{
  HRESULT AgeManyGracefully([in] long nCount,
                            [in] SAFEARRAY(BSTR) psabstrNames,
                            [in] SAFEARRAY(long) psanYears);
}
```

A client can use the single method `AgeManyGracefully` to increment the ages of multiple people. It takes a long, `nCount`, to indicate the number of people affected, an array of BSTRs, `psaNames`, to identify those people, and a parallel array of longs, `psaYears`, to indicate how much older each person should be.

The `PersonMgr` class uses the `Person` class to implement `IPersonMgr`.

```
class PersonMgr : public IPersonMgr,
                … // Other details left out for clarity
{
  STDMETHODIMP AgeManyGracefully(long nCount,
                                 SAFEARRAY *psaNames,
                                 SAFEARRAY *psaYears)
  {
    if (!CallerIsFatherTime()) return E_ACCESSDENIED;
    if (!ValidInput(nCount, psaNames, psaYears))
      return E_INVALIDARG;
    BSTR *rgbstr = 0;
    HRESULT hr = SafeArrayAccessData(psaNames, (void**)&rgbstr);
    if (SUCCEEDED(hr))
    {
      long *rgn = 0;
      hr = SafeArrayAccessData(psaYears, (void**)&rgn);
      if (SUCCEEDED(hr))
      {
        CComPtr<IPersonIdentity> spId;
        hr = spId.CoCreateInstance(__uuidof(Person));
        for (long i = 0; i < nCount; i++)
        {
          if (FAILED(hr)) break;
          hr = spId->put_Name(rgbstr[i]);
          if (FAILED(hr)) break;
          CComPtr<IPerson> spPerson;
          hr = spId->QueryInterface(__uuidof(spPerson),
                                    (void**)&spPerson);
          if (FAILED(hr)) break;
          hr = spPerson->AgeGracefully(rgn[i]);
          if (FAILED(hr)) break;
        }
        SafeArrayUnaccessData(psaYears);
      }
      SafeArrayUnaccessData(psaNames);
    }
    return hr;
  }
  … // Other details left out for clarity
};
```

The `AgeManyGracefully` method checks security privileges and validates input to make sure that the two `SAFEARRAY`s it was given are vectors of the right size and type. Then it iterates through the input, changing each individual's age by the appropriate amount.

Here is a new version of the client, updated to use a single `PersonMgr` object instead of three `Person` objects.

```
' define three people
Dim names(3) As String
names(0) = "Jane"
names(1) = "Bob"
names(2) = "Tazwell"
' define three increments
Dim years(3) As Long
years(0) = 17
years(1) = 29
years(2) = 50
' Age all three people at once
Dim pm As IPersonMgr
Set pm = New PersonMgr
pm.AgeManyGracefully 3, names, years
```

The advantage of this approach is that it realizes the original goal. Assuming that, like the `Person` class, the `PersonMgr` class is registered as using the COM+ transaction service, the client's work now takes place in a single transaction. The burden of transaction management falls entirely to the server, where it belongs. No assumptions are made about the configuration of the client machine, other than that it can create and use a `PersonMgr` object. As an added benefit, the number of roundtrips from the client to the middle tier has been reduced to one, the call to `pm.AgeManyGracefully`. Figure 1-14 shows the new model.

The COM+ plumbing makes sure the `PersonMgr`'s declarative transaction protects the work done by each of the three `Person` objects. It ends the transaction when the client's call to `AgeManyGracefully` completes. This is exactly what the client wants. It has changed all three peoples' ages in a single operation that is guaranteed to execute atomically.

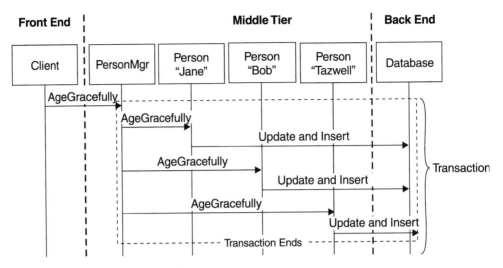

**Figure 1-14   Using a PersonMgr**

### Thinking about Roundtrips Again

The sequence diagram in Figure 1-14 makes it easy to see why using a `PersonMgr` object is a good idea. It does exactly what the client wants, the client doesn't have to worry about transactions, and all the work is done in one roundtrip from the front end to the middle tier. However, the diagram also points out that there are three roundtrips from the middle tier to the back end. Each call to `AgeGracefully` means more time spent on the network, and more time holding RM locks. This is a familiar problem. It is a variation on a theme introduced earlier, in the version of `Person::AgeGracefully` that relied on `get_Age` and `put_Age` to hide the details of data access. That implementation made three calls to the database when only one was necessary. That's exactly what is happening here, and it is happening for exactly the same reason.

In general, there is a fundamental tension between encapsulating the details of data access and making a complex task that involves data access efficient in the aggregate. Hiding details is a good idea, but in this case it means inadvertently making the system significantly slower. This is not good for scalability, which is constrained by contention for resources. If you want scalability, you have to use resources efficiently. That is the reason for Rule 1.2, which this scheme violates by holding locks longer than necessary. Because the `Person` class hides the data access code, `PersonMgr` is forced to make `nCount` roundtrips to the database to service each client request. In this case, it makes three roundtrips where it could make one. The cost of the two extra calls may seem trivial, but consider the cost of updating the ages of 100 people or 1,000 people.

It is the job of the `PersonMgr` class to see the world from the client's point of view. Individual `Person` objects lack that perspective, which makes it impossible for them to supply the transactional semantics the client needs. It also makes it impossible for them to implement access to the back-end database efficiently. They lack the client's or the `PersonMgr`'s understanding of the overall task. The solution to this problem is to revise `PersonMgr` to handle the details of data access itself.

```
STDMETHODIMP PersonMgr::AgeManyGracefully(long nCount,
                                          SAFEARRAY *psaNames,
                                          SAFEARRAY *psaYears)
{
  if (!CallerIsFatherTime()) return E_ACCESSDENIED;
  if (!ValidInput(nCount, psaNames, psaYears))
    return E_INVALIDARG;
  BSTR *rgbstr = 0;
  HRESULT hr = SafeArrayAccessData(psaNames, (void**)&rgbstr);
  if (SUCCEEDED(hr))
  {
    long *rgn = 0;
    hr = SafeArrayAccessData(psaYears, (void**)&rgn);
    if (SUCCEEDED(hr))
    {
      OLECHAR wsz[256];
      CComBSTR bstr;
      for (long i = 0; i < nCount; i++)
      {
        wsprintfW(wsz,
                L"update persons set age = age + %d where name
                                          = \'%s\'\n",
                rgn[i], rgbstr[i]);
        bstr.Append(wsz);
        wsprintfW(wsz,
                L"insert into auditlog (name, age_change) \
                  values(\'%s\', %d)",
                rgbstr[i], rgn[i]);
        bstr.Append(wsz);
      }
```

```
      hr = ExecSQL(bstr, 0);
      SafeArrayUnaccessData(psaYears);
    }
    SafeArrayUnaccessData(psaNames);
  }
  return hr;
}
```

The previous version of `AgeManyGracefully` created a `Person` object to increment each individual's age and record the fact that it did so. This new version simply composes a batch SQL statement that does the same thing. If a stored procedure were being used to isolate the details of the `persons` schema, the batch SQL statement would invoke it three times. When the SQL statement is complete, it calls the `ExecSQL` helper method (which it borrows from the `Person` class) to invoke it. The advantage of this approach—fewer roundtrips—is apparent in Figure 1-15.

As you can see, the overall operation is now as efficient as possible. There is one roundtrip from the client to the middle tier. If the client request is a good one—client has permission to make the call and has provided input that is valid—there is one roundtrip from middle-tier server to back-end database.

### Processor Objects

The `PersonMgr` class's job is to implement the process the client wants to execute. The `PersonMgr` class is an example of a *processor object*. Logically, a processor is part of a client. It models the world from a client's point of view, using that broader knowledge to implement the logic of the task correctly and

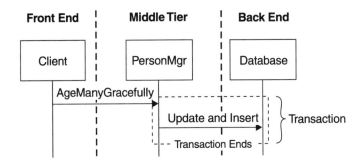

**Figure 1-15   Making PersonMgr more efficient**

TRANSACTIONAL COM+: BUILDING SCALABLE APPLICATIONS

efficiently, protecting it with a transaction when necessary. Physically, a processor executes on a middle-tier server. This is purely for mechanical reasons. The processor has access to back-end databases and the middle-tier server's external TM, so it can use local transactions or distributed transactions as it sees fit. Either way, it can make sure RM locks are held for as short a time as possible.

From an object-oriented (OO) perspective, introducing processor objects may seem unnatural. It certainly flies in the face of the old OO chestnut that "nouns are objects and verbs are methods." However, the notion of using a class to model a task is not new. In fact, there is a lot of precedent for this approach. Well-known terms like *controller, coordinator, manager, façade, service, units-of-work, session,* and *business process object* have all been used (some would argue misused) to describe different versions of essentially this same "verb as object" idea. The term *processor object* avoids all the baggage associated with these other terms.[10]

Whatever the term, the processor idea fits perfectly with the purpose of the middle tier, which is to consolidate logic in a central location. Implementing logic in the middle tier removes the need for each client to connect directly to back-end databases and helps relieve client configuration management headaches. Implementing logic in the middle tier also reduces the load on back-end databases. In general, the purpose of middle-tier code is to execute logic as data is transferred back and forth between clients and databases without making that work a burden for either one. This is exactly what processors are designed to do.

From an object-oriented perspective, downplaying object composition—as in the final version of `PersonMgr`—may also seem unnatural. Remember that scalability is the goal. Scalability requires efficiency, and efficiency requires speed. Calls across the network are slow. You should avoid object models that require lots of them. This is not a new idea either; anyone who has been using DCOM (or any other form of RPC) for any length of time knows that remote invocations are a performance killer. Long-standing conventional wisdom reflects this: Do not access properties or traverse large object hierarchies across the

---

[10] I also wanted to avoid endless debates along the following lines, "A façade cannot model a process," "Gamma's example is a compiler," "A compiler is a thing, not a process," "Just because it ends in 'r'?" "Yes," and so on.

wire, and pass data by value whenever you can. If you are going to apply these guidelines to your client–to–middle-tier communication, *you should apply them to your middle-tier–to–back-end communication too*.

Do not force your processor objects to rely on an underlying "data object" model derived from your database schema. For example, it is not a good idea to make a processor use three different objects—and make three roundtrips to a back-end database—to access customer, order, and inventory tables when a client wants to place an order. It may be easy to code, but it will never be optimal (it probably won't even get close). Instead, encapsulate database schema details with a combination of stored procedures and views. Then let your processors go straight to SQL.

This doesn't mean you should never use a more conventional, hierarchical object model. Pass persisted-object hierarchies as input to and output from processors. Use a conventional object model to build your client's user interface. Use a conventional object model to represent data cached in a middle-tier process. Just don't use a conventional object model when the price is additional network roundtrips.

Processors are key. They bring the notion of large-scale distribution—highly efficient, concurrent operations protected by transactions—to the very heart of your object model. A processor's task-oriented focus gives it the perspective necessary to manage transactions and access back-end data efficiently. A processor's task-oriented focus also makes it easy to implement security policies. Anyone who has the right to use some or all of the methods or interfaces of a particular processor class is, by definition, allowed to perform one or more tasks. A processor's task-oriented focus makes it easy to integrate with connectionless protocols like HTTP too. There is no reason a client needs to stay bound to a machine for longer than it takes a processor to execute a single task. This lack of server affinity makes aggressive load balancing easier and makes your system more reliable as well. All in all, processors provide a great abstraction for implementing a scalable architecture. This is Rule 1.3.

 **RULE** **1.3**

Model client tasks using processor objects that execute on middle-tier servers.

TRANSACTIONAL COM+: BUILDING SCALABLE APPLICATIONS

# Summary

This chapter introduces the basic architectural model used in COM+ systems. The model is derived from the need for scalability, which is the essential problem developers of large distributed applications are facing today. At its core, scalability concerns resources and contention for resources. Scalable systems have to use resources as efficiently as possible. The goal is to avoid enough bottlenecks to achieve the desired level of throughput. Designing scalable systems is difficult. Designing scalable systems using conventional object-oriented techniques is extremely difficult, so COM+ rejects that approach in favor of a much different style.

Every COM+ client uses its own COM object(s) to manipulate the same underlying shared state, which is stored in a back-end database. This is the object-per-client model. It simplifies development because objects do not have to worry about synchronizing access to their data members. However, objects do have to worry about synchronizing access to the data they share. To solve this problem, COM+ objects rely on transactions, a well-known mechanism for protecting concurrent work against a database.

The objects COM+ clients use model processes that clients can invoke. The task-oriented nature of these objects (I call them processors, but you can use whatever name you like) gives them the perspective they need to process requests as efficiently as possible, with a minimum of network roundtrips to back-end databases. By optimizing resource usage, processors promote scalability.

# Chapter 2

# Atoms

Having a general model for building scalable systems using objects is a good starting point, but it is not enough to design and develop a COM+-based system. To use COM+ effectively you need to understand not just its philosophy—it is designed to support the processor model described in the previous chapter—but also how it works. All the runtime services COM+ offers (synchronization, declarative transactions, just-in-time activation, etc.) are built on top of two fundamental atoms called context and causality. To do anything with COM+, you must understand contexts and causalities, why they exist, and how objects interact with them. This chapter introduces both constructs. It starts with a story.[1]

## The Linker Switch Story

Let's climb into the way-back machine and head back to the early days of Win32 development when most people were building stand-alone executables instead of COM components.[2] The Visual C++ project wizard includes two options for generating executables, a graphical Win32 Application or a Win32 Console Application. If you are a developer working in that era, you have to choose one type of executable or the other. This begs the question, What's the key difference between these two types of applications?

Among the many answers to this question, the most common reply is that a graphical windows application uses `WinMain` as an entry point and a console application uses `main`. This is just an artifact of the C Runtime Library (CRT),

---

[1] I first heard this story from my friend Don Box.

[2] See Sherman and Mr. Peabody on Jay Ward's *The Adventures of Rocky and Bullwinkle* for more information about this fantastic device.

which runs some initialization code when your process starts and then calls one or the other entry point, depending on the type of application. The CRT could have been written to use the same entry point for both application types, so I discount this as anything more than a superficial difference. Another common answer is the ability to use graphical elements such as `MessageBoxes` and other sorts of windows. This is also a superficial difference; console applications can call `MessageBox`, `RegisterWindowClass`, `CreateWindow`, and `GetMessage/DispatchMessage` just like a graphical application can (assuming you link to the right import libraries). Similarly, a graphical application can create a console explicitly by calling the `AllocConsole` API and then redirecting the handles defined by the CRT's Standard I/O library (`stdin`, `stdout`, and `stderr`) to use it for input and output. So what *is* the key difference between these two application types? Console applications *expect* to have a console made for them and to have the standard handles bound to it *by default.*

Consider the following code, generated by the Visual C++ Win32 Console Application project wizard using the "Hello World!" option.[3]

```
int main(int argc, char* argv[])
{
  printf("Hello World!\n");
  return 0;
}
```

The implementation of `main` uses `printf` to output its greeting, blissfully happy in the belief that a console will be available at runtime. Graphical applications (and console applications that use graphical windows) make no such assumption; they create their windows from scratch. As it turns out, however, this console application's blind faith is well founded—when it runs, there will be a console for it to use.

### An Experiment

To test this behavior, build a simple "Hello World!" console application, or pick a standard console application, such as `cmd.exe`, and run it from Explorer. When you double click on the executable's icon, what happens? You see a con-

---

[3] Thank goodness this wizard option has been added, otherwise writing "Hello World!" as a console application might take an inordinately long time.

sole appear very quickly and then disappear. It stays on the screen only for a moment because the program ends immediately. Where does the console window come from?

You may think the standard C runtime prolog code, which executes after your application starts but before `main` is called, takes a moment to set up the console on the application's behalf. This is not the case. To verify this, look at the functions the application imports from the Win32 system DLLs. You can do this using the `dumpbin.exe` tool that is included with Visual C++, with the `/imports` switch. To narrow the search, pipe the results into `find.exe`, a shell tool included with the operating system. Look for any imported symbol that includes the word "Console." Here is what you should see (unless you are experimenting with `cmd.exe`, in which case you will see a lot more).

```
C:> dumpbin /imports consoleapp.exe | find "Console"
    26E SetConsoleCtrlHandler
```

If the C runtime prolog code created the application's console, the application would also import `AllocConsole`. To verify this claim, run the console application from a command prompt. This time, you will not get a new console; the application will use the command prompt's console instead! So who is calling `AllocConsole`, and why is it called in some cases and not in others?

## The Windows Process Loader

Whenever an executable is started, the Windows process loader examines the executable image and looks for a marker that indicates whether the application needs a console. If it does need a console and none is available, the loader creates one for the new process to use. This is what happens when a console application is started from Explorer. If the executable needs a console, but one is already available, the loader does not create a new one. In this case, the new process simply reuses the existing console. This is what happens when a console application is started from a command prompt. This brings us to a final question: What does the process loader look at to decide whether the application it is launching needs a console?

All Win32 application binaries are stored on disk in the Portable Executable (PE) format. The PE format includes a set of headers that describe various aspects of the executable. The subsystem header indicates the I/O subsystem an application wants to use. You can see the subsystem header for any given executable using `dumpbin.exe` with the `/headers` switch. If you do this with your console application (or `cmd.exe`), you should get this output:

```
C:> dumpbin /headers consoleapp.exe | find "subsys"
    4.00 subsystem version
       3 subsystem (Windows CUI)
```

All console application executables are marked with a subsystem value of 3, indicating their desire for a console. Graphical applications are marked with a subsystem value of 2, indicating to the loader that they do not need a console. The subsystem header's value is set at build time. It is controlled by the `/subsystem` linker switch. The `/subsystem` switch is esoteric to many modern Windows developers because it is set implicitly when they create a new project in Visual C++. In fact, there is no easy way to set the value with the development environment's Project Settings dialog. However, it is possible to see the switch in use if you scroll through the Project Options edit box on the Link tab. There you'll find `/subsystem:console` for console applications or `/subsystem:windows` for graphical applications.

### How COM+ Works

A console application is fundamentally different from a graphical application because of a linker switch. Console applications declare their need for a console by linking with the `/subsystem:console` option, which brands them with a PE subsystem header that communicates this requirement to the Windows loader. When the loader launches a process of this type, it makes sure that one way or another the new process has access to a console, creating a new one if necessary. *The code in the console application makes no attempt to determine whether a console is available; it trusts the loader to make sure its environment is correct.*

If you understand this idea, you understand how COM+ works.

## From Consoles to Contexts

If an executable is branded as requiring a console, its process's environment will include one, and code executing in that space can safely assume the console is present and make use of it. COM+ leverages this idea and uses it as the abstract model for providing all of its runtime services. COM+ code that needs a runtime service (e.g., security, a distributed transaction, etc.) executes in an environment that provides that service. It would be very inefficient to map these environments directly to processes. If every object with slightly different service requirements had to run in a separate process, there would be many processes, and calls between them would be expensive. So COM+ implements multiple fine-grained runtime environments in a single process, allowing objects with disparate service requirements to interact with a minimum of overhead. These subprocess environments are called contexts.

A *context* is a space within a process that provides a specific set of services to the objects executing inside it. Every object created in a COM+ process is associated with exactly one context that provides the services it requires. If two objects have compatible service requirements, they can share a context; one environment can meet both their needs. If two objects have incompatible service requirements, they must live in different contexts; one environment cannot meet both their needs. A process contains as many contexts as are necessary to satisfy every object's runtime service needs. Figure 2-1 illustrates. In this picture, each process is divided into contexts. Process M contains a single context, A. Process N contains two contexts, B and C. There are two objects in each context. Each pair of objects in each context is, by definition, using the same set of services. In other words, services are mapped to contexts, not objects. This is the basic anatomy of a COM+ process.

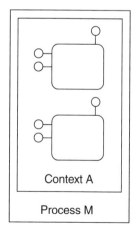
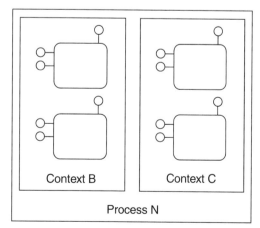

Context A          Context B          Context C

Process M                    Process N

**Figure 2-1   Processes, contexts, and objects**

## Cross-Context Calls

Two objects living in the same context can hold direct references to each other. Calls between them are simply virtual method invocations. Two objects living in separate contexts cannot hold direct references to each other. Instead, cross-context access requires the use of a proxy. Remember that a proxy is a stand-in for a real object that knows how to package method invocations and forward them to the real object, wherever it happens to be. In classic COM, proxies were used only if a call needed to be dispatched on another thread, perhaps in another process. COM+ uses the proxy mechanism to preprocess and postprocess every cross-context method invocation, whether calls need to be serviced on another thread or not. The proxy mechanism gives COM+ a way to provide its services. In essence, proxies tell the runtime when a call is made from one environment to another and give it a chance to transparently invoke service code. The runtime has the opportunity to set up the environment the target context needs before each method call starts and to restore the environment the calling context needs after each method call ends. This technique is known as *interception* and is transparent to both the caller and the object, as Figure 2-2 illustrates.

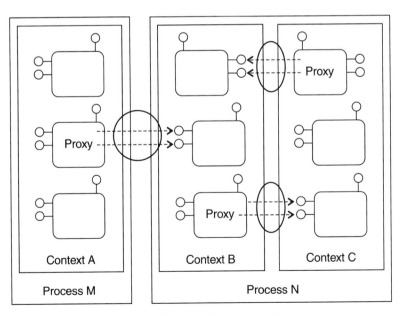

**Figure 2-2** **Cross-context calls are intercepted by proxies.**

TRANSACTIONAL COM+: BUILDING SCALABLE APPLICATIONS

In this figure, each context has a proxy that represents an object in a different context. Context A has a proxy to an object in context B, context B has a proxy to an object in context C, and context C has a proxy to an object in context B. The three circles indicate the points where the COM+ plumbing intercepts calls and triggers the services the code in the target context wants to use.

You may wonder what exactly the plumbing does when it is pre- and postprocessing cross-context method invocations. The answer is . . . it depends. It may do as little as increment a counter to indicate that a call is in progress. It may do as much as move the entire call stack to a thread in another process on another machine. In general, the plumbing always does the minimum amount of work necessary to invoke code in the destination context while making sure that its runtime environment meets its needs.

This description of the plumbing's behavior is vague, but that cannot be helped. Discussions about context in the abstract have to be vague because the context mechanism is completely generic. If you do not know anything about the runtime environment of a context, you cannot say anything about how calls into or out of that context will be pre- and postprocessed. If, on the other hand, you know the exact characteristics of two contexts, you can specify exactly what the plumbing does when a call is made between them. For example, if you know that a call is being made from a context that does not use declarative transactions (remember that a declarative transaction is simply a distributed transaction that is managed by COM+) to a context that does, the interception plumbing makes sure a distributed transaction is available if one is needed while the call executes. You also know that the plumbing can end the transaction after the call completes but before control is returned to the caller. It is this aspect of context—the fact that it is abstract in general and very concrete in specific—that makes it, initially, a difficult construct for many developers to understand. Later chapters explain how specific COM+ services are implemented using pre- and postprocessing code the plumbing invokes around each method call.

## Contexts as Objects

The fact that COM+ implements its runtime services by pre- and postprocessing cross-context method invocations leads to an interesting problem. If services are implemented transparently via call interception, how does an object interact with them? If the code that provides a service is hidden, how can an object use that service to make things happen? For instance, if the object is in a context that provides a declarative transaction, how can the object influence the transaction's outcome?

The COM+ plumbing solves this problem by representing each context as an object called an *object context*. The runtime maintains a unique object context for each context in a process. Each object context implements interfaces that allow an object to interact with the runtime services its context provides. From an object's perspective, its context's object context represents the world the object lives in. If an object's context includes a declarative transaction and the object wants to influence the transaction's outcome, it can do so by using its object context.

An object can acquire a reference to its context's object context by calling the `CoGetObjectContext` API.

```
HRESULT CoGetObjectContext([in] REFIID riid,
                           [out, iid_is(riid)] void **ppv);
```

`CoGetObjectContext` always returns a reference to the object context of the context the calling thread is currently in. The interception plumbing tracks which context a thread is executing in. It updates this information dynamically when a thread moves from one context to another through a proxy. Because the runtime always knows which context a thread is currently in, `CoGetObjectContext` always knows which object context to return a reference to. Figure 2-3 illustrates the object context architecture.

Two threads, A and B, are simultaneously executing code in two contexts, A and B, respectively. The threads are associated with the two *different* object contexts. If thread B finished its work in context B and returned to context A, the interception plumbing would make sure both threads were associated with the *same* object context.

If you are working in Visual Basic 6, you cannot call the `CoGetObject Context` API directly. It requires an IID as an input parameter, a data type VB does not support. COM+ provides another function to make object context available to VB-based objects, `GetObjectContext`:

```
Function GetObjectContext() As ObjectContext
```

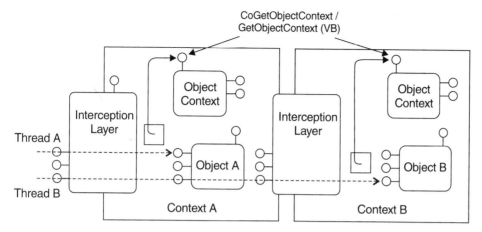

**Figure 2-3  Object context**

It is defined in the COM+ Services Type Library, `COMSVCS.DLL`.

### Object Context Interfaces

Each object context exposes several interfaces, as shown in Figure 2-4. The interfaces on the left of the diagram are designed for use from C++. The interfaces on the right are designed for use from Visual Basic. The interfaces in bold type are preferred in COM+. The ones shown as normal text are available solely for backward compatibility. Their functionality is duplicated by the newer re-factored interfaces.

The first two object context interfaces are `IObjectContextInfo` and `ContextInfo`. Both interfaces allow an object to query its context for information about its configuration. The next object context interface is `IContext State`. It allows an object to control its lifetime and the lifetime and outcome of its declarative transaction, if it has one.[4] The object context's last pair of interfaces, `IGetContextProperties` and `ObjectContext`, allow COM+ objects being used from Active Server Pages (ASP) to access the ASP intrinsic object model (e.g., Request, Response, etc.). (This is the only thing Visual Basic objects need the `ObjectContext` interface for; all the rest of its functionality

---

[4] Chapter 5, Objects, and Chapter 6, Transactions, discuss this interface in detail.

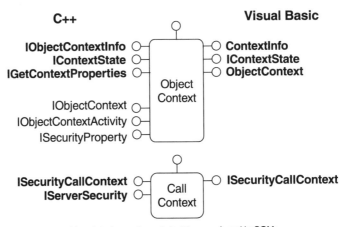

Note: Interfaces shown in **bold** are preferred in COM+.

**Figure 2-4   Object context interfaces**

**Table 2-1   Object context interfaces**

| Interface | Provides |
|---|---|
| IObjectContextInfo/ ContextInfo | Access to information about the environment the context represents |
| IContextState | Control over an object's lifetime and the lifetime and outcome of its declarative transaction, if any |
| IGetContextProperties/ ObjectContext | Access to ASP's object model if object is being used from ASP |

is available from the newer interfaces.)[5] Table 2-1 summarizes the object context interfaces.

## Using Object Context

Here is an example that demonstrates the use of object context. Every context is uniquely identified by a GUID called a context ID. You can ask an object context to return the ID of the context it represents. Although this information is probably not very useful in a production system, it can be quite helpful when debugging (or when spelunking around inside a process figuring out how COM+ works). It also provides the simplest possible example of using object context.

---

[5] Chapter 8, Protocols, discusses these interfaces in detail.

```
HRESULT CSomeCfgClass::WhereAmI(BSTR *pbstrCtxId)
{
  // get reference to object context
  CComPtr<IObjectContextInfo> spCtxInfo;
  hr = CoGetObjectContext(__uuidof(spCtxInfo), (void**)&spCtxInfo);
  // retrieve context ID
  GUID ctxId = GUID_NULL;
  hr = spCtxInfo->GetContextId(&ctxId);
  if (FAILED(hr)) return hr;
  // convert ID to string and return as out parameter
  CComBSTR bstr(ctxId);
  return bstr.CopyTo(pbstrCtxId);
}
```

The `WhereAmI` method calls `CoGetObjectContext` to get an `IObject ContextInfo` reference to its object context. Then it calls the `GetContextId` to retrieve its context's ID, a GUID. Finally, it converts the GUID to a BSTR and returns it to the caller. This style—making use of an object representing the environment in which a chunk of code is executing—makes COM+ code very different from classic COM code.[6]

## Where Do Contexts Come From?

Many developers find contexts a difficult construct to grasp because they seem very abstract. But contexts are actually quite concrete; each one is uniquely identified by a GUID, and the objects within a context can interact with it using object context. One of the reasons that contexts seem so intangible is that there is no documented API for creating them. COM+ does not provide a `CoCreate Context` function or any other way to explicitly manufacture new contexts. Instead, COM+ creates new contexts implicitly, as they are needed to house new objects whose needs cannot be met by their creators' context. In other words, context creation is tied directly to object creation.

---

[6] The act of accessing object context is known colloquially as "reaching into context" or "reaching up into context," as in "An object can reach [up] into context to retrieve its context ID." Often, while uttering this phrase, the speaker raises her right hand just above her head and, with elbow bent forward, wiggles her fingers. This universal hand signal for "reaching [up] into context" is for dramatic effect. It is also appropriate for clandestine communication about COM+ programming. It is derived from the conventional wisdom that the COM+ plumbing maintains context slightly above and to the right of each object.

COM+ offers runtime services to classes that indicate a desire to use them. If a class has indicated that it requires a service, instances of the class execute in a context that makes that service an intrinsic part of the object's runtime environment. Each service's behavior—whether or not it is used and the details of what it does—is controlled by one or more *declarative attributes.* You can think of these attributes as similar to the PE subsystem header that indicates whether a Win32 application expects a console to be part of its environment. A class indicates its desire to use a service by declaring the appropriate attribute(s) when it is registered on a system. Classes that declare one or more attributes—and use one or more services—are called *configured classes.* Classes that do not specify attributes are called *nonconfigured classes*. All classic COM classes are nonconfigured.

When an instance of a class is created via the Service Control Manager (SCM), the SCM checks the declarative attributes defined by the class. Then it examines the context where the code that called `CoCreateInstance[Ex]` (or the `CreateObject` function in Visual Basic) is executing.[7] If the SCM decides the current context *can* meet the environmental needs of the new object without additional interception, it assigns the new object to the current context, and returns a raw reference to the object to the creator. If the SCM decides the current context *cannot* meet the environmental needs of the new object without additional interception, it builds a brand new context, assigns the new object to it, and returns a reference to a proxy to the creator. This is how new contexts are created. All of this happens within the scope of the object creation call.

### The Catalog

The declarative attributes for each configured class are stored in the COM+ *catalog.* The SCM consults the catalog to see which services a configured class wants to use. The catalog is an abstraction that hides the location of information about configured classes. Some of the information about each configured class is in the Registry for backward compatibility with classic COM.

---

[7] The SCM is a distributed entity, implemented partially in a service—RPCSS.DLL loaded into the surrogate process SVCHOST.EXE—and partially in the standard COM library—OLE32.DLL—loaded into every COM process. This makes it easy to examine the context where the creation request originated.

Specifically, each configured class has a key entry under `HKEY_CLASSES` `_ROOT\CLSID`. All the new declarative attributes are not stored in the Registry. They are recorded in a series of component library (CLB) files stored in the `%systemroot%\Registration` directory. The format of CLB files is not documented. The catalog encapsulates all this information on a per-machine basis. Each machine running Windows 2000 has a catalog of its own. For efficiency's sake, the contents of the catalog are cached in memory so that the SCM does not have to access a disk as part of each creation request.

The catalog can be managed programmatically through a hierarchical object model with `COMAdminCatalog` at its root. These catalog administration objects are designed to be script-friendly, so catalog management can be done entirely with JScript or VBScript files executed from command lines using the Windows Scripting Host. The catalog can also be managed interactively via the Component Services Explorer (CSE), a Microsoft Management Console snap-in built on top of the catalog's object model. Note, however, that not all of the catalog's settings are exposed via the CSE; some can be set only programmatically. At installation time, configured classes are registered in the catalog either directly via the administrative object model or interactively through the CSE. Either way, COM+ has the opportunity to verify that classes are registered correctly and possibly to change the format of registration information over time. This new layer of indirection should help put an end to the Registry-related configuration bugs that have plagued COM developers for several years.

**Applications**

The catalog divides configured classes into logical groupings called *applications*. Each configured class belongs to exactly one application. Every application has a set of attributes that apply to all the classes it contains. Table 2-2 lists the basic application attributes. (Additional application attributes are discussed as they come up in later chapters.[8])

Notice that each application has a name, description, and COM+-assigned unique ID, a GUID.

---

[8] For a complete list of all the application attributes, see the Applications Collection documentation in the Platform SDK.

**Table 2-2  Basic application attributes**

| Attribute | Type | Default | Notes |
|---|---|---|---|
| Name | String | "New Application" | Name of application |
| Description | String | "" | Description of application |
| ID | GUID | Generated by COM+ | Unique ID, assigned by COM+ when application is created |
| Activation | COMAdminActivationOptions | COMAdminActivationLocal | Controls the process that an application's classes activate in |
| ShutdownAfter | Long, 0 to 1,440 minutes (24 hours) | 3 | How long to idle before shutting down, after last object goes away; 0 means shutdown immediately |
| RunForever | Boolean | False | If true, process never shuts down, overrides ShutdownAfter |
| Changeable | Boolean | True | Advisory lock to protect application from configuration changes; false = locked |
| Deletable | Boolean | True | Advisory lock to protect application from deletion; false = locked |

## Libraries and Servers

Beyond these basic identifiers, the most important application attribute is its activation type. Each application is configured as either a *library* or a *server,* and the choice determines how the classes in the application are mapped to processes.

Library applications (`Activation = COMAdminActivationInproc`) always activate directly in a caller's process. When a client requests a new instance of a class that is part of a library application, the SCM makes sure the code for the application's classes is loaded into the caller's process. Then the SCM creates the new object either in the context of the code calling `CoCreateInstance[Ex]` or in a new context in the same process, depending on its environmental needs as specified in the catalog.

Server applications (`Activation = COMAdminActivationLocal`) always activate in a process of their own. When a client requests a new instance of a class that is part of a server application, the SCM makes sure the code for the application's classes is loaded into a dedicated process, starting the process if necessary. Then the SCM creates the new object in a brand-new context in the server process, configured to meet the object's requirements.

Each configured class is added to either a library or a server application at deployment time. In essence, we're deferring the decision about which process a class's code should be loaded into until the code is installed on a system. To support this degree of flexibility, configured classes are always implemented using in-process servers, DLLs that can be loaded into a caller's process, or a separate surrogate server process as needed. Loading a DLL into a caller's process is easy, but loading a DLL into a separate process requires that some sort of basic bootstrapping program be running. COM+ leverages the classic COM surrogate process, the appropriately named `dllhost.exe`, for this purpose. One side effect of this approach is that it is no longer possible to consult the Registry to discover where instances of a class will be activated. Every configured class is registered with an InprocServer32 key. The only way to know where instances of a configured class will be activated is to look in the catalog to see what type of application the class belongs to.

COM+ maps each server application to a separate instance of `dllhost.exe`, launched with the `/ProcessId:{application ID}` command line flag to tell it which server application it represents. The lifetime of each server application process depends on the application's `ShutdownAfter` and `RunForever` attributes. Specifically, the `ShutdownAfter` property determines how many minutes an application's instance of `dllhost.exe` will idle after its last object is released before shutting down. The default for new applications is 3 minutes, the minimum is 0 minutes (shutdown immediately), and the maximum is 1440 minutes (24 hours). If an application's `RunForever` property is set to true, its instance of `dllhost.exe` will not shut down unless it is explicitly stopped. The purpose of both these settings is to avoid the cost of continually starting and stopping commonly used server processes, which is expensive. These properties have no meaning for a library application; its lifetime is limited by the lifetime of the process that loaded it.

It is important to note that the mapping of classes to applications is completely independent of the mapping of classes to DLLs. In general, $x$ classes from $y$ DLLs can be mapped to $z$ applications, as shown in Figure 2-5. In this example, each DLL implements two classes, and each application contains two classes, but the mapping from DLLs to applications is not one to one.

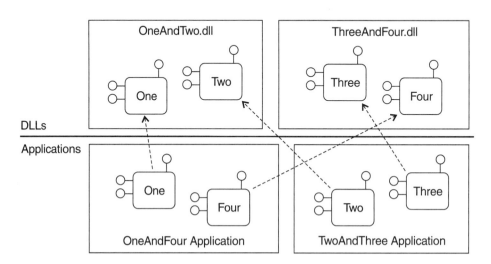

**Figure 2-5** *x* classes, *y* DLLs, and *z* applications

## Why Library Applications?

Server applications are more common than library applications simply because they run in separate processes that can be accessed remotely by clients. If you are using COM+ to develop a three-tier system, with the majority of object code running on middle-tier machines, server applications are necessary. If your client code and COM+ code are typically installed on different machines, what is the point of library applications, which are loaded into a calling process? Library applications provide a useful way to deploy utility classes that you want to use from more than one server application. Imagine you have developed an auditing class that writes information to a log. Multiple classes in multiple server applications may want to use auditing objects while they do their work. You cannot deploy the auditing class in *every* server application that wants to use it; configured classes are always contained in a *single* application. You could deploy the auditing class in a server application of its own, but then its instances would run in a separate process, and accessing them from other server applications would require cross-process calls. A much better approach is to deploy the auditing class in a library application.

The library application can be loaded into as many server applications' processes as necessary. Instances of the auditing class can be created in each server application process and accessed with much less overhead (though a cross-context call may still be necessary). In essence, you are using a library application to overcome the restriction that each configured class must be in exactly one application. Library applications are also useful if we want to load code into a process other than dllhost.exe. For instance, you may want to load code directly into a Web server process in order to respond to an HTTP request.

Here is a general example to help reinforce the relationship between library applications and processes. Consider four configured classes called A, B, C, and D. Classes A, B, and C are deployed in server applications named ASrv, BSrv, and CSrv, respectively. D is a utility class deployed in a library application named DLib. A and B objects create and use instances of C and D to do their work. Figure 2-6 shows all these applications mapped to processes.

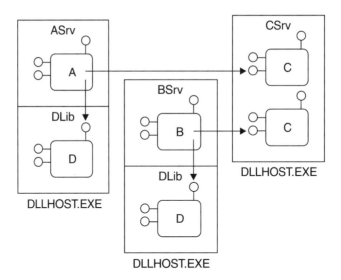

**Figure 2-6   Applications and processes**

### Configured Classes

Each configured class in an application has an individual set of attributes that controls how it uses COM+ runtime services. Table 2-3 lists the basic attributes for a configured class. (As I introduce specific services in later chapters, I'll talk about the additional attributes that control them.[9])

### Custom Attributes

The set of declarative attributes COM+ defines for controlling runtime services is fixed and cannot be extended (today). However, the catalog can store a single custom attribute for each class that can be used to encode arbitrary configuration information. This custom attribute is called a *constructor string*. The string is stored as up to 512 characters of plain text, and the catalog treats it as opaque data. If a class has a constructor string in the catalog, the COM+ plumbing hands the string to new instances of the class as they are created.

You have to do two things to enable this functionality. First, you have to register your class as using object construction (ConstructionEnabled =

---

[9] For a complete list of all the application attributes, see the Components Collection documentation in the Platform SDK.

TRANSACTIONAL COM+: BUILDING SCALABLE APPLICATIONS

**Table 2-3  Basic class attributes**

| Attribute | Type | Default | Notes |
|---|---|---|---|
| CLSID | GUID | Required | Unique name of class |
| ProgId | String | Required | Text-based name of class (not unique) |
| DLL | String | Required | Path to file that implements class |
| Description | String | "" | Description of class |
| ConstructionEnabled | Boolean | False | Each new class instance expects runtime to hand it ConstructorString |
| ConstructorString | String | "" | String for runtime to hand to each new class instance |

true) and store its constructor string in the catalog (ConstructorString = "This string will be passed to every new instance of this class"). Second, you have to implement the standard construction interface, IObjectConstruct.

```
IObjectConstruct : public IUnknown
{
  HRESULT Construct([in] IDispatch *pCtorObj);
}
```

The COM+ plumbing will call Construct to deliver a class's constructor string to each object of that type that is created. Notice that the argument to Construct is not a string, but an object reference, pCtorObj. This argument points to a constructor object, which implements IDispatch and IObject ConstructString.

```
IObjectConstructString : public IDispatch
{
  [propget] HRESULT ConstructString([out, retval] BSTR *pVal);
}
```

An implementation of Construct can extract its constructor string by calling IDispatch::Invoke, which is painful in C++ but easy in Visual Basic, or it can call QueryInterface to get an IObjectConstructString reference and then access the `ConstructString` property directly. Here is an example.

```
class CSomeCfgClassWithCustomAttr : IObjectConstruct,
                              … // Other details left out
                                          for clarity
{
  // data member to hold constructor string
  CComBSTR m_bstr;
public:
  // Construct method is called when object is created
  HRESULT Construct(IDispatch *pCtorObj)
  {
    // query constructor object for string interface
    CComPtr<IObjectConstructString> spCtorString;
    HRESULT hr = pCtorObj->QueryInterface(__uuidof(spCtorString),
                                    (void**)& spCtorString);
    if (FAILED(hr)) return hr;
    // retrieve constructor string
    return spCtorString->get_ConstructString(&m_bstr);
  }
  … // Other details left out for clarity
};
```

Assuming the `CSomeCfgClassWithCustomAttr` class is registered correctly, the COM+ plumbing will call `IObjectConstruct::Construct` as each instance is created. This implementation extracts its initialization data by querying the passed-in constructor object for `IObjectConstructString` reference, calling `get_ConstructString`, and storing the result in the `m_bstr` data member.

Here are some observations about the constructor string mechanism. First, it might seem that this solution is somewhat overengineered. It would be a lot simpler to have the `Construct` method simply accept a string as input and do away with the constructor object. The motivation for the existing model is support for future expansion; someday COM+ may support construction arguments of more complex types.

If the `Construct` method returns a failure code (e.g., `E_FAIL`), object creation fails, and `CoCreateInstance[Ex]` returns `CO_E_INITIALIZATION FAILED`. If you register a class as using a constructor string and it does not implement `IObjectConstruct`, object creation always fails, and `CoCreate Instance[Ex]` returns `E_NOINTERFACE`.

Finally, while this feature uses constructor strings and constructor objects, it has nothing whatsoever to do with constructors in the classic sense. A client does not pass these construction parameters to a new object it is creating. From the client's point of view, COM+, like classic COM, supports only default construction. Given that, what purpose do constructor strings serve? They provide an easy way to initialize classes with database connection strings (the `PersonMgr` class in Chapter 1 needs to know where to find the `persons` table), MSMQ queue names, or any other information they might need at runtime while retaining a great deal of flexibility. Because constructor strings are simply an aspect of a class's registration, they can be changed as needed without rebuilding any code.

### Changing the Contents of the Catalog

The contents of the catalog may be changed either programmatically or via the Component Services Explorer (CSE) while applications are in use. The catalog administration objects propagate information about changes to all processes executing configured class code, that is, each server application process and any other processes using library applications. None of the processes have to be restarted to see the modified settings. Changes to a class's declarative attributes affect all *new* objects of that type created *after* the changes are made. Existing objects of that type are *not* affected. For example, if an existing class is reconfigured to use a new constructor string, new instances of the class created after the change is made will be handed the new string when they are created. Existing instances of the class will not be handed the new string.

Allowing the configuration of a class to be changed dynamically without restarting any processes is a powerful feature. Being able to change a class's construct string so that objects of that type start using a different database provides a great deal of flexibility, for example. Being able to change a class's security settings to grant or deny users access to objects of that type is also very useful. There are, however, many declarative settings that should not be changed. Remember the Win32 console application from the beginning of this chapter? Its implementation was written with the expectation that a console would be present in its process's environment at runtime. The program trusts the Windows loader to guarantee that its needs would always be met. If, however, you relinked the console application with the `/subsystem:windows` switch, the Windows loader would *not* make sure the program's process had a console as part of its environment. In fact, the loader would make sure a console *was not* present! If you did not also modify the application's source code either to manufacture its own console or to not use a console, you would end up with a major bug.

The application's environment would satisfy the requirement declared by the binary executable's PE subsystem header, but it would *not* meet the source code's expectations. Similarly, modifying many of a configured class's declarative attributes—including synchronization, transaction, just-in-time activation, object pooling, and other settings—can have a dramatic impact on how instances of that class behave. Configured classes, like console applications, are written with certain attribute settings in mind. If you change a class's attributes without also changing its code, you will almost certainly introduce a significant bug, perhaps even putting the integrity of your system at risk.

So why aren't configured classes written to execute properly in different environments? Consider a processor class that needs to use a distributed transaction. If it is configured to use a declarative transaction, COM+ will make sure a distributed transaction is part of each instance's context. If the processor class had to be coded to create and manage a distributed transaction itself as well, just in case someone decides to reconfigure the class as *not* relying on declarative transactions, the benefit of relying on COM+ to provide services would be lost. The COM+ programming model is simple: With a few exceptions (e.g., constructor strings and security settings), classes do not expect their attributes to be changed. I realize that this statement belies the claim that COM+ classes can be reconfigured as needed by "application assemblers" who enable or disable services at will. While that is a beautiful idea, it is not realistic in practice. In fact, it is downright dangerous! Unfortunately, there is no good way for a class to make sure that its attributes do not get changed. Nor is there a way for an object to verify that the context it lives in actually meets all of its requirements. Object context does not provide enough information to figure this out. Like console applications, COM+ classes simply have to have faith.[10]

If all this is true, why does Windows 2000 provide a friendly user interface that allows these options to be changed? The answer is simple: The development tools you use to build COM components do not yet allow you to specify all these options using linker switches (or the moral equivalent). Until a new set of tools is available, it is up to you *and everyone else* to follow Rule 2.1.

 **2.1**

> Do not change any configured class's declarative attributes (other than constructor string and security settings) without the express permission of the author, who is the only one who can verify which settings are safe.

If you do not think everyone else is going to follow Rule 2.1, there are two things you can do in an effort to protect a class's configuration. One is to mark each application as locked (`Changeable = False`) so that neither its attributes nor any of its classes' attributes can be changed. These locks are simply advisory, however, and anyone with access to the catalog can unlock them. The other is to restrict access to the catalog so that only trusted users can modify its contents. The catalog administration objects (`COMAdminCatalog`, etc.) are classic COM nonconfigured classes that always load into a client's process. They manipulate the catalog indirectly using instances of `CatalogServer`, a configured class in the System Application. When a client attempts to change the contents of the catalog, the `CatalogServer` class checks to see if the user is a member of the System Application's Administrator role. If so, access to the catalog is allowed; if not, access is denied. By default, the local system Administrators group is included in the `Administrator` role.

## Context Flow

When a context is being built for a newly created object, some of its properties may be "inherited" from the environment of the object's creator. This phenomenon is called "context flow." In essence, the creator's context is a template

---

[10] If COM is Love, as has so often been said, perhaps COM+ is Trust.

for the context being created. For example, a configured class can specify via its attributes that it wants to share its creator's declarative transaction. As instances of this class are created, COM+ makes sure that their creators' declarative transactions are included in their new contexts, as shown in Figure 2-7.

The declarative transaction that is part of context A is inherited by context B when object B is created. This is how the previous chapter's less efficient version of the `PersonMgr` class was able to propagate its declarative transaction to multiple instances of the `Person` class (before they were removed in favor of the call to `ExecSQL`). What if object B were created from a context that did not include a declarative transaction? In that case, COM+ could create a new declarative transaction just for context B, or it could create context B without a transaction. The precise behavior would depend on the specific attribute settings for object B's class.

In the initial version of COM+, there are only two context properties that can flow to new contexts, activities and declarative transactions. (Both of these topics are discussed in great detail in Chapter 4, Threads, and Chapter 6, Transactions, respectively.) Future versions of COM+ may include additional examples of context flow as well.

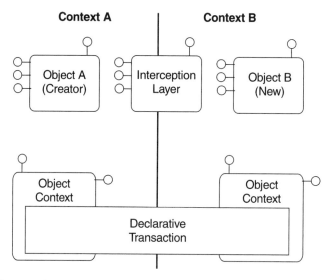

**Figure 2-7   Context flow: sharing a distributed transaction**

# Causality

COM+ processes are divided into contexts. A context is a space that provides particular runtime services to meet one or more objects' needs. COM+ implements its runtime services by pre- and postprocessing calls across context boundaries. Some services need to know whether multiple calls across context boundaries are causally related, that is, whether one call caused another. In a stand-alone application that uses multiple threads, the causal relationship between calls can be determined by thread ID. But in COM+-based systems, calls may be dispatched on different threads, perhaps in different processes. The only way to detect the relationships between calls in this scenario is to add an abstraction that's similar to a thread, but not bound to any particular process. In COM+ this abstraction is called a causality.

A *causality* is a distributed chain of COM method calls that spans any number of contexts in any number of processes. Where contexts are static spatial constructs, causalities are dynamic temporal constructs. Each causality represents a single *logical* thread of action that is doing work in a system as it winds its way from one context to another. Each causality is uniquely identified by a GUID called a causality ID, or CID; CIDs are logical thread IDs. Each causality can involve any number of physical threads. As Figure 2-8 illustrates, two

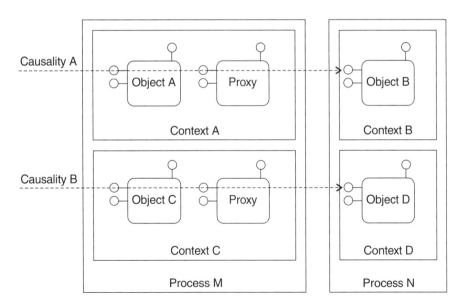

**Figure 2-8  Causalities represent logical threads of action in a system.**

causalities, A and B, are executing work in multiple contexts across multiple processes. Each call chain is uniquely identified by a CID, independent of the physical threads used to service each method call.

## How Causality Works

The implementation of causality is very simple. Whenever a new causality starts, the interception plumbing assigns it a CID. A causality's CID is automatically propagated from context to context as COM method calls are made. The same CID identifies a causality for as long as it is running. Support for this is built into the DCOM wire protocol.[11]

To make this work, the interception plumbing has to know when a new causality starts. Remember that a causality is just a chain of COM method calls. Whenever a thread that *is not* currently processing a COM method call makes a COM method call, it is by definition starting a *new* call chain and therefore a new causality. The new causality's CID is automatically propagated as part of the call. Whenever a thread that *is* currently processing a COM method call makes another COM method call, it is by definition *continuing* an existing call chain and therefore simply participating in the ongoing causality. In this case, the ongoing causality's CID is automatically propagated as part of the call.

The current implementation of causality caches CIDs on a per-thread basis. Every thread that uses COM is assigned a CID that it keeps for life. The interception plumbing uses a thread's CID to identify causalities that thread starts. A causality is always identified by the initiating thread's CID; the CIDs of all the other threads participating in a causality are ignored. The fact that a thread keeps the same CID for its entire life and reuses it for each causality it starts seems to contradict the claim that causalities are uniquely identified. Since COM method calls are blocking, however, a given thread's causality ID will represent only a single call chain at a time. A single CID will never represent two call chains executing simultaneously. In this sense, CIDs are unique.[12]

---

[11] The CID is embedded in each DCOM request message as part of the implicit ORPCTHIS parameter. See the DCOM Wire Protocol Specification for more information.

[12] There is an exception to this rule. Windows 2000 supports making multiple, *nonblocking* COM calls from the same thread. The interception plumbing gives each of these calls a brand new CID when it starts, so in this case too, CIDs are unique. In this release of Windows 2000, nonblocking calls are incompatible with configured classes and are beyond the scope of this book.

An object can retrieve the ID of the current physical thread by calling the standard Win32 API, `GetCurrentThreadId`. Unfortunately, there is no documented way for an object to retrieve the ID of the current logical thread, that is, the current causality ID. There is, however, an *undocumented* function called `CoGetCurrentLogicalThreadId` that does the trick. This API is exported by `OLE32.DLL`; if you want to call, it you have to declare its signature yourself. Here's the definition.

```
STDAPI CoGetCurrentLogicalThreadId(GUID *pcid);
```

Here is an example of its use.

```
HRESULT CSomeCfgClass::WhichCallIsThis(BSTR *pbstrCausalityId)
{
  // retrieve causality ID
  GUID causalityId;
  HRESULT hr = CoGetCurrentLogicalThreadId(&causalityId);
  if (FAILED(hr)) return E_FAIL;
  // convert ID to string and return it as out parameter
  CComBSTR bstr(causalityId);
  return bstr.CopyTo(pbstrCausalityId);
}
```

The `WhichCallIsThis` method calls `CoGetCurrentLogicalThreadId` to the current causality ID. It converts the CID to a BSTR and returns it to the caller. You cannot call `CoGetCurrentLogicalThreadId` directly from Visual Basic 6, because it returns a GUID. It would be easy, however, to implement a VB-friendly version that delegated to this API and converted its output to a BSTR, exactly like the method just discussed.

The `CoGetCurrentLogicalThreadId` function is not officially supported. It should be. Causality is a basic atom of COM+, and this API is key to working with causalities, just as `GetCurrentThreadId` is key to working with threads. Whether it uses this API or not, the COM+ plumbing can retrieve a causality's CID whenever it needs it. This same functionality should be made available to all developers as a documented part of COM+. Until it is, you use this function at your own risk.

## Causalities as Objects

The primary purpose of causality is to allow a service to detect reentrant calls into a context or a group of contexts. But one service, security, uses causalities in a different way. It leverages causality to aggregate information about every security principal participating in a given call chain and make it available to objects while method calls are executing. It does not make sense to expose this data via object context because there might be multiple causalities involving different principals doing work in the same context at the same time. Instead, the security service provides this information using objects that represent individual causalities. They are called *call context* objects. Call contexts are just like object contexts, except that, where object contexts model the space an object lives in, call contexts model work being done in that space.

An object can acquire a reference to a call context object representing the current causality by calling the `CoGetCallContext` API.

```
HRESULT CoGetCallContext([in] REFIID riid,
                         [out, iid_is(riid)] void **ppv);
```

`CoGetCallContext` always returns a reference to a call context for the causality the calling thread is currently participating in. Interception plumbing tracks which causality a thread is executing in at any given time, updating the information dynamically as a thread is used to service different COM method calls. Because the runtime always knows which causality a thread is currently participating in, `CoGetCallContext` always knows which call context to return a reference to.

Figure 2-9 illustrates call context and its relationship to object context. Two threads, A and B, are simultaneously executing code in the same context, A. The threads are part of two different causalities, so they are associated with the two *different* call contexts. The threads are working in the same context, so they are associated with the *same* object context.

You cannot call the `CoGetCallContext` API directly if you are working in VB6, because, like `CoGetObjectContext`, it requires an IID as an input parameter. COM+ provides another function to make the call context, `GetSecurityCallContext` available to VB-based objects.

```
Function GetSecurityCallContext() As SecurityCallContext
```

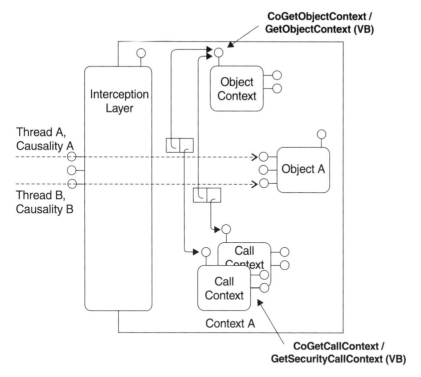

**CoGetObjectContext /
GetObjectContext (VB)**

Object
Context

Interception
Layer

Thread A,
Causality A

Object A

Thread B,
Causality B

Call
Context

Call
Context

Context A

**CoGetCallContext /
GetSecurityCallContext (VB)**

**Figure 2-9   Call context**

It is defined in the COM+ Services Type Library, COMSVCS.DLL.

### Call Context Interfaces

Each call context object exposes multiple interfaces, as shown in Figure 2-10.[13]
The interfaces shown on the left of the diagram are designed for use from C++.
The interfaces on the right are designed for use from Visual Basic.

The first call context interface is ISecurityCallContext. It provides
access to security information about every caller in a causality and allows you
to test a direct caller's right to do something. The second call context interface,
IServerSecurity, provides access to lower-level COM security features,
including impersonation. It is only usable from C++. Table 2-4 summarizes the
call context interfaces.

---

[13] There are some other call context interfaces as well, but none are relevant to this story. See the
Platform SDK documentation for CoGetCallContext for more information.

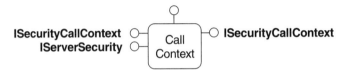

**Figure 2-10   Call context interfaces**

**Table 2-4   Call context interfaces**

| Interface | Provides |
|---|---|
| ISecurityCallContext | Access to role-based security features and information about all callers in causality |
| IServerSecurity | Access to low-level COM security functionality (C++ only) |

Before continuing, I have to mention one unpleasant detail. Unlike object context, which is a relatively new idea, call context has been a part of classic COM since Windows NT4. When call context was extended to support COM+, the new features were added not to the existing call context object, but to an additional call context object. In other words, while the description of call context just given is *conceptually* correct, call context is actually implemented using two objects, one for the classic COM functionality and one for the new COM+ functionality. Both call context objects are retrieved using `CoGetCall Context`. Which one you get depends on which interface you ask for.

In Figure 2-11 there are two call context objects, one inherited from classic COM and one added for COM+. `CoGetCallContext` returns a reference to one or the other depending on which call context interface you ask for. The diagram shows the mapping by highlighting interfaces in bold. If an object calls `CoGetCallContext` asking for either `IUnknown` or `IServerSecurity`, it gets the classic COM implementation. If an object calls `CoGetCallContext` asking for `ISecurityCallContext`, it gets the new COM+ implementation. Note that the `GetSecurityCallContext` API used by Visual Basic always returns a reference to the new call context object.

Hopefully some future version of COM+ will correct this quirk.

*Note:* Interfaces shown in **bold** determine which call context CoGetCallContext returns.

**Figure 2-11   An unpleasant call context implementation detail**

## Using Call Context

Here is an example that demonstrates the use of call context. Every causality involves one or more method calls executing as particular security principals. You can ask a call context to return the name of the security principal that invoked a particular method in a causality.

```
HRESULT CSomeCfgClass::WhoAmI(BSTR *pbstr)
{
  // get a reference to call context
  CComPtr<ISecurityCallContext> spCtxSec;
  HRESULT hr = CoGetCallContext(__uuidof(spCtxSec),
                                (void**)&spCtxSec);
  if (FAILED(hr)) return hr;
  // retrieve information about direct caller
  CComVariant vCaller;
  hr = spCtxSec->get_Item(CComBSTR("DirectCaller"), &vCaller);
  if (FAILED(hr)) return hr;
  if (vCaller.vt != VT_UNKNOWN && vCaller.vt != VT_DISPATCH)
    return E_FAIL;
  CComPtr<ISecurityIdentityColl> spSecId;
  hr = vCaller.punkVal->QueryInterface(__uuidof(spSecId),
                                       (void**)&spSecId);
  if (FAILED(hr)) return hr;
  // retrieve direct caller's account name
  CComVariant vName;
  hr = spSecId->get_Item(CComBSTR("AccountName"), &vName);
  if (FAILED(hr)) return hr;
  if (vName.vt != VT_BSTR) return E_FAIL;
  // return account name as out parameter
  *pbstr = vName.bstrVal;
  vName.bstrVal = 0;
  return S_OK;
}
```

The `WhoAmI` method calls `CoGetCallContext` to get an `ISecurity CallContext` reference to call context. Then it calls the `get_Item` method to retrieve a reference to the collection of information about the direct caller and uses the collection object's `get_Item` method to retrieve the direct caller's account name. Finally, it converts the name to a BSTR and returns it to the caller.

## Summary

This chapter introduces context and causality, the two basic atoms that all the COM+ runtime services are built with. COM+ processes are subdivided into contexts, spaces that provide specific runtime services. When a new object is created, the SCM puts it into a context that provides the services it needs—either in its creator's context or a brand new context—as determined by its class's configuration in the COM+ catalog. Some properties of a new context can be inherited from the context of an object's creator. This is called context flow. Calls between contexts are intercepted by the COM+ plumbing. The interception layer pre- and postprocesses each method invocation and transparently invokes service code.

The interception layer also tracks the causal relationships between calls across context boundaries. This information is captured by causality. A causality is a logical thread of action in a system. COM+ services use causality to detect reentrant calls into contexts or groups of contexts. The security service also provides information about every security principal participating in a given causality.

An object can interact with its context using object context and with a given causality using call context. These two objects provide interfaces for interacting with COM+ runtime services. This style of coding, "reaching into context," makes COM+ development very different from classic COM development.

# Chapter 3

# Mechanics

Atoms are complicated things, and the atoms of COM+ are no exception. This is particularly true of context, the mechanics of which are more complex than they appear at first glance. If you want to apply COM+ successfully, you need to know more about how contexts work. You need to understand the relationship between contexts and references to objects, that is, interface pointers. This association is integral to the correct behavior of the COM+ plumbing. You need to manage interface pointers properly for interception to work correctly. If you do not, interception will not work, and neither will any of the runtime services COM+ provides. You also need to understand the relationship between contexts and objects themselves. By default, every instance of every configured class gets a brand-new context of its own. This implies a nontrivial amount of overhead in both time (for interception) and space (for context data structures). Although you get runtime services in return, you should not simply accept these costs. You can reduce runtime overhead by creating multiple objects in a single context, but you need to know how to configure classes to exhibit this behavior. This chapter deals with these basic mechanical topics.

## Context Relativity

COM+ does a lot of work to make sure new objects live in contexts configured to meet their needs. The goal, of course, is to make sure that when an object's method is invoked, it executes in an appropriate environment that provides the services the object requires. The details are handled by the interception plumbing, which "does the right thing" when a causality crosses a context boundary to do work against an object. While COM+ makes sure an object's environment is *initially* correct, you bear some responsibility for making sure it *remains* correct. To make sure the interception plumbing always works correctly, you have to treat interface pointers as *context-relative* resources that cannot be used outside the context where they were initially acquired. In general this is not a burden; however, in some rare circumstances it requires some extra work on your part.

**The Problem**

First, let me explain the problem. Remember that when a new object is created, the SCM has to decide whether it should exist in the same context as its creator or in a brand-new context of its own. In the former case `CoCreate Instance[Ex]` returns a raw interface pointer that refers to the new object directly. In the latter case it returns an interface pointer to a proxy set up to intercept each method call and provide whatever additional runtime services the new object requires.

Assume that the SCM decides a new object can exist in its creator's context and returns a raw reference to it, as shown in Figure 3-1. What would happen if the raw reference to the new object, A' in the diagram, were handed to an object in another context? Figure 3-2 depicts this situation. If the object in the foreign context, object B, were to call a method of object A' directly, no interception would occur. The method of object A' would execute in object B's environment, using whatever runtime services context B was configured to use. If the method of object A' attempted to access object context, the call to `CoGet ObjectContext` would succeed, but it would return a reference to an object representing B's world. That is not at all what object A' expects. If object A' expects a declarative transaction, it might not get one or it might get object B's. Neither of these situations is good; in fact, either result could be catastrophic.

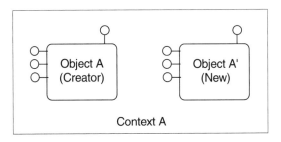

Context A

**Figure 3-1  A new object in its creator's context**

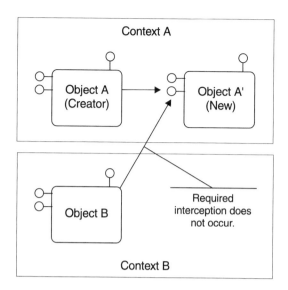

**Figure 3-2　Raw reference passed across a context boundary**

What happens if the SCM decides a new object needs to live in a new context and `CoCreateInstance[Ex]` returns a reference to a proxy, as shown in Figure 3-3? Does the same problem exist in this case? Can a reference to a *proxy* safely be handed to other contexts? The answers are yes, the problem remains, and no, the proxy cannot be used from other contexts. To understand why, you have to know a little bit more about the COM+ interception plumbing.

In Chapter 2, I explained that COM+ uses proxies to intercept cross-context calls and to "do the right thing" to provide the services' objects in the target context expect. Proxies, however, are just one part of the picture. The interception plumbing's *logical* model has three separate pieces, shown in Figure 3-4.

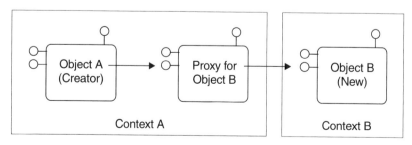

**Figure 3-3　A new object in a new context**

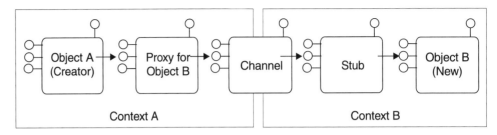

**Figure 3-4   The logical architecture of the COM+ interception plumbing**

A proxy represents an object in a foreign context. Proxies convert method calls into messages that can be sent through a channel. A channel is a conection to a foreign context, a pipe. Channels move messages from one context to another. A stub represents an object from a channel's point of view. Stubs convert messages back into method invocations on real objects. The *physical* structure of the interception plumbing differs depending on the distance between the two contexts it connects. Specifically, channels that move calls to other threads are more complex than channels that do not. Channels that do not move calls to other threads do not use full-blown stubs. Instead, the stub is merged with the channel. For simplicity's sake, the rest of this book focuses on the logical model of the interception plumbing and assumes there is always a stub.

COM+ runtime services are implemented in the stub side of the channel, where they can expose functionality as part of an object's context. (In some cases, such as just-in-time activation, the stub gets involved, too.) For example, if a declarative transaction is going to be made available as part of an object's environment, it makes no sense to try to do that on the proxy side. The declarative transaction has to be available to the real object, where it lives, not where the caller (and proxy) live. This architecture is shown in Figure 3-5.

COM+ gains great flexibility by invoking runtime services in the channel instead of the stub. Each channel represents a connection to a stub from a *particular* proxy; there can be as many channels to a stub and object as required. Each proxy is permanently affixed to its channel when it is created. Stubs, on the other hand, are simply handed a channel long enough to process an inbound call. Within the scope of each call, the stub uses the channel to allocate memory for out parameters and to optimize their marshaling based on how far away the proxy is. COM+ tunes each channel's behavior so that it does the

TRANSACTIONAL COM+: BUILDING SCALABLE APPLICATIONS

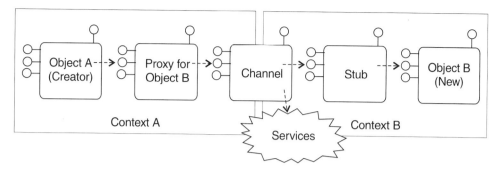

**Figure 3-5   Runtime services are invoked by stub side of channel.**

minimum amount of work necessary to bridge the difference between the proxy's context and the real object's context.

As Figure 3-6 illustrates, each channel is tuned to bridge the specific differences between its proxy's context and the real object's context. It might be, for instance, that calling from context A to context B mandates a security check and initiates a new declarative transaction, while calling from context C to context B initiates a new declarative transaction but does nothing in terms of security.

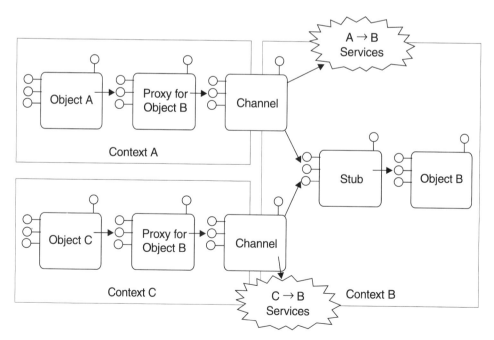

**Figure 3-6   Multiple channels to the same object**

What would happen if a reference to a proxy were handed to an object in another context, as shown in Figure 3-7? In this case, object C in context C holds a reference to the proxy in context A. Calls through the proxy will be intercepted, but because the proxy was created in context A, its channel cannot do the right thing. The channel's behavior is specifically optimized to deal with the difference between context A and context B. It knows nothing about context C. If calls from object C were allowed to go through, the results would be hard to predict and might be disastrous. So the channel does not let the call go through.

Channels actively enforce the context relativity of their proxies. The proxy side of the channel records the context it is initially created in. As each call comes in, the channel examines the current context ID, which is available as part of object context (remember `IObjectContextInfo::GetContextId`). If its original context ID and the current context ID match, the channel processes the call. If the IDs do not match, the channel returns a standard error code, `RPC_E_WRONGTHREAD`. COM+ inherited this constant from classic COM and uses it to indicate that a proxy is being used from a context other than its own, even if the problem has nothing to do with which thread is making the call. You should think of it as `RPC_E_WRONGCONTEXT`, which is what it really means.

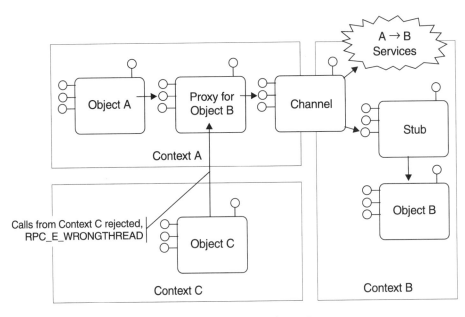

**Figure 3-7**   **Proxy reference passed across context boundary**

You have to treat interface pointers as *context-relative* resources, or the interception plumbing will not work correctly. If you use a raw pointer to a real object in any context other than the one the object was created in, no interception will occur. If you use a pointer to a proxy in any context other than the one the proxy was created in, the channel will reject the call because it knows the right interception cannot occur. In either case, the resulting behavior is undesirable. In the former case, it is probably dangerous as well. All this leads to an inevitable question: How can you pass interface pointers to real objects or proxies from one context to another safely?

**Marshaling Interface Pointers**

Obviously COM+ has to provide a way to translate an interface pointer that is valid in one context into one that is valid in another context. If a pointer to a real object is passed to another context, it should be converted to a pointer to a proxy that is appropriate for that context and can forward calls back to the real object. If a pointer to a proxy is passed to another context, it should also be converted to a proxy appropriate for that context, with one exception. If a pointer to a proxy is passed to the context where the real object it refers to lives, the pointer to the proxy should be converted to a pointer to the real object instead.

COM+ enables all this functionality through an API it inherited from classic COM, `CoMarshalInterface`. `CoMarshalInterface` is one of a set of APIs designed to facilitate moving interface pointers from one context to another. `CoMarshalInterface` translates, or marshals, interface pointers into context-neutral byte streams called OBJREFs. An OBJREF contains the addressing information necessary to make calls back to an object. If you pass a pointer to a real object to `CoMarshalInterface`, it will create a stub for the object (if one does not already exist) and return an OBJREF identifying where the object lives. If you pass a pointer to a proxy to `CoMarshalInterface`, it will not create a stub, and it will return an OBJREF identifying where the real object the proxy refers to lives.

Once you have an OBJREF, you can take it to any context anywhere in the world and then convert it back into an interface pointer by calling `CoUnmarshalInterface`. `CoUnmarshalInterface` interprets, or unmarshals, the contents of an OBJREF and returns a pointer either to a proxy or to a real object if you happen to be in the context where the object the OBJREF refers to lives. If CoUnmarshalInterface returns a pointer to a proxy, the proxy is attached to a channel that is specifically tuned for the difference between the proxy's context and the real object's context.[1]

The context relativity of interface pointers is not a burden in general. You do not have to call these low-level plumbing APIs on a regular basis. Whenever you pass interface pointers to or receive them from the methods of COM interfaces or system APIs, you do not have to worry about marshaling; the plumbing takes care of all the details as needed. If you call CoCreateInstance[Ex] and the SCM decides the new object being created needs to live in a new context of its own, CoMarshalInterface and CoUnmarshalInterface are called automatically. If you pass an interface pointer through an existing proxy/stub connection, the proxy and stub call CoMarshalInterface and CoUnmarshal Interface on your behalf again. If you pass an interface pointer directly to an object in your own context, nothing happens because no translation is necessary. As long as you always pass interface pointers from one context to another using one of these techniques—COM APIs or the methods of COM interfaces— you never have to worry about marshaling interface pointers.

There are, however, two situations where you may want to pass interface pointers between contexts without using either a system API or a COM method call. First, you may want to put an interface pointer into a global variable that is accessible from multiple contexts in your process. Second, you may want to pass an interface pointer to a new thread you are starting. These are the rare circumstances where you have to do some extra work. In both these cases, you are responsible for making sure interface pointers are marshaled correctly.

### The Global Interface Table
Even when you are responsible for marshaling interface pointers by hand, you do not have to use the low-level marshaling APIs. Most application developers

---

[1] My coverage of this topic is purposefully brief because, although this aspect of the plumbing is important to understand, the details are not relevant to this story and have been copiously documented elsewhere. For more information on these APIs and the contents of OBJREFs, see the COM Specification and the DCOM Protocol Internet Draft, available from MSDN or online at http://www.microsoft.com/com, or Essential COM by Box.

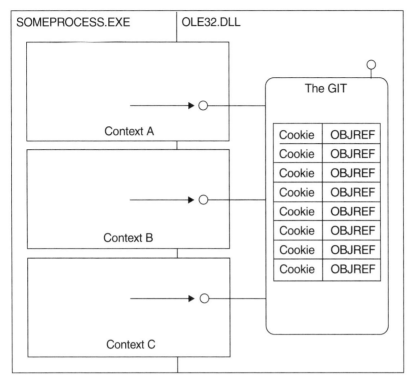

**Figure 3-8   The Global Interface Table**

use the Global Interface Table (GIT) instead. The GIT is a processwide lookup table that maps back and forth between context-relative interface pointers and context-neutral cookies. The GIT is implemented in `OLE32.DLL`. You can instantiate it by calling `CoCreateInstance[Ex]` and passing `CLSID_Std GlobalInterfaceTable`. A reference to the GIT is implicitly context neutral. It can be cached in a global variable and safely accessed from any context. This is a special exception to the context-relativity rule that does not apply in the general case. Figure 3-8 shows the architecture of the GIT.

The Global Interface Table implements a standard interface called `GlobalInterfaceTable`.

```
interface IGlobalInterfaceTable : IUnknown
{
   HRESULT RegisterInterfaceInGlobal([in]  IUnknown *pUnk,
                                     [in]  REFIID riid,
                                     [out] DWORD *pdwCookie);
```

```
HRESULT RevokeInterfaceFromGlobal([in] DWORD dwCookie);
HRESULT GetInterfaceFromGlobal([in] DWORD dwCookie,
                               [in] REFIID riid,
                               [out, iid_is(riid)] void **ppv);
};
```

`RegisterInterfaceInGlobal` inserts an interface pointer into the GIT and returns a context-neutral cookie to represent it. The cookie is a DWORD that is guaranteed not to be 0 (the null cookie, like a null pointer, is never valid). A GIT cookie can be passed to another context using any technique you like, including via a global variable or as an argument to a new thread. `GetInterface FromGlobal` converts a valid cookie into an interface pointer that is appropriate for the current context. A cookie remains valid until the interface pointer it refers to is removed from the GIT by a call to `RevokeInterfaceFrom Global`. This explicit clean-up mechanism allows the GIT to easily support a "marshal-once/unmarshal-many times" scheme, which is preferred if you're going to store a GIT cookie in a global variable. It also means that the GIT holds a reference to a registered object until it is explicitly revoked. If you fail to revoke a reference held by the GIT, the object it refers to will remain in memory until the GIT releases it when the process shuts down.

Here is an example demonstrating how the GIT can be used to pass an interface pointer to a new thread. The `StartSomething` function creates a new object and passes it as input to a new thread. It uses the GIT to marshal the interface pointer.

```
// Global GIT reference initialized elsewhere
extern IGlobalInterfaceTable *g_pGIT;
// Declaration of thread proc implemented below
DWORD WINAPI DoSomething(void *pv);
// Function that starts a new thread
HRESULT StartSomething(void)
{
  // Create new object
  CComPtr<IObject> spObj;
  HRESULT hr = spObj.CoCreateInstance(__uuidof(SomeObject));
  if (FAILED(hr)) return hr;
  // Put reference to object into GIT
  DWORD cookie = 0;
  hr = g_pGIT->RegisterInterfaceInGlobal(spObj, __uuidof(spObj),
                                         &cookie);
```

```
    if (FAILED(hr)) return hr;
    // Start new thread, passing cookie as argument
    HANDLE thread = CreateThread(0, 0, &DoSomething,
                                 (void*)cookie, 0, 0);
    // If CreateThread fails, remove reference from GIT
    if (thread == 0)
    {
      g_pGIT->RevokeInterfaceFromGlobal(dwCookie);
      return E_FAIL;
    }
    CloseHandle(thread);
    return hr;
}
```

Notice that this function removes the interface pointer from the GIT if CreateThread fails. Here is the implementation of the thread function, DoSomething. It uses the cookie that StartSomething passed as an input argument to retrieve an interface pointer to the object from the GIT.

```
// implementation of thread proc
DWORD WINAPI DoSomething(void *pv)
{
  // initialize COM
  HRESULT hr = CoInitializeEx(0, COINIT_MULTITHREADED);
  if (FAILED(hr)) return hr;
  // retrieve reference from GIT
  DWORD cookie = (DWORD) pv;
  CComPtr<IObject> spObj;
  hr = g_pGIT->GetInterfaceFromGlobal(cookie, __uuidof(spObj),
                                      (void**)&spObj);
  // remove reference from GIT
  g_pGIT->RevokeInterfaceFromGlobal(cookie);
  // if attempt to get reference failed, exit
  if (FAILED(hr)) return hr;
  … // use object
  // clean things up
  spObj.Release();
  CoUninitialize();
  return hr;
}
```

This function retrieves an interface pointer to the object and then removes it from the GIT. When this thread function completes, the object is released.

### Context Relativity in Day-to-Day Life

Although you have to be aware of context relativity and the importance of marshaling interface pointers between contexts, you typically do not have to spend much time worrying about these issues in your day-to-day development work. None of the code in Chapter 1 had to worry about context relativity at all. COM+ designs are based on the object-per-client model (remember Rule 1.1), so it is unlikely that you will need to put an interface pointer into a global variable. Similarly COM+-based classes typically rely on the thread pool provided by the runtime and do not create their own threads. Still, there may be cases where you want to share an interface pointer using one of these techniques, especially if you are building some relatively low-level plumbing of your own, an efficient middle-tier cache, for example. There may also be situations where you violate context relativity accidentally and need to be able to figure out why your code is not working correctly. Just remember that context relativity boils down to one simple, tremendously important guideline, Rule 3.1. If you do not follow this rule, the interception plumbing and, therefore, the context programming model will not work correctly.

 **RULE** 3.1

Do not pass interface pointers from one context to another without using a system-provided facility (e.g., system API, COM interface method, the Global Interface Table) to translate the reference to work in the destination context.

## The Cost of Contexts

Now that you understand the relationship between contexts and interface pointers, it is time to focus on the relationship between contexts and objects. Whenever the SCM is asked to instantiate a new instance of a configured class, it consults the catalog to see what services the class requires. The SCM uses this information to decide whether the current context can meet the environmental needs of the new object without additional interception. If it can, the SCM decides to put the new object in its creator's context. If it cannot, the SCM puts the new object in a new context of its own. As it turns out, the SCM makes the latter choice the vast majority of the time. In practice, that means that there are likely to be lots of contexts in a COM+ process.

## A Context for Every Object

Most configured classes' declarative attribute settings are such that each new instance of the class has to live in a new context of its own. This is certainly the case for classes that use the default settings assigned by the catalog when they are initially deployed. This "context for every object" approach is not mandated by the context programming model itself; it is simply a result of how the runtime's services are currently implemented.

Consider the seemingly innocuous class attribute described in Table 3-1, `EventTrackingEnabled`, which controls the COM+ statistics service. If a class is registered with this option set to true (the default), the interception plumbing gathers statistics about its usage, including how many instances of the class exist, how many method calls those objects are currently processing, and the aggregate time the processing is taking in milliseconds. These bits of information are fed to Component Services Explorer, which displays them so that an administrator can monitor ongoing work in a system. To keep these counters accurate for each class, interception plumbing has to know when each call enters and leaves each object. The only way to get this information is to intercept every call. The only way to guarantee that every call will be intercepted is to put each object in a context of its own and never let anyone have direct access to it. This is exactly what the SCM does for classes deployed with `EventTrackingEnabled = true`.

The revelation that the mechanism COM+ uses to gather usage statistics forces each object into a context of its own may prompt you to turn this option off. However, this will not resolve the issue. The declarative transaction and just-in-time activation services require that objects live in contexts of their own as well. Further, even if you turn these services off for a particular class, its *application's* security settings may force each instance into its own context anyway. If an application is configured to support component-level security, regardless of whether it is enabled, every instance of every class in that application

**Table 3-1   The EventTrackingEnabled class attribute**

| Attribute | Type | Default | Notes |
|---|---|---|---|
| EventTrackingEnabled | Boolean | True | Runtime tracks work in progress |

will be in its own context. In this case, it does not matter how individual classes are configured.

### The Cost of Contexts in Time

If every object lives in its own context, every call to every object will be intercepted. How much time does all this interception take? Not surprisingly, many factors influence the speed of interception, including the types of the arguments being passed to a method, the sort of marshaler (type library or proxy/stub DLL) being used, whether the call stack has to be moved to another thread, the services the destination context is using, and, of course, the hardware resources COM+ has at its disposal. The only way to know how long interception takes in a particular situation is to test it.

It is possible, however, to talk about the relative performance of interception in a general way. The left column of Table 3-2 lists the three possible degrees of interception. The right column lists the order of magnitude of the number of calls per second you can expect to make at each level, assuming the methods do nothing other than return s_ok. If a caller has a raw pointer to an object, no interception occurs. This is degree 0. Each method call is nothing more than a C++ virtual invocation. In this case, you can expect to make on the order of ten million calls per second.

If a caller has a pointer to a proxy that forwards calls without a thread switch, interception occurs, and performance is three orders of magnitude

**Table 3-2   Degrees of interception and relative throughput**

| Degree | Description | Order of Magnitude of Calls per Second |
|--------|-------------|----------------------------------------|
| 0 | None, raw pointer to object | 10,000,000 |
| 1 | Interception without thread switch | 10,000 |
| 2 | Interception with thread switch* | 1,000 or less |

*Note:* Cross-thread, cross-process, and cross-machine calls are lumped into one category for simplicity's sake. Obviously there are performance differences among these three cases, but they are not always intuitive. Some cross-thread calls in a process run more slowly than calls across processes, for instance. In general, they all provide roughly the same degree of performance degradation, so treating them as one is not unreasonable.

TRANSACTIONAL COM+: BUILDING SCALABLE APPLICATIONS

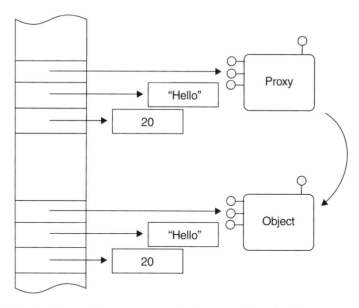

**Figure 3-9   A stack frame for a cross-context, same-thread call**

lower. This is degree 1. In this case, you can expect to make on the order of ten thousand calls per second. The cost here, in addition to services being invoked, is in making a deep copy of each call's stack frame and translating each context-relative interface pointer, as required. For example, if a caller invokes this method:

```
HRESULT DoStuff([in] IUnknown pObj, [in] BSTR bstr, [in] long *pn);
```

the entire stack frame will be duplicated, as shown in Figure 3-9, so that the IUnknown pointer, pUnk, can be converted to a pointer to a proxy that is appropriate for the destination context. Copying the entire stack frame may seem like overkill when a call is going to be serviced on the caller's thread. Interface pointers are the only arguments that really need to be marshaled in this situation; in theory, everything else could be left as is. The type library marshaler, which is used by interfaces marked with either the oleautomation or dual keyword, actually makes some optimizations along these lines. Unfortunately, they apply only to primitive types like longs and shorts, not more complex types like BSTRs and SAFEARRAYs, as shown in Figure 3-10. This makes the type

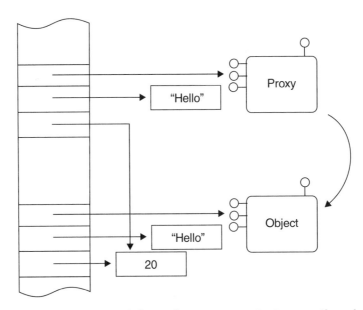

**Figure 3-10   An optimized stack frame for a cross-context, same-thread call**

library marshaler marginally faster in some cases, but it turns out to be marginally slower in others; therefore, in general, it does not offer a consistent performance advantage. Hopefully some future version of COM+ will optimize further the behavior of cross-context, same-thread calls.

If a caller has a pointer to a proxy that forwards calls with a thread switch, performance drops at least one more order of magnitude. This is degree 2. In this last case, you can expect to make on the order of one thousand calls per second. In these situations, a deep copy of the stack frame is always necessary to move a call to another thread. The additional reduction in performance reflects the additional overhead of the thread switch and whatever cross-process or cross-machine communication is necessary.

### The Cost of Contexts in Space

Contexts exact a price in space as well as time. Each context is represented by a set of data structures maintained in OLE32.DLL, and they consume memory. Each proxy, channel, and stub also consumes memory. Again, the exact overhead depends on several factors, including what exactly a context is configured to do and whether the interception plumbing has to worry about moving call stacks to other threads or processes. COM+ uses entirely different channel implementations depending on whether a thread switch is required. As a general guideline, the price of a context is between 2,048 and 3,072 bytes, or 2K and 3K. Contexts accessed through channels that switch threads use approximately 3K each. Contexts accessed through channels that do not switch threads are closer to 2K. By contrast, each instance of a generic wizard-generated ATL class—without additional data members—consumes 32 bytes of memory (a minimal ATL class can whittle this down to 8 bytes). Each instance of a generic class implemented in Visual Basic 6 consumes approximately 165 bytes.

Here is a formula for estimating the memory footprint of a COM+ process. It is based on the assumption that each object resides in its own context and is used by a single client (i.e., you are following the object-per-client model). It accounts for the difference in memory consumption of the two types of channels. It ignores the additional overhead introduced by other DLLs your objects might be using.

$$((n_2 \times (s_2 + 3{,}072)) + (n_1 \times (s_1 + 2{,}048))) \div 1{,}024 = k \text{ KB.}$$

The variables $n$ and $s$ refer to the number and average size of objects being used. The subscripts 2 and 1 indicate the degree of interception necessary to access those objects. Specifically, the variable $n_2$ is the number of objects in contexts accessed via a proxy and a thread switch—degree 2 interception. The variable $n_1$ is the total number of objects in contexts accessed via a proxy but no thread switch—degree 1 interception. The variable $s_2$ is the average size of the $n_2$ objects in bytes. The variable $s_1$ is the average size of the $n_1$ objects in bytes. The result, $k$, is the estimated memory footprint of the process in kilobytes (KB).

For example, if you have 500 clients in other processes accessing one object each, $n_2 = 500$. If *each* of those 500 objects uses three additional objects in contexts that can be reached without a thread switch, $n_1 = (500 \times 3) = 1{,}500$. Altogether, in this case, there are 2,000 objects in 2,000 contexts. If the average size of these objects is $s_2 = s_1 = 32$ bytes (the size of a generic ATL object), the memory consumed by the process is approximately $k = 4{,}560$ KB, or just under 4.5 megabytes (MB). The actual memory consumed by the objects themselves is 62 KB, about 1.5 percent of the total.

Figure 3-11 shows the memory consumption statistics for this same scenario with four different average sizes for objects. The vertical axis measures memory consumption in kilobytes. The horizontal measures average object size. The shaded area at the bottom of each bar represents the space consumed by contexts and interception plumbing. It is the same in all four cases because there are always 2,000 contexts. The white area at the top of each bar represents the space consumed by objects themselves. It varies across all four cases because each case represents a different average object size. The numbers above the bars indicate the percentage of overall memory the objects consume in each case.

The leftmost bar represents the case just described. The other three bars represent the same usage scenario with larger objects. If the average size of the objects is 165 bytes (the size of a generic VB object), the process uses close to $k = 4,820$ KB, or 4.7 MB, of which 320 KB is consumed by the objects, or 7 percent. If the average size of the objects is 500 bytes, the process consumes $k = 5,470$ KB, or 5.4 MB. The objects themselves account for around

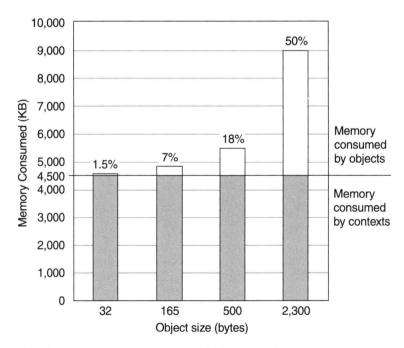

**Figure 3-11  Memory consumed by 2,000 objects in 2,000 contexts**

TRANSACTIONAL COM+: BUILDING SCALABLE APPLICATIONS

970 KB, or 18 percent of the total. In this example, objects would have to average 2,300 bytes apiece to account for 50 percent of the memory consumed by their processes.

### Are Contexts Worth the Price?

If these numbers are depressing, remember that contexts and interception are not all pain and no gain. You get runtime services in return. How much overhead in time and space would your own version of these services incur? More important, how long would it take to implement and maintain them? Unless you are prepared to integrate your objects with transactions by hand, build your own security framework, and so on, the benefit of contexts and interception cannot be overlooked.

That being said, however, you also have to remember that a COM+ process has a limited set of hardware resources. There is a limit to the number of threads a COM+ process can use to handle client requests effectively without introducing contention for CPU cycles. Every COM+ process also has access to a finite amount of physical memory. Its allotment is assigned by the operating system, which is doing its best to share physical memory—a very precious resource—among all the processes running on a machine. If your COM+ system is accessed via the Web, for instance, you have to share memory with Internet Information Server (IIS), which wants lots of it to cache files. If a process's virtual memory consumption outstrips its physical memory allotment, the operating system starts swapping the process's virtual memory pages out to disk. A virtual page will be swapped back into physical memory when an attempt to reference it generates a page fault. The more virtual memory a process consumes, the more likely it is to generate page faults. The cost of paging virtual memory into and out of physical memory is very high because disks are very slow, at least compared to RAM. In other words, the cost of memory consumption in space ultimately becomes a cost in time, because more and more time is spent waiting for virtual pages to move to and from disk.

If the goal is scalability, you need to use each middle-tier server's hardware resources as efficiently as possible. You need to free threads as fast as you can so they can be used to process other requests. You certainly want to minimize the time threads spend waiting for virtual memory to be paged in from disk.

Obviously, as Chapter 1 explains, efficient use of these resources will take you only so far; eventually you will need more hardware. But the thriftier you are, the more throughput you will squeeze out of each middle-tier server and the longer you will postpone the acquisition of additional machines. Interception takes time, and contexts take space. You should take care to use contexts and interception *only when you really need them*.

## Limiting Context

If a class uses one or more COM+ runtime services, each instance of that class needs a context configured to suit its needs. But what if a class does not use any services? Consider a class that encapsulates the details of validating some sort of data. Other classes use this helper class to validate input passed to them by client programs, but client programs never use the validation class directly. The implementation of the validation class simply examines the data it receives and returns a boolean value indicating whether it is valid. Classes that use the validation class interpret its boolean return code to decide whether to proceed with a client request. The validation class neither knows nor cares about context; it does not rely on it and does not do anything with it. It never calls either `CoGetObjectContext` or `CoGetCallContext`. Each instance of the validation class can do its job in any environment because it is oblivious of the fact that there is an environment. Each validation class instance can accomplish its task without the additional space overhead of a new context or the additional time overhead of calls through the interception layer. Given that, the validation class should not be a normal configured class. If it were, the default catalog settings would force each instance into a new context of its own, which is neither necessary nor efficient. Instead, the validation class should be registered such that the SCM always puts each new instance directly in its creator's context.

### Nonconfigured Classes

One way to achieve this effect is by using a nonconfigured class. Nonconfigured classes have entries in the Registry, but not in the catalog. Remember that the SCM puts a new object into a new context and introduces interception only if its creator's context cannot meet its needs. If the creator's context is a suitable environment for the new object, the SCM will put the object there and return a raw pointer to it. The SCM assumes that nonconfigured classes do not know and do not care about context; if they did, they would be configured classes with specific declarative attributes recorded in the catalog. The SCM always puts new instances of nonconfigured classes directly into their creators' contexts, and `CoCreateInstance[Ex]` always returns a raw reference, never a proxy, to the new object. (There is one exception to this rule related to threading, which is addressed in Chapter 4.)

## Raw-Configured Classes

It is possible to set a configured class's declarative attributes so that the SCM treats it like a nonconfigured class at creation time. If a configured class is registered this way, each new instance will always live in its creator's context. Here too `CoCreateInstance[Ex]` will always return a raw reference to the new object, so I call configured classes that are registered this way *raw-configured classes*.

Raw-configured classes turn off all the runtime services that are implemented via interception, which is just about all of them. (Later chapters explain how raw-configured classes should set their attributes to turn these features off.) Raw-configured classes can use a constructor string (`Construction Enabled = true, ConstructorString = "This string will be passed to every new instance of this class"`) if they want to. They can also use the object pooling service if they want to.[2] Neither of these features is implemented via interception, so turning them on does not force a new object into a new context.

You should also set a raw-configured class's `MustRunInClientContext` attribute, described in Table 3-3, to true. This boolean flag tells the SCM that

**Table 3-3   The MustRunInClientContext class attributes**

| Attribute | Type | Default | Notes |
|---|---|---|---|
| MustRunInClientContext | Boolean | False | If SCM cannot put new instances in creator's context, activation fails |

---

[2] Chapter 5, Objects, addresses object pooling in detail.

**Table 3-4** **The AccessChecksLevel application attribute**

| Attribute | Type | Default | Notes |
|---|---|---|---|
| AccessChecks Level | COMAdmin AccessChecks | COMAdminAccess ChecksApplication ComponentLevel | Controls granularity of security access checks |

instances of a class *must* activate in their creator's context. If the SCM cannot meet this requirement for some reason, it fails the activation request and returns `CO_E_ATTEMPT_TO_CREATE_OUTSIDE_CLIENT_CONTEXT`. Whether or not a runtime services requires interception may vary depending on the configuration of a creator's context. By enabling a raw-configured class's `MustRunInClient Context` attribute, you can ensure that its instances will use services only when interception is not required.[3]

Raw-configured classes are typically installed in a library application of their own. This makes it possible to load their code into any process where a context might exist. It also solves a thorny security problem. The SCM always puts new instances of classes deployed in an application configured to support component-level security into individual contexts of their own. To avoid this, you have to disable support for component-level security by setting an application's `AccessChecksLevel` attribute, which is shown in Table 3-4, to `COMAdmin AccessChecksApplicationLevel`.

If raw-configured classes are deployed in a library application of their own, you can disable component-level security for that application without affecting other applications. In other words, the configured classes in other server or library applications that use your raw-configured classes can still use component-level security if they want to.

Figure 3-12 shows how a raw-configured class is deployed and used. In this case, object A is an instance of a normal configured class. The SCM put it in its own context A when it was created. Object A creates object B, an instance of a

---

[3] Chapter 4, Threads, provides an excellent example of why the `MustRunInClientContext` attribute is useful.

TRANSACTIONAL COM+: BUILDING SCALABLE APPLICATIONS

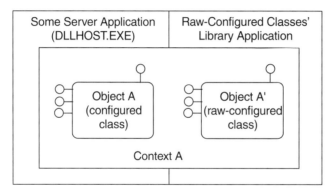

Some Server Application
(DLLHOST.EXE)

Raw-Configured Classes'
Library Application

Object A
(configured
class)

Object A'
(raw-configured
class)

Context A

**Figure 3-12   Using a raw-configured class**

raw-configured class deployed in a library application with component-level security turned off. The SCM puts object B in context A.

There are three advantages to using raw-configured classes instead of non-configured classes. First, raw-configured classes have entries in the catalog. Nonconfigured classes do not appear in the catalog; they are registered directly in the Registry using classic COM techniques. Having all your classes in the catalog makes it easier to manage your system's configuration because you can find all your classes' configuration information in one place.

Second, raw-configured classes are part of an application, usually a library application. Applications are the standard unit of deployment in COM+. Because there are tools for exporting applications and installing them on other machines, being in an application can help ease configuration management.

Third, as mentioned before, raw-configured classes can use the constructor string mechanism and the object pooling service because neither relies on interception. For all these reasons, in general, raw-configured classes are preferred. The rest of this book discusses raw-configured classes and ignores nonconfigured classes except in situations where their behavior differs.

### Context-Aware Code Revisited

Each new instance of a raw-configured class lives in its creator's context. If a class is aware of that context and its implementation calls `CoGetObject Context` or `CoGetCallContext`, can it still be a raw-configured class? The answer is a qualified yes. Remember that COM+ maps runtime services to contexts, not to individual objects. Any code executing in a context can make use of the services the context provides. Developing a context-aware raw-configured class is fine as long as you guarantee that it behaves correctly in *any* context. Consider a class that encapsulates, sending event notifications using Microsoft Message Queue (MSMQ). MSMQ relies on transactions to guarantee that messages are delivered in the order they were sent and that each message arrives exactly once. The event notification class can be implemented as a raw-configured class that uses a context's declarative transaction *if there is one,* or an internal MSMQ transaction if there is not. In short, this class can be used from any context. Its instances do not need new contexts of their own because their environmental needs are always the same as the environmental needs of their creators.

This may seem a risky way to design your classes, but it is not. It is simply leveraging your understanding of how contexts and interception work. Consider a method call into an instance of a configured class running in some context. The COM+ plumbing intercepts the call and makes sure the appropriate run-time services are invoked. Inside the method, the object can access context by calling either `CoGetObjectContext` or `CoGetCallContext`. If the object calls another one of its own methods, that method can access context by calling one of these APIs as well. If the object creates a language-level object and calls one of its methods, that method can also access context. Finally, if the object creates another COM object *in the same context* and calls one of its methods, then that method can access context, too. This is exactly what happens when a configured class makes use of a raw-configured class, as shown in Figure 3-13.

If object A' is an instance of a raw-configured class, it can acquire references to context A's object context because it is executing on a thread in context A. It can retrieve a reference to the current call context, too. Remember that both `CoGetObjectContext` and `CoGetCallContext` retrieve references to context based solely on the calling thread. Neither API cares which *object* is calling it. Any code a *thread* executes can retrieve either reference, until the thread passes through another interceptor and they are either removed or replaced. If object A called another one of its own methods, that second method could access context. Object A' accesses context the same way. Putting context-aware

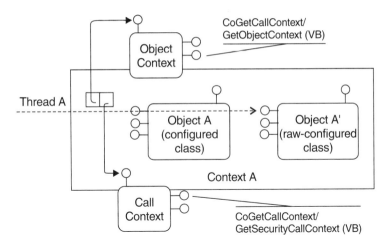

**Figure 3-13** How a context-aware raw-configured class works

code into a nonconfigured or raw-configured class makes it a reusable, updatable, deployable unit that can be written in any language you like. In short, it gives you all the advantages of traditional in-process classic COM *without* the additional overhead of a new context and interception incurred by each instance of a configured class using the same services as its creator.

There is no real risk in this approach as long as your raw-configured classes behave correctly no matter what services the context they are created in provides. Remember that, while a class can use the current object context to find out about its environment, it cannot find out everything about its context. It is up to you to ensure that your raw-configured classes do not depend on aspects of context that cannot be detected. This is not hard once you understand how the COM+ services work.

If this seems to be taking advantage of some kind of undocumented loophole that might someday be closed, consider three things. First, key pieces of the COM+ infrastructure rely on nonconfigured and raw-configured classes. OLE DB and ADO use nonconfigured classes so they execute in their creator's context specifically so they can access and automatically enlist against a declarative transaction if one is present. Internet Information Server (IIS) uses raw-configured classes to dispatch HTTP requests. If the basic system plumbing relies on this feature, you can too.

Second, the `MustRunInClientContext` attribute exists specifically to allow a configured class to insist that it wants to run in its creator's context, as a raw-configured class does. As you will see in later chapters, other services provide attribute settings specifically designed to support raw-configured classes. The creators of COM+ designed the runtime with the notion of raw-configured classes in mind.

Third, if for some reason the context and interception architecture were changed such that new instances of raw-configured classes were no longer put in their creators' contexts, classes that are not aware of context will not care, and classes that are aware of context can simply be redeployed as configured classes with the right options set.

**A Different Way of Looking at the World**

Using raw-configured classes may seem like a strange idea, especially if they make use of context. It definitely represents a very different way of looking at the world of contexts. It reduces the number of contexts that exist, lowering memory consumption. It also reduces the number of calls through the interception plumbing, because calls to instances of raw-configured classes are not intercepted.

Here is an extended version of the formula introduced earlier for estimating the memory consumption of a COM+ process. This version still assumes the object-per-client model, but it has been extended to consider the impact of using instances of raw-configured classes.

$$((n_2 \times (s_2 + 3{,}072)) + (n_1 \times (s_1 + 2{,}048)) + (n_0 \times s_0)) \div 1{,}024 = k \text{ KB}$$

The new variable $n_0$ represents the total number of objects that can be accessed without a proxy—degree 0 interception. Instances of raw-configured classes fall into this category. The new variable $s_0$ is the average size of the $n_0$ objects in bytes.

In the earlier example, 500 clients each used a single object in a server application process, so $n_2 = 500$. Each of those objects used three additional objects that lived in contexts of their own that could be reached without a thread switch, so $n_1 = 1{,}500$. All together, there were 2,000 objects in 2,000 contexts. With objects that consumed an average of $s_2 = s_1 = 32$ bytes of memory, the total footprint for the process was approximately $k = 4{,}560$ KB, or 4.5 MB. However, if each of the $n_2 = 500$ clients' objects used three additional objects *that did not have to live in their own contexts,* memory consumption would be greatly reduced. If each of those additional objects' requirements could be met by their *creator's context*—either because they do not care about context or because they rely on the same services their creator needs—they could live there and be accessed directly. In this case, $n_2 = 500$, $n_1 = 0$, and $n_0 = (500 \times 3) = 1,500$. Assuming the objects are still the same average size, $s_2 = s_0 = 32$ bytes, the total memory consumed by the process drops to approximately $k = 1,560$ KB, or 1.5 MB. At 62 KB, the object still represent only 4 percent of that total; however, there is a 66 percent reduction in the memory consumed by contexts.

Figure 3-14 shows the memory consumption statistics for this new scenario with four average sizes for objects. Again the vertical axis measures memory consumption in KB, and the horizontal measures average object size. The shaded area at the bottom of each bar still represents the space consumed by contexts and interception plumbing. It is the same in all four cases because there are always 500 contexts. It is 66 percent lower than the previous case,

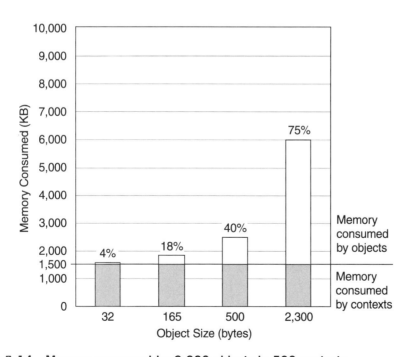

**Figure 3-14   Memory consumed by 2,000 objects in 500 contexts**

shown in Figure 3-11, because 1,500 fewer contexts exist. The numbers that are above the bars indicate the percentage of memory the objects consume in each case. They are all higher than in the previous case because the amount of memory consumed by contexts has decreased.

Two things should be apparent from these numbers. First, reducing the number of contexts dramatically reduces the overall memory consumption of a process and dramatically increases the percentage of memory dedicated to objects themselves. Second, the larger the objects get, the less beneficial this reduction is. However, as noted earlier, objects would have to be quite large indeed to dull the impact of putting each one in a new context of its own.

Some might argue that this is a premature optimization that is too dependent on the implementation details of the COM+ plumbing, but I do not see it that way. This approach simply uses contexts efficiently, never paying more than is necessary to leverage the services COM+ provides. It is codified in Rule 3.2.

 **RULE** **3.2**

Give raw-configured classes preference over configured classes whenever possible to reduce context and interception overhead. Always use this technique for classes that do not care about context. Consider using this technique for classes that do care about context if you can guarantee that they will behave correctly in any context.

### Subtle Complexities

Using an instance of a raw-configured class within a single context is fine; however, returning a reference to one of these objects to a caller in another context can lead to some subtle complexities. A reference to an object must be marshaled when it is passed from one context to another. This happens automatically when interface pointers are passed as arguments to and from calls to COM methods and APIs. If a client calls to an instance of a configured class living in a context, and that object returns a reference to an instance of a raw-configured class living in the same context, the interface pointer it returns will be marshaled. The client will get a reference to a proxy that forwards calls directly to the instance of the raw-configured class. Figure 3-15 illustrates this situation.

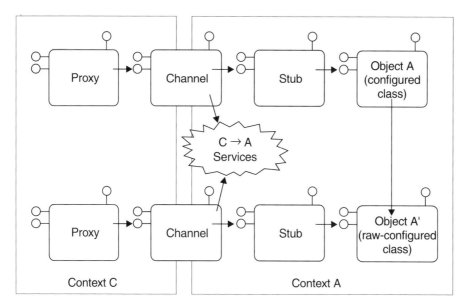

**Figure 3-15    An external reference to an instance of a raw-configured class**

In Figure 3-15, a client created object A, an instance of a configured class that the SCM put into context A. Object A created object A', an instance of a raw-configured class that the SCM also put into context A. Object A returned a reference to object A' to its client. What exactly happens when the client calls to object A' depends on the configuration of context A.

Remember that runtime services are applied to contexts, not objects. A new context is configured to provide the services an initial new object needs, as defined by its class's declarative attributes. That first object is known as the context's *distinguished object* because it is the object the context was originally constructed for.[4] COM+ implements services by intercepting calls and invoking infrastructure code as needed. This happens not for calls to a distinguished object, but for all calls into a context. In the example, the client's calls directly to object A' will be intercepted at the context boundary, and whatever runtime services the distinguished object A requires will be applied. This may or may not present a problem.

---

[4] As you'll see in later chapters, some runtime services are tied directly to a context's distinguished object.

Imagine that object A is an instance of a configured class set up to use the COM+ statistics service (it is registered in the catalog with `EventTracking Enabled = true`). The SCM makes sure context A is set up to supply this service. All calls into context A are intercepted so statistics about the use of class A can be gathered. If the client calls to object A' in context A, the call will still be intercepted, and the statistics service will record the call as an invocation on an instance of class A. This may or may not be a problem. It is certainly misleading.

Now imagine that object A is an instance of a configured class set up to use role-based security. Assume it is configured to allow the user Alice to call any method of the interface IA and to deny calls from any other users or through any other interfaces. This security check is implemented automatically via interception when calls to object A enter context A. The reference to object A' that object A returns to the client is of type IA'. If the client attempts to call to object A' the call will be intercepted at the context boundary. Context A's environment is configured only to allow Alice to call through interface IA. Calls through IA', even if Alice makes them, are not allowed. So the client's attempt to call IA' will be rejected with the standard error code `E_ACCESSDENIED`. This is a problem.

What exactly happens when a client calls to an instance of a raw-configured class running in a context originally created for an instance of some other configured class depends on the specific combination of services the configured class is using. The exact behavior is difficult to predict and, in some cases, can be very strange indeed. You should avoid this situation by following Rule 3.3.

 **RULE 3.3**

> Use instances of raw-configured (or nonconfigured) classes to help implement the methods of configured classes, but do not return references to them to callers.

## Custom Marshaling

Actually, there is one exception to Rule 3.3. In the example above, it would be okay for object A to return a reference to object A' to the client if object A' supported some form of custom marshaling, such as, marshal-by-value or free-threaded marshaling. Custom marshaling allows a COM object to control what happens when its interface pointers are passed from one context to another. An object expresses its desire to custom marshal by implementing the standard `IMarshal` interface. If an object exposes this interface, it will never be attached to a standard proxy/channel/stub connection. Without that, there is no interception, runtime services are never invoked, and the problems outlined never occur.

It is a common misconception that instances of configured classes cannot custom marshal; this is not the case. It is the case that a context's distinguished object cannot custom marshal. If the SCM creates a new context to meet a new object's needs, the object *is* going to live there, and calls to it *are* going to be intercepted. Many configured classes use runtime services that make each instance the distinguished object in its own context, so it is natural to assume that instances of configured classes cannot custom marshal. However, the SCM never creates new contexts for instances of raw-configured classes, and they can custom marshal if they want to. In fact, this is exactly how ADO's disconnected Recordsets—instances of a nonconfigured class—work. If you are planning to return a reference to an instance of a raw-configured class to a caller outside the context the object lives in, the object should definitely custom marshal. This is Rule 3.4.

 **RULE** ▷ **3.4**

> If a configured class does return a reference to an instance of a raw-configured class to a caller, make sure the raw-configured class uses custom marshaling.

## Some Other Observations

There are three more observations I need to make about contexts. First, for the context architecture to work, object creation requests must be routed through the SCM. If one object creates another using language-level techniques, such as operator `new`, the SCM is not involved. It has no chance to put the new object into an appropriate context and set up interception. As a result, objects created with language-level techniques are treated as if they were nonconfigured classes, even if they are configured or raw-configured classes with entries in the catalog. For example, one object should *not* create a second object using a direct call to ATL's creator plumbing, which ultimately invokes the `new` operator.

```
HRESULT CSomeCfgClass::CreateSubObject(void)

{
  if (m_spSubObject == 0)
    // Creation request by-passes SCM
    return CSomeOtherCfgClass::CreateInstance(&m_spSubObject);
  return S_OK;
}
```

In this case, the new instance of `CSomeOtherCfgClass` will be instantiated in its creator's context no matter what declarative attributes it specifies. To solve this problem, you must use `CoCreateInstance[Ex]`.

```
HRESULT CSomeCfgClass::CreateSubObject(void)

{
  if (m_spSubObject == 0)
    // Creation request is sent to SCM
    return m_spSubObject.CoCreateInstance(__uuidof
    (CSomeOtherCfgClass);
  return S_OK;
}
```

If you are implementing classes in Visual Basic 6, this means they cannot reliably use operator `new` for object construction. VB's `new` operator calls `CoCreateInstance` if the class being instantiated is not implemented in the same DLL. If the class being instantiated is in the same DLL, `new` uses an internal creation mechanism instead. VB class should use `CreateObject` instead of `new` to make sure all object creation requests are routed through the SCM.

Second, for the context architecture to work, `IClassFactory::CreateInstance` must return a reference to a new object each time it is called. The SCM assumes that each object it creates is unique. If you implement a classic COM singleton by always returning a reference to the same object from `CreateInstance`—ATL makes this trivial with the DECLARE

`_CLASSFACTORY_SINGLETON` macro—the SCM will assign your object to multiple contexts, one for each creation call. Your object will have multiple proxies, channels, and stubs. How the runtime services your class uses behave in this situation varies from service to service. Suffice it to say that many of them will not provide the desired semantics. While it is possible to implement a non-configured or a raw-configured class as a singleton, it is far from trivial.[5] It is much simpler to achieve singleton semantics using some form of logical identity to map multiple physical objects to shared state. In short, the use of a classic COM singleton is entirely outside the COM+ object-per-client model.

Third, the life of a context is tied to the interception plumbing used to reach that context. New contexts are created by the SCM as needed to meet the requirements of new objects. A context will remain in existence as long as it contains at least one stub. A stub will remain in existence as long as there are extant proxies or a reference to it stored in the GIT. When a stub's last proxy is released—or its GIT reference is revoked—the stub will go away, releasing its object in the process. When the last stub in a context is torn down, the context itself goes away.

## Summary

This chapter looks closely at the mechanics of contexts. There is an intrinsic relationship between contexts and interface pointers. Specifically, interface pointers are context-relative resources that are inexorably bound to the contexts in which they were originally acquired. You cannot use an interface pointer acquired in one context directly from another context safely. Instead, you must translate the interface pointer into one that is appropriate for use from the foreign context using the system-provided marshaling application programming interfaces (`CoMarshalInterface`, etc.). This happens automatically when you pass interface pointers as parameters to COM methods or standard APIs. If you pass interface pointers between contexts in other ways, such as by storing them in global variables or passing them as input to new threads, you have to marshal them by hand using either the low-level marshaling APIs or the GIT.

---

[5] For a description of the essence of the problems you face, see Item 4 in *Effective COM* by Box et al.

If you invoke the methods of an interface pointer that was not marshaled across context boundaries, the results are undefined.

There is also a relationship between contexts and objects. By default, the SCM maps new instances of most configured classes to contexts of their own. This is not a restriction of the context model. It is simply the result of the way several of the COM+ runtime services are currently implemented. The one-to-one mapping of objects to contexts produces significant overhead in both time and space. You may choose simply to accept this as the price of runtime services that you would otherwise have to implement yourself, or you may choose to reduce this overhead without losing functionality by using raw-configured classes. The SCM always puts new instances of raw-configured classes directly in their creators' contexts. They can take advantage of the services their creators' contexts provide as they see fit. They can also custom marshal. The notion of raw-configured classes may seem to go against the COM+ grain (i.e., "services are applied transparently; don't worry about the details"), but the creators of COM+ designed the runtime with the notion of raw-configured classes in mind. You should consider them an integral part of the COM+ programming model and leverage them whenever possible to make your system more efficient.

# Chapter 4

# Threads

Scalable systems are highly concurrent by nature. Writing code that is both safe and efficient in the face of high concurrency is a challenge. COM+ adopts the object-per-client model to simplify things. The object-per-client model allows each COM+ object to pretend the world is single-threaded. A single object will never execute multiple methods simultaneously, so objects do not have to worry about synchronizing access to their data members. This makes implementing COM+ classes significantly easier. The COM+ runtime uses two spatial constructs to support its preferred concurrency model: apartments and activities. These two molecules are built on top of the basic atoms of context and causality. Apartments determine which threads are allowed to do work in a given set of contexts. Activities influence the assignment of contexts to apartments and also control which causalities are allowed to do work in a given set of contexts at a given time. Both structures play an integral role in maintaining the illusion that an object exists in its own single-threaded world. This chapter introduces apartments and activities and explains how they control how work is done concurrently in a COM+ process.

## Apartments

The term *thread affinity* describes the relationship between a piece of code and threads. Code with high thread affinity can only be executed on a specific thread. Windows user-interface code is a good example; the thread that creates a window must also process the messages sent to that window. Code with no thread affinity can be executed on any thread at all. Non-user-interface code is likely to have no thread affinity; it typically does not matter which thread it executes on.

Both configured and nonconfigured classes can specify a degree of thread affinity. When the SCM instantiates a class, it has to put the new object in an environment that meets its needs, including providing the necessary relationship with the threads in the process. COM+ needs a way to define associations between contexts and threads. It does this using an additional abstraction called an apartment.

An *apartment* is a group of contexts in a process that share the same degree of thread affinity. Calls and callbacks into a context are always serviced on a thread in that context's apartment. Every context created in a COM+ process is associated with exactly one apartment that provides the degree of thread affinity it needs. A process can contain multiple apartments with different degrees of thread affinity.

Figure 4-1 illustrates the relationships among processes, contexts, objects, and apartments. In this picture, each process is divided into apartments. Process M contains a single apartment, X. Apartment X has a single context, A. Process N contains two apartments, Y and Z. Apartment Y has a single context, B. Apartment Z has two contexts, C and D. There are two objects in each context. All the objects in all the contexts associated with a particular apartment

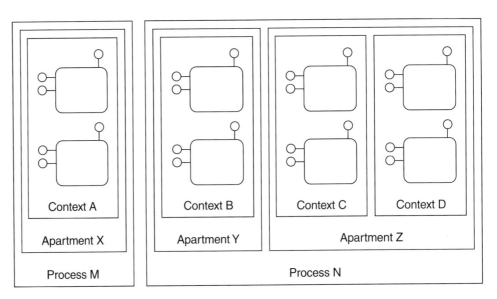

**Figure 4-1  Processes, contexts, objects, and apartments**

TRANSACTIONAL COM+: BUILDING SCALABLE APPLICATIONS

have, by definition, the same degree of thread affinity. An apartment's degree of thread affinity depends on its type.

## Apartment Types

COM+ defines three apartment types: single-threaded, multithreaded, and thread neutral. Each apartment type provides a different degree of thread affinity.

Single-threaded apartments (STAs) have high thread affinity. An STA always contains exactly one thread. Calls into contexts in an STA have to be serviced on the STA's one and only thread. If a call into a context in an STA originates on another thread, a thread switch is necessary. The interception plumbing serializes concurrent calls into contexts in an STA using its thread's Windows message queue. This reflects the STA's original purpose, which was to integrate COM code with user interface code. It also poses a number of interesting problems, which are explained later. There can be any number of STAs in a process. This is necessary to support concurrent execution across objects that require a high degree of thread affinity.

Multithreaded apartments (MTAs) have low thread affinity. An MTA can contain many threads. All calls into contexts in an MTA have to be serviced on one of the MTA's threads. If a call into a context in an MTA originates on a thread that is not in the same MTA, a thread switch is necessary. The interception plumbing makes no attempt whatsoever to serialize calls into contexts in an MTA. Because work in an MTA can execute concurrently, there is no need for more than one MTA in a process.

Thread-neutral apartments (TNAs), or neutral apartments (NAs), have no thread affinity. A TNA does not contain threads of its own. All calls into contexts in a TNA are always serviced on the caller's thread. MTA and STA threads normally execute work only in their respective apartments, but they can temporarily visit a TNA to call methods on objects that live there. After each method call completes, a visiting thread leaves the TNA and returns to its home apartment. This meets the requirement that calls into contexts in a TNA be serviced by a thread in that apartment. An MTA or STA thread is in the TNA while it is executing a method. Calls into a TNA require interception, but not a thread switch. An MTA or STA thread that is visiting a TNA may call back into a context in its home apartment. Again this requires interception, but not a thread switch. The interception plumbing makes no attempt whatsoever to serialize calls into contexts in a TNA. Because work in a TNA can execute concurrently, there is no need for more than one TNA in a process. MTAs and TNAs are very similar; both support concurrent access to objects. At first glance, TNAs often seem preferable because of the lower overhead of calls. However, the TNA is rarely the best apartment type for a COM+ object to live in.

Figure 4-2 shows the relationships among a process, its apartments, and threads (indicated by the circular arrows). The process M has four apartments, each with two contexts. Apartments W and X are STAs, each with a dedicated thread. Apartment Y is the process's MTA, with multiple threads. Apartment Z is the process's TNA, with no threads. The STA and MTA threads from apartments W, X, and Y temporarily enter apartment Z as necessary to service calls.

### Where Do Apartments Come From?

Apartments, like contexts, cannot be created explicitly. Just as there is no `CoCreateContext` API, there is no `CoCreateApartment` API. Instead, like contexts, apartments are created implicitly. Apartments exist to map threads to

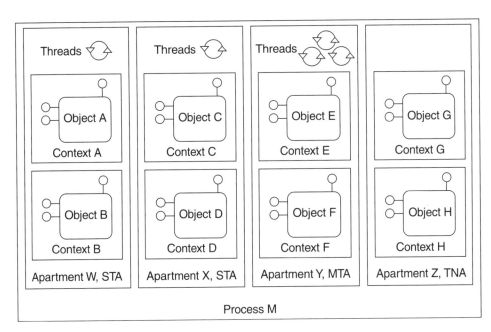

**Figure 4-2  A process, its apartments, and their threads**

contexts so that objects live in environments with the right degree of thread affinity. New apartments may be implicitly created when new threads start using COM+ or when new objects are created.

Before a thread can do anything COM+ related, it has to tell the runtime that it plans to do so. It also has to tell the runtime the type of apartment it would like to join, that is, whether it wants to interact with objects that have high or low thread affinity. A thread does both these things by calling `CoInitializeEx`; here is its signature.

```
HRESULT CoInitializeEx(void *pvReserved, DWORD dwCoInit)
```

The `CoInitializeEx` API tells the runtime about a new thread and adds the new thread to an apartment, creating one if necessary. This is one way a new apartment can be created. The first parameter to `CoInitializeEx` is always 0; the second parameter indicates which type of apartment the calling thread wants to live in. If a thread passes `COINIT_MULTITHREADED` as the second parameter, it joins the process's single MTA. If a thread passes `COINIT_APARTMENTTHREADED` as the second parameter, it enters a brand new STA created just for it. The older `CoInitialize` API delegates to `CoInitializeEx` and passes this value. Note that there is no way for a thread to enter a process's TNA; that is, there is no `COINIT_NEUTRALTHREADED`. What would be the point, when all calls into a TNA are processed on the caller's thread?

When a new instance of a class is created, the SCM may have to create not just a new context for it, but a new apartment as well. Each class defines its relationship to apartments at installation time by setting an attribute called *threading model*. A class's threading model determines the type of apartment that instances of the class can reside in. When the SCM creates an instance of a class, it has to decide whether the new object should be loaded into its creator's context or a brand new context all its own. The class's threading model is a primary factor influencing the SCM's decision. In fact, threading model takes precedence over all other declarative attributes. If a new object has a threading model that is compatible with its creator's apartment type, its ability to live in its creator's context depends on the other services it needs. If a new object's threading model is incompatible with its creator's apartment type, it cannot possibly live in its creator's context, even if it provides all the runtime services the new object needs. The SCM has to put the new object in a different apartment instead. The SCM may have to create a new apartment to do this. This is the other way a new apartment can get created.

### Threading Models

All configured, raw-configured, and nonconfigured classes have threading models; that is part of the legacy of classic COM. Each class's threading model is stored in the Registry using the `ThreadingModel` subkey of the class's `InprocServer32` key. Each configured and raw-configured class's threading model is also stored in the catalog using the `ThreadingModel` attribute described in Table 4-1. A class's threading model is stored in the Registry for backward compatibility with COM client code, which expects to find it there. It is stored in the catalog for forward compatibility with future versions of COM+. Unfortunately, it is up to you to keep the two values synchronized for each class. If the COM+ runtime detects a difference for a given class, all attempts to use that class will fail, returning the well-known error code `CO_E_THREADING MODEL_CHANGED`. The only way to fix this problem is to reinstall the class in the catalog. COM+ cannot fix this problem automatically because it cannot make assumptions about which threading model—the one in the Registry or the one in the catalog—is correct.

A class can choose from five possible threading models. They are listed in Table 4-2. The first column lists the symbolic names of the values stored in the catalog. The middle column lists the text string stored in the Registry using the `ThreadingModel` named value of a components `InprocServer32` key. These are the terms developers typically use when discussing threading models. The last column lists the type of apartment instances a class with a given threading model can execute in.

**Table 4-1   The ThreadingModel class attribute**

| Attribute | Type | Default | Notes |
|---|---|---|---|
| ThreadingModel | COMAdminThreadingModel | None | Describes class's relationship to apartments |

**Table 4-2  Threading model choices**

| Catalog (Configured and raw-configured classes only) | Registry (All classes) | Apartment Type |
|---|---|---|
| COMAdminThreadingModelBoth | Both | Any |
| COMAdminThreadingModelFree | Free | MTA |
| COMAdminThreadingModelNeutral | Neutral | TNA |
| COMAdminThreadingModelApartment | Apartment | STA |
| COMAdminThreadingModelMain | <none> | Main STA |

Note that Both is poorly named. It really means "any" apartment type will do.

The apartment type a new object ends up in depends on its class's threading model and on the apartment type of the thread calling CoCreate Instance[Ex]. Table 4-3 explains the relationship between these two factors. The first column in this table lists two thread types, STA and MTA. Each of the other columns represents one of the five threading models. The intersection of each row and column identifies the apartment where a new object will be created based on the type of thread calling CoCreateInstance[Ex] and on the threading model of the class being created.

The SCM always puts instances of classes marked COMAdminThreading ModelBoth (i.e., Any) into contexts in their creator's apartment, whatever type it happens to be. The benefit of this threading model is that it guarantees that

**Table 4-3  Threading model decoder ring**

| CoCreateInstance Called from . . . | Class Registered as ThreadingModel = . . . | | | | |
|---|---|---|---|---|---|
| | Apartment | Free | Neutral | Both | <absent> |
| STA | Current STA | MTA | TNA | Creator's Apartment (any type possible) | Main STA |
| MTA, TNA, or Remote Apartment | Host STA | | | | |
| | The SCM Puts a New Object in a Context in the . . . | | | | |

a new object can always be accessed by its creator without the overhead of a thread switch.

The SCM always puts instances of classes marked `COMAdminThreading ModelFree` into contexts in a process's MTA. It always puts instances of classes marked `COMAdminThreadingModelNeutral` into contexts in a process's TNA. The SCM puts instances of classes marked `COMAdmin ThreadingModelApartment` that are created from an STA in a context in that same STA. It puts instance of classes marked `COMAdminThreadingModel Apartment` that are created from an MTA or a TNA into a process's Host STA. The Host STA is created and managed by the plumbing specifically to house objects that require a high degree of thread affinity (i.e., an STA environment), but that are created from the MTA or TNA.

Finally, the SCM always puts instances of classes marked `COMAdmin ThreadingModelMain` or without a defined threading model into contexts in the Main STA. The Main STA is the first STA created in the process. If the Host STA is the first STA created in the process, then the Host STA is the Main STA. If the Main STA is explicitly created before the Host STA, then Host STA is not the Main STA. All instances of all classes without threading models are put into the Main STA and share one thread.

### Default Contexts

Every apartment has a special context called the *default context*. A default context is different from all the other, nondefault contexts in an apartment because it does not provide runtime services. Code executing in a default context can call `CoGetObjectContext` to retrieve a reference to its object context, but it does not support any of the normal object context interfaces, that is, `IObjectContextInfo`, `IContextState`, or `IGetContextProperties` (or `ContextInfo`, `IContextState`, or `ObjectContext` in VB). In fact, this is how an object can tell it is running in the default context of its apartment.

```
HRESULT CSomeClass::IsInDefaultContext(VARIANT_BOOL *pvb)

{
  *pvb = VARIANT_FALSE;
  CComPtr<IObjectContextInfo> spCtxInfo;
  HRESULT hr = CoGetObjectContext(__uuidof(spCtxInfo),
                                  (void**)&spCtxInfo);
```

TRANSACTIONAL COM+: BUILDING SCALABLE APPLICATIONS

```
    if (FAILED(hr) && hr != E_NOINTERFACE) return hr;
    if (hr == E_NOINTERFACE) *pb = VARIANT_TRUE;
    return S_OK;
}
```

The `IsInDefaultContext` method calls `CoGetObjectContext` to get a reference to its object context, asking for interface pointer of type `IObject ContextInfo`. This interface is exposed by the object context in all nondefault contexts. If the interface is not present `IsInDefaultContext` returns true; otherwise it returns false.

A new thread that has just entered an apartment executes in that apartment's default context. The COM+ process architecture is based on the premise that all COM-related code is executed in a context. After a thread has called `CoInitializeEx`, it is free to execute whatever COM-related code it likes, so it must be in an apartment and also in a context. Threads do not specify environmental needs beyond their apartment type, so they execute in the plain-vanilla default context their apartment provides.

The default context is also used by instances of nonconfigured classes when they are created from an apartment that does not support their threading model. In other words, if an object in an apartment creates an instance of a nonconfigured class and the new object cannot be added to its creator's context because of its threading model, the new object will be added to the default context of an apartment of the appropriate type instead. This is the only time the SCM puts a new object into an *existing* context other than its creator's. (For simplicity's sake, I ignored this esoteric case when I introduced context in Chapter 2.)

Interestingly, this rule does not apply to raw-configured classes. If an object in an apartment creates an instance of a raw-configured class and the new object cannot be added to its creator's context because of its threading model, the new object will be added to a brand-new, nondefault context in an apartment of the appropriate type instead. This disparity is a quirk of the current implementation of the COM+ plumbing. This is the only situation where non-configured and raw-configured classes behave differently during instantiation.

Default contexts can be confusing. Just remember that a new thread executes in the default context of its apartment and that new instances of classes are assigned to contexts and apartments as summarized in Table 4-4.

**Table 4-4  Threading model and context decoder ring**

| Current Apartment Type and Threading Model Are . . . | Creating an Instance of a . . . | | |
|---|---|---|---|
| | Configured Class | Nonconfigured Class | Raw-configured Class |
| Compatible | New Context, Same Apartment | Same Context, Same Apartment | Same Context, Same Apartment |
| Incompatible | New Context, Other Apartment | Default Context, Other Apartment | New Context, Other Apartment |
| | SCM Puts New Object in . . . | | |

The first column in Table 4-4 lists the two options for compatibility between an apartment and a threading model; that is, they are compatible or they are not compatible. Each of the other columns represents one of the three class configuration types—configured, nonconfigured, and raw-configured. The intersection of each row and column identifies the context and apartment where a new object will be created based on the level of compatibility between the type of thread calling CoCreateInstance[Ex] and the threading model of the class being created and on the class's configuration type. Figure 4-3 shows an example to help drive this point home.

The STA thread of apartment X lives in the apartment's default context A. It created object A, an instance of a raw-configured class marked either COMAdminThreadingModelApartment or COMAdminThreadingModelBoth. Because it has a compatible threading model and does not need additional interception, object A lives in context A as well. Object A created object B, an instance of a configured class also marked either COMAdminThreading ModelApartment or COMAdminThreadingModelBoth. It lives in a new context B in the same apartment X. Object B created object B', another instance of a raw-configured class marked either COMAdminThreadingModelApartment or COMAdminThreadingModelBoth. Object B created object C, an instance of a *nonconfigured* class marked COMAdminThreadingModelFree. It lives with the MTA threads in the default context C of apartment Y. Object B also created object D, an instance of a *raw-configured* class marked COMAdmin ThreadingModelFree. The object has to live in apartment Y to satisfy its threading requirements. Because it is an instance of a raw-configured class, the

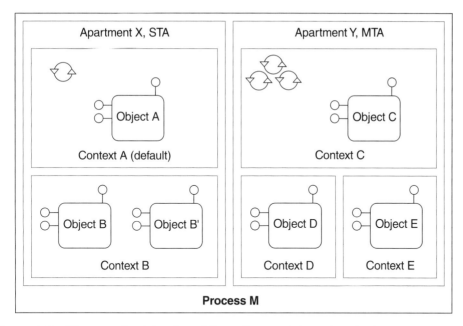

**Figure 4-3   The complex interplay of threading models and contexts**

SCM puts object D into a new context without services, context D. Finally, object B created object E, an instance of a configured class marked COMAdmin ThreadingModelFree. It lives in a context E configured to provide the run-time services its needs.

### Remote Object Creation

Up to this point, the discussion of apartments has focused on the creation of objects in a process. Often, however, objects are created by code executing in a separate process. This adds a new dimension to the SCM's decision about where to put a new object. Specifically, if a remote client creates an instance of a configured class deployed in a server application, the SCM cannot possibly put the new object into its creator's context or apartment. It has no choice but to put the new object into a context and apartment in the server process.

Obviously, the apartment in a server process that a new, remotely created object goes into depends on its class's threading model. Instances of classes marked COMAdminThreadingModelFree or COMAdminThreadingModel Both are created in contexts in a server process's MTA. Instances of classes marked `COMAdminThreadingModelNeutral` are created in contexts in a server process's TNA. The SCM puts remotely created instances of classes marked `COMAdminThreadingModelApartment` into contexts in one of a server process's STAs. Each process includes a Host STA and a pool of additional STAs for housing new objects that require a high degree of thread affinity. The pool allows requests to STA-based objects to be processed concurrently.

The size of the STA pool is limited by number of CPUs installed in the machine an application is running on. Both the upper and lower bounds of the pool are determined by CPU count using this formula:

$$7 + n_{CPU} \leq n_{STA} \leq n_{CPU} \times 10.$$

In other words, the number of STAs available in COM+ process $n_{STA}$ ranges from 7 plus the number of CPUs in the machine, $n_{CPU}$, to 10 times the number of CPUs in the machine, inclusive. On a box with a single CPU, the range is 8 to 10 STAs; on a box with two CPUs, the range is 9 to 20 STAs; on a box with four CPUs, the range is 11 to 40 STAs, and so on. The size of the pool is adjusted dynamically based on the number of inbound requests to all STAs. There is no documented way to change the size of this pool.

When a new STA-based object is created from an MTA or a TNA or a remote client, the SCM puts the new object into a context in the process's Host STA. The STA pool does not get used in any of these cases. However, this is only the SCM's default behavior, which is based solely on a class's threading model. The SCM will put a new instance of a class marked `ThreadingModel = Apartment` into an STA in a process's pool if the class uses activities. (The second half of this chapter addresses activities in detail.)

## Cross-Apartment Calls

The apartment mechanism requires that all calls and callbacks into a context be serviced on a thread in that context's apartment. With the exception of calls into a TNA from other apartments in the same process, that means that all cross-apartment calls require a thread switch. Chapter 3 mentions that COM+ uses an entirely different channel implementation when a thread switch is required. More precisely, COM+ uses an entirely different channel implementation if calls have to cross an apartment boundary. If the SCM puts a new object into an apartment other than its creator's—either because its threading model wasn't compatible with its creator's apartment type or because it resides in a separate process—`CoCreateInstance[Ex]` will return a reference to a proxy. The proxy will be attached to a channel that is prepared to move call stacks from one thread to another by executing remote procedure calls (RPCs). (Different optimized RPC mechanisms are used for in-process, cross-process, and cross-machine calls.) This is true even when an object lives in a context in a TNA and can be called without switching threads. This is done for consistency's sake, so that all cross-apartment calls use the same interception mechanism.

The COM+ runtime maintains a per-process pool of threads for receiving and servicing cross-apartment RPCs. This thread pool is dynamically sized. It expands and contracts as workload varies and has no documented lower or upper bound. The RPC receive thread pool is allowed to grow as needed because its threads can be terminated if there is no work to do. This is obviously different from the per-process STA pool that COM+ maintains for instances of classes marked `COMAdminThreadingModelApartment`. STA threads need to exist as long as there are connections to contexts in their apartments, a factor that is ultimately controlled by clients. If lots of STA threads were created, they might all have to stay alive for a long time. To avoid a large number of threads contending for resources over an extended period, the COM+ plumbing strictly limits the number of STA threads that exist. This is not an issue for the RPC receive threads, which have to live only as long as they are servicing method calls.

## STA Complexities

Calls and callbacks into contexts in a process's MTA are serviced directly by the process's RPC receive threads, which live in that apartment. Calls and callbacks into contexts in an STA have to be serviced on the STA's one and only thread. RPC calls into an STA are queued as messages on its thread's Windows message queue, and each caller blocks until its message gets pumped and its call gets serviced.[1] This means that an STA thread must continually pump

---

[1] In some cases, a cross-apartment, same-machine call can be dispatched into an STA without using an RPC receive thread, but this optimization does not change the logical model for STA behavior.

messages to ensure that calls into its apartment get processed in a timely manner. It also means that an STA thread must never be blocked indefinitely. If an STA thread were blocked indefinitely, calls or callbacks into its apartment would have to wait as well. The potential for deadlock in this situation is very high. For example, if the STA thread were waiting infinitely for a mutex and the thread that currently owned the mutex tried to call into the STA, both threads would grind to a halt. This significant limitation does not apply to threads in an MTA. In an MTA, where calls can be serviced concurrently using multiple threads, blocking a single thread for an extended period of time is not nearly so dangerous.

COM method calls are synchronous, blocking operations. But issuing a COM method call cannot stop an STA thread. If it did, and the outbound call could not complete without making a call back into the STA, the calls would deadlock. So the COM+ interception plumbing goes to a lot of trouble to make sure that an STA thread is never really blocked. When an STA thread makes an outbound call through a proxy and a *cross-apartment* channel that mandates a thread switch, the thread seems to block waiting for a response. But the thread is not really stopped. Instead, it is inside the channel in a message loop, while another thread makes the outbound, genuinely blocking RPC call. If a call arrives while an STA thread is in the channel, it will be queued on the STA's message queue. Then it will be serviced because the STA thread—still in the channel—is pumping messages. All this is necessary to support callbacks. (And to make sure Windows messages are processed. This is important when an STA is executing user-interface code, which is irrelevant in COM+-based, middle-tier server processes.)

While the interception plumbing works this way to support callbacks, the message loop inside the channel does not discriminate between callbacks and new calls entering an STA. It dispatches incoming calls either way.[2] If a causality—remember that a causality is a logical thread of action—enters an STA and

---

[2] In theory, it is possible to tailor the behavior of the channel's message loop by registering an implementation of the `IMessageFilter` interface that accepts or rejects calls that arrive in an STA based on whatever criteria you choose. In practice this is not a good idea unless you have complete knowledge of what's happening in a process. You have no idea to what extent the COM+ plumbing and services rely on the STA reentrancy mechanism, so tinkering with that behavior is verboten.

then makes an outbound call to another apartment, a second causality can enter the STA. The second causality will use the STA thread to service its call, as per the plumbing's requirement. The first causality cannot return to the STA to finish its work until the second causality is done. In other words, if a method dispatched on an STA thread makes an outbound call through a cross-apartment proxy, it is implicitly yielding the STA thread to *another* caller and cannot use the thread again until that other caller's invocation completes.

As Figure 4-4 illustrates, causality A entered context A in apartment X, an STA, to execute a method of object A. In the midst of that call, causality A made an outbound call to an object in some other apartment. When causality A left apartment X, the apartment's thread entered a message loop inside the channel. Because the STA thread is pumping messages, causality B is able to enter context B in the same apartment to execute a method of object B. The fact that causality B is calling to a different object in a different context is irrelevant. It could just as easily have entered context A to execute a method of object A. Once causality B enters the apartment, it has possession of the STA thread, which it has borrowed from causality A. Causality A cannot return to the apartment until causality B completes and relinquishes the STA thread. This type of nesting can go arbitrarily deep. If causality B called out to another apartment,

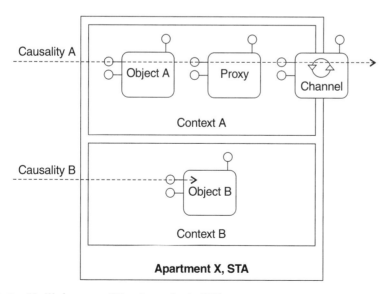

**Figure 4-4   Multiple causalities in a single STA**

a third causality, C, could enter apartment X to service a call. Or causality A could reenter the STA to service a callback. In either case, the third call would have to complete before the second call could continue, and so on until the entire nested series of calls is unwound.

This behavior explains why, if a class marked `COMAdminThreadingModel Apartment` uses the COM+ statistics service (`EventTrackingEnabled = True`), the value Component Services Explorer displays for the number of calls currently being serviced by instances of the class can exceed the maximum number of STAs in an application's pool. If an object in an STA calls out to another apartment, another call can enter that STA. In this case, the same thread is servicing two calls simultaneously; one is simply nested in the other.

This behavior also makes it very hard to predict how long it will take to complete an invocation in an STA if the method being called makes outbound calls to objects in other apartments. One of your goals in developing scalable systems is to write tight code that executes as quickly as possible in order to free resources to service other requests. If a method calls out to another apartment from an STA, there is no telling how long it will have to wait to reclaim the STA thread and finish its work. This isn't a problem for thread consumption; the STA thread is kept busy servicing other calls. But this is a potential problem where other resources, such as RM locks, are concerned because they may be held for an arbitrarily long time.

Calls and callbacks into contexts in a process's TNA are serviced directly by the calling thread. If an STA thread calls into a TNA in the same process, no thread switch is required, and none of the issues described above arise. If an STA thread that is visiting a TNA calls back into its home apartment, again no thread switch is required, and none of the issues described above arise. However, if an STA thread that is visiting a TNA calls out into some other apartment, a thread switch is necessary, and all the issues described above arise; that is, the channel puts the STA thread into a message loop to service callbacks and avoid deadlocks.

None of these issues arise when an MTA thread calls into or out of a TNA. If an MTA thread calls into a TNA, no thread switch is required. If an MTA thread that is visiting a TNA calls back into its home apartment, again no thread switch is required. If an MTA thread that is visiting a TNA calls out into another apartment, a thread switch is required, and the MTA thread blocks. Remote calls into a TNA are serviced directly by the RPC receive threads living in a process's MTA, so none of these issues arise for remote calls independent of the type of the caller's thread.

### Cross-Apartment Call Overhead

In general, cross-apartment calls are at least one order of magnitude slower than cross-context calls. Call stacks have to be marshaled in either case, but cross-apartment calls also require a thread switch, that is, degree 2 interception. In-process calls into a TNA are the exception to this rule. If a thread in an STA or MTA calls a method of an object in the same process's TNA, marshaling occurs, but no thread switch is required—this is degree 1 interception. Despite this fact, the performance of calls into contexts in a TNA is noticeably lower than the performance of cross-context calls in the same apartment. Calls into the default context of a TNA take roughly twice as long as cross-context calls in the same apartment. Calls into nondefault contexts in a TNA take roughly four times as long as cross-context calls in the same apartment.

Also, as explained when I derived the formula for estimating the memory footprint of a COM+ process, contexts accessed with a thread switch (i.e., with a cross-apartment channel), consume more memory than contexts accessed without a thread switch (i.e., with a simpler cross-context channel). The difference in weight between the two channels is approximately 1 KB.

## Apartment Guidelines

You have to pick a threading model for each new class you create. Threading model Both is preferred in COM+ simply because instances of classes marked COMAdminThreadingModelBoth always activate as close to their creator as possible. Although interception may be necessary to cross a context boundary, no thread switch will be necessary as long as the object and its creator are in the same process. If the object and its creator are in different processes, the object will be put into a context in the server's MTA. This is preferable for performance reasons because the object is not bound to a particular thread. Many classic COM developers shied away from threading model Both because they didn't want their objects to inadvertently end up in the exciting, dynamic, highly concurrent, and potentially dangerous world of the MTA. Remember, however, that the MTA is dangerous only if multiple threads access an object simultaneously. If you follow the object-per-client model (Rule 1.1), this is not a concern. If some clients do not follow the object-per-client model, you can rely on activities to protect your objects from concurrent access. In general, threading model Both is the way to go.

While threading model Both is the preference in COM+, there are several situations when another threading model is appropriate. First, if you are implementing classes using Visual Basic 6, they must use threading model Apartment. (The next version of Visual Basic does away with this restriction.)

If a class uses instances of other classes, it might want to share their threading model. Imagine a class that is written in C++ and marked `COMAdminThreadingModelBoth`. When a client in another process creates an instance of that class, the SCM will put the new object in the server process's MTA. If that object creates several instances of classes implemented in Visual Basic and marked `COMAdminThreadingModelApartment`, the SCM will put those objects into an STA. Every call from the MTA-based object to one of the STA-based objects will require a thread switch. In this case, it would be better to mark the original class `COMAdminThreadingModel Apartment` as well. That way, the client's new object and all the STA-based objects it creates will go to the same apartment and calls between them can be serviced on the same thread. Bear in mind that this situation may arise when you use standard classes provided by the Windows platform. Many of them were designed for use from Visual Basic 6 and use threading model Apartment (e.g., the various ADO classes and MSXML 2's `XMLHttpRequest` class). Instances of these types are expensive to call from an MTA.

If a class has a method that blocks a thread indefinitely without pumping messages, the class must use threading model Free. Remember that the COM+ plumbing never blocks an STA thread indefinitely without pumping messages, because it could easily lead to deadlock. You should never block an STA thread indefinitely without pumping messages either. This does not mean, however, that you cannot stop an STA thread temporarily. For example, if a method executing on STA thread wanted to test an event to see if it was signaled, it could call `WaitForSingleObject` without blocking.

```
dwRes = WaitForSingleObject(g_hEvent, 0); // don't wait
```

This call is fine because the timeout of 0 guarantees that the API will always return quickly. Calling `WaitForSingleObject` with longer timeouts is acceptable also.

```
dwRes = WaitForSingleObject(g_hEvent, 1000); // don't wait long
```

In this case, the STA thread would wait for one second to find out if the event were set. This will never result in deadlock. If another thread is waiting to call into the STA before it signals the event, both threads will stop, but only for one second until the STA thread returns from this call. Calling `WaitForSingle Object` with an indefinite timeout is not acceptable.

```
dwRes = WaitForSingleObject(g_hEvent, INFINITE); // just wait
```

If the thread that is responsible for signaling this event is waiting to access this STA, this call will lead to a deadlock.

Windows 2000 introduces a new COM-aware synchronization API called `CoWaitForMultipleHandles` that makes blocking an STA thread safer.

```
WINOLEAPI CoWaitForMultipleHandles (DWORD dwFlags,
                                     DWORD dwTimeout,
                                     ULONG cHandles,
                                     LPHANDLE pHandles,
                                     LPDWORD  lpdwindex);
```

`CoWaitForMultipleHandles` understands that STA threads cannot block indefinitely without pumping messages. If it is called from an STA thread, its implementation puts the thread into a message loop. It will break out of the loop if the kernel object(s) that the thread is waiting for becomes available or the timeout expires. Here is an example of this function's use:

```
DWORD dwIndex = 0;
HRESULT hr = CoWaitForMultipleHandles(COWAIT_ALERTABLE,
                                      60000, 1, &g_hEvent,
                                      &dwIndex);
```

If an STA thread executes this code, it waits up to one minute for `g_hEvent` to be signaled. Meanwhile, `CoWaitForMultipleHandles` will pump messages sent to the STA and dispatch inbound COM calls or callbacks, which lowers the risk of deadlock significantly.

However, using `CoWaitForMultipleHandles` does not eliminate STA deadlock concerns. It helps only in situations where an STA thread is waiting for a resource that will not be released unless a new call into the STA can be processed. If an STA thread is waiting for a resource that will not be released unless an ongoing causality that *left* the STA to service an outbound call can *return* to complete its work, `CoWaitForMultipleHandles` cannot help. In this case, even if you are using `CoWaitForMultipleHandles`, the only answer is not to block indefinitely.

`CoWaitForMultipleHandles` makes it easier, but not easy, to block an STA thread safely. It also works correctly from MTA threads, where it is the moral equivalent of a call to `WaitForMultipleObjectsEx`. Instances of classes marked `COMAdminThreadingModelBoth` or `COMAdminThreading ModelNeutral` do not know in advance what type of thread they will be called from. They should use `CoWaitForMultipleHandles`, which detects the thread's type—MTA or STA—and behaves accordingly, and they should *never wait indefinitely* just in case they are executing work on an STA thread.

Unfortunately, sometimes you have no choice about what blocking calls your threads make or how long they wait for them to complete. Perhaps you have legacy code or a third-party library that calls `WaitForSingleObject` with an infinite timeout or calls `recv` and blocks until data arrives at a socket. If a class calls code like this, it cannot use threading model Apartment, Both, or Neutral. Under the right circumstances, all three of those options could allow an object to be called from an STA thread. But this code cannot be executed from an STA thread; the potential for deadlock is too high. If a class calls code like this, it must use threading model Free.

If an object is called from more than one apartment in a process, it should use threading model Neutral. All the calls to the object will be intercepted, but none of them will require a thread switch. This is different from using custom marshaling to do away with interception (à la the classic COM Free-Threaded Marshaler, or FTM). These calls will still go through a standard COM+ proxy/ stub connection, which can invoke any services the object wants to use. This is also different from threading model Both, which allows an object to be created in any apartment, but then requires a thread switch to service calls from other apartments (unless the object happened to be created in a TNA).

As a corollary, if an object is called from exactly one apartment in a process, it should not use threading model Neutral. Calls into a TNA are always more expensive than cross-context calls in the same apartment. By definition, an object that can live safely in a TNA makes no assumptions about the type of thread—MTA or STA—that is invoking its methods. In that case, if the object is called from exactly one apartment, it should use threading model Both and live as close as possible to its one and only client. This corollary applies to the vast majority of objects used in COM+-based systems. The object-per-client model means there is no reason for processor objects to use threading model Neutral; they are never called from more than one apartment. The one place threading model Neutral might be useful in a COM+-based system is in building relatively low-level plumbing like a middle-tier cache.

Finally, a class should never use threading model Main (the default if a class does not have a threading model at all). The SCM puts all instances of every class using Main into a process's Main STA. All calls into contexts in the Main STA have to be serviced by its one and only thread, making concurrent access to objects impossible. In short, the Main STA is a tremendous bottleneck. Threading model Main was devised for classic COM in-process servers that were developed before apartments became mainstream. This option destroys scalability and has no place in modern COM+ development.

All of these apartment guidelines are summarized in Rule 4.1.

 **RULE** **4.1**

Use threading model Both (Any) whenever possible, with the following caveats:

- Use threading model Apartment when there is no alternative.
- Match a class's threading model to the threading model of the classes it depends on, where appropriate.
- Use threading model Free for classes with methods that block the calling thread indefinitely.
- Use threading model Neutral for classes whose instances are called from multiple apartments in the same process (rare, but may be useful for building plumbing).
- Never use threading model Main.

### Raw-Configured Classes Revisited

The fact that threading model takes precedence over all other declarative attributes has an impact on the behavior of raw-configured classes. If a raw-configured class really wants to make sure the SCM always puts its new instances in their creators' contexts, it should use threading model Both. If a raw-configured class uses a more specific threading model, a new instance can go in its creator's context only if its creator is in an apartment of the appropriate type. If all your classes use the same threading model (e.g., they are all implemented in Visual Basic 6 and use threading model Apartment), this is not a problem. If all your classes do not use the same threading model, you have to be more careful, especially if your raw-configured classes expect to access their creator's object context. One way to avoid problems is to enable a raw-configured class's `MustRunInClientContext` attribute to ensure that instances can be created only from apartments that are compatible with the class's threading model.

## Activities

Now that you are familiar with apartments, let me return to a perplexing problem with STA-based objects. The SCM's default behavior is to put new instances of classes marked `COMAdminThreadingModelApartment` that are being created from an MTA or a TNA or a remote client into a server process's Host STA. All calls into contexts in the Host STA have to be serviced by its one and only thread, making concurrent access to objects impossible. It is not good for STA-based objects to live in a process's Host STA because the Host STA, like the Main STA, is a tremendous bottleneck. Each COM+ process contains a pool of STAs specifically designed to house high-thread affinity objects and still execute work concurrently. The question is, Why doesn't the SCM use those STAs by default and how can you change its mind?

There are two reasons for the SCM's behavior. First, it reflects classic COM, which did exactly the same thing when an STA-based object was created from an MTA thread or a remote client. Second, a threading model alone does not give the SCM enough information to allocate STA-based objects to single-threaded apartments efficiently in all cases. The SCM could use a simple round-robin allocation scheme to map new STA-based objects into apartments in a process's pool. But if an object in one process created multiple STA-based objects in another process, they could easily end up in different apartments. If they needed to invoke each other's methods, calls between them would require a thread switch and servicing a single client request would tie up multiple STA threads. The SCM really has no idea whether STA objects are going to talk to each other or not. But it is afraid of making an expensive mistake. So it chooses to avoid the situation and puts new STA-based objects in the Host STA instead (definitely a *very* expensive mistake)—unless it has additional information that explains how the new object it is creating relates to the other objects in a process. This is where activities come in.

## Enter Activities

An *activity* is a group of contexts in one or more processes that were created to do work for a single client. COM+ assumes, based on the object-per-client model, that access to contexts in an activity can and should be serialized. The reasoning is simple: If clients don't share objects, they don't share contexts, and therefore contexts will never be used concurrently. Every context created in a COM+ process is associated with at most one activity. Activities are a part of context and can flow to new contexts as they are created. When a new context is created, it can be added to its creator's activity, a new activity of its own, or no activity at all. A process can contain multiple activities for multiple clients. However, unlike apartments, activities can extend across process boundaries.

Figure 4-5 illustrates the relationships among processes, contexts, objects, and activities. In this picture, each process is divided into contexts. Process M contains a single context, A. Process N contains three contexts, B, C, and D. There are two activities, X and Y. Each activity contains two contexts that were created to do work for a single client. Activity X spans process boundaries. It contains context A from process M and context B from process N, so work in those contexts can and should be serialized. Activity Y does not span a process boundary. It contains contexts C and D from process N, so work in those contexts can and should be serialized.

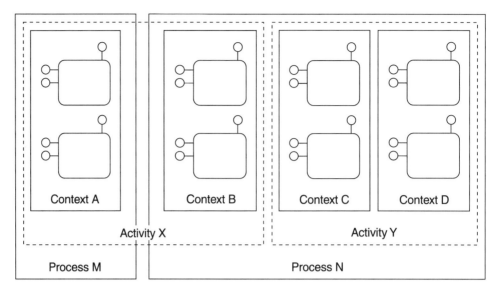

**Figure 4-5   Processes, contexts, objects, and activities**

### Where Do Activities Come From?

Like contexts and apartments, activities cannot be created explicitly. Just as there is no `CoCreateContext` API or `CoCreateApartment` API, there is no `CoCreateActivity` API. Activity creation and propagation is implicitly tied to context creation, which is implicitly tied to object creation. How each instance of a configured class relates to activities (e.g., whether creating a new object also creates a new activity) is determined by the value of the class's *synchronization* attribute in the catalog. The synchronization attribute is described in Table 4-5.

The five possible synchronization settings are listed in the first column of Table 4-6. The second column lists the corresponding name for each setting used by the Component Services Explorer (CSE) user interface. These are the

**Table 4-5   The Synchronization class attribute**

| Attribute | Catalog Type | Default Value | Notes |
|---|---|---|---|
| Synchronization | COMAdmin Synchronization | COMAdmin Synchronization Required | Determines class's use of activities |

**Table 4-6  Synchronization options**

| Attribute | CSE Name | Is in Activity? | Shares Creator's Activity? |
|---|---|---|---|
| COMAdminSynchronization None | Not_Supported | Never | Never |
| COMAdminSynchronization Supported | Supported | If creator is in activity | If creator is in activity |
| COMAdminSynchronization Required | Required | Always | If creator is in activity |
| COMAdminSynchronization RequiresNew | Requires_New | Always | Never |
| COMAdminSynchronization Ignored | Disabled | If creator is in activity and object shares creator's context | If creator is in activity and object shares creator's context |

terms developers typically use when discussing synchronization options. The third column indicates whether a new object will be in a context in an activity. The last column indicates whether a new object will be in a context that inherits an activity from its creator. Note that Not_Supported and None are synonymous, as are Ignored and Disabled.

All five of these options provide different semantics for controlling the flow of an activity from a creator's context to a new context. The first four options are straightforward variations on a theme. The fifth option is more complex and is designed specifically for raw-configured classes. The default synchronization setting for a new configured class is Required.

New instances of a class marked `COMAdminSynchronizationNone` never inherit their creator's activity. If a new object's creator is in an activity, the SCM must put the new object into a new context that is not in an activity.

New instances of a class that is marked `COMAdminSynchronization Supported` inherit their creator's activity, if it has one; otherwise, they are not in an activity. This happens implicitly if the SCM puts a new object in its creator's context. If the SCM puts a new object in a new context and its creator has an activity, the activity is extended to encompass the new context. Otherwise the new context is not in any activity.

New instances of a class marked `COMAdminSynchronizationRequired` inherit their creator's activity, if it has one; otherwise they get a new activity. This happens implicitly if a new object's creator is in an activity and the SCM puts the new object in its creator's context. If the SCM puts the new object in a new context and its creator is in an activity, the SCM extends the activity to encompass the new context. If a new object's creator is not in an activity, the SCM must put the new object into a new context that is part of a new activity.

New instances of a class marked `COMAdminSynchronizationRequires New` always get a new activity; they never inherit activities from their creators. The SCM always puts the new object into a new context that is part of a brand-new activity.

New instances of a class marked `COMAdminSynchronizationIgnored` do not care about activities. If the SCM puts a new object in its creator's context and its creator is in an activity, the new object inherits that activity implicitly. If the SCM puts a new object in its creator's context and its creator is not in an activity, the new object is not in an activity. If the SCM puts a new object into a new context, the new context is not in an activity. Think of this Disabled setting as being somewhere between Supported and Not_Supported. Like Supported, Disabled means a new object should inherit its creator's activity if it has one, *but only if the new object ends up in its creator's context*. Like Not_Supported, Disabled means a new object should never inherit its creator's activity, *but only if the new object ends up in a new context*.

The Disabled option is designed for raw-configured classes that never want the presence or absence of an activity to have an effect on the SCM's decision about what context they should live in. A raw-configured class can also use the Not_Supported or Required options to ensure that its instances always exist in contexts outside an activity or inside an activity, respectively. These settings do not require interception if a creator's context already has the desired synchronization semantics. If a creator's context does not have the desired synchronization semantics, these options do require interception and will force instances of raw-configured classes into contexts of their own. You can avoid this by enabling a raw-configured class's `MustRunInClientContext` attribute so that object creation fails in these cases.

Consider the example in Figure 4-6. A single client created the contexts and objects in this diagram. The order of creation proceeded from left to right; that is, object A in context A was created first, then it created object B in context B, and so on. Object A is an instance of a class marked `COMAdmin SynchronizationRequired` or `COMAdminSynchronizationRequires New`. Either one would cause the creation of a new activity X. Object B is an instance of a class marked `COMAdminSynchronizationRequired` or `COMAdminSynchronizationSupported`. Either one would allow it to inherit its creator's—object A's—activity. Object C is an instance of a class marked `COMAdminSynchronizationNone`. That forced it outside its creator's activity. Object D, like object A, is an instance of a class marked `COMAdmin SynchronizationRequired` or `COMAdminSynchronizationRequires New`. Either one would cause the creation of a new activity Y. Object D' is an instance of a raw-configured class marked `COMAdminSynchronization Ignored`. That forced it into its creator's context D and therefore activity Y. Object E is an instance of a class marked `COMAdminSynchronization RequiresNew`. That caused the creation of one last activity, Z.

**Detecting the Presence of an Activity**

Any object can detect whether it is in a context that is part of an activity. This is useful for an instance of a configured class marked `COMAdmin SynchronizationSupported` that wants to know whether its context inherited an activity from its creator. It is also useful for an instance of a raw-configured class marked `COMAdminSynchronizationIgnored` that wants to know whether its creator's context (where it lives) is in an activity. Every activity has a unique ID, a GUID. If a context is in an activity, the activity's ID can

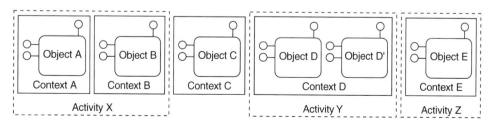

**Figure 4-6   Activity creation and propagation**

be retrieved from object context using the `IObjectContextInfo` interface's `GetActivityId` method. If a context is not in an activity, `GetActivityId` returns `GUID_NULL`. Here is some code that uses `GetActivityId` to determine if it is executing in a context in an activity.

```
HRESULT CSomeCfgClass::IsInActivity(VARIANT_BOOL *pvb)
{
  CComPtr<IObjectContextInfo> spCtxInfo;
  HRESULT hr = CoGetObjectContext(__uuidof(spCtxInfo),
                                  (void**)&spCtxInfo);
  if (FAILED(hr)) return hr;
  GUID activityId;
  hr = spCtxInfo->GetActivityId(&activityId);
  if (FAILED(hr)) return hr;
  *pvb = (activityId != GUID_NULL ? VARIANT_TRUE : VARIANT_FALSE);
  return S_OK;
}
```

The `IsInActivity` method calls `CoGetObjectContext` to get an `IObjectContextInfo` reference to its object context. It calls the `GetActivityId` method to retrieve the GUID representing the current activity. If the value it retrieves is not `GUID_NULL`, it returns true; otherwise it returns false.

## Allocating STA Objects to Apartments

The SCM puts STA-based objects created from an MTA or a TNA or a remote client into a server process's Host STA by default. The SCM does not use the pool of STAs available in each COM+ process because it is worried about using them inefficiently. However, if the SCM knows which STA-based objects in a process are being used together, it can map them all to a single apartment. Calls between the objects would be less expensive and a single client request would use only a single STA thread, alleviating the SCM's concerns. Activities tell the SCM what it needs to know to do this.

Remember that an activity is a group of contexts created to do work for a single client and that access to the contexts in an activity can be serialized. The SCM takes this to heart. It knows about activities and uses them to make more informed decisions about which apartment a new object should reside in. Its main goal is to conserve threads and minimize cross-apartment calls by putting all the objects in contexts in a single activity as close to each other as possible. It also tries to minimize contention for threads by putting objects in contexts in one activity as far from objects in contexts in other activities as possible. The SCM realizes its goals by implementing two specific behaviors. First, it puts all the STA-based objects that are in the same activity and process into a single STA from the process's pool. Second, it allocates a whole activity to an unused STA in a process's pool, if possible. If all the STAs in a process's pool are in use, the SCM allocates activities to STAs using a round-robin algorithm.

These rules override the normal threading model rules for assigning new objects to apartments. Table 4-7 summarizes how activities change the way the SCM maps STA-objects to apartments. The first column lists the four pertinent combinations of apartment type—STA or MTA/TNA/remote—and the presence of an activity (a thread is executing in a context in an activity or it is not). Each of the columns represents one of the five synchronization settings a class marked `COMAdminThreadingModelApartment` can use. The intersection of each row and column identifies the activity and STA where a new object will be created based on the type of thread calling `CoCreateInstance[Ex]`, the presence of an activity, and the synchronization setting of the class being created.

**Table 4-7  Activity and STA decoder ring**

| CoCreateInstance Called from a Context in . . . | Class Registered as ThreadingModel = Apartment and Synchronization = | | | | |
|---|---|---|---|---|---|
| | Not_Supported | Supported | Required | Requires_New | Disabled |
| An Activity and an STA | No Activity, Same STA | Creator's Activity, Same STA | | New Activity, a Different STA | Same Activity/ STA, If Other Settings Allow |
| An Activity and an MTA, TNA, or Remote Apartment | No Activity, Host STA | Creator's Activity, Host STA | Creator's Activity, that Activity's STA | | No Activity, Host STA |
| No Activity and an STA | No Activity, Same STA | | New Activity, a Different STA | | No Activity, Same STA |
| No Activity and an MTA, TNA, or Remote Apartment | No Activity, Host STA | | | | No Activity, Host STA |
| The SCM Puts a New Object in a Context in . . . | | | | | |

The SCM's behavior varies according to the creator's apartment type. Assume that a new STA-based object is created from an MTA, a TNA, or an apartment in a remote client. If the new object is an instance of a class marked either `COMAdminSynchronizationRequired` or `COMAdminSynchronization RequiresNew`, the SCM does not put it into the Host STA. It puts it into the pooled STA to which its activity has been assigned. If the new object is an instance of a class marked `COMAdminSynchronizationNone`, the SCM puts it into the Host STA. If the new object is an instance of a class marked `COMAdminSynchronizationSupported`, the SCM puts it into the Host STA, *even* if it inherits an activity from its creator. This is a quirk of the current implementation of the runtime; the new object should end up in its activity's pooled STA.

If a new STA-based object is created from an STA, the SCM behaves differently. If the new object is an instance of a class marked `COMAdmin SynchronizationSupported` or `COMAdminSynchronizationNone`, the SCM puts it in its creator's STA. If the new object is an instance of a class marked `COMAdminSynchronizationRequired`, the SCM puts it in its creator's STA *only* if it inherits its creator's activity. If there is no activity to inherit and the object has to be given a new activity, the SCM puts it in a different STA from the pool. Finally, if a new object is an instance of a class marked `COMAdminSynchronizationRequiresNew`, the SCM does not put it into its creator's apartment. It puts the new object into another STA from the pool instead.

For example, the five objects in Figure 4-7 all belong to a single activity, X. The activity includes context A in the MTA of process M, where object A lives. Contexts B and C in STA 1 of process M, where objects B and C live, are also part of activity X. Finally, contexts D and E in STA 4 of process N, where objects D and E live, are part of activity X as well. If more STA-based objects are created in contexts that inherit activity X, they will end up in STA 1 or STA 4, depending on whether they live in process M or N, respectively. This allocation of objects to apartments results from the fact that all the objects are in the same activity; for example, they are all instances of classes marked `COMAdmin SynchronizationRequired`.

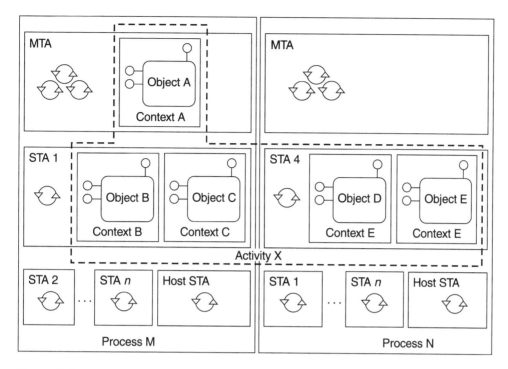

**Figure 4-7   Activities and STA-based object creation**

The order in which the objects in the diagram were created and which object created which does not matter. As long as they all propagate their creator's activity, the mapping to apartments works out the same way. This is true even when objects are created from other processes. If object B creates object D and object D creates object C, the SCM knows object C should be in the same apartment as object B because they are part of the same activity. This is why activities extend across process boundaries.

Activities are propagated from one context to another as new objects are created. When a client creates a new object, there is no activity to propagate. If the client is creating an instance of a class marked either COMAdmin SynchronizationRequired or COMAdminSynchronizationRequiresNew, the SCM will put the new object in a new context in a new activity. If a client creates two objects that require activities, they will end up in two *different* activities. If the objects are STA-based, they will end up in different apartments, making calls between them expensive. This is not a problem for MTA- or TNA-based objects, which always end up in the same apartment. Frankly, COM+ does not expect this situation to arise. It expects a client to create one object to accomplish a given task. If that one object creates additional objects, they can inherit the original object's activity, and the SCM can keep them all as close together as possible so that calls between them will always be as cheap as possible. In short, COM+ expects clients to use processor objects.

## Serializing Calls

The SCM uses activities to map new STA-based objects to apartments based on the assumption that, because all the contexts in an activity belong to a single client, access to those contexts *can* be serialized. Activities have a second, entirely different purpose. It is based on the assumption that, because the class code executing in a client's contexts was written with the object-per-client model in mind and is not thread-safe, access to those contexts *should* be serialized. Whether this is true or not is irrelevant; the interception plumbing serializes calls into activities just in case.

Every COM+ process maintains a table of data structures describing the activities in that process. The table is indexed based on activity ID. The most interesting element in the activity data structure is an exclusive lock. When a call into a context in an activity is preprocessed, the interception plumbing acquires the activity's lock before dispatching the call. The lock is released when the call is postprocessed. In effect, this serializes work in the activity. Figure 4-8 shows the data structure associated with an activity. The causality entering the context has to acquire the activity's lock before it can proceed.

Activity synchronization is completely orthogonal to apartments. Figure 4-9 shows an activity that includes contexts in two apartments in the same process. The interception plumbing will not let a client's call enter either context A or context C without acquiring the lock for activity A first. Once the lock is acquired, other clients' calls into either context will be forced to wait. For instance, if a call is in progress inside object A in context A, it must have acquired activity A's lock. If another client's call attempts to enter context C to invoke a method of object C, it has to wait, even though nothing is happening in context C and there are plenty of MTA threads available because work in an

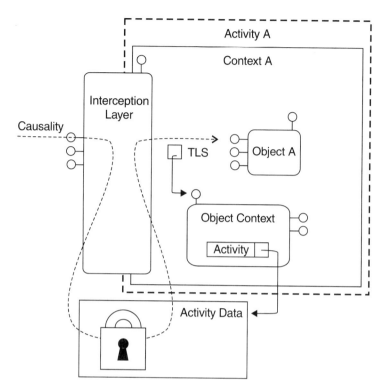

**Figure 4-8  Acquiring an activity lock**

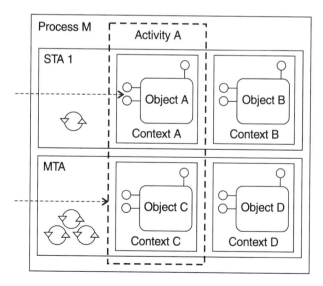

**Figure 4-9  Activity serialization and apartments**

activity is serialized. Context C cannot be used until the call into context A completes and activity A's lock is released.

There is one exception to this serialization rule. The COM+ runtime does not serialize access to an activity across process boundaries. Each process an activity touches maintains its own lock. If two concurrent calls enter two contexts in the same activity but two different processes, they will each acquire a per-process lock, and their work will execute in parallel. As Figure 4-10 illustrates, if a call enters context A, it will acquire the lock for activity A in process M. If another call enters context C, it will acquire the lock for activity A in process N. The two calls will execute in parallel. The runtime does not try to prevent this simply because guaranteeing serialized access to portions of a group of processes, possibly on different machines, is a very difficult problem to solve without radically impacting performance. Activities span process boundaries solely to provide hints to the SCM about how to allocate objects to apartments, not to enforce cross-process serialization.

You may wonder why your objects need to be protected from concurrent access. In theory, if you follow the object-per-client model, each activity will be

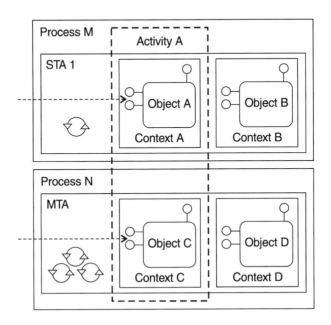

**Figure 4-10  Activity serialization and processes**

used only by a single causality, and these problems will never arise. (This assumes that if a client has more than one thread, either each thread has its own set of objects or the client makes sure only one thread uses the objects at a time.) However, the interception plumbing does not want to leave things to chance. One of the benefits of the object-per-client model is that it simplifies development by allowing you to assume that objects will not be accessed concurrently and will not have to worry about protecting their data members. If an object implemented this way ends up in an MTA or a TNA, it is counting on the client to make sure only one method is invoked at a time. Needless to say, this can be risky. If the client decides to start passing out references to an object to other threads to start making calls in parallel, the object is likely to get hurt. To prevent this, the interception plumbing serializes access to activities.

## Activity Reentrancy

What happens when an object in an activity calls out to another object that is not in the activity? The activity lock cannot be released because the original call that acquired the object has not completed. If the lock is held, a callback from the second object back into any context in the activity must not cause a deadlock. Remember that activities may include contexts in any type of apartment, so work in an activity may be done on different physical threads. That makes locking activities based on thread ID essentially impossible. Instead, activities are locked on a per-causality basis. When the interception plumbing acquires an activity's lock, the lock is owned by the current causality, as identified by its CID. If a reentrant call is part of the same causality that owns an activity's lock, the call is processed.

In Figure 4-11, for example, causality A enters activity A to execute a method of object A in context A in an MTA. While that call is in progress, the causality makes an outbound call through a proxy and leaves the context, the activity, and the apartment. While that outbound call is in progress, the causality makes another, *nested* call back into activity A. Because this work is being done inside an MTA, this callback will be dispatched on a different thread. The MTA thread servicing the causality's original call is blocked inside the proxy and the channel while it waits for the causality's outbound call to complete. If the activity locking mechanism were based on thread ID, dispatching the callback

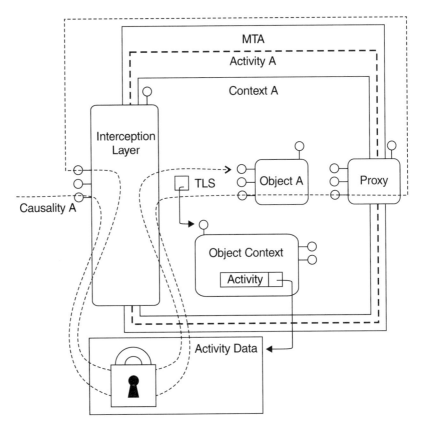

**Figure 4-11   Causality-based reentrancy**

on different thread would cause a deadlock. Because activity locking is based on causality, the callback can use whatever thread it likes. If another causality attempts to enter activity A, it will block until the current causality leaves the activity permanently. It is important to note that this behavior is markedly different from, and far preferable to, the reentrancy behavior of STAs, which allows a second causality to enter an apartment if the causality that's using the apartment's thread makes an out-of-apartment call.

## Activity Deadlock

While activities make synchronization easier by working with causalities instead of threads, they do not make synchronization easy. You cannot specify how long a call should wait to acquire an activity lock; it will wait indefinitely. If you are not careful, this makes it easy to create deadlocks with activities. There are many ways to create activity-based deadlocks; I'm going to point out three cases where they can occur.

The simplest way to cause an activity deadlock is by having two causalities, each of which already owns an activity lock, call into each other's activities. Assume causality A owns the lock for activity A, and causality B owns the lock for activity B. If causality A tries to enter activity B while causality B tries to enter activity A, the result is a deadlock. This is an example of the infamous "deadly embrace" problem so familiar to developers of concurrent systems. Deadly embrace can also occur within a single activity that spawns process boundaries because activity locking occurs on a per-process basis (see Figure 4-10).

Another way to create an activity deadlock is by spawning a thread. Assume causality A owns the lock for activity A. Causality A is executing a method on an object, and the method decides to start a new thread and then wait indefinitely for it to complete. Remember that a new thread executes in the default context of its respective apartment; it does *not* execute in the context where `CreateThread` was called. Also remember that a new thread is assigned a new causality ID; it is *not* part of the causality that spawned it. If the new thread tries to call into activity A, the interception plumbing will stop it and make it wait for the activity's lock. But the thread is part of causality B and will not be allowed into activity A until causality A, which is waiting indefinitely for the thread to complete, leaves the activity. Again, deadlock.

A third way to create a deadlock is to rely on the activity serialization mechanism to work with STA-based objects. Assume causality A owns the lock for activity A. Causality A is executing a method on an STA-based object, and the method decides to make an outbound call through a proxy and leaves the context and the apartment. It does not matter if it also leaves the activity; it still owns the activity's lock. The outbound call deposits the STA-thread in the channel, where it pumps messages. While the outbound call is in progress, another causality, B, arrives at the same apartment. The STA thread, which is pumping messages, dispatches the call. Causality B tries to enter activity A, but it cannot. Causality A owns the lock for activity A until its original call completes. Unfortunately, causality A cannot return from its outbound call because causality B, which is waiting for causality A to complete its work and release the activity lock, is using the STA's thread. Once more, deadlock. Using `CoWaitFor` `MultipleHandles` to acquire the activity lock cannot help here. This is exactly the type of problem it cannot solve. The only solution is not to let causality B wait indefinitely on the STA thread. Unfortunately, you cannot control this time-out because the interception plumbing makes the STA thread wait to acquire the activity lock.

It is important to note that all three of these deadlocks occur in situations where multiple causalities are trying to enter the same activity. The objects in the activities caused the first two problems by doing things they should not have. You can easily avoid both problems by careful coding. The third problem had nothing to do with the object itself. It can hardly be blamed for making a call to another object in another apartment. In this case, the client is at fault because it shared its object with another caller that introduced a second causality. Activities are *supposed* to provide serialized access on a per-causality basis specifically to deal with situations like this. Unfortunately, the STA call-dispatching mechanism and the activity locking mechanism do not play well together and can cause deadlocks. The only solution is to count on clients to never let two causalities try to access the *same STA* and the *same activity* simultaneously. Having two causalities try to access the *same STA* but *different activities* is fine.

## Activity Guidelines

You have to pick a synchronization setting for each new class you create. Synchronization Required is the preference in COM+ for a wide range of reasons. STA-based objects use activities to gain access to a process's pool of STAs. MTA- and TNA-based objects use activities to ensure serialized access to their data members. And all objects need activities if they want to use other COM+ services that rely on them, (i.e., just-in-time activation and declarative transactions). For all these reasons, `SynchronizationRequired` is generally the way to go.

This is true even for raw-configured classes. You should mark raw-configured classes `COMAdminSynchronizationRequired` and enable their `MustRunInClientsContext` attributes in order to stop creation from contexts that are not in activities. If you do not, instances of your raw-configured classes can be used from contexts that are not in activities, and you will be responsible for protecting their data members from concurrent access.

The other synchronization settings are useful only if you are planning on stepping outside COM+'s object-per-client model or starting your own threads. For example, if you are going to share an object and want work to proceed in parallel, you should mark its class `COMAdminSynchronizationNone`. If you are creating a new object for a new thread to use, you might want to mark its class `COMAdminSynchronizationRequiresNew`, again so that work can proceed in parallel. Or, if you are creating a raw-configured class that you want to use from any context, you could mark its class `COMAdmin SynchronizationIgnored` to disable the influence of activities on the SCM's decision about where its instances should live. If you choose to use any of these other options, perhaps because you are implementing some relatively low-level plumbing, keep your wits about you. They definitely impact the mapping of STA objects to apartments. They may also influence the semantics of other runtime services or simply make some services impossible to use.

All these activity guidelines are summarized in Rule 4.2.

 **RULE** **4.2**

> Use synchronization Required whenever possible. Use the other synchronization settings only if you are stepping outside the object-per-client model or starting your own threads.

## Summary

This chapter introduces the two constructs the COM+ runtime uses to control concurrency in a process, apartments, and activities. An apartment is a group of contexts in a process that share the same degree of thread affinity. There are three apartment types: single-threaded, multithreaded, and neutral. Each type offers a differing degree of thread affinity. Every context in a process is associated with exactly one apartment that provides the degree of thread affinity the context needs. Threads are assigned to apartments when they call `CoInitializeEx`. Objects are assigned to contexts in apartments based on their classes' threading models.

Calls and callbacks into a context are always serviced on a thread in that context's apartment. As a result, most calls across apartment boundaries require a thread switch. That makes cross-apartment calls significantly more expensive than calls across context boundaries in an apartment. It also radically increases the complexity of single-threaded apartments, which have to work hard to provide synchronous method invocation semantics and the ability to service callbacks simultaneously using only one thread.

A COM+ process can contain a single MTA, a single TNA, and any number of STAs. Each COM+ process includes a pool of STAs for housing contexts for objects with high thread affinity that are created from contexts in that process's MTA or TNA or any remote apartment. The size of the STA pool is constrained by the number of processors in a machine. A process's STA pool is used to house only STA-based objects that are also in an activity.

An activity is a group of contexts that were created to do work for a single client, access to which can and should be serialized. A context may or may not belong to an activity. Objects are assigned to contexts in activities based on their classes' synchronization attribute. Activities influence the allocation of STA-based objects to apartments. Specifically, they provide the SCM with the information it needs to map those objects to a process's pool of STAs. Activities also serialize access to the contexts they contain. The serialization mechanism is based on causality and works on a per-process basis for efficiency's sake.

# Chapter 5

# Objects

COM+ is designed to simplify the development of highly concurrent systems by allowing you to pretend that each client's objects exist in their own single-threaded world. This is the basic reasoning behind the object-per-client model, and it does in fact make COM+ classes easier to implement. But you do not get this development-time benefit for free. This model incurs significant overhead at runtime because lots of objects have to be created, which takes both time and space. COM+ provides two services intended to mitigate this unfortunate side effect of its preferred architecture. Both services focus on efficiently managing objects and the resources they use. Both services fundamentally change the classic COM relationship between a client and an object by taking control of the object's lifecycle out of the client's hands. The first service is object pooling, which is designed to recycle objects instead of continually creating and destroying them. This is beneficial because it amortizes the cost of object initialization across multiple client uses. The object pooling service also supports putting both lower and upper bounds on the number of instances of a class that exist in memory at any given time. This is useful if you want to make sure some small number of objects always exists in case a client needs one or if you want to limit the number of objects that can be used to restrict concurrency. The second service is just-in-time activation (JITA), which is designed to allow an object to detach from its stub and remove itself from its context *before* it is released by its client. Many argue that this mechanism enables better resource sharing and is therefore the key to improved scalability. As you will see later in this chapter, however, this position is somewhat naïve and won't stand up to a critical analysis. In fact, JITA was designed for something else entirely (explained in Chapter 6, Transactions). But first, let me tell you how these two services work.

## Object Pooling

The basic object pooling mechanism is simple. Within each COM+ process, the object pooling service maintains pools of objects not in use. There is one pool for each class configured to support object pooling. When a new instance of a pooled class is needed, the object pooling service provides one. It looks for an existing object first and reuses one from the class's pool if possible. Only when there are no objects in the class's pool will the service consider creating a new one. When a client no longer needs a pooled object, it can be returned to its class's pool to be reused later. You can specify an upper and a lower bound for the size of a class's pool in order to control the number of objects of each type that exist in memory at any given time.

### Enabling Object Pooling

Configured classes indicate their desire to use object pooling by setting attributes in the catalog. Table 5-1 lists the object pooling attributes. The `Object PoolingEnabled` attribute is a boolean flag that enables or disables the object pooling services on a per-class basis. It is set to false by default for all new configured classes. The other attributes influence the behavior of the object pooling service in various ways. I'll talk about them shortly.

Beyond setting these declarative attributes, there are additional requirements for classes that use the object pooling service. First, they must support

**Table 5-1  Object pooling attributes**

| Attribute | Type | Default | Notes |
|---|---|---|---|
| ObjectPoolingEnabled | Boolean | False | Turns on object pooling |
| MinPoolSize | Long | 0 | Minimum number of instances that will exist at any given time |
| MaxPoolSize | Long (1–1048576) | 1048576 | Maximum number of instances that can exist at any given time |
| CreationTimeout | Long (0–2147483647) | 0 | Number of milliseconds client waits for object to be available |

COM aggregation. Aggregated objects always forward calls to the methods of `IUnknown` to their aggregator. The object pooling service aggregates each pooled object so it can intercept calls to `AddRef` and `Release` and take control of the object's lifetime. Aggregation allows the service to know when an object is released by its client and should be returned to its class's pool. It also allows the service to keep an accurate count of the instances of a class in memory.

It is important to note that because the object pooling service traps `IUnknown` method calls using aggregation instead of the normal interception plumbing, it does not force new objects to live in contexts of their own. This makes it one of the services that raw-configured components can use. It is also important to note that because the object pooling service relies on aggregation, it does not work with objects implemented using the current version of Visual Basic 6. The next version of Visual Basic will include support for aggregation.

In addition to supporting aggregation, classes that use the object pooling service must *not* use threading model Apartment. Once an object is bound to a specific STA, it cannot be reused to satisfy another STA's request to create an object. Further, STA-based objects cannot be precreated to satisfy a lower bound on the size of a class's pool without knowing what apartment they will be used in, which cannot be determined in advance. For both these reasons, STA-based objects cannot be pooled. Although neither of these issues arises with instances of classes marked `COMAdminThreadingModelMain`, they cannot be pooled either (you shouldn't be using this threading model anyway). Only classes with threading model Both, Free, or Neutral can use the object pooling service.

Finally, classes that use the object pooling service typically implement the `IObjectControl` notification interface.

```
interface IObjectControl : IUnknown
{
  HRESULT Activate(void); // Called before first use in a context
  void Deactivate(void);  // Called before removal from context
  BOOL CanBePooled(void); // Called before return to pool
};
```

The object pooling service calls the methods of `IObjectControl` to keep a pooled object informed about how it is being used. The object pooling service can work with objects that do not implement `IObjectControl`, but it has to make some assumptions to do so.

### Reusing Objects

By default, COM+ objects, like classic COM objects, are destroyed when their clients release them. Pooled objects, however, are not destroyed when they are released. Instead, they are stored in their classes' pools for later reuse. The fundamental difference between pooled objects and nonpooled objects is that pooled objects move between contexts over time.

When pooled objects are not in use, that is, when they are in their pools, they live in their apartments' default contexts. Specifically, pooled objects that use thread model Free or Both sit in the default context of their process's MTA. Pooled objects that use threading model Neutral sit in the default context of their process's TNA. Before a pooled object can be used, it must be moved to a context that provides the services the object requires. You don't have to worry about pooled objects being moved to contexts that don't meet their needs because the object pooling service maintains its pools on a per-class basis. A pooled object is reused only where a new instance of the same class would otherwise be required. By definition, pooled objects that use either threading model Free or threading model Neutral can move to contexts only in their respective apartments. Pooled objects that use threading model Both can move to contexts in *any* apartment in a process. When a client releases a pooled object and it returns to its class's pool, the object moves back to its apartment's default context. Pooled objects that use threading model Both return to the default context of the MTA.

The basic series of events in a pooled object's lifecycle—that is, moving into a context, being used in that context, and leaving that context to return to the pool—is called an *activation cycle.* A pooled object can go through any number of activation cycles and migrate through any number of contexts in its lifetime. This may seem to contradict the statement in Chapter 2 that objects live in exactly one context; more precisely, pooled objects live in exactly one context *at a time.*

The object pooling service notifies pooled objects when it moves them from one context to another by calling the methods of `IObjectControl`. The service calls `Activate` just *after* moving an object into an appropriately con-figured context to satisfy a client's object creation request, that is, a call to `CoCreateInstance[Ex]`. The call to `Activate` marks the beginning of an activation cycle. The service calls `Deactivate` just *before* removing an object from the context it is in when it is released by its client.[1] The call to `Deactivate` marks the end of an activation cycle. The object pooling service does not assume that a just-deactivated object wants to return to its class's pool. Instead, it asks the object whether it wants to be reused. The question is phrased as a call to the object's implementation of the last `IObjectControl` method, `CanBePooled`. If the object returns true, it is put back in its class's pool. If it returns false, the object is destroyed.

An object that opts to return to its class's pool cannot remain there indefi-nitely. The object pooling service periodically sweeps each class's pool and cleans up stale objects. The exact definition of *stale* is not documented, but empirical study shows that a pooled object that hasn't been used for approxi-mately 6 minutes is destroyed (if it isn't required to satisfy the lower-bound con-straint on the size of the class's pool).

Figure 5-1, a UML state diagram, shows the complete lifecycle of a pooled object. The solid black dot represents an object's initial state. The black dot with a circle around it represents an object's final state. Rounded rectangles represent states an object may remain in over time. Circles represent transient states an object passes through but does not remain in over time. Transitions between states are labeled with three optional elements, using the following syntax:

```
event[constraint]/action
```

An object moves from one state to another when an event occurs and/or a con-straint is met. When it moves from one state to another, an action may occur.

This diagram shows all the possible states of a pooled object. Like all objects, a pooled object starts life (the black dot is its initial state) as raw memory. (It's just a twinkle in the heap manager's eye.) A new object is created when a client's creation request arrives and there are no objects in a class's

---

[1] As explained later in this chapter, the relationship between a client's actions and activation and deactivation notifications change if the pooled object is also using the JITA service.

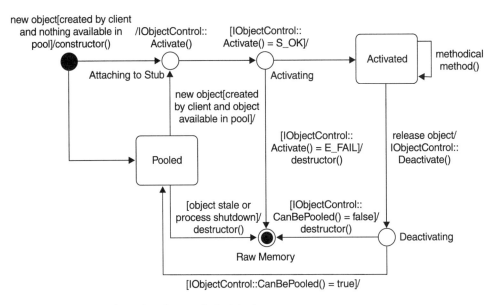

**Figure 5-1**  **The lifecycle of a pooled object**

pool. The new object is added to an appropriately configured context and attached to a stub (it moves to the transient attaching-to-stub state), and the `Activate` method is called immediately (it moves to the transient activating state). If `Activate` succeeds, the object can be used to service its client's method calls (it is in the activated state). If `Activate` fails, the object is destroyed, and `CoCreateInstance[Ex]` returns the well-known error code `CO_E_INITIALIZATIONFAILED`. Note that in this case the `Deactivate` method is never called, so `Activate` is responsible for cleaning up any resources it acquired before it failed.

When a client finally releases an object, the object's `Deactivate` method is called (it moves to the transient deactivating state). Immediately after `Deactivate` completes, the object's `CanBePooled` method is called. If `CanBePooled` returns True, the object returns to its class's pool (it is in the pooled state). If `CanBePooled` returns False, the object is discarded. Its destructor executes, and its memory returns to the heap (it is in its final state).

Once an object is in its class's pool (it is in the pooled state), it can be used to service incoming client creation requests. In this case the object is moved to an appropriately configured context and attached to a stub (it moves to the transient attaching-to-stub state), `Activate` is called, and the cycle repeats. If an object remains in its class's pool (in the pooled state) long enough to be considered stale, the object pooling service discards it. Its destructor executes, and its memory returns to the heap (it is in its final state).

It is important to note that if a pooled object does not implement `IObjectControl`, it will not receive notifications about how it is being used. The object will still pass through all the lifecycle states shown in Figure 5-1, but it won't know when it moves from one state to another. The object pooling service assumes that objects that don't implement `IObjectControl` are always willing to be activated and reused. In other words, it behaves as if `Activate` always succeeds and `CanBePooled` always returns True. This means that a pooled object that does not implement `IObjectControl` can be moved from one context to another without knowing it. Depending on what a pooled object does in its methods, this can be downright dangerous. So even though the runtime plumbing doesn't require it, implementing `IObjectControl` for classes that use object pooling should not be optional. This is Rule 5.1.

 **5.1**

Classes that use object pooling should implement `IObjectControl`.

## Controlling the Size of a Class's Pool

The object pooling service supports putting lower and upper bounds on the number of instances of a pooled class that can exist in a process's memory at any given time. By setting a lower bound for a pooled class, you can force the runtime to keep a minimum set of objects of that type in existence, even if they are not being used. This is useful if you want to keep objects "warmed up" and ready to use. By setting an upper bound for a pooled class, you can force the runtime to stop creating new objects of that type, even if clients are clamoring for more. This is useful if you want to limit concurrency to avoid contention for the resources a particular class encapsulates.

The `MinPoolSize` and `MaxPoolSize` attributes specify the inclusive lower and upper bounds for a pooled class, respectively. If a pooled class specifies a `MinPoolSize` greater than the default value 0, the object pooling service makes sure that at least that many instances of the class always exist. Notice that I did *not* say that the service would make sure that `MinPoolSize` instances of the class always exist *in the pool*, as the attribute's name implies. If a class's `MinPoolSize` is 3, the object pooling service will precreate three objects and put them in the pool when the class's application is started. If three clients ask for new objects of that type, the SCM will use the three existing objects from the pool. Then the pool will be empty. But the class's `MinPool Size` requirement, which really defines the minimum number of instances *in memory*, will still be satisfied. If the destruction of a pooled object that returns False from `CanBePooled` causes the number of instances in memory to drop below a class's `MinPoolSize`, the object pooling service will create a replacement object and put it into the pool. A pooled object that has grown stale will not be destroyed if that would violate the class's `MinPoolSize` constraint.

The `MaxPoolSize` attribute determines the number of instances of a pooled class that can exist in memory at any given time. Like `MinPoolSize`, `MaxPoolSize` controls the total number of objects, not the number of objects available, in a class's pool. When the SCM asks the object pooling service for an instance of a pooled class, the service checks to see if there are objects available in the pool. If there are no objects in the pool, the service checks to see how many instances of the class already exist. The object pooling service will not create another object if `MaxPoolSize` objects already exist. Although specifying a lower bound for a pooled class is optional, specifying an upper bound for a pooled class is not. In other words, although a pooled class can leave its `MinPoolSize` at 0, it must define a `MaxPoolSize` greater than 0.

If `MaxPoolSize` objects already exist, the object pooling service will not create another one. But neither will it simply reject an object creation request. Instead, when a request for a new object arrives, the object pooling service will wait for the number of milliseconds specified by a pooled class's `CreationTimeout` attribute. If, in that time, an object is returned to the pool, the service reuses it, and the creation request succeeds. Or if, in that time, the number of existing instances of the class drops below `MaxPoolSize` because an object is destroyed, the service creates a new object, and the creation request succeeds. If neither of these things happens before `Creation Timeout` milliseconds pass, the creation request fails, and the plumbing returns

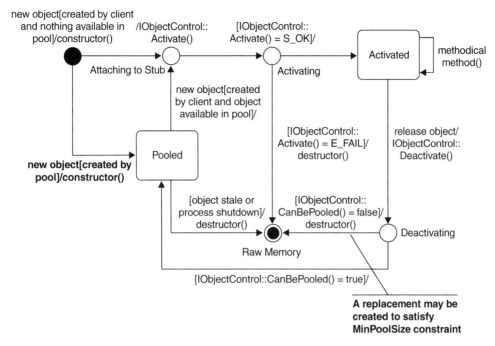

**Figure 5-2** The lifecycle of a pooled object with a constrained pool

`CO_E_ACTIVATIONFAILED_TIMEOUT`. While the use of a timeout makes the most sense when `MaxPoolSize` objects already exist, a class's `Creation Timeout` actually applies to *all* attempts at instantiation, whether `MaxPool Size` objects exist or not. If you are tempted to set `CreationTimeout` to 0 with the intent of rejecting creation requests immediately when `MaxPoolSize` objects already exist, resist. The 0 millisecond limit will apply to all creation requests, and it can never be satisfied. If a pooled class's `CreationTimeout` is 0, all attempts to create instances of that type will time out and fail.

The diagram in Figure 5-2 shows how constraining the size of a pool affects the lifecycle of a pooled object. The only difference between this diagram and Figure 5-1 is the addition of a transition, shown in bold, from an object's initial state (the black dot) to the pooled state to indicate that objects may be precreated to satisfy a class's `MinPoolSize` requirement before a client needs one.[2]

---

[2] There is also a note that if the destruction of an object that returns false from `CanBePooled` reduces, the number of existing instances below a class's `MinPoolSize` value, a replacement object will be created and put into the pool.

A class's `MaxPoolSize` has no effect on the lifecycle of objects; it simply prevents creation of new objects.

## Implementing Pooled Classes

Pooled objects are different from nonpooled objects. A nonpooled object lives in one context for its entire lifetime. A pooled object can live in multiple contexts in its lifetime. This makes pooled objects harder to implement. They have to address issues nonpooled objects never face.

### Accessing Context

First, pooled objects have to be careful about when they access context. When they are not in use (i.e., in between activation cycles), pooled objects live in their apartments' default contexts, which provide no services at all. A pooled object is in a context that provides the services it needs only when it is in use (i.e., during an activation cycle). Therefore, a pooled object should access context only during an activation cycle. In practical terms, an instance of a pooled class should not access context in its language-level constructor (or ATL's `FinalConstruct`) or destructor (or ATL's `FinalRelease`). Instead, any code that depends on context must execute after `Activate` starts and before `Deactivate` ends. This is Rule 5.2.

 **RULE 5.2**

A pooled object should access context only during an activation cycle.

Remember that the implementation of `CoCreateInstance[Ex]` examines context to determine whether a new object should get a new context of its own. If a pooled object creates other objects *before* `Activate` is called, `CoCreateInstance[Ex]` will not behave as desired. Consider a pooled class that requires an activity, that is, it is marked `COMAdminSynchronization Required`. An instance of that pooled class, A, creates another object, B, which also requires an activity. Object A wants object B to inherit its activity, but it creates object B *before* `Activate` is called. Since object A still resides in its apartment's default context, the SCM puts object B into a new context in a new activity of its own. Object A won't have an activity until *after* its

`Activate` method starts to execute. When `Activate` is called, object A will be in a context in an activity, but not object B's activity. If object A and object B are STA based, they may be forced into different apartments too. This clearly is not what object A wants. To produce the desired result, object A needs to follow Rule 5.2 and create object B only after `Activate` begins.

## Managing Resources

Pooled objects have to deal with a second issue. Because they can live in more than one context over time, pooled objects have to manage resources very carefully. Many resources are *context neutral,* meaning they can be used from any context. Strings, structures, arrays, and other simple types are generally context neutral. For instance, it probably doesn't matter from which context a BSTR is accessed, as long as its pointer value is valid in the process. I say "probably" because storing certain information in an instance of a simple type can make it *context relative,* meaning it can be used only in a particular context. For example, if a pooled object stores its client's security principal in a BSTR when it activates, that value is context relative and should not be kept across activation cycles.

Interface pointers are always context relative. As explained in Chapter 3, an interface pointer is valid only in the context in which it is initially acquired. You cannot use a reference to either a proxy or a real object in a foreign context without marshaling the reference first (remember Rule 3.1). The behavior of a reference to a proxy that is used out of context (so to speak) is predictable. The proxy rejects all calls and returns `RPC_E_WRONGTHREAD`, which really means `RPC_E_WRONGCONTEXT`. The behavior of a direct reference to an object that is used out of context is unpredictable. Neither of these situations is acceptable. Because interface pointers are context relative, they cannot be held across activation cycles.

Rule 5.3 summarizes these observations about resource management.

 **5.3**

> Classes that use object pooling must not hold *context-relative* resources across activation cycles.

The following example of Rule 5.3 shows the code for a pooled class. Some of its data members are context neutral, and some are context relative.

```
class CPooledClass : public IPooledClass,
                     public IObjectControl
                     ... // Other details removed for clarity
{
  long m_nTimesActivated; // count of times activated
  GUID m_ctxId; // current context id
  DWORD m_nProcessId; // current process id
  CComPtr<IObject> m_spObject; // reference to object
public:
  CPooledClass() : m_nTimesActivated(0),
                   m_ctxId(GUID_NULL),
                   m_nProcessId(0) {}
  STDMETHODIMP Activate(void)
  {
    // increment activation counter
    m_nTimesActivated++;
    // record context id
    CComPtr<IObjectContextInfo> spCtxInfo;
    HRESULT hr = CoGetObjectContext(__uuidof(spCtxInfo),
                                    (void**)&spCtxInfo);
    if (FAILED(hr)) return hr;
    hr = spoci->GetContextId(&m_ctxId);
    if (FAILED(hr)) return hr;
    // record process id if it hasn't been recorded already
    if (!m_nProcessId) m_nProcessId = GetCurrentProcessId();
    // acquire context-relative interface pointer
    return m_spObject.CoCreateInstance(__uuidof(Object));
  }
  STDMETHODIMP_(void) Deactivate(void)
  {
    // reset context-relative context id
    m_ctxId = GUID_NULL;
    // release context-relative interface pointer
    m_spObject.Release();
  }
  ... // Other details removed for clarity
};
```

CPooledClass has four data members. m_nTimesActivated counts the number of times an instance of the class has been reused. m_nProcessId keeps track of the process an instance lives in. `m_ctxId` stores the ID of the context an instance is currently in. `m_spObject` holds a reference to another object. All four values are initialized to zero (`GUID_NULL` for the context ID) when an instance of `CPooledClass` is constructed. Each time it is called, the `Activate` method increments `m_nTimesActivated`, sets `m_ctxId`, and creates a new object to store in `m_spObject`. `Activate` sets `m_nProcessId` only the first time it is called. The implementation of `Deactivate` resets `m_ctxId` to `GUID_NULL` and releases the interface pointer stored in `m_spObject`, but leaves the other two data members alone. `m_ctxId` and `m_spObject` are the only two of the four that are context relative. As you can see, implementing pooled objects can be a little tricky!

### The GIT Trick (and Why It Doesn't Work)

Rule 5.3 means, among other things, that you cannot pool a group of objects as a single entity. A pooled object must acquire any objects it uses each time it is activated, as shown in the `CPooledClass` example just given. If a pooled object always uses another object to accomplish its tasks, having to acquire, use, and then release that object during each activation cycle may be a hard pill to swallow, even if the second object is also pooled. You might be tempted to solve this problem by putting a reference to the pooled object's secondary object into the Global Interface Table (GIT). Interface pointers are context-relative resources, but GIT cookies are context-neutral resources. A pooled object can hold a GIT cookie as it moves across contexts. This GIT trick sounds promising, but it won't work. Here is an example that explains why.

```
// Global GIT reference initialized elsewhere
extern IGlobalInterfaceTable *g_pGIT;
// A pooled class that stores object references in the GIT
class CTrickyPooledClass : public ITrickyPooledClass,
                           public IObjectControl,
                           ... // Other details left out for
                               clarity
{
  CComPtr<IObject> m_spObject; // reference to object
  long m_nCookie; // GIT cookie
```

```
public:
  CTrickyPooledClass() : m_nCookie(0) {}
  ~CTrickyPooledClass()
  {
    // remove reference from GIT if necessary
    if (m_nCookie) g_pGIT->RevokeInterfaceFromGlobal(m_nCookie);
  }
  STDMETHODIMP Activate(void)
  {
    // create object or retrieve reference from GIT
    if (m_nCookie == 0)
      return m_spObject.CoCreateInstance(__uuidof(Object));
    else
      return g_pGIT->GetInterfaceFromGlobal(m_nCookie,
                                            __uuidof(m_spObject),
                                            (void**)&m_spObject);
  }
  STDMETHODIMP_(void) Deactivate(void)
  {
    // store object reference in GIT and release it
    if (m_nCookie == 0)
      g_pGIT->RegisterInterfaceInGlobal(m_spObject,
                                        __uuidof(m_spObject),
                                        &m_nCookie);
    m_spObject.Release();
  }
  ... // Other details left out for clarity
};
```

The CTrickyPooledClass class has two data members. m_spObject is a
context-relative reference to a second object, and m_nCookie is a context-
neutral GIT cookie. Both are initialized to zero. When an instance of CTricky
PooledClass activates, it checks to see if m_nCookie is zero (the null
cookie). If m_nCookie is zero, the object creates a new helper object and stores
its interface pointer in m_spObject. As long as an instance of CTricky
PooledClass is active, it can use m_spObject whenever it needs to. When
an instance of CTrickyPooledClass deactivates, it again checks to see if
m_nCookie is zero. If m_nCookie is zero, the object registers its helper object in the GIT and stores its cookie in m_nCookie. Then it releases its context relative reference. If the call to RegisterInterfaceInGlobal fails,
m_nCookie will still be zero, and the helper object will be destroyed. The next

time it is activated, the `CTrickyPooledClass` object will reacquire a context-relative reference to its helper object by "dereferencing" its GIT cookie. Or, if the GIT cookie is zero, it will create another helper object. Either way, once the `CTrickyPooledClass` object is activated, `m_spObject` holds a valid context-relative interface pointer. When the `CTrickyPooledClass` object destructs, it revokes the GIT cookie, and the helper object is released.

The problem with this approach is that the GIT helps a pooled object conform only to the letter, not the intent, of the law. Consider Figure 5-3. Pooled object A in context A is holding onto a proxy to object B in context B. Both objects are instances of classes marked `COMAdminSynchronization Required` and are in the same activity, X.

Figure 5-4 shows what could happen if object A used the GIT to transfer its reference to the proxy to object B when it is recycled into another context, C. Now object A is in context C. It is still holding onto a proxy to object B in context

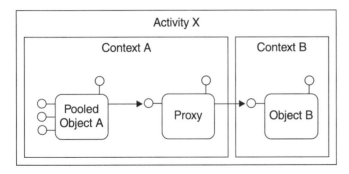

**Figure 5-3   Setting up for the GIT trick**

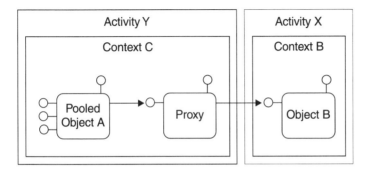

**Figure 5-4   The aftermath of the GIT trick**

B, so everything appears to be fine. But object A and object B are no longer in the same activity. This does not violate object A's synchronization requirement, which is now satisfied by activity Y. If object A and object B are STA based, they might not be in the same apartment anymore either. In any case, the semantics of calling from object A to object B have changed in an unpredictable manner, which could lead to tremendous problems. Pooled objects should avoid this situation by not using the GIT trick.

### An Exception to the Rules

There is one exception to these pooled object rules, and it involves raw-configured (and nonconfigured) classes. Instances of raw-configured classes can be *created* in any context. If an instance of a raw-configured class never stores any context-relative resources over time, it can also be *used* from any context. A pooled object could hold onto such an instance for as long as it liked, even across multiple activation cycles. But how does a pooled object know which objects it can hold onto and which ones it must discard? Unfortunately there is no programmatic way for a pooled object to determine if an object reference is safe to keep. If an object implements the `IProxyManager` signaling interface, it is a context relative proxy that has to be released. If an object implements `IMarshal` using the Free-Threaded Marshaler (FTM), it is context neutral and does not have to be released. However, there are objects that can be used safely from any context that do not aggregate the FTM, so this is a heuristic mechanism at best. In the end, a pooled object just has to "know" whether an object is safe to hold onto. When in doubt, a pooled object should always follow Rules 5.3 and release all interface pointers when it is deactivated.

Given the uncertainty and inherent risk in this exception to the rules governing pooled objects, you might well wonder why I even mention it. I am compelled to divulge it simply because it is at the heart of a scheme for pooling database connections with a level of flexibility and performance that outstrips the connection pooling mechanism built into OLE DB (and used by ADO). The technique is described in Appendix B, Building a Better Connection Pool. While it uses this somewhat ugly technical loophole to good advantage, the idea that pooled objects can safely hold some objects across activation cycles should not be generally applied.

# Object Pooling Guidelines

The object pooling service is turned off by default. This is good because most classes are not implemented with object pooling in mind. You must leave it off for any class that does not follow Rules 5.1 through 5.3 (i.e., implement `IObjectControl`, access context only during an activation cycle, and discard context relative resources between activation cycles). Of course you must also leave it off for any class that does not support aggregation or uses threading model Apartment, including all classes implemented using Visual Basic 6.

Given that it takes extra work to make a class support pooling, the obvious question is, When will it be worth the effort? In the abstract, object pooling is beneficial when the cost of creating and destroying an object, including memory management and context-neutral initialization, is greater than the cost of activating and deactivating an object, including pool management and context-relative initialization. The following formula expresses this idea in pseudo-mathematical terms:

$$\text{Benefit of object pooling} = \frac{\text{cost of object creation and destruction}}{\text{cost of object activation and deactivation}}$$

In general, it is beneficial to pool objects that use context-neutral resources that are expensive to acquire. The database connection pooling technique described in Appendix B provides one concrete example, but there is another example that is much less obvious and much more interesting.

All objects acquire one common resource: memory. Instantiating a class requires allocating enough space in a process's address space to hold an object's data members, v-pointers, and so on. Most developers do not think of memory allocation as particularly expensive; it is not, as long as the load on a system is low. As load increases, however, the cost of allocating memory rises. This happens because a language's memory management engine has to serialize access to some of its internal data structures in order to avoid corrupting the heap at runtime. As the number of requests to allocate and free memory increases, contention for a memory manager's internal locks also climbs. When load gets high enough, a memory management engine can itself become a bottleneck. Empirical testing shows that the object pooling service can, in some circumstances (e.g., when load is high), provide better performance than a language's memory management engine (i.e., the one used by Visual C++). The benefits of applying object pooling to this end depend heavily on what a system is doing and on what tools it was implemented with. For example, a third-party memory manager might provide similar benefits without the extra development effort required to implement objects that can be pooled.

Finally, in some cases, object pooling may be useful simply because it allows you to constrain how many instances of a particular type exist in memory at any given time.

These object pooling guidelines are summarized in Rule 5.4.

 **RULE 5.4**

Use object pooling when the following is true:

- The cost of creating and destroying an object is greater than the cost of activating and deactivating an object.
- You want to specify a lower or upper bound on the number of instances of a class that can exist in memory at a time.

## Just-in-Time Activation

In addition to the object pooling service, COM+ provides a second service related to object lifecycle management, just-in-time activation (JITA). The basic JITA mechanism is simple. By default, objects—whether pooled or not—remain in their contexts and attached to their stubs until their clients release them. An object that uses the JITA service has the option of detaching from its stub and being removed from its context *before* its client releases it. The object can then be replaced the next time its client invokes a method.

### Enabling JITA

Table 5-2 lists the attributes that control the JITA service. The `JustInTime Activation` attribute is a boolean flag that enables or disables the JITA services on a per-class basis. It is set to true by default for all new configured classes. The SCM always puts new instances of classes using the JITA service into a new context of their own, so raw-configured classes should set `JustIn TimeActivation` to false. The `AutoComplete` attribute influences the behavior of the JITA service on a per-method basis.

**Table 5-2   JITA attributes**

| Attribute | Type | Default | Notes |
|---|---|---|---|
| JustInTimeActivation | Boolean | True | Turns on JITA |
| AutoComplete | Boolean | False | Automatically deactivates object when method completes |

Beyond setting these declarative attributes, there is one additional require-ment for classes that use the JITA service: They must support activities. There are potential race conditions around concurrent calls to a JITA-based object. What should happen if one call to an object causes it to detach from its stub while a concurrent call is in process? To avoid this sort of question, the JITA service insists that calls to objects be serialized. So COM+ forces classes that use the JITA service to use activities as well. If a class is not marked `COMAdminSynchronizationRequired` or `COMAdminSynchronization RequiresNew`, it cannot use JITA, that is, `JustInTimeActivation = False`.

Like the object pooling service, the JITA service notifies objects about how they are being used by calling the methods of `IObjectControl`. Unlike the object pooling service, the JITA service works with classes implemented using Visual Basic 6; they implement `ObjectControl`, a slight variation on `IObjectControl`, to receive notifications. This is not a strict requirement, as it is for classes that use the object pooling service. JITA by itself does not move objects from one context to another, so ignoring its notifications is not nearly so dangerous. If a class uses both JITA *and* object pooling, it should implement `IObjectControl` as dictated by Rule 5.1.

## How JITA Works

The JITA service allows an object to deactivate itself before its client releases it. When the SCM instantiates a class that uses JITA, it puts the new object into a new context configured to include a "done" bit, as shown in Figure 5-5. The interception plumbing examines the done bit when a call into a JITA context completes. The done bit's default state is off. If the done bit is on at the end of a method call, the runtime deactivates the context's distinguished object

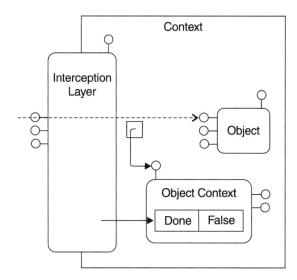

**Figure 5-5   JITA context and its done bit**

(the first object created in the context). If the object is an instance of a class that is configured to support object pooling, it can be reused. If the object is an instance of a class that is not configured to support object pooling, it is destroyed.

When a JITA-based object is deactivated, the stub it was attached to and the context it lived in remain in place. (Remember that, as explained in Chapter 3, the life of a context is tied to the life of a stub, not an object.) The stub simply sets its internal object reference to null. The proxy and channel connecting the client and the stub also remain. If the client issues another call, the interception plumbing acquires another instance of the same class to service the request (hence the term *just-in-time activation*). If the class supports object pooling, the object may come from the pool. If the class does not support object pooling, a new object is created. In either case, an object is acquired, and the client's method call is dispatched to it.

### Flipping the Done Bit

The done bit is a part of an object's context and can be manipulated using the object context object's `IContextState` interface.

```
interface IContextState : IUnknown
{
  HRESULT SetDeactivateOnReturn([in] VARIANT_BOOL bDeactivate);
  HRESULT GetDeactivateOnReturn([out] VARIANT_BOOL *pbDeactivate);
  … // other methods removed for clarity
}
```

GetDeactivateOnReturn and SetDeactivateOnReturn read and write the state of the done bit, respectively. They each take one argument of type VARIANT_BOOL, reflecting the fact that this interface is used from both C++ and Visual Basic. The VARIANT_BOOL type corresponds to Visual Basic's values for true and false, −1 and 0. If you are working in C++, use the constants VARIANT_TRUE and VARIANT_FALSE for these values. Calling SetDeactivateOnReturn with VARIANT_TRUE turns the done bit on. Calling it with VARIANT_FALSE turns the done bit off. Here is a method that uses IContextState to change the state of the done bit.

```
HRESULT CSomeCfgClassUsingJITA::DeactivateAtTheEndOfThisCall(void)
{
  CComPtr<IContextState> spCtxState;
  HRESULT hr = CoGetObjectContext(__uuidof(spCtxState),
                                  (void**)&spCtxState);
  if (FAILED(hr)) return hr;
  hr = spCtxState->SetDeactivateOnReturn(VARIANT_TRUE);
  if (FAILED(hr)) return hr;
  return S_OK;
}
```

The implementation of DeactivateAtTheEndOfThisCall calls CoGetObjectContext to retrieve an IContextState reference to object context. Then it calls SetDeactivateOnReturn, passing in VARIANT_TRUE, to turn the done bit on. When this call is postprocessed by the interception plumbing, the object will be deactivated.

Note that changing the state of the done bit has no effect on an object until the interception plumbing examines it at the end of a method call. That means that a method can change the state of the done bit as many times as it likes. It is only the final state of the done bit when the call completes that matters. If there are multiple, nested calls through the interception plumbing to an object in a JITA context, the done bit will not be interpreted until the outermost call completes. Figure 5-6 illustrates this situation.

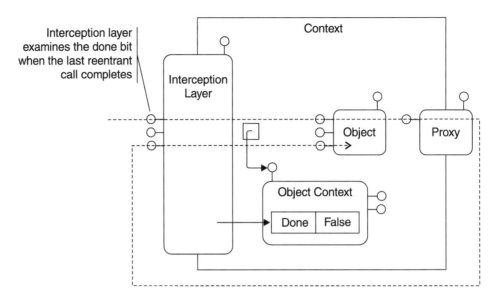

**Figure 5-6   Reentrant calls and examining the done bit**

A causality enters a context to invoke a method on an object. During the call, the causality makes an outbound call through a proxy and leaves the context. In the process of servicing that outbound call, the causality reenters the context to invoke another method on an object in the original context. If the reentrant method turns the done bit on, the plumbing will ignore it when the call completes. Deactivating the object at this point would be quite dangerous because the original, outstanding invocation of one of the object's methods is still in progress. To be safe, the plumbing will interpret the done bit and deactivate the object only after the original, outermost method call completes. If the original call into the context turns the done bit off *after* its outbound call through the proxy completes, the object will *not* be deactivated, even if the inner reentrant method turned the done bit on.

Instances of raw-configured classes can change the state of a JITA-based context's done bit. However, this is considered bad style. The JITA service is tied to a context's distinguished object—the instance of the class that declared its desire to use the JITA service—and it should always be left to that object to decide whether it wants to deactivate at the end of a call.

Finally, if a context is not configured to use JITA, it doesn't have a done bit. If an object in a context that is not configured to support JITA attempts to set or get the state of the done bit through `IContextState`, the methods will fail with the well-known error code `CONTEXT_E_NOJIT`.

### The AutoComplete Attribute

The interception plumbing resets a JITA context's done bit in between method calls. If a method turns the done bit on and deactivates the object, the interception plumbing will turn the done bit off again before dispatching the next call. In essence, this means that each method that wants to force deactivation has to turn the done bit on explicitly by calling `IContextState::Set DeactivationOnReturn`. You can override this behavior if you want to by configuring a method to deactivate an object automatically when it completes.

COM+ defines a declarative attribute called `AutoComplete` that can be applied to the *methods* of a class configured to use JITA. It is set to false for all of a class's methods by default. Setting it to true for a given method changes the JITA service's deactivation logic when that method is invoked. When a method marked with this attribute completes, the plumbing will automatically deactivate the object even though the method did not explicitly set the state of the done bit. If the method did set the state of the done bit explicitly by calling `SetDeactivationOnReturn`, the `AutoComplete` attribute is ignored. This allows a method to override its declarative setting and avoid deactivation (of course, if a method explicitly turns the done bit on, the object will deactivate anyway).

It is worth noting that while the `AutoComplete` attribute affects the logic of deactivation, it does not actually change the default state of the done bit. In other words, just because a method is autocompleting, doesn't mean the plumbing turns the done bit on before dispatching that method. If an auto-completing method examines the default state of its done bit by calling `GetDeactivateOnReturn` it will see that the bit is off.

### JITA Notifications

The JITA service tells objects how they are being used by calling the methods of `IObjectControl` (or `ObjectControl` in VB). The JITA service calls

**Table 5-3  IObjectControl (ObjectControl) notification decoder ring**

| Class Configured to Use . . . | IObjectControl(ObjectControl) Method . . . | | |
|---|---|---|---|
| | Activate | Deactivate | CanBePooled |
| Neither Service | Never | Never | Never |
| Object Pooling Only | When Client Calls CoCreate Instance[Ex] | When Client Releases Object | Right After Deactivate |
| JITA Only | When Client Calls First Method | When Client Releases Object or Method Ends with Done Bit On | Never |
| Both Object Pooling and JITA | | | Right After Deactivate |
| | Method Is Called . . . | | |

`Activate` to notify an object just before the first time it is *used* in a context, that is, just before dispatching its client's *first method call.* This is different from the object pooling service, which calls `Activate` when an object is *moved* into a new context to satisfy a client's *creation request.* The JITA service calls `Deactivate` just before removing an object from its context, either because it returned from a method with its done bit turned on or because its client released it. This is also different from the object pooling service, which calls `Deactivate` only when a client finally releases an object.

If an object is an instance of a class that uses both JITA and object pooling, the JITA notification scheme takes precedence, as summarized in Table 5-3. The left column lists the four possible configurations of a class: a class uses neither object pooling nor JITA, object pooling by itself, JITA by itself, or both services together. The other three columns describe when the methods of `IObjectControl` will be called. Notice that the JITA scheme for `Activate` and `Deactivate` notifications takes precedence if a class uses both JITA and

TRANSACTIONAL COM+: BUILDING SCALABLE APPLICATIONS

object pooling and that `CanBePooled` is called only for classes that use object pooling.

With that information in mind, consider the lifecycle of a *nonpooled* object that uses the JITA service, as shown in Figure 5-7. Like all objects, a JITA-based object starts life (the black dot is its initial state) as raw memory. When a client calls `CoCreateInstance[Ex]` and a new object is created, its language-level construction code is executed, and the object is attached to a stub (it is in the attached-to-stub state). When the client's first method invocation arrives, the object's `Activate` method is called (the object is in the transient activating state). What happens next depends on whether the `Activate` method succeeds or fails.

If `Activate` succeeds, the object is activated (it is in the activated state), and the actual method the client called executes. The object remains activated as it processes further method requests (it stays in the activated state). Eventually, when the object returns from a method call with the done bit set or when the client releases its proxy and the connection to the object is torn down, the object's `Deactivate` method is called (it is in the transient deactivating state). After `Deactivate` is called, the object is discarded. Its destructor executes, and its memory returns to the heap (the object is in its final state).

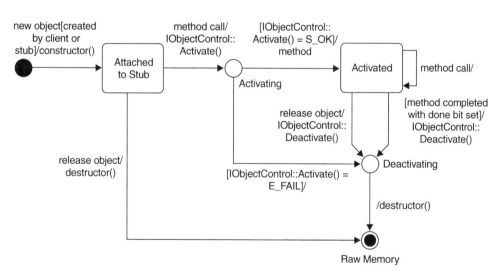

**Figure 5-7  Lifecycle of a nonpooled object using JITA**

If `Activate` fails, the client's initial method invocation returns `CO_E_ INITIALIZATIONFAILED`, and the object is deactivated (it is in the transient deactivating state) and immediately discarded. Note that, in this case, the `Deactivate` method is never called, so `Activate` is responsible for cleaning up any resources it acquired before it failed. The object's destructor executes, and its memory returns to the heap (it is in its final state). In this case, the client's connection to the object's stub and context remains intact. When an object is destroyed because it failed to activate, the stub simply sets its internal reference to the object to null, as it does when an object deactivates itself by setting its done bit. When the client issues its next call, the plumbing creates a new object to service the request and calls the new object's `Activate` method, and the same logic is applied again. If `Activate` succeeds, the client's request is processed. If `Activate` fails, the client's request fails, the new object is discarded, and the client's connection to the stub and context is left intact in case the client wants to try another call.

It is worth noting that if a JITA-based object does not implement `IObject Control` (or `ObjectControl` in VB), it will not receive notifications about how it is being used. The object will still pass through all the lifecycle states shown in Figure 5-7, but it won't know when it moves from one state to another. The JITA service assumes that objects that don't implement `IObjectControl` are always willing to be activated (i.e., it behaves as if `Activate` always succeeds).

Now consider the lifecycle of a *pooled* object that uses the JITA service, as shown in Figure 5-8. This diagram essentially merges the object lifecycle models shown in Figures 5-2 and 5-7. In this model, with both services applied, an object can be returned to its class's pool when it is deactivated, possibly between method calls.

## JITA Guidelines

The JITA service is turned on by default, but has no effect unless an object sets its done bit during a method call (or a method's `AutoComplete` attribute is turned on). So when should a class support JITA, and when should a JITA-based object set its done bit?

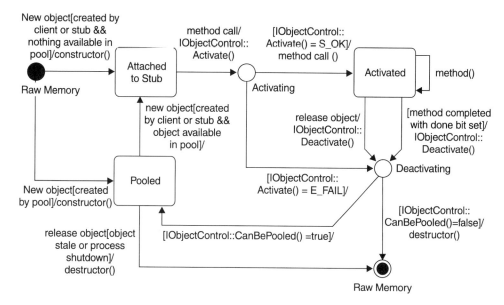

**Figure 5-8   Lifecycle of a pooled object using JITA**

Many people argue that *every* class should use JITA and that *every* object should set its done bit at the end of *every* method call. Instances of classes that adopt this philosophy are called *stateless objects* because they do not keep state between method calls.[3] From a traditional COM perspective, this is very strange indeed. It means that a client request is not sent to an object, but to a context where a stub lives. In essence, an object becomes just another resource, like an activity lock or a declarative transaction, which the COM+ plumbing must acquire in order to process a client method invocation. This could be called the "object-per-method" model.

The outspoken proponents of this approach—the JITAratti—claim that stateless objects offer phenomenal benefits in terms of resource sharing and, therefore, scalability. While I agree that efficient resource management is key to implementing scalable systems, I steadfastly disagree with the claim that state-less objects enable better resource sharing. In fact, in many cases, stateless objects are actually less efficient. Let me explain why.

---

[3] Some people use the term *stateless object* more loosely to refer to any object that doesn't hold state over time. Throughout the book, I use the strict COM+ definition of stateless object to mean an object that uses the JITA service and deactivates at the end of each method call.

The general argument people make in favor of stateless objects is simple: Deactivating an object at the end of each method call ensures that it will not hold valuable resources any longer than necessary. Consider an object that, in the classic COM style, acquires some resources when it is constructed and stores references to them in its data members. The object holds onto the resources until it is destroyed. If such an object is accessed via DCOM, it will not be destroyed until its client releases its proxy. Unfortunately, that means it is the client, not the object, that ultimately controls how long the resources are held. This is a problem if the resources (e.g., database connections) are precious; there probably aren't enough to give one to each client's object.

Making objects stateless solves this problem. If an object is forced to deactivate at the end of each method call, it cannot store references to precious resources in its data members. When a client invokes a method, the JITA service automatically replaces the previous stateless object with another one. Each stateless object acquires any resources it needs when `Activate` is called just before the desired method is invoked, then releases them when `Deactivate` is called just after the method completes.

There are several problems with this model. First, it assumes a one-to-one mapping of client requests to method calls. If that's the case, as it is when a client is accessing an object directly via DCOM, the overhead of activating an object is incurred only once per client request. But what if a client request is sent over HTTP and does not correspond to a single method invocation on a single object? For instance, what if a client requested an ASP page with a script that made five calls to an object, as shown here.

```
<script runat=server language=jscript>
   var obj = new ActiveXObject("SomeSrv.SomeCfgClass");
   obj.One();
   obj.Two();
   obj.Three();
   obj.Four();
   obj.Five();
</script>
```

In this scenario, making the `SomeCfgClass` object referred to by `obj` stateless would actually hurt performance. The object would have to be activated not once but five times in order to service a single client request. Any resources the object needs to service a call would have to be reacquired each time the object is activated. All of this represents additional overhead, even if `SomeCfgClass` supportes object pooling. In this example, it would be better to service all five calls using a single object, especially since the object will be deactivated when the script is done executing.

It is important to note that this same situation arises with "helper" objects that are not used directly by clients, as follows.

```
HRESULT CSomeCfgClass::One(void)
{
  CComPtr<ISomeCfgHelperClass> spObject;
  HRESULT hr = spObject.CoCreateInstance
                  (__uuidof(SomeCfgHelperClass));
  if (FAILED(hr)) return hr;
  hr = spObject->Beginning();
  if (FAILED(hr)) return hr;
  hr = spObject->Middle();
  if (FAILED(hr)) return hr;
  hr = spObject->End();
  if (FAILED(hr)) return hr;
  return S_OK;
}
```

In this example, the client uses an instance of the `CSomeCfgClass`, which in turn uses an instance of the `CSomeCfgHelperClass`. Making the helper object stateless would add overhead for the reasons outlined above. Again, it would be better to service all three calls using a single object, especially since it will be deactivated when the `One` method completes.

Beyond the additional overhead the stateless model incurs when more than one method is called to service a client request, there is a second serious flaw. The general idea with stateless objects is that they consolidate their resource management code in `Activate` and `Deactivate`. This is convenient, but it is often inefficient. The JITA service makes sure that `Activate` is called just before the first call to an object is dispatched. For stateless objects, which deactivate at the end of every call, every call is the first one and is therefore preceded by `Activate`. It doesn't make sense to acquire a resource in `Activate` if it is not going to be used in the particular method a client is calling. Unfortunately, because `Activate` doesn't know which method a client is calling, it can't tailor its behavior along these lines. The best `Activate` can do is to acquire the union of all resources all methods need. Unless all of an object's methods use exactly the same set of resources, this scheme will sometimes result in the acquisition of resources the stateless object does not need to service its one and only method call.

There are similar problems with implementing resource cleanup code in `Deactivate`. Specifically, holding the resources an object acquires until it deactivates prevents other objects from using those resources in the meantime. For example, imagine an object that acquires a resource in `Activate` and uses it in a method. During that method, the object makes a blocking call to another object that wants to reuse the same resource. If the first object is holding onto the resource until `Deactivate` is called, the second object cannot reuse it. The second object must acquire a different resource or fail.

The solution to both these problems is to implement more aggressive fine-grained resource management directly in an object's methods, where it can be tuned for efficiency. Instead of acquiring resources in `Activate`, objects should acquire resources in each method so that they can be sure they get only the resources a particular method needs. (If several methods need the same resources, encapsulate acquisition in a private method that public methods can call.) Instead of releasing resources in `Deactivate`, objects should release resources as soon as they are done with them, generally at the end of a method, if not earlier. This approach is often more efficient and never less efficient than making an object stateless and forcing it to deactivate at the end of each method call.

If a class's resource management code is moved into its methods for efficiency's sake, there is no reason to store references to valuable resources in data members. Forcing an object to release valuable resources it held in its data members was the motivation for using stateless objects in the first place. If objects don't store references to valuable resources in data members, why should they deactivate at the end of each method call? People have proposed several answers to this question, none of which make sense.

First, many have argued that making objects stateless saves memory. But remember that when an object is deactivated, its context remains in place—consuming 2 KB to 3 KB of memory. Unless your objects are huge, you'll end up on the wrong side of this equation. You cannot legitimately claim that deactivating objects provides any significant benefit in terms of reducing memory consumption. If that is your goal, you should pursue the idea of raw-configured classes as a means of reducing the number of contexts in a process. This argument is spurious.

Many have also argued that stateless objects are better about sharing threads. But again, remember that when an object is deactivated, its context remains in place, and in the same apartment where it was created. If a context is in an MTA or a TNA, it has little or no thread affinity. If a context is in an STA, it has high thread affinity. Pulling a stateless object out of a context after each method call doesn't change this; COM+ does not move contexts and stubs to other apartments (or processes or machines, for that matter).[4] This argument is spurious too.

Finally, many have argued that using stateless objects saves developers from themselves. Their basic position is that most developers are simply not capable of writing code that manages resources efficiently. They need to use stateless objects because they *might* hold on to a valuable resource for too long, even if you tell them they shouldn't. This argument is the most spurious of the three, and I reject it outright. If developers have trouble managing resources, they will have trouble building systems that scale, whether they use stateless objects or not. I believe that developers are perfectly capable of gaining the skill and experience they need to develop efficient scalable systems without accepting the tremendous, inefficient, and draconian oversimplification the stateless object model represents.

Ultimately, there is really only one motivation for deactivating an object at the end of each method, and it is very subtle indeed. A class that uses both object pooling and JITA may want to make its instances stateless in order to alter the semantics of its `MaxPoolSize` attribute. Remember that the `MaxPoolSize` attribute specifies the upper bound on the size of a class's pool, the total number of objects that can exist in memory at any given time. Normally, for pooled objects that are not stateless, the `MaxPoolSize` setting determines how

---

[4] This functionality would be nice, but it would require a radical reworking of the DCOM wire protocol.

many clients can be concurrently attached to objects of a given type. However, for pooled objects that are stateless and used only for a single method call, the `MaxPoolSize` setting determines how many methods can be concurrently executing against objects of a given type. This slight variation is important, but only if the objects are pooled and their pools are constrained by upper bounds.

The best advice on how to use JITA is, turn it off unless it is required by another service (i.e., declarative transactions). Discard the notion of stateless objects as automatically enabling resource sharing and scalability and implement your classes as you see fit. Pay attention to how your objects are used and how that affects their use of resources (Are they accessed directly by clients or only by other objects in the same process? Are they accessed via DCOM or HTTP?). *Above all, make sure that your objects manage resources, including memory, efficiently.*

These JITA guidelines are summarized in Rule 5.5.

 **RULE 5.5**

Do not use JITA unless another service (i.e., declarative transactions) requires it. Implement your classes to manage resources efficiently.

As Rule 5.5 suggests, the declarative transaction service relies on the JITA service to help guarantee correct transactional semantics. In fact, that's what JITA is really for, as explained in detail in Chapter 6, Transactions.

## Lies, Damn Lies, and Statistics

I can't end this chapter without quoting Mark Twain, who said in his autobiography that "figures often beguile me, particularly when I have the arranging of them myself; in which case the remark attributed to Disraeli would often apply with justice and force: 'There are three kinds of lies: lies, damned lies, and statistics.'" He might have been thinking about the usage numbers the Component Services Explorer (CSE) displays for classes configured to use object pooling, JITA, and the COM+ statistics service.

If a configured class uses the COM+ statistics service (`EventTracking Enabled = true`), the interception plumbing gathers data about its usage and feeds it to the CSE for display. The service reports three statistics about how objects are being used. They are listed in the CSE in columns labeled Objects, Activated, and Pooled. Unfortunately, these names represent a tour-de-force of misinformation in that not one of them accurately reflects the meaning of the values its column displays. If it were up to me, the columns would be relabeled with the names listed in Table 5-4.

The value in the CSE's first column, Objects, is not a count of objects. It tells how many clients have connections (i.e., stubs) to instances of a given type, whether they are attached to objects or not. This column should be labeled Connections. The value in the CSE's second column, Activated, has nothing to do with how many objects have had their `Activate` methods called and entered the activated state. It is really a count of the number of client connections that are attached to objects. Since objects can be attached to client connections for extended periods without being activated, this column should be labeled Attached. The value in the CSE's third column, Pooled, is not the number of objects available for use in a class's pool. It is the number of objects in existence. This value minus the value in the second column is the number of objects currently in the pool. This column should be labeled Objects.

I should point out two other things. First, the CSE does not display statistics for configured classes deployed in library applications. A library application can be loaded into any number of different processes. Reporting aggregate class usage statistics gathered from all those processes would not help you understand what was going on in any one of them. Displaying a per-process breakdown of the statistics would be useful, but also more complicated. The current version of the CSE doesn't do either; no statistics are reported for classes in library applications. Second, while the CSE does display usage statistics for

**Table 5-4   CSE class usage statistics decoder ring**

| CSE Column | Preferred Label | Meaning |
| --- | --- | --- |
| Objects | Connections | The number of existing client connections (i.e., stubs) |
| Activated | Attached | The number of objects attached to stubs |
| Pooled | Objects | The number of objects in existence |

configured classes deployed in server applications, this is considered a low-priority task. If a server application gets very busy, the statistics displayed in the CSE will not be kept up to date.

## Summary

This chapter introduces two services that COM+ provides in an effort to mitigate the overhead introduced by the object-per-client model. Both services change the relationship between clients and objects in fundamental ways.

The object pooling service allows objects to be reused by multiple clients. Unlike nonpooled objects, pooled objects move between contexts over time. When a pooled object is not being used, it sits in its apartment's default context. When a pooled object is being used, it sits in a context configured to meet its needs. The basic series of events in a pooled object's lifecycle (i.e., moving into a context, being used, and returning to its class's pool) is called an activation cycle.

A class must be specifically implemented to take advantage of the object pooling service. It must support aggregation, must use a threading model other than Apartment or Single, and should implement `IObjectControl` to receive notifications about how they are being used. Also, a class that supports object pooling should access context only during an activation cycle and must not hold context-relative resources across activation cycles. The extra effort required to use the object pooling service is worthwhile when the cost of constructing and destructing an object is greater than the cost of activating and deactivating an object. It is also worthwhile when you want to constrain the number of instances of a class that can exist in memory at any given time.

The JITA service allows objects to detach from their contexts before their clients release them. Specifically, a JITA-based object can set its context's done bit to tell the COM+ plumbing to deactivate it when the current method call completes. When the JITA service deactivates an object, it leaves the client's connection to the object's stub and context in place. When the client invokes another method, the JITA service provides another object to service the call. As with object pooling, a class must be implemented with JITA in mind. It must use activities, and it should implement `IObjectControl` (`ObjectControl` in Visual Basic) in order to receive notifications about how it is being used.

JITA is often positioned alongside object pooling as a way to help compensate for the overhead of the object-per-client model, but it is not nearly so useful as its counterpart. Forcing an object to detach from its context after each method call is a heavy-handed and often inefficient way to promote resource sharing, largely predicated on the belief that developers cannot do better themselves. This argument simply does not stand up to a thorough critique.

# Chapter 6

# Transactions

Transactions provide a uniform model for managing changes to state in a distributed system. Transactions are at the very center of the COM+ programming model and are integral to the framework's ability to support scalable systems. COM+ adopts the object-per-client model to simplify development by allowing objects to pretend the world is single-threaded. It uses transactions to extend that single-threaded model from middle-tier server processes to back-end databases.

Chapter 1 explains the basics of transactions. Clients use transactions to protect changes to system state. Each transaction represents work done on behalf of a single client, and each transaction exhibits the ACID properties; that is, a transaction is guaranteed to succeed or fail atomically, leave the system in a consistent state when it ends, execute in isolation from other transactions, and be durable in the face of random process failures. Transaction managers (TMs) create transactions for clients and manage their commit or abort processing. Transaction-aware resource managers (RMs) track changes to durable system state on a per-transaction basis. There are two kinds of transactions. Local transactions protect work done by a single client process against a single RM. They are simple and efficient. Distributed transactions protect work done by multiple client processes against multiple RMs. Distributed transactions are quite powerful. They allow you to integrate operations against multiple databases, message-based communication systems, and other RMs into a single unit of work. However, this power comes at a price. Compared to local transactions, distributed transactions are significantly harder to use and less efficient.

COM+ classes can be implemented to use either local or distributed transactions directly. They can also be implemented to use distributed transactions implicitly. COM+ provides the declarative transaction service to simplify distributed transactions programming. Declarative transactions are distributed transactions that are managed by the COM+ runtime and implicitly merged with object context. They are designed to provide both the flexibility of distributed transactions and the ease of use (but not the efficiency) of local transactions. Declarative transactions are supported by an undocumented spatial construct called a *transaction stream.* Like apartments and activities, transaction streams are molecules built on top of the basic atoms of context and causality; they must be well understood if you want to apply declarative transactions effectively. The first half of this chapter explains the mechanics of local and distributed transactions. The second half describes the declarative transaction service and transaction streams.

## Local Transactions

Most developers who have used transactions have used local transactions. With local transactions, an RM acts as its own TM, and a client's connection is implicitly enlisted so that all the requests the client submits are automatically protected. Modern relational databases process client requests expressed in an extended version of the industry standard Structured Query Language (SQL-92). SQL Server uses Transact-SQL (T-SQL), Oracle uses PL/SQL, and other databases use other SQL-92 dialects. In general, the lowest-level API for local transactions is a database's implementation of the SQL itself. For example, here is a piece of T-SQL code that uses a local transaction to insert an order and its line items into two tables in a SQL Server database.

```
begin transaction
  insert into orders (orderid, customerid, cancelled)
          values (1795, 1001, 0)
  insert into orderitems (orderid, productid, unitprice, quantity)
          values (1795, 49, 10.50, 7)
  insert into orderitems (orderid, productid, unitprice, quantity)
          values (1795, 134, 23.95, 2)
commit
```

This is T-SQL, and not SQL-92, because the BEGIN TRANSACTION statement is actually an extension to that language. SQL-92 itself expects transactions to be started implicitly when a "transaction initiating" statement (e.g., INSERT) is executed. (SQL-99 defines the `StartTransaction` statement to explicitly start new local transactions.)

The fact that a statement as fundamental as BEGIN TRANSACTION is actually a vendor-specific, albeit widely implemented, extension to SQL-92 is somewhat problematic. It means that there is no guarantee that the seemingly innocuous code just listed will work with a given SQL-92–compliant database. In an effort to address this problem, modern data access technologies like OLE DB and ADO provide support for managing local transactions indirectly. They hide vendor-specific local transaction control statements behind standard abstract interfaces and rely on the database-specific code that implements them to "do the right thing."

## OLE DB

OLE DB defines the `ITransactionLocal` interface to encapsulate the management of local transactions. OLE DB providers for data sources that support local transactions implement this interface on their session objects. They map its methods to whatever vendor-specific SQL statements are appropriate for the database they represent. `ITransactionLocal` has a base interface, `ITransaction`. Here are the definitions of both interfaces.

```
interface ITransaction : IUnknown
{
  HRESULT Commit([in] BOOL fRetaining,
                 [in] DWORD grfTC,
                 [in] DWORD grfRM);
  HRESULT Abort([in] BOID *pboidReason,
                [in] BOOL fRetaining,
                [in] BOOL fAsync);
  HRESULT GetTransactionInfo([out] XACTTRANSINFO *pinfo);
};
interface ITransactionLocal : ITransaction
{
  HRESULT GetOptionsObject([out] ITransactionOptions **ppOptions);
  HRESULT StartTransaction([in] ISOLEVEL isoLevel,
                           [in] ULONG isoFlags,
                           [in] ITransactionOptions
                                *pOtherOptions,
                           [out] ULONG *pulTransactionLevel);
};
```

The `ITransactionLocal::StartTransaction` method explicitly starts a new local transaction. `ITransaction::Commit` and `ITransaction::Abort` commit and abort a local transaction, respectively. The OLE DB specification does not define what should happen if a session object is released while a local transaction is running, that is, whether it should commit or abort. This detail is left to individual providers. The OLE DB provider for SQL Server (SQLOLEDB) aborts local transactions that are running when their sessions are released. This echoes SQL Server's low-level T-SQL transaction semantics; if a local transaction is running when a connection is closed, the transaction is automatically aborted.

Here is an example that shows how `ITransactionLocal` is used.

```
HRESULT ExecSQLInLocalTransaction(void)
{
  // given a pointer to a session
  CComPtr<IDBCreateCommand> spCreateCmd;
  HRESULT hr = GetSessionSomehow(__uuidof(spCreateCmd),
                                 (void**)&spCreateCmd);
  if (FAILED(hr)) return hr;
  // start a local transaction for the session
  CComPtr<ITransactionLocal> spLocalTx;
  hr = spCreateCmd->QueryInterface(__uuidof(spLocalTx),
                                   (void**)&spLocalTx);
  if (FAILED(hr)) return hr;
  hr = spLocalTx->StartTransaction(ISOLATIONLEVEL_SERIALIZABLE,
                                   0, 0, 0);
  if (FAILED(hr)) return hr;
  // create a command for session
  CComPtr<ICommandText> spCmdText;
  hr = spCreateCmd->CreateCommand(0, __uuidof(spCmdText),
                                  (IUnknown**)&spCmdText);
  if (FAILED(hr)) return hr;
  hr = spCmdText->SetCommandText(DBGUID_DBSQL,
                                 L"insert into...");
  if (FAILED(hr)) return hr;
  CComPtr<ICommand> spCmd;
  hr = spCmdText->QueryInterface(__uuidof(spCmd),
                                 (void**)&spCmd);
  if (FAILED(hr)) return hr;
  // execute command within local transaction
  LONG cRows = 0;
  hr = spCmd->Execute(0, IID_NULL, 0, &cRows, 0);
```

```
  // end local transaction
  if (FAILED(hr))
    hr = spLocalTx->Abort(0, FALSE, FALSE);
  else
    hr = spLocalTx->Commit(FALSE, XACTTC_SYNC, 0);
  return hr;
}
```

The `ExecSQLInLocalTransaction` function executes a SQL statement within the scope of a local transaction. It starts by acquiring a reference to an OLE DB session object that encapsulates a connection to an underlying data source (the details of this are not important). The reference is of type `IDBCreateCommand`, the OLE DB interface for manufacturing new command objects. The function calls `QueryInterface` to acquire an `ITransaction Local` reference. Then it calls `StartTransaction` to start a new local transaction. The first three parameters control the new transaction's isolation characteristics.[1] The last parameter returns the nesting depth of the new local transaction, typically 1.[2]

Once the transaction is started, `ExecSQLInLocalTransaction` builds and executes a SQL statement using normal OLE DB techniques. If the statement fails, the function aborts the transaction by calling `Abort`. The first parameter to `Abort`, `pboidReason`, is a pointer to a byte-ordered ID (BOID)—a structure containing an array of 16 bytes—that tells the RM why the client is aborting the transaction. There are no well-known BOIDs; you can pass 0 for this value. The second parameter to `Abort`, `fRetaining`, is a boolean flag that tells a session to start another transaction immediately after the current transaction completes. Support for this style of transactional programming, sometimes called chained transactions, varies; some providers may not accept true. The third parameter to `Abort`, `fAsync`, is a boolean flag that tells the provider to perform an asynchronous abort. The only value that OLE DB providers generally support for local transactions is false, which tells `Abort` to block until the transaction is aborted.

---

[1] They are discussed in detail in Chapter 7, Isolation.

[2] The value returned may be greater than 1 if the data source supports nested transactions. Many databases, including SQL Server, support only flat transactions and will never return a value greater than 1. For more information on nested transactions, see *Principles of Transaction Processing* by Bernstein and Newcomer or *Transaction Processing Fundamentals* by Gray and Reuter.

If the statement succeeds, the function commits the transaction by calling `Commit`. The first parameter to `Commit`, `fRetaining`, is identical to the second parameter to `Abort`; it controls the use of chained transactions. The second parameter to `Commit`, `grfTC`, is a DWORD that tells the provider if the client wants to wait to discover the transaction's outcome. It is analogous to the third parameter to `Abort`. You can pass either 0 or a value from the `XACTTC` enumerated type.

```
typedef enum XACTTC
{
  XACTTC_SYNC_PHASEONE = 1,
  XACTTC_SYNC_PHASETWO = 2, XACTTC_SYNC    = 2,
  XACTTC_ASYNC_PHASEONE = 4, XACTTC_ASYNC = 4
} XACTTC;
```

The only `XACTTC` value that OLE DB providers generally support for local transactions is `XACTTC_SYNC`, which tells `Commit` to block until the outcome of a local transaction is known. If you pass 0, a provider applies its default behavior, typically `XACTTC_SYNC`. The third parameter to `Commit`, `grfRM`, is reserved and must be zero.

There is no guarantee that a call to `Commit` will succeed. If it does, it returns `S_OK`, and the client knows the changes it made within the scope of its transaction have been kept. If it fails, it returns an error code, and the client knows the changes it made within the scope of its transaction have been discarded.[3]

## Higher Level APIs

Most developers do not have the time, patience, or finger strength necessary to write data access code using the OLE DB interfaces in the raw. (The previous example doesn't include the code for loading, configuring, and initializing a provider or extracting results from a rowset.) Instead, they prefer to use either the ATL OLE DB consumer templates or ADO. Both libraries do their best to simplify local transaction management.

The ATL OLE DB consumer templates expose local transaction functionality as part of the `CSession` class, which wraps a reference to an OLE DB session

---

[3] See `transact.h` in the Platform SDK for a complete list of possible transaction error codes.

object. The `CSession` class implements all the methods of `ITransaction Local` and `ITransaction`, but takes advantage of C++ support for default arguments to make calling them easier. Here is an example.

```
HRESULT ExecSQLInLocalTransaction(void)
{
  // given a reference to a session
  CSession sess;
  HRESULT hr = GetSessionSomehow(&sess);
  if (FAILED(hr)) return hr;
  // start a local transaction
  hr = sess.StartTransaction(ISOLATIONLEVEL_SERIALIZABLE);
  if (FAILED(hr)) return hr;
  // build and execute a command
  CCommand<CNoAccessor, CNoRowset, CNoMultipleResults> cmd;
  long cRows = 0;
  hr = cmd.Open(sess, "insert into...", 0, &cRows,
                DBGUID_DBSQL, false);
  // end the local transaction
  if (FAILED(hr))
    hr = sess.Abort();
  else
    hr = sess.Commit();
  return hr;
}
```

ADO exposes more limited local transaction functionality as part of the `Connection` class, which wraps references to both an OLE DB data source object and an OLE DB session object. The `Connection` class implements its own set of methods with simplified signatures that map to the underlying OLE DB session interface. Here is an example.

```
Sub ExecSQLInLocalTransaction()
  ' given a reference to a session
  Dim conn As Connection
  Set conn = GetSessionSomehow()
  ' start local transaction
  conn.IsolationLevel = adXactSerializable
  conn.BeginTrans
  ' build and execute command
  Dim cRows As Long
  On Error Resume Next
  conn.Execute "insert into...", cRows
  ' end local transaction
```

```
    If Err.Number < 0 Then
      conn.RollbackTrans
    Else
      conn.CommitTrans
    End If
  End Sub
```

## Distributed Transactions

Local transactions are simple and fast, but limited. If a client wants to protect changes to state stored in multiple RMs, it needs to use a distributed transaction. Clients that use distributed transactions cannot rely on any single RM to play the role of transaction manager because transactions are not RM-specific. Instead, they rely on an external TM, whose job it is to create distributed transactions and manage their commit or abort processing via the two-phase commit protocol. Clients of distributed transactions must explicitly enlist their RM connections in the external TM if they want their work to be protected. The use of the two-phase commit protocol makes distributed transactions significantly slower than local transactions.

### Enter the Distributed Transaction Coordinator

The Distributed Transaction Coordinator (DTC) is an external transaction manager that ships with Windows 2000. The DTC's job is to dispense distributed transactions for clients to use, facilitate the propagation of those transactions between processes, and manage the process of committing or aborting those transactions upon completion. The DTC has a proprietary communication protocol to do all these things, which works well in a homogeneous environment. To integrate better with heterogeneous environments, the DTC also supports a number of additional communication protocols, including the Transaction Internet Protocol (TIP), a wire-protocol based on TCP messaging.[4]

The DTC is implemented as a service called `msdtc.exe`. Every process, client or RM, that is participating in a distributed transaction needs to commu-

---

[4] Microsoft and Tandem submitted TIP to the Internet Engineering Task Force (IETF) as a proposed standard, RFC 2371. See the IETF Web site, http://www.ietf.org, for more information. DTC also supports bridging to the X/Open DTP XA protocol popular on Unix systems and IBM's LU 6.2 sync level 2 protocol for CICS and IMS integration. See the DTC documentation in the Platform SDK for more information.

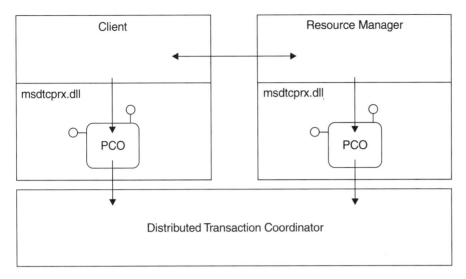

**Figure 6-1  Single DTC architecture**

nicate with the DTC its machine is configured to use. Windows 2000 servers are configured to run an instance of the DTC service locally by default. They can also be configured to rely on a DTC running on another machine.[5] This can improve performance in a system where a middle-tier server always works with the same back-end machine. Configuring the server to use the DTC on the back-end machine reduces the number of DTCs involved in each distributed transaction to one. Of course, if a middle-tier server is working with a single RM on a back-end machine, local transactions would offer better performance still.

Programs always interact with a DTC indirectly using an in-process library called `msdtcprx.dll`. The library exposes a fairly simple object model that's defined by the OLE Transactions (OLETX) specification. The heart of the model is called the DTC Proxy Core Object (PCO). Every process that interacts with a DTC uses a PCO.[6] Figure 6-1 illustrates the architecture.

It is possible that multiple processes that are participating in the same transaction are executing on separate machines that are configured to use

---

[5] This per-machine declarative setting is controlled using the MSDTC tab on a computer's property sheet in the CSE.

[6] This is an excellent example of the notion of logical identity being provided implicitly through type.

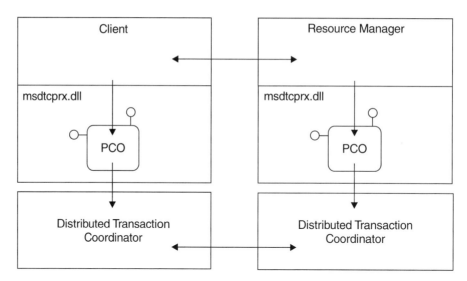

**Figure 6-2  Multiple DTC architecture**

different instances of the DTC service. In this case, the DTCs will collaborate to manage the transaction and its outcome. Figure 6-2 shows this variation.

You can acquire a PCO by calling `DtcGetTransactionManager`, the well-known bootstrap function.

```
HRESULT DtcGetTransactionManager([in] char *pszHost,
                                 [in] char *pszTmName,
                                 [in] REFIID riid,
                                 [in] DWORD dwReserved1,
                                 [in] WORD wcbVarLenReserved2,
                                 [in] void *pvVarDataReserved2,
                                 [out, iid_is(riid)] void** ppv);
```

`DtcGetTransactionManager` returns a reference to a PCO that represents the particular instance of the DTC service, either local or remote, that a server is configured to use. Here is an example.

```
CComPtr<IUnknown> spuPCO;
hr = DtcGetTransactionManager(0, 0, __uuidof(spuPCO), 0, 0, 0,
                              (void**)&spuPCO);
```

Only two of the parameters passed to `DtcGetTransactionManager` are generally useful. The third parameter specifies the type of reference you'd like to get back, and the seventh parameter provides a place to return a valid interface pointer if the call succeeds. All the other parameters should be 0.[7]

## Starting a Distributed Transaction

With a reference to a PCO in hand, you can interact with the DTC service. The PCO exposes quite a few interfaces. Some are for clients that want to create and manage distributed transactions. Some are for RMs that want to enlist against distributed transactions and participate in the two-phase commit protocol. Only the client interfaces are relevant in this discussion. The basic client interfaces are shown in Figure 6-3.[8]

A PCO exposes the `ITransactionDispenser` interface to allow clients to start new distributed transactions, each of which is represented as a separate COM object. Each distributed transaction object implements `ITransaction`, the same interface used by OLE DB session objects to represent local transactions. Like a PCO, a distributed transaction object is really just an in-process representation of some information managed by a DTC. Here is the definition of `ITransactionDispenser`.

```
interface ITransactionDispenser : IUnknown   {
  HRESULT GetOptionsObject([out] ITransactionOptions **ppOpts);
  HRESULT BeginTransaction([in]  IUnknown *punkOuter,
                           [in]  ISOLEVEL isoLevel,
                           [in]  ULONG isoFlags,
                           [in]  ITransactionOptions *pOptions,
                           [out] ITransaction **ppTransaction);
}
```

---

[7] The first parameter, `pszHost`, is the name of the machine where an instance of DTC is running. If you pass 0, the function will return a reference to a PCO that represents the DTC a server is configured to use. If you pass a string, the function checks to make sure it is a valid machine name and fails if it is not. If the string is a valid machine name, the function ignores it and behaves as if you had passed 0. So always pass 0 for the first parameter. The second parameter is an extensibility hook to allow the API to select a particular TM by name if multiple TMs are installed on a system. Passing 0 tells the API to use the default TM—DTC. You can also pass either "MSDTC" or "msdtc." The fourth, fifth, and sixth parameters were reserved until recently when SQL Server decided that it wanted to give the PCO a hint about how many threads it could use to make callbacks into a database process. To specify this, you can pass the flag `dwUSER_MS_SQLSERVER` as the fourth argument and the size of and a pointer to an instance of the `PROXY_CONFIG _DATA` structure as the fifth and sixth arguments. See the Platform SDK documentation for more information.

[8] See the Platform SDK documentation on the DTC for a complete list of the interfaces PCOs support.

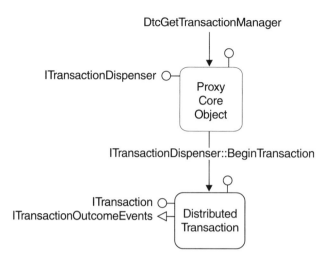

DtcGetTransactionManager

ITransactionDispenser

Proxy
Core
Object

ITransactionDispenser::BeginTransaction

ITransaction
ITransactionOutcomeEvents

Distributed
Transaction

**Figure 6-3    The Proxy Core Object basic client interfaces**

`BeginTransaction` is used to explicitly start a new distributed transaction. If the call succeeds, it returns an `ITransaction` reference to an object representing the new distributed transaction. The methods of `ITransaction` are used to commit or abort the distributed transaction. Here is an example.

```
// given a pointer to a PCO
CComPtr<ITransactionDispenser> sptdPCO = GetPCOSomehow();
// start a distributed transaction
CComPtr<ITransaction> sptDistTx;
hr = sptdPCO->BeginTransaction(0, ISOLATIONLEVEL_SERIALIZABLE, 0, 0,
                               &sptDistTx);
```

The first parameter to `BeginTransaction` is a pointer to a controlling unknown that wants to aggregate the new transaction object. The current implementation of the distributed transaction object does not support aggregation, so this parameter should be 0. The second, third, and fourth parameters are identical to the first three parameters of `ITransactionLocal::Start Transaction`. They control the new distributed transaction's isolation characteristics (explained in the next chapter.) The fifth parameter to `Begin Transaction` is output; it returns a reference to a new distributed transaction object if the call to `BeginTransaction` succeeds.

## Enlisting a Connection

Having a new distributed transaction does not do a client much good unless it has a way to tell RMs about it. Each RM a client interacts with needs to know that the work that client is submitting should be protected by the client's distributed transaction. A client tells an RM about its transaction by enlisting its connection. The way you enlist a connection against a distributed transaction varies depending on the data access API you are using. OLE DB defines the `ITransactionJoin` interface for this purpose. OLE DB providers for data sources that can participate in DTC-managed distributed transactions implement `ITransactionJoin` on their session objects. The interface definition follows.

```
interface ITransactionJoin : IUnknown
{
  HRESULT GetOptionsObject([out] ITransactionOptions **ppOptions);
  HRESULT JoinTransaction([in] IUnknown *punkTransactionCoord,
                          [in] ISOLEVEL isoLevel,
                          [in] ULONG isoFlags,
                          [in] ITransactionOptions *pOtherOptions);
};
```

The `JoinTransaction` method explicitly enlists the connection represented by an OLE DB session against a DTC-managed distributed transaction. Here is an example.

```
// given a reference to a distributed transaction
CComPtr<ITransaction> spDistTx = GetDistributeTransactionSomehow();
// given a reference to a session
CComPtr<IUnknown> spSess;
hr = GetSessionSomehow(__uuidof(spSess), (void**)&spSess);
if (FAILED(hr)) return hr;
// enlist session against distributed transaction
CComPtr<ITransactionJoin> spJoinTx;
hr = spSess->QueryInterface(__uuidof(spJoinTx),
                            (void**)&spJoinTx);
if (FAILED(hr)) return hr;
hr = spJoinTx->JoinTransaction(spDistTx,
                               ISOLATIONLEVEL_SERIALIZABLE, 0, 0);
```

All of the parameters to `JoinTransaction` are input. The first parameter is a pointer to an object that represents the distributed transaction you want to enlist the connection against. Remember that OLE DB providers are generally implemented as in-process libraries. Calling `JoinTransaction` really just presents an in-process session object with a reference to an in-process distributed transaction object. So what is happening behind the scenes? Basically, a session's implementation of `JoinTransaction` conveys information about the distributed transaction to the RM process it's connected to. The RM presents that information to its own in-process PCO in order to enlist against the transaction.[9] Once that happens, any changes to state the RM makes in response to requests sent through the session are included in the scope of the distributed transaction. The second, third, and fourth parameters to `JoinTransaction` are the seemingly ubiquitous transaction isolation characteristics.

If you want to use an enlisted connection after its distributed transaction completes, you must break the link between them. This is known as unenlisting a connection. It tells an RM that work done in response to future requests sent through the connection should not be associated with any distributed transaction. You can unenlist a connection from a transaction by calling `Join Transaction` and passing 0 as the first parameter. You can also enlist a connection against a different distributed transaction after its current distributed transaction commits. In this case, you do not have to explicitly unenlist the connection first.

Neither the ATL OLE DB consumer templates nor ADO provide simplified support for explicitly enlisting a connection against a distributed transaction. If you want to enlist a connection with either API, you must acquire a reference to the underlying OLE DB session object and call `ITransactionJoin::JoinTransaction` yourself. An ATL `CSession` object stores a reference to an OLE DB session object in a public data member called `m_spOpenRowset`. The reference is of type `IOpenRowset`, but you can call `QueryInterface` to cast it to a reference of type `ITransactionJoin`. An ADO connection object stores its reference to an OLE DB session object in an internal data member. You can extract a reference to it using the `Session` property of the little-known `ADOConnectionConstruction15` interface, which is implemented

---

[9] See the Platform SDK documentation for the `IResourceManager` interface for more information.

by the ADO `Connection` class. The reference is returned as an `IUnknown` pointer; you can acquire an `ITransactionJoin` reference by calling `Query Interface`.[10]

## The Two-Phase Commit Protocol

A distributed transaction ends when the client calls the distributed transaction object's `ITransaction::Commit` or `ITransaction::Abort` method. If a distributed transaction object is released prior to a call to `Commit`, it is automatically aborted. Committing a distributed transaction is much more complicated than committing a local transaction. When a client commits a local transaction, it is making a request to a single RM. The RM will or will not be able to commit the local transaction, and there the matter ends. When a client commits a distributed transaction, it is in effect making a request to multiple RMs, and somehow they must coordinate their answer. The DTC service handles this task using the two-phase commit protocol.

The two-phase commit concept is easy to understand. Just think of a wedding. Every wedding has an official (a DTC), partners (RMs), and witnesses (a client). The wedding ceremony proceeds in two steps. First, the official asks each partner if he or she is willing to commit. This is phase one: vote collection, or *preparation*. Second, after each partner has prepared, the official announces the outcome. If either partner is unwilling to commit—"I don't"—the marriage does not take place. Only if both partners say they are willing to commit—"I do"—is the marriage complete. In either case, the official notifies the witnesses and the partners of the outcome. This is phase two: *notification*. It is important to note that once partners are prepared, they cannot change their votes.

And so it is with distributed transactions. When a client asks its DTC to commit a distributed transaction, the client's DTC asks each RM participating in the transaction to prepare to commit. If an RM is using a different DTC, the client's DTC asks the RM's DTC to collect and return the RM's vote. If all the RMs vote yes during the preparation phase, the client's DTC tells the client the transaction committed and tells the RMs (through their intermediate DTCs, if

---

[10] See `adoint.h` in the Platform SDK documentation for the definition of `ADOConnection` `Construction15`.

necessary) to save the client's changes. If any RM votes no during the preparation phase, the client's DTC tells the client the transaction aborted. If the client asks its DTC to abort a distributed transaction, the client's DTC tells the client the transaction aborted and tells the RMs (through their intermediate DTCs, if necessary) to undo the client's changes.

Note that RMs must guarantee that during phase one, preparation, they will save to disk all the information they need to complete the transaction one way or another. In other words, each RM has to store before and after images of all the client's changes so it can keep them or undo them during phase two, notification. Note that DTCs also log information about the transactions they manage or participate in so that they can recover in the face of failure as well. It follows from all this that it is impossible for phase two to fail.[11]

It also follows that the client's DTC knows the outcome of a distributed transaction at the end of phase one. Every RM has voted by that point, so the client's DTC knows if they all voted yes (commit) or if any of them voted no (abort). Either way, it can tell the client immediately, so the client believes the transaction is over at the end of phase one. Each RM is told the transaction outcome during phase two, notification. All this work runs in parallel, and each RM completes the transaction asynchronously. When all the RMs involved in a transaction finish phase two, the DTCs involved in the transaction consider it complete.

Finally, the two-phase commit protocol can be optimized if only one RM is participating in a distributed transaction. In this case, the DTC asks the RM to execute a one-phase commit, as it would with a local transaction. However, even if a given RM chooses to honor this request, committing a distributed transaction still has higher overhead than committing a local transaction because of the extra interprocess communication with the DTC.

Although a client uses the same methods to end a local and a distributed transaction (i.e., `ITransaction::Commit` or `ITransaction::Abort`), the

---

[11] You may be legitimately skeptical of this claim. Phase two *can* fail in catastrophic cases when hardware is damaged (e.g., a disk is corrupted). In these cases, completing the transaction requires manual intervention from a system administrator. You should strive to avoid these situations by using robust hardware—multiple power supplies, RAID subsystems, and the like. For more information on this aspect of two-phase commit, refer to *Principles of Transaction Processing* by Bernstein and Newcomer or *Transaction Processing Fundamentals* by Gray and Reuter.

values you are allowed to pass as arguments are different in each case. The DTC does not support chained distributed transactions, so you must always pass False for `fRetaining`. Nor does the DTC support synchronous completion of the two-phase commit protocol. While a call to commit a local transaction blocks until the local transaction is entirely committed, a call to commit a distributed transaction blocks only until phase one of the two-phase commit protocol completes. Remember that a client's DTC knows a transaction's outcome at the end of phase one, and that phase two cannot fail; thus, there is no reason `Commit` should wait for phase two to complete. In practical terms this means that you cannot pass `XACTTC_SYNC` (or `XACTTC_SYNC_PHASETWO`) as the second argument to `Commit`. You must pass 0 or `XACTTC_SYNC _PHASEONE` instead. If you pass 0, DTC applies its default behavior, that is, `XACTTC_SYNC_PHASEONE`.

The DTC does support committing and aborting transactions asynchronously; functionally OLE DB providers generally do not provide for local transactions. If you want to end a distributed transaction asynchronously, you can pass true for the `fAsync` parameter to `Abort` or `XACTTC_ASYNC` (or `XACTTC _ASYNC_PHASEONE`) to `Commit`. In either case, the method will return `XACT_S _ASYNC`, indicating that the transaction will be completed asynchronously. If you want to know the outcome of an asynchronously completed transaction, you must use the classic COM connection point mechanism to attach an implementation of the `ITransactionOutcomeEvents` notification interface to the distributed transaction object. Unfortunately, the implementation of this feature is not robust. In some cases the DTC may not notify the client about its transaction's outcome. It may also leak memory. You should avoid ending distributed transactions asynchronously.

As with local transactions, there is no guarantee that an attempt to commit a distributed transaction will succeed. If `Commit` succeeds, it returns `S_OK`, and the client knows that the changes it made in the scope of its distributed transaction have been kept. If `Commit` fails, it returns an error code, and the client knows that the changes it made in the scope of its distributed transaction have been discarded.[12] If a distributed transaction is committed asynchro-

---

[12] Again, see `transact.h` in the Platform SDK documentation for a complete list of possible transaction failure codes.

nously, the HRESULT indicating the transaction's outcome is passed to the client's implementation of `ITransactionOutcomeEvents`. If the client does not provide this interface, it will not know the transaction's outcome.

## Distributed Transaction Complexities

At first glance, using distributed transactions doesn't look much harder than using local transactions. But looks can be deceiving. As soon as you move beyond the simplest scenarios, using distributed transactions becomes quite a bit more complicated. Before you start programming with distributed transactions, you need to be aware of several issues involving distributed transaction propagation, management of enlisted connections, and a commit-related race condition.

### Distributed Transaction Propagation

Multiple client processes can participate in the same distributed transaction. Once a client has acquired a reference to a distributed transaction from its DTC, it can pass that reference to another process, possibly on another machine, and that process can use the distributed transaction too. While the notion of passing references to transactions back and forth is very simple, the mechanics of distributed transaction propagation are quite complex.

You can pass references to distributed transaction objects as arguments to COM methods. However, you have to be aware of the object's special marshaling semantics. Distributed transaction objects are instances of a nonconfigured class, so they always live in their creators' contexts and custom marshal. When a reference to a distributed transaction object is marshaled between contexts in the same process, it passes its raw four-byte pointer address.[13] In other words, distributed transaction objects are context neutral.

When a reference to a distributed transaction is marshaled between processes on the same machine, it marshals by value. In other words, a distributed transaction object is copied from a source process to a destination process. The distributed transaction object that is created in the destination process is a copy of the original object in the source process and does not have its full

---

[13] This is exactly what the Free-Threaded Marshaler (FTM) does, although the distributed transaction object doesn't actually use the FTM.

functionality. First, its `Commit` method is disabled and always returns `XACT_E` `_COMMITPREVENTED`. This is not surprising. Remember that only a transaction's client knows when all the work necessary to make a valid change to system state is done and a transaction can be committed. The DTC plumbing simply reflects and enforces this fact by making it impossible to commit a distributed transaction using a duplicate of a client's original distributed transaction object. Also, the lifetime of a copy of a distributed transaction object has no effect on the lifetime of the transaction it represents. In other words, releasing a copy of a distributed transaction object does not cause the transaction to abort. Similarly, holding onto a copy of a distributed transaction object does not stop a transaction from aborting if the original object created by the call to `ITransactionDispenser::BeginTransaction` is released before the transaction is committed. Other than that, a copy of a distributed transaction object behaves like an original. You can use it to enlist connections to RMs. You can also use it to explicitly abort the distributed transaction it represents.

Although a reference to a distributed transaction object can be marshaled between processes on a single machine, it cannot be marshaled between processes on different machines. More precisely, the interface pointer can be converted to a custom `OBJREF` in the source process—`CoMarshalInterface` succeeds—but the custom `OBJREF` cannot be converted back to a valid interface pointer in the remote destination process—`CoUnmarshalInterface` fails and returns an undocumented HRESULT. Cross-machine marshaling of a distributed transaction object could certainly be made to work, but it is not surprising that it does not. The enlistment process provides the most obvious example of a situation in which information about a distributed transaction (which is all a distributed transaction object represents) needs to be passed from a process on one machine to a process on another. However, most OLE DB providers do not communicate with their underlying data sources using DCOM. They use the data source's native protocol instead. For example, SQLOLEDB uses SQL Server's Tabular Data Stream (TDS) protocol. Given that, there is not a lot of incentive to make distributed transaction objects marshal across machines correctly, at least not via DCOM.

Still, there has to be some way to pass a distributed transaction object from a process on one machine to a process on another. In general, this involves two steps. First, you have to tell the source machine's DTC and the destination machine's DTC (which may or may not be the same, depending on configuration) that the latter is going to participate in the former's distributed transaction. There are two ways to do this. You can ask the source machine's DTC to *push* a distributed transaction to the destination machine's DTC, or you can ask the destination machine's DTC to *pull* a distributed transaction from the source machine's DTC. Either way, once you've propagated a distributed transaction to a destination machine's DTC, you have to create an object to represent it in the destination process. The resulting object is a copy of the original distributed transaction object in the source process. It has the same limitations as the copies that are created when distributed transaction objects are marshaled between processes on a single machine; that is, its Commit method is disabled, and its lifetime does not affect the lifetime of the transaction it represents.

The PCO supports two sets of interfaces for moving distributed transactions between processes on different machines. They are shown in Figure 6-4. The interfaces on the upper right can be used to push a distributed transaction using the DTC's native communication protocol. The interfaces on the lower right can be used to pull a distributed transaction using the DTC's native communication protocol. The interfaces on the left can be used to push or pull a distributed transaction via TIP. The TIP interfaces are simpler, and I'm going to focus on them.[14]

The ITipHelper interface is implemented by Proxy Core Objects and the ITipTransaction interface is implemented by distributed transaction objects. Here are the definitions.

```
interface ITipHelper : IUnknown
{
  HRESULT Pull([in] char *i_pszTxUrl,
               [out] ITransaction **o_ppITransaction);
  HRESULT PullAsync([in] char *i_pszTxUrl,
                    [in] ITipPullSink *i_pTipPullSink,
                    [out] ITransaction **o_ppITransaction);
  HRESULT GetLocalTmUrl([out] char **o_ppszLocalTmUrl);
};
```

---

[14] See the Platform SDK documentation for more information on the interfaces on the upper right. See txdtc.h for the definitions of the interfaces on the lower right. There is no documentation for these interfaces, but it's easy to figure out how to use them.

```
interface ITipTransaction : IUnknown
{
  HRESULT Push([in] char *i_pszRemoteTmUrl,
               [out] char **o_ppszRemoteTxUrl);
  HRESULT GetTransactionUrl([out] char **o_ppszLocalTxUrl)
};
```

Both interfaces are used when you push or pull a distributed transaction via TIP.

To push a distributed transaction to a destination process with TIP, you must first call `ITipHelper::GetLocalTmUrl` in the destination process to acquire a URL that identifies the destination machine's DTC, for example,

```
tip://dest.xyz.develop.com/
```

This URL is handed back to the source process, where it is passed as an argument to `ITipTransaction::Push`. This call actually pushes a given distributed transaction from the source machine's DTC to the destination

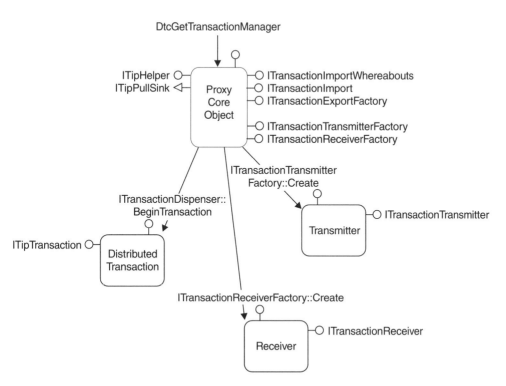

**Figure 6-4　Distributed transaction propagation interfaces**

machine's DTC. It also returns a URL that identifies the transaction, for example,

```
tip://dest.xyz.com/?OleTx-687E90B0-E0DC-4658-956D-21D3BD493DBC
```

Notice that the transaction's URL includes the name of the destination machine the transaction has been pushed to and the transaction's unique identifier (the serialized GUID at the end).[15] This URL is handed to the destination process, where it is passed as an argument to `ITipHelper::Pull`. This call returns a reference to a copy of the original distributed transaction object that resides in the destination process.

To pull a distributed transaction to a destination process with TIP, you must first call `ITipTransaction::GetTransactionUrl` in the source process to acquire a URL that identifies a given distributed transaction, for example,

```
tip://source.xyz.com/?OleTx-687E90B0-E0DC-4658-956D-21D3BD493DBC
```

Notice that this URL includes the name of the source machine the transaction will be pulled from and the transaction's unique identifier. This URL is handed to the destination process, where it is passed as an argument to `ITip Helper::Pull`. This call actually pulls the distributed transaction from the source machine's DTC to the destination machine's DTC. It also returns a reference to a copy of the original distributed transaction object that resides in the destination process.[16]

The push and pull techniques for moving distributed transactions between machines are equally efficient, both involve a cross-process call from one DTC to the other. From a developer's perspective, the pull model is preferable because the data that represents a transaction (e.g., the TIP transaction URL) can be generated in advance, without knowing which machine a transaction is being propagated to. The push model, by contrast, requires information about the destination DTC (e.g., the TIP TM URL) before the transaction can be prop-

---

[15] You can get either a local or distributed transaction's unique ID by calling `ITransaction:: GetTransactionInfo`. See the Platform SDK documentation for more information.

[16] Pulling a transaction takes time. You can pull a transaction asynchronously by calling `ITipHelper::PullAsync`, passing a reference to an implementation of `ITipPullSink` so that you receive a notification when the pull completes.

agated. The pull model makes it easy to propagate a transaction in a single RPC call. Here is some sample code that shows how to pull a transaction using `ITipTransaction` and `ITipHelper`.

```
HRESULT PassDistributedTransToObject(ITransaction *pDistTx,
                                     ISomeClass *pObj)
{
  // get TIP interface for given transaction
  CComPtr<ITipTransaction> spTipTx;
  HRESULT hr = pDistTx->QueryInterface(__uuidof(spTipTx),
                                       (void**)&spTipTx);
  if (FAILED(hr)) return hr;
  // extract TIP URL
  char *pszTipTxURL = 0;
  hr = spTipTx->GetTransactionUrl(&pszTipTxURL);
  if (FAILED(hr)) return hr;
  // pass TIP URL to remote object
  hr = pObj->SomeMethod(pszTipTxURL);
  CoTaskMemFree(pszTipTxURL);
  if (FAILED(hr)) return hr;
  return S_OK;
}
```

The `PassDistributedTransactionToObject` function uses the `ITipTransaction` interface to retrieve a URL representing the transaction it passed as a parameter. It passes the URL as an argument to `SomeMethod` on a remote object.[17] The implementation of `SomeMethod` follows.

```
HRESULT CSomeClass::SomeMethod(char *pszTipTxURL)
{
  // acquire reference to PCO
  CComPtr<ITipHelper> spTipHelper;
  HRESULT hr = DtcGetTransactionManager(0, 0, __uuidof(spTipHelper),
                                        0, 0, 0, (void**)&spTipHelper);
  if (FAILED(hr)) return hr;
  // pull transaction via TIP
  CComPtr<ITransaction> spDistTx;
  hr = spTipHelper->Pull(pszTipTxURL, &spDistTx);
  if (FAILED(hr)) return hr;
  ... // enlist connection and do some work with pulled transaction
  return S_OK;
}
```

---

[17] In the real world you would need to convert the TIP URL to a wide character string or a BSTR to comply with standard COM style.

The implementation of `SomeMethod` acquires a PCO and uses its `ITipHelper` interface to pull the distributed transaction identified by the URL that it was passed as a parameter to its process. If the call to `ITipHelper::Pull` succeeds, `SomeMethod` has a copy of the original distributed transaction object from the source process and can use it to enlist a connection.

### Connection Management

A single database connection can, over time, be used without transactions, with local transactions, and with distributed transactions. The only restriction is that a given connection can participate in at most one transaction of either type at any given time. This sounds simple enough, but the mechanics differ depending on the RM you are talking to and the data access library you are using. And they can be quite tricky.

For example, if you enlist a connection to SQL Server by calling `ITransactionJoin::JoinTransaction` and then execute a BEGIN TRANSACTION statement to start a local transaction, the statement has no effect.[18] Executing a COMMIT statement through an enlisted connection has no effect either.[19] Executing a ROLLBACK statement, however, does have an effect; it aborts the *distributed* transaction. This behavior is quite intentional, and you can use it to your advantage. Consider the T-SQL example from the beginning of this chapter.

```
begin transaction
  insert into orders (orderid, customerid, cancelled)
            values (1795, 1001, 0)
  insert into orderitems (orderid, productid, unitprice, quantity)
            values (1795, 49, 10.50, 7)
  insert into orderitems (orderid, productid, unitprice, quantity)
            values (1795, 134, 23.95, 2)
commit
```

If you execute these statements through a connection that *is not* enlisted against a distributed transaction, they will run in a local transaction. If you execute these statements through a connection that *is* enlisted against a dis-

---

[18] Actually, it increments the connection's @@TRANCOUNT variable, but that's not important now.

[19] Actually, it decrements the connection's @@TRANCOUNT variable, but that's not important now either.

tributed transaction, it will take precedence. The BEGIN TRANSACTION and COMMIT statements will be ignored, and the changes will not be made permanent until the distributed transaction commits. This is actually very useful; unfortunately there is no guarantee that other RMs will work the same way. If you use an RM other than SQL Server, you should investigate how it behaves in these same circumstances. Interestingly, if you enlist a connection to SQL Server by calling ITransactionJoin::JoinTransaction and then call ITransactionLocal::StartTransaction to start a local transaction, the call fails and returns XACT_E_XTIONEXISTS. This is an aspect of the SQLOLEDB provider, not SQL Server itself. As I said, the interplay between connections and local and distributed transactions can be quite tricky!

Additional concerns about connection management arise when you work with distributed transactions. All the connections that are enlisted against a given distributed transaction must stay open and enlisted until that transaction completes. Attempts to unenlist a connection or to enlist it against another distributed transaction before its current distributed transaction commits ties things up in knots. If you attempt either operation against SQLOLEDB, Join Transaction will simply hang. If you close an enlisted connection before its distributed transaction commits, any attempt to commit the transaction will fail. Worse, Commit will return XACT_E_INDOUBT, and the outcome of the distributed transaction will not be known. Needless to say, you must avoid both of these situations.

Obviously, you can close a connection after its distributed transaction ends. You can also reuse a connection after its distributed transaction ends, as long as you explicitly unenlist it or enlist it against another distributed transaction first. If you don't, the RM the connection is attached to will reject your requests because it knows the distributed transaction the connection is enlisted against is over. If you attempt this with SQLOLEDB, it will return the semantically questionable DB_E_ERRORSINCOMMAND. You must avoid this situation, too.

## A Race Condition

Developers who work with distributed transactions must address one more issue. A distributed transaction must not be committed if it is still being used to do work.[20] Consider a DTC client process that starts a distributed transaction and then hands a reference to its distributed transaction object off to a second process. The second process gets a copy of the original distributed transaction object, uses it to enlist a connection against the distributed transaction, and uses the connection to do some work. Then, before the second process can finish its work, the DTC client process commits the transaction. The transaction ends, and the participating RMs save their changes, even though the second process's work is not done. The second process won't know something is wrong until it tries to do more work and an RM rejects its request because the distributed transaction its connection is enlisted against just ended. Unfortunately, because the second process only partially completed the work it needed to do, the consistency of the durable state maintained by the system is probably compromised. The only way to avoid this problem is for the client processes to coordinate their work. Somehow, the second process needs to signal the first process when it's done working with the distributed transaction. There is no standard way to do this. Note that the second process cannot commit the distributed transaction while the first process is still working because it has a copy of the original distributed transaction object with its `Commit` method disabled.

## Declarative Transactions

You can implement COM+ classes that use either local or distributed transactions directly if you want to. If you do, you have complete control over how transactions are used. But you are also solely responsible for using them correctly. Many developers have experience working with local transactions. Far fewer developers have experience working with distributed transactions, which, as the previous section explained, can be quite complicated. COM+ provides the declarative transaction service as a way to simplify programming with distributed transactions. The declarative transaction service merges DTC-managed distributed transactions into the context model and, in so doing, hides many of their inherent complexities.

---

[20] Strictly speaking, this is true of any transaction, but it is not usually an issue when you're using local transactions.

## Transactional Objects

By default, COM+ classes do not use declarative transactions. This is good because using a declarative transaction changes an object's very nature. Instances of classes that use declarative transactions are called *transactional objects* because they run inside distributed transactions. *Inside* may seem like an odd preposition to use, but it accurately describes the relationship between a transactional object and its transaction. The declarative transaction service hides all the details of creating and committing or aborting distributed transactions. Transactional objects can influence the outcome of their distributed transactions indirectly (i.e., whether they should commit or abort), but the interception plumbing actually calls `ITransaction::Commit` or `ITransaction::Abort`.

Because this happens transparently and because there is always a chance that `ITransaction::Commit` will fail, a transactional object may never know its distributed transaction's outcome. Given that, it would be dangerous for a transactional object to keep any data that reflects changes it made to RM-managed system state because it has no way of knowing whether its changes were kept or rolled back. Even if a transactional object did know its transaction's outcome, once its transaction ends, the data it accessed can be changed by other transactions, making any cached data obsolete. So, to avoid consistency problems, a transactional object cannot outlive its distributed transaction; when its transaction ends, a transactional object must deactivate and discard any data it holds.

A transactional object must deactivate even if a client is still holding a reference to it. To that end, classes that use the declarative transaction service always use JITA as well. In fact, this is JITA's real purpose. It is an integral part of the declarative transaction model. Because transactional objects use JITA, they always live in contexts of their own. It is possible, however, for multiple transactional objects to participate in the same distributed transaction. In order to support this, COM+ needs a way to define associations between contexts and distributed transactions. It does this using an additional abstraction called a transaction stream.

## Enter Transaction Streams

A *transaction stream* is a group of contexts within an activity that always share the same distributed transaction. Every context created in a COM+ process is associated with at most one transaction stream. Like activities, transaction streams are a part of context and can flow to new contexts as they are created.[21] When a new context is created, it can be added to its creator's transaction stream, a new transaction stream of its own, or no transaction stream at all. When a new context is added to a new transaction stream of its own, it becomes that stream's *root context*. All the other contexts that are added to a transaction stream after that point are *nonroot contexts*. The root context of a transaction stream is of special significance because a transaction stream's distributed transaction ends only when the distinguished object in the stream's root context—also called the *root object*—deactivates. (Remember that the distinguished object is the first object created in a context.) In essence, a root object is the client of a declarative transaction. A process can contain multiple transaction streams. Transaction streams are scoped to activities, and, like activities, they can extend across process boundaries.

Figure 6-5 illustrates the relationship between processes, activities, contexts, objects, and transaction streams. In this picture, each process is divided into contexts. Process M contains two contexts, A and B. Process N contains six contexts, C, D, E, F, G, and H. All of the contexts in both processes are in a single activity, Q. There are two transaction streams, X and Y. Each transaction stream contains a single root context and one or more nonroot contexts. Transaction stream X spans process boundaries. It contains contexts A and B from process M and contexts C and D from process N. Work within those contexts uses the same distributed transaction, which ends when the distinguished object in the root context A deactivates. Transaction stream Y does not span a process boundary. It contains contexts E and F from process N. Work within those contexts uses the same distributed transaction, which ends when the distinguished object in the root context E deactivates. Contexts G and H are not in a transaction stream. Work in those contexts is not done within the scope of a distributed transaction.

---

[21] That's how the original implementation of the `PersonMgr` class presented in Chapter 1 was able to create multiple `Person` objects that participated in its declarative transaction.

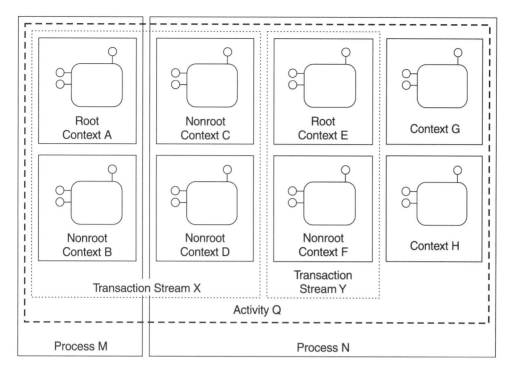

**Figure 6-5 Processes, activities, contexts, objects, and transaction streams**

It is important to understand the difference between a transaction stream and a transaction. A transaction stream is a space within which a distributed transaction executes. In a sense, it is similar to an apartment within which one or more threads execute or an activity within which a single causality executes. While only one distributed transaction is available in a stream at a time, multiple transactions may execute within the same stream over time. By definition, work done in two separate transaction streams is done in two separate distributed transactions. It makes sense to use multiple transaction streams any time you want two tasks to be protected by transactions, but you want them to commit or abort independently.

## Where Do Transaction Streams Come From?

Like contexts, apartments, and activities, transaction streams cannot be created explicitly. Instead, as with activities, transaction stream creation and propagation is implicitly tied to context creation and, therefore, object creation. How each instance of a configured class relates to transaction streams, that is, whether creating a new object also creates a new transaction stream, is determined by the value of the class's *transaction* attribute in the catalog. Table 6-1 describes the transaction attribute.

The five possible transaction settings are listed in the first column of Table 6-2. The second column lists the corresponding name for each setting used by the Component Services Explorer (CSE) user interface. These are the terms developers typically use when discussing declarative transaction options. The third column indicates whether a new object will be in a context in a transaction stream. The fourth column indicates whether a new object is in a context that inherits a transaction stream from its creator. The fifth column indicates whether a new object will be in the root context of its transaction stream. The sixth column indicates whether a new object will be the root object, that is, the distinguished object in the root context.

The five transaction options are analogous to the five synchronization settings described in Chapter 4. All five of these options provide different semantics for controlling the way a transaction stream flows from a creator's context to a new context. The first four options are straightforward variations on a theme. The fifth option is more complex and is designed specifically for raw-configured classes. The default transaction setting for a new configured class is Not_Supported.

New instances of a class marked `COMAdminTransactionNone` never inherit their creator's transaction stream. If a new object's creator is in a transaction stream, the SCM must put the new object into a new context that is not in a transaction stream.

New instances of a class marked `COMAdminTransactionSupported` inherit their creator's transaction stream if it has one. Classes marked `COMAdmin TransactionSupported` must also use JITA, and the SCM will always put a new object in a context of its own. If a new object's creator has a transaction

**Table 6-1   The transaction class attribute**

| Attribute | Catalog Type | Default Value | Notes |
|---|---|---|---|
| Transaction | COMAdminTransaction | COMAdminTransaction NotSupported | Defines class's use of transaction streams |

**Table 6-2** Transaction options

| Attribute | CSE Name | Is in Transaction Stream? | Shares Creator's Transaction Stream? | Is in Stream's Root Context? | Is Stream's Root Object? |
|---|---|---|---|---|---|
| COMAdminTransactionNone | Not_Supported | Never | Never | Never | Never |
| COMAdminTransactionSupported | Supported | If creator is in transaction stream | If creator is in transaction stream | Never | Never |
| COMAdminTransactionRequired | Required | Always | If creator is in transaction stream | If creator is not in transaction stream | If creator is not in transaction stream |
| COMAdminTransactionRequiresNew | Requires_New | Always | Never | Always | Always |
| COMAdminTransactionIgnored | Disabled | If creator is in transaction stream and object shares creator's context | If creator is in transaction stream and object shares creator's context | If creator is in root context and object shares creator's context | Never |

stream, the transaction stream is extended to encompass the new *nonroot* context. Otherwise, the SCM must put the new object in a new context that is not in any transaction stream.

New instances of a class marked `COMAdminTransactionRequired` inherit their creator's transaction stream if it has one. Classes marked `COM AdminTransactionRequired` must also use JITA, and the SCM will always put a new object in a context of its own. If a new object's creator is in a transaction stream, the transaction stream is extended to encompass the new *nonroot* context. Otherwise, the SCM must put the new object into a new *root* context in a new transaction stream.

New instances of a class marked `COMAdminTransactionRequiresNew` always get a new transaction stream; they never inherit transaction streams from their creators. The SCM always puts the new object in a new *root* context in a new transaction stream.

New instances of a class marked `COMAdminTransactionIgnored` don't care about transaction streams. If the SCM puts a new object in its creator's context and its creator is in a transaction stream, the new object inherits that transaction stream implicitly. If the SCM puts a new object in its creator's context and its creator is not in a transaction stream, the new object is not in a transaction stream. If the SCM puts a new object into a new context, the new context is not in a transaction stream. As with the synchronization attribute, the semantics of this Disabled setting are somewhere in between Supported and Not_Supported. Like Supported, Disabled means a new object should inherit its creator's transaction stream if it has one, *but only if the new object ends up in its creator's context*. Like Not_Supported, Disabled means a new object should never inherit its creator's transaction stream, *but only if the new object ends up in a new context*.

The Disabled option is designed for raw-configured classes that never want the presence or absence of a transaction stream to affect the SCM's decision about what context they should live in. A raw-configured class can also use the Not_Supported option to ensure that its instances always exist in contexts outside a transaction stream. This setting does not require interception if a creator's context is part of a transaction stream. If a creator's context is part of a transaction stream, this option does require interception and will force instances of raw-configured classes into contexts of their own. You can avoid this by enabling a raw-configured class's `MustRunInClientContext` attribute so that object creation fails in these cases.

Note that, while an instance of a raw-configured class can be created in a transaction stream's root context, it can never be the transaction stream's root object, that is, the distinguished object in the root context. As a result, deactivating an instance of a raw-configured class that happens to live in a transaction stream's root context has no effect on the stream's distributed transaction.

I mentioned earlier that transactional objects always use the JITA service. More specifically, if a class is marked `COMAdminTransactionSupported`, `COMAdminTransactionRequired`, or `COMAdminTransactionRequiresNew`, it must also be marked `JustInTimeActivation = True`. I also mentioned that transaction streams are scoped by activities (I haven't explained why, but I will shortly). More specifically, if a class is marked `COMAdminTransaction Supported` or `COMAdminTransactionRequired`, it must also be marked `COMAdminSynchronizationRequired`, so that if new instances inherit a transaction stream they also inherit an activity. If a class is marked `COM AdminTransactionRequiresNew`, it must be marked either `COMAdmin SynchronizationRequired` or `COMAdminSynchronizationRequiresNew`, so that new instances always end up in an activity.

Consider the example in Figure 6-6. A single client created the contexts and objects in this diagram. The order of creation proceeded from left to right, that is, object A in context A was created first, it created object A' in context A, and so on. Object A is an instance of a class marked `COMAdminTransaction Required` or `COMAdminTransactionRequiresNew`. Either one would cause the creation of a new transaction stream, X. Object A' is an instance of a

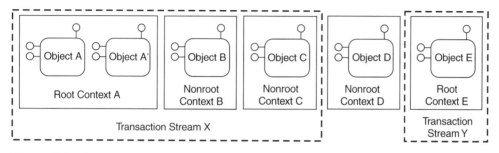

**Figure 6-6** Transaction stream creation and propagation

raw-configured class marked COMAdminTransactionIgnored. That forced it into its creator's context A and therefore transaction stream X. Objects B and C are instances of classes marked COMAdminTransactionSupported or COMAdminTransactionRequired. Either setting would cause the two objects to join transaction stream X. Object D is an instance of a class marked COMAdminTransactionNone. That forced it outside its creator's transaction stream. Object E, like object A, is an instance of a class marked COMAdmin TransactionRequired or COMAdminTransactionRequiresNew. Either one would cause the creation of a new transaction stream Y.

### Detecting the Presence of a Transaction Stream

Any object can detect whether it is in a context that is part of a transaction stream. This is useful for an instance of a configured class marked COMAdmin TransactionSupported that wants to know whether its context inherited a transaction stream from its creator. It is also useful for an instance of a raw-configured class marked COMAdminTransactionIgnored that wants to know whether its creator's context is in a transaction stream. Detecting the presence of a transaction stream is straightforward. The IObjectContext Info interface's IsInTransaction method returns a boolean value that tells you whether the context it is called from is part of a transaction stream. It does not tell you whether the context is the root of the transaction stream. There is no documented way to determine this. Here is an example.

```
HRESULT CSomeCfgClass::IsInTransactionStream(VARIANT_BOOL *pvb)
{
  CComPtr<IObjectContextInfo> spCtxInfo;
  HRESULT hr = CoGetObjectContext(__uuidof(spCtxInfo),
                                  (void**)&spCtxInfo);
  if (FAILED(hr)) return hr;
  *pvb = spCtxInfo->IsInTransaction() ? VARIANT_TRUE :
   VARIANT_FALSE;
  return S_OK;
}
```

The IsInTransactionStream method calls CoGetObjectContext to get an IObjectContextInfo reference to its object context. It calls the IsIn Transaction method to determine whether the current context is in a transaction stream and returns the result as output.

## Creating and Propagating a Distributed Transaction

Transaction streams exist to hide the details of distributed transaction creation and propagation. Each transaction stream maintains a reference to a DTC-dispensed distributed transaction object. Figure 6-7 shows this aspect of the transaction stream architecture.

If a transaction stream includes contexts in multiple processes on one or more machines, the COM+ plumbing copies the stream's distributed transaction object to each process using the techniques described in the previous section.[22] References to the copies are stored in a "well-known" location in each process.

Code executing in a context in a transaction stream can retrieve a reference to the stream's distributed transaction object by calling the GetTransaction

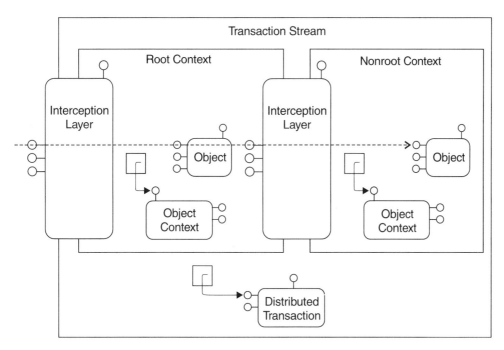

**Figure 6-7 A transaction stream and its transaction**

---

[22] Cross-machine propagation is done with the DTC's native mechanisms for pushing and pulling transactions, not with the TIP.

method of the `IObjectContextInfo` interface exposed by object context.[23] Here is an example.

```
CComPtr<IObjectContextInfo> spCtxInfo;
HRESULT hr = CoGetObjectContext(__uuidof(spCtxInfo),
                                (void**)&spCtxInfo);
if (FAILED(hr)) return hr;
CComPtr<IUnknown> spDistTx;
hr = spCtxInfo->GetTransaction(&spDistTx);
if(FAILED(hr)) return hr;
```

The declarative transaction service does not actually start a new distributed transaction when a transaction stream is created. Instead, it calls `ITransactionDispenser::BeginTransaction` to create a distributed transaction on demand the first time a piece of code in the transaction stream needs one. Typically this happens when a database connection is acquired. The OLE DB infrastructure, and therefore ADO, knows about transaction streams and can extract a reference to a stream's distributed transaction and automatically enlist against it (I'll talk more about this later). The call to `IObject ContextInfo::GetTransaction` in the code above would also cause a new distributed transaction to start if the transaction stream it was executed in didn't already have one.

The declarative transaction service ends a transaction stream's distributed transaction when the stream's root object deactivates. But if a quick call to `GetTransaction` retrieves a reference to a stream's distributed transaction object, what stops any object in a transaction stream from ending the stream's transaction directly? In fact, the declarative transaction service plumbing is prepared for this. The distributed transaction object that's available through object context is actually a copy of an original and cannot be used to commit a stream's transaction. Its `ITransaction::Commit` method always fails with the well-known error code `XACT_E_COMMITPREVENTED`. This is true even when the code retrieving the reference to the distributed transaction object is executing in the process where the transaction was originally started, that is,

---

[23] There is a second method called `GetTransactionId` that retrieves the unique ID of a transaction stream's distributed transaction.

even if the distributed transaction object has not been marshaled across a process boundary.[24]

The distributed transaction object that's available through object context can be used to abort a stream's transaction. In short, the object emulates the behavior of the SQL statements for local transactions when they are executed within the scope of a distributed transaction. COMMIT is ignored, and ROLL-BACK aborts the distributed transaction. While it is possible to abort a transaction this way, be aware that you are bypassing the declarative transaction service's normal transaction management code. In other words, it works, but you are stepping outside the intended usage model and exercising code paths in the COM+ plumbing that are not commonly used. It's hard to say how risky this is. In general, it is best to avoid it.

### Autoenlisting Connections

The declarative transaction plumbing takes care of distributed transaction creation and propagation. However, a distributed transaction is not useful unless you can enlist RM connections against it. So the service also collaborates with OLE DB to manage the enlistment process. Specifically, transaction streams rely on OLE DB to automatically enlist connections created within their contexts against their distributed transactions. Transaction streams also rely on OLE DB to help make sure that connections enlisted against their transactions remain open and enlisted until their transactions complete. In short, transaction streams work with OLE DB to handle the complexities of managing enlisted database connections for you.

Support for automatically enlisting database connections against declarative transactions is actually provided by the OLE DB Service Components. The Service Components are a set of helper objects that merge with an OLE DB provider's objects via COM aggregation, which gives them the opportunity to intercept method calls. The basic architecture is shown in Figure 6-8.

When new OLE DB data sources and sessions are created, the OLE DB Service Components intercept the calls. The Service Components know how to

---

[24] Distributed transaction objects implement an undocumented interface called `ITransaction Cloner` with a single method called `CloneWithCommitDisabled` to support in-process duplication. See `transact.h` in the Platform SDK documentation for more information.

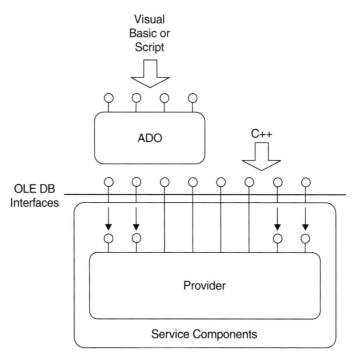

**Figure 6-8　OLE DB Service Component architecture**

detect the presence of a transaction stream and how to acquire a reference to a stream's distributed transaction (forcing the plumbing to ask the DTC for a new one if necessary). If a connection is established from within a context in a transaction stream, the Service Components will autoenlist the connection against the stream's distributed transaction by calling `ITransactionJoin::JoinTransaction`. All of this happens transparently, and the object that is acquiring the database connection is none the wiser. Here is an example that shows you all the code that's necessary to autoenlist against a transaction stream's distributed transaction.

```
HRESULT CSomeTxClass::ExecSQLInDeclarativeTransaction(BSTR bstrSQL)
{
  // create data source
  CDataSource dataSrc;
  HRESULT hr = dataSrc.OpenFromInitializationString(L"Provider=...");
  if (FAILED(hr)) return hr;
  // create session
```

```
    CSession sess;
    hr = sess.Open(dataSrc);
    if (FAILED(hr)) return hr;
    // create and execute command
    CCommand<CNoAccessor, CNoRowset, CNoMultipleResults> cmd;
    hr = cmd.Open(sess, "insert into...", 0, 0,
                    DBGUID_DBSQL, false);
    if (FAILED(hr)) return hr;
    return S_OK;
};
```

If this code is executed in a context in a transaction stream, the work it does will be automatically protected by the transaction stream's distributed transaction.

Of course, there are some caveats to all this. Autoenlistment is a feature of the OLE DB Service Components, and they must be loaded for it to work. The Service Components are bootstrapped through a special factory class called MSDAINITIALIZE that is used to load OLE DB providers. If you don't use MSDAINITIALIZE to load your providers, the Service Components will not be loaded, your connections will not autoenlist against declarative transactions, and you will receive no warning that something is amiss. If you are using the ATL OLE DB consumer templates, you should use the CDataSource class's OpenWithServiceComponents or OpenFromInitializationString to load providers; both methods call to MSDAINITIALIZE. If you are using ADO, you don't have to worry about a thing because ADO always loads providers using MSDAINITIALIZE.

Even if the OLE DB Service Components are loaded, they may not automatically enlist connections. Individual OLE DB providers are configured to support a default set of services. If a provider is not configured to support autoenlistment, the Service Components will not autoenlist new connections against declarative transactions. An OLE DB provider's service configuration is specified by the OLEDB_SERVICES value of its CLSID in the Registry. OLEDB _SERVICES is a DWORD of bit-flags; the second lowest bit controls auto-enlistment. When a provider is initialized, its default service settings can be overridden by either an "OLE DB Services" clause in an OLE DB (or ADO) connection string or by a DBPROP_INIT_OLEDBSERVICES property passed to a provider's data source object.[25] If you manually disable a provider's use of the autoenlistment service using either one of these techniques, the Service Components will not autoenlist new connections against declarative transactions.

Finally, the Service Components only support autoenlistment for the first session acquired from a data source object. If you are using OLE DB in the raw or the ATL OLE DB consumer templates, and you want your connections to autoenlist, you should create only one session object from each data source object. ADO does this implicitly.

Database connections that are enlisted against a distributed transaction must remain open and enlisted until the transaction commits. Since the declarative transaction service does not commit a transaction stream's distributed transaction until *after* the stream's root object deactivates, there is little a transactional object can do to ensure that the database connections it uses are managed correctly. Luckily, the Service Components help out here too. In addition to implementing autoenlistment, the Service Components also implement OLE DB's connection pooling service. The connection pooling service is aware of declarative transactions and makes sure that autoenlisted connections are managed properly so that a transaction stream's distributed transaction can commit.

The connection pooling service handles all requests for OLE DB (and ADO) connections. It maintains pools of connections on a per-process and per-provider basis. When a request for a connection with a given set of properties (e.g., provider type, target server, user name, etc.) arrives, the connection pooling service looks for an existing connection that fits the bill. If the service finds one, it returns it. If the service doesn't find one, it creates and returns a new connection with the desired properties.

The OLE DB connection pooling service differentiates between connections that are enlisted against declarative transactions and connections that are not. When a request for a connection comes from a context within a transaction stream, the connection pooling service looks for a connection that is already enlisted against the stream's distributed transaction. If it finds one, the ser-

---

[25] For more information, see the section "Overriding Provider Service Defaults" in the Platform SDK documentation.

vice returns the already enlisted connection. If it does not find one, the service looks for an unenlisted connection instead. If it finds one of those, it asks the autoenlistment service to enlist the connection against the distributed transaction from the requesting context's transaction stream (possibly causing the stream to start a new distributed transaction in the process). Then it returns the newly autoenlisted connection. If the connection pooling service does not find an unenlisted connection either, it creates a new connection. Then it asks the autoenlistment service to enlist the new connection against the distributed transaction from the requesting context's transaction stream (again, possibly causing the stream to start a new distributed transaction in the process). Finally, it returns the newly created and autoenlisted connection.

When an autoenlisted connection is released, the connection pooling service keeps it aside in a special, transaction-specific pool. An autoenlisted connection can be reused only in a context in the transaction stream whose distributed transaction it is enlisted against. When a transaction stream's distributed transaction ends, the connection pooling service drains the corresponding transaction-specific pool. It asks the autoenlistment service to unenlist any connections and then returns them to the appropriate unenlisted pool. By pooling autoenlisted connections this way, the Service Components guarantee that they will be kept open and enlisted until after a transaction stream's distributed transaction ends. This approach has the added benefit of reusing autoenlisted connections whenever possible, thereby minimizing the overhead of the enlistment process.

Again, there are some caveats. First, all the requirements related to autoenlistment apply. The Service Components must be loaded, and a provider must be configured to support connection pooling, as indicated by the lowest-bit of its CLSID's OLEDB_SERVICE value in the Registry. In addition, you must release your OLE DB data source objects when you are done with them, but you must not uninitialize them by calling IDBInitialize::Uninitialize. The Uninitialize method closes an underlying database connection, period. If you forcibly close a connection that is autoenlisted against a transaction stream's distributed transaction, the transaction cannot commit. When the transaction stream's root object deactivates, the transaction will abort, and the well-known error code CONTEXT_E_ABORTED will be returned. This is definitely better than the XACT_E_INDOUBT outcome you get when you program directly against the DTC and explicitly close a manually enlisted OLE DB connection, but it still isn't desirable. This is an issue only if you program OLE DB in the raw. ATL CDataSource objects and ADO Connection objects do not uninitialize their underlying OLE DB data source objects when they are closed.

### Controlling a Declarative Transaction's Outcome

A transaction stream's distributed transaction ends when the stream's root object deactivates. A stream's root object deactivates when it is released by its client, when it returns from a method with its done bit turned on (remember that transactional objects always use JITA), or when it returns from a method marked AutoComplete = True. The moment one of these things happens, the declarative transaction service has to decide whether it should commit or abort a stream's distributed transaction. It makes this decision by considering the happiness of all of the transactional objects in all the contexts in the stream.

Every context in a transaction stream has a "happy" bit in addition to a done bit, as shown in Figure 6-9. A context's happy bit is turned on by default. When a root object deactivates, the COM+ plumbing examines the state of the happy bit of every context in the root object's transaction stream. If all of the contexts' happy bits are turned on, the plumbing commits the stream's distributed transaction. If any of the contexts' happy bits are off, the plumbing aborts the stream's distributed transaction.

It is very important that a distributed transaction not be committed by one thread while it is still being used by another thread. If you follow the object-per-client model, this situation should never arise. But in case you don't, the declarative transaction service eliminates this race condition by insisting that a transaction stream exist within an activity. If access to a transaction stream's contexts is serialized, the stream's distributed transaction cannot be committed while it is being used. However, as explained in Chapter 4, access to the contexts within an activity is serialized only on a per-process basis. If a transaction stream spans process boundaries, what stops a thread in one process from deactivating the stream's root object while a thread in another process is still working in a context in the stream? The answer is simple. In order to examine the happy bit of each context within a transaction stream, the declarative trans-

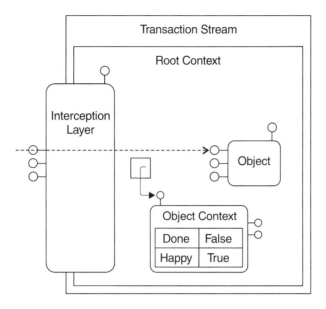

**Figure 6-9  A transaction stream context and its happy and done bits**

action service has to acquire an activity lock *in each process*. If work is being done in a nonroot context in a stream when its root object deactivates, the plumbing will wait until that work is done before reading that nonroot context's happy bit. This does not stop concurrent work from executing within a transaction stream, but it does stop a transaction stream's distributed transaction from committing while it is in use.

It is possible that a context in a transaction stream will not exist when the stream's root object deactivates. For instance, if a root object creates, uses, and releases a nonroot object within a single method, the nonroot object's context will be created, accessed, and destroyed before the root object's method completes. Since the root object can't possibly deactivate until after its method completes, the nonroot object and its context will be gone before the declarative transaction plumbing has a chance to check the state of its happy bit. To solve this problem, each transaction stream has a "doomed" bit, as shown in Figure 6-10.

If a nonroot object is unhappy (i.e., its context's happy bit is turned off) when it deactivates, the interception plumbing turns the transaction stream's doomed bit on. In the example in Figure 6-10, the nonroot object deactivated

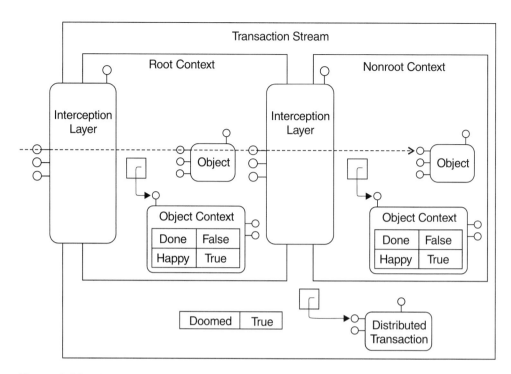

**Figure 6-10   A transaction stream and its doomed bit**

when the root object released it. A nonroot object will also deactivate—and potentially set its transaction stream's doomed bit—when it returns from a method with its done bit set or when it returns from a method marked `AutoComplete = True`. Turning a transaction stream's doomed bit on does not immediately abort the stream's distributed transaction. Instead, the state of the doomed bit simply influences the declarative transaction service's decision about whether a transaction stream's distributed transaction should be committed or aborted when the stream's root object deactivates. If a transaction stream's doomed bit is turned on when its root object deactivates, the stream's distributed transaction is aborted, even if all of the stream's remaining objects are happy.

   The doomed bit is a latch that can be reset only by the declarative transaction service. Once a transaction stream's doomed bit is turned on, it stays on until the plumbing resets it after the stream's root object deactivates and its current distributed transaction aborts. In other words, once a transactional object has doomed its declarative transaction, there is nothing any object in the same transaction stream can do to save it. The stream's distributed transaction *will* abort; it is just a matter of time. So once a transaction stream's doomed bit is on, the objects in that stream have only one priority. They must complete their work as quickly as possible so the root can deactivate, the stream's distributed transaction can be aborted, and any locks the transaction holds can be released.

## Flipping the Happy Bit

Like the done bit, the happy bit is part of an object's context. It is manipulated using the `IContextState` interface introduced in Chapter 5. Here is the interface's complete definition.

```
interface IContextState : IUnknown
{
  HRESULT SetDeactivateOnReturn([in] VARIANT_BOOL bDeactivate);
  HRESULT GetDeactivateOnReturn([out] VARIANT_BOOL *pbDeactivate);
  HRESULT SetMyTransactionVote(TransactionVote txVote);
  HRESULT GetMyTransactionVote(TransactionVote *ptxVote)
}
```

`GetMyTransactionVote` and `SetMyTransactionVote` read and write the state of the happy bit, respectively. They each take one argument of enumerated type `TransactionVote`.

```
typedef  enum tagTransactionVote
{
  TxCommit = 0,
  TxAbort = TxCommit + 1
} TransactionVote;
```

Calling `SetMyTransactionVote` with `TxCommit` turns the happy bit on. Calling it with `TxAbort` turns the happy bit off. Here is a method that uses `IContextState` to change the state of its context's happy bit and done bit.

```
HRESULT CSomeTxClass::ExecSQLInDeclarativeTransaction(void)
{
  // get IContextState reference to context
  CComPtr<IContextState> spCtxState;
  HRESULT hr = CoGetObjectContext(__uuidof(spCtxState),
                                  (void**)&spCtxState);
  if (FAILED(hr)) return hr;
  // turn done bit on
  hr = spCtxState->SetDeactivateOnReturn(VARIANT_TRUE);
  if (FAILED(hr)) return hr;
```

```
    // turn happy bit off in case of failure
    hr = spCtxState->SetMyTransactionVote(TxAbort);
    if (FAILED(hr)) return hr;
    hr = ... // do work with RMs, use decl. tx. implicitly
    if (FAILED(hr)) return hr;
    // every thing succeeded, turn happy bit on again
    hr = spCtxState->SetMyTransactionVote(TxCommit);
    if (FAILED(hr)) return hr;
    return S_OK;
}
```

This new version of ExecSQLInDeclarativeTransaction uses an IContextState reference to object context to manipulate the state of its context's happy and done bits. When it starts, the method calls SetDeactivateOnReturn, passing in VARIANT_TRUE, to turn the done bit on and indicate that the object should be deactivated when the call completes. It also calls SetMyTransactionVote, passing in TxAbort, to turn the happy bit off and indicate that if the method does not complete successfully, the declarative transaction should be doomed. After setting both bits, the method does its transactional work. Then, if everything succeeds, it calls SetMyTransactionVote, passing in TxCommit, to turn the happy bit back on and indicate that the method has completed successfully and the declarative transaction should commit. This idiom—setting the initial state of the bits to indicate failure at the beginning of a method and resetting them to indicate success at the end of a method—is typical transactional object style.

As with the done bit, you can change the state of the happy bit as many times as you like during a method call. Only the happy bit's final state when the call completes matters. Also, as with the done bit, if there are multiple, nested calls through the interception plumbing to an object in a context in a transaction stream, the happy bit will not be interpreted until the outermost call completes.

Instances of raw-configured classes can change the state of a transactional context's happy bit. However, like setting a context's done bit, this is considered bad style. The declarative transaction service is tied to a context's distinguished object—the instance of the class that declared its desire to use the declarative transaction service and the object that will deactivate when its distributed transaction ends—and it should be left to that object to decide whether it is happy or unhappy at the end of a call.

If a method of a transactional object is marked `AutoComplete = True`, the interception plumbing will set the happy bit automatically, based on the method's HRESULT.[26] If the method returns `S_OK`, the happy bit is turned on; otherwise, the happy bit is turned off. The interception plumbing will not change the value of the happy bit if an autocompleting method sets it explicitly by calling `SetMyTransactionVote` independent of the method's HRESULT. Unfortunately, this mechanism does not work correctly when a method is invoked from script. If a client calls an autocompleting method through `IDispatch::Invoke`, the object will always deactivate with its happy bit turned on unless the method sets the bit's value explicitly. This happens even if the method returns a failure code. This behavior is a quirk of the current implementation that should be fixed in the future. Meanwhile, transactional objects should not rely on autocompleting methods to manage their declarative transactions' outcomes.

Finally, if a context is not part of a transaction stream, it does not have a happy bit. If an object in a context that is not configured to use a declarative transaction attempts to set or get the state of the happy bit through `IContextState`, the methods will fail with the well-known error code `CONTEXT_E_NOTRANSACTION`.

### The Four Possible States of a Transactional Object

In general, a transactional object ends every method call in one of four possible states. Each state corresponds to a unique combination of an object's context's done and happy bits. Each state also corresponds to a method of the old `IObjectContext`—`ObjectContext` in Visual Basic—interface that can be used to set a context's happy and done bit in one call. An object's state at the end of a method indicates its disposition toward its declarative transaction. The meaning of some states differs for root objects and nonroot objects. The states are described in Table 6-3. The first column lists the four states by name. The second and third columns list the corresponding values of the context's happy and done bits, respectively (remember that completing a method that is marked to `AutoComplete` is functionally equivalent to turning the done bit on).

---

[26] This is how the Person and PersonMgr classes in Chapter 1 controlled their declarative transactions' activities.

**Table 6-3  The four possible states of a transactional object**

| Name | Happy Bit | Done Bit | Meaning |
|---|---|---|---|
| EnableCommit | On | Off | Object *won't* object if transaction commits. |
| SetComplete | On | On | Commit transaction if object is root; all contexts are happy, and doomed bit is off. |
| SetAbort | Off | On | Set doomed bit *or* abort transaction if object is root. |
| DisableCommit | Off | Off | Object *will* object if transaction commits. |

The fourth column lists the meaning of each state, that is, how it affects an object's declarative transaction.

If an object ends a method call happy but not done, it is in the Enable Commit state. If a transaction stream's root object deactivates in order to commit the stream's distributed transaction, objects in the EnableCommit state will not object. By ending a method in the EnableCommit state, an object is indicating that it has left the system in a consistent state and that it is standing by, ready to be used again. A context's happy and done bits are on and off, respectively, by default, so all new transactional objects start life in the EnableCommit state.

If an object ends a method call happy and done, it is in the SetComplete state. If a root object ends a method call in the SetComplete state, the plumbing commits the transaction stream's distributed transaction unless another context in the stream is unhappy or the stream's doomed bit is turned on. If a nonroot object ends a method in the SetComplete state, it is simply deactivated. If the `ExecSQLInDeclarativeTransaction` method in the example succeeds, it leaves its object in the SetComplete state.

If an object ends a method call unhappy and done, it is in the SetAbort state. If a root object ends a method call in the SetAbort state, the plumbing aborts the transaction stream's distributed transaction. If a nonroot object ends a method in the SetAbort state, it is deactivated, and the transaction stream's doomed bit is turned on. Once a declarative transaction is doomed, there is no reason to continue working with it, and every reason to abort it as quickly as possible in order to release RM locks. When a nonroot object completes a method in the SetAbort state, it must raise an error so its caller knows its goal has changed from successfully completing the transaction to simply ending it as quickly as possible. When a root object completes a method in the SetAbort state, it must raise an error so its caller knows its transaction has aborted. This is Rule 6.1. There is no compelling mechanical reason why root objects should follow this rule, but they often do (especially if they are sometimes used as non-root objects). If the `ExecSQLInDeclarativeTransaction` method in the example fails, it leaves its object in the SetAbort state and raises an error.

**RULE 6.1**

A transactional object must raise an error when it completes a method in the SetAbort state (unhappy and done).

If an object ends a method call unhappy but not done, it is in the DisableCommit state. If a transaction stream's root object deactivates in order to commit the stream's distributed transaction, objects in the DisableCommit state will object, and the transaction will be aborted. DisableCommit is useful if you design transactional objects that require multiple method calls to accomplish a task. An object can return from an initial method call in the DisableCommit state, remain in that state across several additional method calls, and then return from a final method call in the SetComplete state. The advantage of this approach is that the object does not have to guarantee that system state is consistent until the final method call completes. Prior to that point, any attempt to commit the transaction stream's distributed transaction will fail, and the transaction will be aborted.

Rule 6.1 is quite difficult to implement correctly if nonroot objects ever return from methods in the DisableCommit state. If you release a nonroot object that is in the DisableCommit state, it deactivates, silently entering the SetAbort state (i.e., unhappy and done) and dooming its declarative transaction. Unfortunately, an object's caller does not know when this happens because `IUnknown::Release` does not return an HRESULT. There are three things you can do to solve this problem. First, you can simply avoid DisableCommit and make sure that all your objects always end their methods in one of the other three states. Second, you can make your objects return a special error code whenever they end methods in the DisableCommit state so that their callers know what will happen if the objects are released. And third, you can document the semantics of each of your transactional objects methods very carefully so that anyone who is writing code that uses your objects knows exactly which methods leave them in the DisableCommit state. If you do not do at least one of these things, you are likely to end up with a bug in your system that is very difficult to find, especially since there is no documented way to examine the state of a transaction stream's doomed bit to see if and when it is turned on.

Many argue that transactional objects should end every method call in either the SetComplete or SetAbort state so that they end their declarative transactions as quickly as possible in order to release any RM locks they hold. In other words, they argue that transactional objects should be stateless. I agree that ending transactions quickly in order to release locks is of paramount importance and that transactional objects need to be deactivated to avoid consistency problems, but it doesn't follow from either observation that all transactional objects should be stateless. If a root object makes five calls to a nonroot object, there is no need to make the nonroot object stateless because deactivating it does not end the objects' declarative transaction. In this case, making the nonroot object stateless will actually slow things down, and RM locks will be held longer.

Similarly, if an ASP page makes three calls to a root object, there is no need to make the root object stateless because its declarative transaction will end when it is released, at the end of the page at the latest. As long as the root object runs in the same process as the ASP page, it does not hurt to allow its declarative transaction to span method calls. It will not be holding locks across multiple network roundtrips. With transactional objects, as with all JITA-based objects, the stateless style is a dramatic oversimplification. As long as you pay attention to managing RM locks efficiently, you can implement your transactional objects however you see fit. This is rule 6.2.

 **6.2**

A transactional object must manage RM locks efficiently (however, this does not imply that it must be stateless.)

## Root Objects and HRESULTs

The declarative transaction plumbing commits a transaction stream's distributed transaction when the stream's root object deactivates in the SetComplete state. However, there is no guarantee that its call to `ITransaction::Commit` will succeed. It may fail because a nonroot object in another context is unhappy or the transaction stream has been doomed. Or it may fail because an RM that is participating in the transaction votes no during phase one of the two-phase commit protocol. If an attempt to commit a transaction stream's distributed transaction fails, the declarative transaction service replaces the HRESULT the root object returned with the well-known failure code `CONTEXT_E_ABORTED`. It also walks the call stack and frees all the out parameters because COM clients do not expect to have to clean up out parameters when a method invocation fails. Note that this change is made only when a root object ends a method in the SetComplete state and its declarative transaction aborts. In all other cases, the root object's HRESULT is simply passed through to the client. Table 6-4 summarizes the relationship between root objects, the outcomes of their declarative transactions, and the HRESULTs returned to clients.

## Transaction Stream Caveats

There is one major caveat to programming with transaction streams. It springs from the fact that a transaction stream's root context never changes. Imagine a set of three transactional objects that represents a company's organizational chart. The first object represents the company, the second object represents a

**Table 6-4   Root objects and HRESULTs**

| Root Object Deactivates . . . | Declarative Transaction . . . | |
|---|---|---|
| | Commits | Aborts |
| Happy (SetComplete) | Root Object's HRESULT | CONTEXT_E_ABORTED |
| Unhappy (SetAbort) | Not Applicable | Root Object's HRESULT |
| | Client Sees . . . | |

department in the company, and the third object represents a group in a department. A client wants to use these three objects to give everyone in a particular group a raise. To do that, the client creates a company object and asks it for the appropriate department object. Then it asks the department object for the appropriate group object. Finally, the client asks the group object to update the human resources database to reflect a raise for all its members.

Figure 6-11 illustrates this object model. Obviously, if the client is accessing these three objects via DCOM, this scenario has some issues with regard to roundtrips. However, there is a much larger problem. The work done by the group object on the client's behalf cannot be committed until the transaction stream's root object deactivates. In this example, the company object is the root. So in order to finish its work, the client has to call back to the company object simply so it can deactivate and the declarative transaction can end. That means, however, that the client has to be aware of the special relationship between the company object and the group object. The client can never work with the group object alone; it always has to work with both objects in tandem. If the client releases the company object, the group object is useless. And if the special relationship between the two objects changes, that is, if the next version of the company object is nontransactional and the department object

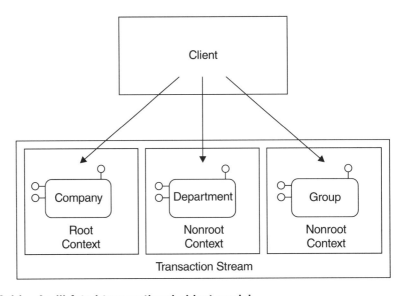

**Figure 6-11   An ill-fated transactional object model**

becomes the root of the transaction stream, the client has to be updated to reflect that.

This model puts far too heavy a burden on the client and leads to software that cannot be maintained over time. The solution to all these problems is simple, effective, and has a huge impact on how you design classes that use declarative transactions. A root object's use of nonroot objects is an implementation detail that should remain hidden from clients. Clients should create and call root objects and never see nonroot objects. In short, *do not expose a transaction stream's nonroot objects to clients*. This is Rule 6.3.

**RULE 6.3**

A transactional object should not expose a transaction stream's nonroot objects to clients.

It is important to note that Rule 6.3 does not prohibit *different* instances of a single class from being used as root objects that clients can access in some situations, and as nonroot objects that must remain hidden in other situations. Rule 6.3 only prohibits using the *same* instance both ways.

If a client can only see a transaction stream's root object, you cannot create transactional object models like the one just described. In fact, if a client can only see a transaction stream's root object, the only model for transactional objects that makes any sense is the one introduced in Chapter 1. Transactional objects should be processors that model client tasks, not just because a task-oriented focus leads to greater efficiency but also because the implementation of the COM+ declarative transaction service demands it. Together, Rule 6.3 and Rule 1.3 lead to Rule 6.4.

**RULE 6.4**

A transactional object must be a processor.

## Transaction Guidelines

Local transactions are significantly faster than distributed and declarative transactions because much less interprocess communication is required to create and commit or abort them. To optimize performance, COM+ classes should use local transactions whenever possible, that is, whenever they are working with individual RMs. COM+ classes should use declarative transactions whenever necessary, that is, whenever they are working with multiple RMs. Declarative transactions are favored over raw distributed transactions because they are significantly easier to work with. This approach minimizes the overhead transactions introduce, promotes better resource sharing, and increases scalability. It is codified in Rule 6.5.

 **6.5**

COM+ classes should use local transactions to protect work against a single RM and declarative transactions to protect work against multiple RMs.

Some COM+ developers reject Rule 6.5. Despite the performance benefits of local transactions, they choose to use declarative transactions in all cases because it provides a single programming model and is flexible in the face of change. I understand their position, but I do not accept it. First, there is no harm in having two programming models for local and declarative transactions as long as both are easy to use. You cannot convincingly argue that it is easier to end a transaction by calling `IContextState::SetMyTransactionVote` instead of `ITransaction::Commit` or `ITransaction::Abort`. Second, if you have to modify a class that works with one RM to work with multiple RMs, you have to change its code anyway, and you can easily switch it from using local transactions to using distributed transactions at the same time. Implementing classes to use declarative transactions "just in case" they will need to access multiple RMs increases overhead without providing any real benefit.

## Summary

COM+ adopts the object-per-client model to simplify development. COM+ uses transactions to extend its preferred concurrency model from middle-tier server processes to back-end databases. There are two types of transactions, local transactions and distributed transactions. Local transactions protect work done by a single client process against a single RM. You can control local transactions using SQL statements or using OLE DB or a higher-level data access API, such as the ATL OLE DB consumer templates or ADO. Distributed transactions protect work done by multiple client processes against multiple RMs. You can control distributed transactions using the DTC, which is made accessible through a simple COM object model. Distributed transactions are much more flexible than local transactions, but they are also a lot more complicated and significantly slower.

The COM+ declarative transaction service simplifies programming with distributed transactions by merging them with object context. Instances of classes that use declarative transactions are called transactional objects because they execute "inside" of distributed transactions. Transactional objects must support JITA and therefore always reside in their own contexts. The declarative transaction service uses transaction streams to map distributed transactions to collections of contexts. Transaction streams are created implicitly when transactional objects are created. The first context created in a transaction stream is the stream's root context. All the other contexts created in a transaction stream are nonroot contexts. A transaction stream stores a reference to a distributed transaction in a "well-known" place where code that wants to can access it. The OLE DB Service Components access a transaction stream's distributed transaction to autoenlist database connections. A transaction stream's distributed transaction ends when the stream's root object (i.e., the distinguished object in the stream's root context) deactivates. Every context in a transaction stream has a happy bit that can be manipulated via object context. Every transaction stream also has a doomed bit which gets set by the plumbing if a transactional object deactivates while it is unhappy. A transaction stream's distributed transaction can only commit if all of the objects in the stream are happy and the stream has not been doomed. The fact that a transaction stream's root never changes makes it impossible to build conventional object models using transactional objects. Transactional objects should always use the processor model.

For performance and scalability reasons, your COM+ classes should use local transactions to protect work against a single RM and declarative transactions to protect work against multiple RMs.

# Chapter 7
# Isolation

The introduction to transactions in Chapter 1 started with a discussion of the ACID properties (atomicity, consistency, isolation, and durability) exhibited by both local and distributed transactions. From a developer's perspective, consistency requires special attention. In COM+, middle-tier objects are transactional clients. Only the middle-tier object that starts a transaction can commit it because only that object knows when it has made all the changes necessary to leave a system in a new consistent state. If you are implementing a COM+ class that uses local, distributed, or declarative transactions, consistency is ultimately your responsibility. Databases help by enforcing constraints encoded in their schemas, but this doesn't work in all cases. For instance, you can't define a cross-database foreign-key constraint to guarantee that records in one database refer to existing records in another database. In situations like these, any mistake in the design or implementation of your transactions can easily damage the integrity of your system.

Consistency cannot be maintained if one transaction is allowed to see the intermediate results of a second transaction's ongoing work. If it does, the first transaction might make a decision based on a change to state that is undone when the second transaction aborts; for example, it might see an order that never gets placed or a stock purchase that is never made. It is impossible to maintain a system's integrity if these kinds of problems arise. The only solution is to make sure that a transaction's work completes—successfully or not—before any other transaction can see its results. Transactions must be isolated. In essence, each transaction must see the world as its own—as if it were the only transaction doing work in the system.

There is an unmistakable parallel between this idea and the COM+ object-per-client model. In fact, transactions are both the inspiration for that concurrency model and, as explained in Chapter 6, a natural extension to it. The object-per-client model is about isolation. Instead of forcing developers to implement classes that are both thread-safe and efficient, which is difficult, the object-per-client model simply replicates objects so that client tasks can be executing concurrently without interfering with one another. Clearly this approach will not work for *shared* state stored in a back-end database. The object-per-client model is reasonable, but the database-per-client model is not. It is up to individual databases to implement isolation using a combination of locking and versioning techniques. Rule 1.2 says that to maximize throughput (and, therefore, scalability), you must lock as little data as possible for as short a time as possible. You can't do that without understanding how your RM implements isolation and how you can tune your transactions to get the highest possible degree of concurrency. This chapter explores isolation in detail.

## Correctness versus Performance

Resource managers shoulder the burden of implementing transaction isolation efficiently. One way to implement isolation is to execute transactions one at a time. This approach guarantees consistency; each transaction sees the world, quite literally, as its own. But it is not efficient; this approach creates a massive bottleneck, lowering throughput and destroying scalability. To achieve high throughput, an RM must execute transactions concurrently, *but only when it is safe to do so*. Assume for a moment that a given RM naïvely favors performance over correctness and simply allows all transactions to execute concurrently, no matter what they do. In this case, four well-known problems may arise. They are described in Table 7-1, which lists them in order of decreasing severity, from lost updates to phantoms.[1]

All four of these problems represent violations of consistency that can damage the integrity of your system. If an RM favors correctness over performance, it constrains the concurrent execution of transactions just enough to ensure that

---

[1] These problems are well documented in both the transaction and database literature. However, most texts ignore the problem of lost updates. This reflects the position of the SQL-92 standard, which assumes that RMs will simply not allow them to occur. For complete coverage of all four problems, see *Transaction Processing: Concepts and Techniques* by Gray and Reuter.

**Table 7-1   Four potential problems**

| Problem | Description |
|---------|-------------|
| Lost updates | A transaction's changes to a record are overwritten by a second transaction *before* the first transaction commits or aborts. |
| Dirty reads | A transaction's changes to a record are visible to a second transaction *before* the first transaction commits. |
| Unrepeatable reads | A transaction reads the same *record* twice and gets different results because, in between the reads, a second transaction modified the record. |
| Phantoms | A transaction reads the same *set of records* twice and gets different results because, in between the reads, a second transaction added a record to or removed a record from the set. |

none of these four problems arises. This presents a challenging problem: How does an RM know if it is safe to allow concurrent execution of transactions?

An RM can safely assume that two transactions can run in parallel if they do not access the same data. When two transactions do access the same data, an RM has to decide whether it is safe for both of them to continue or whether one should be temporarily blocked. An RM makes this decision based on what the transactions are doing. If they are simply reading the same data, they can execute concurrently. If one or both transactions are writing the same data, they may or may not be able to execute concurrently. This seems straightforward, but it has some fairly far-reaching implications. For example, an RM cannot *assume* that a transaction that reads some data once will not read it a second time. Instead, an RM must ensure that once a reading transaction has accessed some data, that data does not change until that reading transaction ends. If the data did change and the reading transaction accessed it a second time, it would get different results—this is the essence of both the unrepeatable read and phantom problems. The illusion that the transaction is the only one in the world would be shattered, and consistency might be lost. To avoid these problems, an RM must block writing transactions from accessing data a reading transaction has accessed until that reading transaction ends. An RM could behave differently if it *knew* what a transaction was going to do. For instance, if an RM knew that a reading transaction that accesses some data accesses it only once (or accesses it twice but doesn't care if it gets different results), the RM could let other writing transactions access the data *before* the reading transaction ended. That would increase concurrency and, therefore, throughput. But how can an RM know what a transaction is going to do? An RM has no idea what a transaction is going to do until it does it, that is, until an object submits a request through an enlisted connection. In the absence of that knowledge, RMs must err on the side of caution, even if concurrency and throughput suffer.

Unlike RMs, which have no way of knowing in advance what transactions are going to do, an object that uses a transaction knows exactly what it is going to do. An object can give the RM(s) it works with categorical hints about the problems its transaction is implicitly guaranteed *not* to encounter simply because of its logic. For instance, the phantom problem can arise only when a transaction reads the same set of records twice. If an object knows that its transaction will not reread any records, it can tell its RM(s) not to bother protecting against phantoms. This improves concurrency and throughput.

**Five Degrees of Isolation**

When an object starts a transaction, it marks it with a necessary *degree of isolation*. A transaction's degree of isolation indicates which, if any, of the four problems listed in Table 7-1 the transaction is implicitly guaranteed *not* to encounter simply because of its logic. An RM can use a transaction's degree of isolation to tune its isolation behavior and improve concurrency. There are five well-known degrees of isolation, or *isolation levels*. They are listed in Table 7-2, which shows that each degree or level of isolation is identified by number and by name (some levels have alternative names as well). Each level represents a point on the spectrum between performance, on the left, and consistency, on the right. At level 3, consistency is ensured. None of the four potential problems listed in Table 7-1 can arise. Level 3 is appropriately named "Serializable" because it allows transactions to execute concurrently while maintaining the illusion that transactions are executing serially, one after another. At each isolation level below 3, performance is higher, but one or more of the possible problems can arise. At isolation level 0, performance is highest, but all four of the possible problems can arise. Level 0 is appropriately named "Chaos" because consistency is forsaken.

**Table 7-2  The five well-known isolation levels**

| Degree | 0 | 1 | 2 | 2.99 | 3 |
|---|---|---|---|---|---|
| Name | Chaos | Read Uncommitted | Read Committed | Repeatable Reads | Serializable |
| Alternative Name | | Browse | Cursor Stability | | Isolated |
| Lost Updates? | Yes | No | No | No | No |
| Dirty Reads? | Yes | Yes | No | No | No |
| Unrepeatable Reads? | Yes | Yes | Yes | No | No |
| Phantoms? | Yes | Yes | Yes | Yes | No |

The implementation of isolation varies from RM to RM. Databases take one of two general approaches to the problem. One is based on locking data; the other is based on versioning data. You cannot implement a transactional system that is correct, let alone efficient, without knowing which approach a given database takes and without understanding that technique.

## Implementing Isolation Using Locks

Many databases, including SQL Server 7+, implement isolation using two types of record-level locks. Read locks, also called shared locks, allow multiple transactions to read a piece of data simultaneously. Write locks, also called exclusive locks, allow an individual transaction to write a piece of data only when no other locks are held. Table 7-3 shows how read and write locks affect each other. If a transaction attempts to acquire a read lock for data that is either not locked for write access or is locked for read access, the request is granted. If a transaction attempts to acquire a read lock for data that is locked for write access, the request is blocked until the write lock is released. If a transaction attempts to acquire a write lock for data that is not locked, the request is granted. Finally, if a transaction attempts to acquire a write lock for data that is locked by another transaction for either read or write access, the request is blocked until all the locks are released. In short, used in concert, read locks and write locks provide multireader, single-writer access to data.

**Table 7-3    Read locks and write locks**

| Attempt to Acquire . . . | If . . . | | |
|---|---|---|---|
| | No Lock Is Held | A Read Lock Is Held | A Write Lock Is Held |
| Read Lock | Granted | Granted | Blocked |
| Write Lock | Granted | Blocked | Blocked |
| | Request Is . . . | | |

Some databases use page-level locking instead of record-level locking. A page is the basic unit of storage in a database (in SQL Server 7, a page is 8 KB). Page-level locking is less efficient than record-level locking when transactions access few records because they block other transactions from acquiring locks against other records that happen to be on the same page. Page-level locking is more efficient than record-level locking when transactions access lots of records on the same page because less lock data has to be maintained. Databases that use record-level locking typically switch to page-level (or even table-level) locking dynamically for queries that access lots of contiguous records.

Before I can show you how read and write locks are used to implement isolation, I have to introduce two academic terms that describe how they are used by transactions. A transaction is *well formed* if it acquires the appropriate type of lock (i.e., a read lock or a write lock) before it attempts a particular action and releases it after the action completes, as follows.

```
ReadLock(A)
Read(A)
ReadUnlock(A)
ReadLock(B)
Read(B)
ReadUnlock(B)
```

A well-formed transaction is also *two-phase* if it acquires all the locks it needs before it releases any of them, as follows.

```
ReadLock(A)
Read(A)
ReadLock(B)
Read(B)
ReadUnlock(A)
ReadUnlock(B)
```

A two-phase transaction acquires locks incrementally when it touches data and holds them until it ends. A two-phase distributed transaction releases locks during phase two of the two-phase commit protocol.

With these two terms in mind, I can now explain how the five degrees of isolation are realized through locking. Table 7-4 is an extended version of Table 7-2 with three additional rows inserted in the middle. The extra rows show how transactions at each isolation level use read locks, write locks, and locks against metadata to address the four problems listed in Table 7-1. The abbreviation EOT stands for "end of transaction" and indicates when a two-phase transaction releases its locks, that is, when it ends. If you read from left

**Table 7-4   Implementing isolation using locks**

| Degree | 0 | 1 | 2 | 2.99 | 3 |
|---|---|---|---|---|---|
| Name | Chaos | Read Uncommitted | Read Committed | Repeatable Reads | Serializable |
| Alternative Name | | Browse | Cursor Stability | | Isolated |
| **Write Locks** | **Well-formed** | **Two-phase (EOT)** | **Two-phase (EOT)** | **Two-phase (EOT)** | **Two-phase (EOT)** |
| **Read Locks** | **None** | **None** | **Well-formed** | **Two-phase (EOT)** | **Two-phase (EOT)** |
| **Read Locks against Metadata** | **None** | **None** | **None** | **None** | **Two-phase (EOT)** |
| Lost Updates? | Yes | No | No | No | No |
| Dirty Reads? | Yes | Yes | No | No | No |
| Unrepeatable Reads? | Yes | Yes | Yes | No | No |
| Phantoms? | Yes | Yes | Yes | Yes | No |

to right, it becomes apparent that each incremental step in isolation uses more locks and exhibits fewer problems.

Transactions running at isolation level 0 are well formed with respect to writes. Because they acquire write locks before changing data, they will not overwrite changes made by transactions running at isolation levels higher than 0. Level 0 transactions suffer from lost updates, dirty reads, unrepeatable reads, and phantoms.

Transactions that execute at isolation level 1 or higher are two-phase with respect to writes. Because they acquire *and hold* write locks before changing data, other transactions cannot overwrite their changes while they are in progress. Level 1 or higher transactions do not suffer from lost updates.

Transactions that execute at isolation level 2 or higher are *at least* well formed with respect to reads. Because they acquire read locks before examining data, they cannot examine data that other transactions have write locked. Level 2 or higher transactions do not suffer from dirty reads.[2]

Transactions that execute at isolation level 2.99 or higher are two-phase with respect to reads. Because they acquire *and hold* read locks before examining data, other transactions cannot change data they have read until they end. Level 2.99 or higher transactions do not suffer from unrepeatable reads.

Transactions that insert or delete records have to acquire write locks against the records they affect. They also have to acquire write locks against the metadata that describe the range of data (e.g., either portions of an index or the size of a table) they are changing. Transactions that execute at isolation level 3 or higher are two-phase with respect to *reading* the metadata that describe a range of data. Because they acquire and hold read locks against metadata before examining a range of data, other transactions cannot add to or remove from the range. Level 3 transactions do not suffer from phantoms.

### Implementing Isolation Using Versions
Other RMs, including Oracle 8i, implement isolation by keeping multiple versions of a piece of data, each one representing the data's value at a given time.

---

[2] Actually, changes made by a level 0 transaction are visible to a level 2 transaction before the level 0 transaction commits because level 0 transactions are only well formed with respect to writes. If anyone uses isolation level 0, the result is chaos.

Table 7-5 illustrates the idea. There are multiple versions of the data X that represent its value at given points in time. Specifically, X was 10 from time $t0$ until time $t1$; it was 35 from time $t1$ until time $t2$; it was 47 from time $t2$ until time $t3$; and it has been 50 since time $t3$.

A transaction reads data by examining one of the versions in its history. Because old versions of data are never updated, read operations do not have to acquire locks. A transaction writes data by appending a new version (or a marker indicating that the data has been deleted) to its history. A new version is not actually appended, and so cannot be seen by *other* transactions, until a transaction commits. Up to that point, a new version of data is visible only to the transaction that writes it. Versions of data must be recorded in sequence, so if one transaction appends a new version to a history, other transactions must be blocked from appending versions until the first transaction successfully commits. This rule is enforced using two-phase, exclusive record-level write locks. A transaction must acquire a write lock before it can create a new version of a piece of data.

The versioning scheme eliminates the lost update problem implicitly. Because data is never updated in place, one transaction's changes to a record cannot overwrite another's. Instead, each transaction's changes simply become separate versions of the record as it appeared at different times. Because a new version of a record is not visible to other transactions until the transaction that

**Table 7-5  Multiple versions of a piece of data**

| X | |
| --- | --- |
| At Time $t$ ... | Value Is ... |
| $t3 \leq t \leq$ present | 50 |
| $t2 \leq t < t3$ | 47 |
| $t1 \leq t < t2$ | 35 |
| $t0 \leq t < t1$ | 10 |

writes it commits, dirty reads are also implicitly resolved. In short, under the versioning system, transactions cannot run at either isolation level 0 or 1.

Whether the unrepeatable read or phantom problems arise depends on which version of data a transaction reads. Every transaction is marked with the time that it started. When a transaction reads a piece of data, it can read either the latest visible version or the version that existed when the transaction started. If a transaction reads the latest visible version of data, it can see changes made by other transactions that have committed since it started. That means it can suffer from both unrepeatable reads and phantoms; that is, it runs at isolation level 2. If a transaction reads the versions of data from the time it started, it cannot see changes made by other transactions that have committed since then. That means it cannot suffer from either unrepeatable reads or phantoms; that is, it runs at isolation level 3. Since the unrepeatable read problem cannot be solved without solving the phantom problem too, transactions cannot run at isolation level 2.99.

It is worth noting that the versioned histories of data can be truncated to save space. An old version of a piece of data needs to be kept only as long as there is a level 3 transaction that started *before* that version was created that might want to read it. Only the latest visible version of a piece of data needs to be kept to satisfy transactions running at isolation level 2. They never read anything else.

Table 7-6 is another extended version of Table 7-2 with two additional rows inserted in the middle. The extra rows summarize how transactions at each isolation level use versioned data to address the four problems listed in Table 7-1.

Many people like the versioning approach to isolation because there are no read locks and, therefore, attempts to read data never block. Certainly in cases where transactions *only* read data, this is good. However, if transactions read and then write data, the lack of read locks can be problematic. Imagine a record that represents a counter. A level 3 transaction, A, starts, but before it can do anything, another transaction, B, increments the value of the counter by 1, changing it from 5 to 6. When transaction B commits, a new version of the counter record with the value 6 is appended to the record's history and becomes visible to other transactions. However, transaction A is running at isolation level 3 and cannot see the new counter value. Instead, transaction A sees

Table 7-6 Implementing isolation using versioning

| Degree | 0 | 1 | 2 | 2.99 | 3 |
|---|---|---|---|---|---|
| Name | Chaos | Read Uncommitted | Read Committed | Repeatable Reads | Serializable |
| Alternative Name | | Browse | Cursor Stability | | Isolated |
| **Write Locks** | Not Applicable | Not Applicable | **Two-phase (EOT)** | Not Applicable | **Two-phase (EOT)** |
| **Data Read** | Not Applicable | Not Applicable | **Latest Visible Version** | Not Applicable | **Version When Transaction Started** |
| Lost Updates? | Not Applicable | Not Applicable | **No** | Not Applicable | **No** |
| Dirty Reads? | Not Applicable | Not Applicable | **No** | Not Applicable | **No** |
| Unrepeatable Reads? | Not Applicable | Not Applicable | Yes | Not Applicable | **No** |
| Phantoms? | Not Applicable | Not Applicable | Yes | Not Applicable | **No** |

the version of the counter record that existed at the time it started, when the counter's value was 5. If transaction A were allowed to increment the counter, it would append another version with a duplicate value of 6, and the usefulness of the counter would be lost. So transaction A cannot be allowed to update the counter. In general, a transaction that is running at isolation level 3 cannot safely update a record that has been changed by another transaction since it started.[3] This problem makes designing a system more difficult because there is an implicit race condition between level 3 transactions and other transactions that attempt to write the same data concurrently.

If transaction A ran at isolation level 2, it would be allowed to update the counter, whether transaction B had updated it after transaction A started or not. That's because level 2 transactions see the latest visible versions of data, not the versions that existed when they started.

This problem gets a bit more complicated if transaction A wants to read the counter in one SQL statement and then update it in a later SQL statement. In

---

[3] Oracle returns ORA-08177; it cannot serialize access for this transaction to indicate that this problem has occurred.

this case, transaction A has to have a way to guarantee that the counter does not get modified between the time it is read and the time it is updated. In short, transaction A needs a way to force a write lock against the counter when it *reads* it. RMs that implement isolation using versioning typically provide a way to do this. For example, transactions in Oracle can forcibly acquire a write lock using the PL/SQL SELECT ... FOR UPDATE statement.

### Choosing an Isolation Level

A transaction's isolation level is a key part of its design. However, determining which isolation level is appropriate for a given transaction can be quite tricky. The answer depends on what a transaction does and what other transactions do. It also depends on whether the target RM implements isolation using locking or versioning.

Consider a simple order-tracking system that stores information in an order table and a line-item table. Records in the two tables are linked by a foreign key relationship. Two transactions interact with this system. One transaction removes an order by deleting first its line items and then the order itself using the following SQL statements. The line items are removed first to avoid violating the table's foreign key constraint.

```
delete from lineitems where orderid = n    [w1]
delete from orders where orderid = n        [w2]
```

The other transaction reads an entire order using these SQL statements.

```
select * from lineitems where orderid = n  [r1]
select * from orders where orderid = n      [r2]
```

If these two transactions run at the same time, there is a chance that their statements will be interleaved. To avoid consistency problems when both transactions affect the same records, both transactions must be properly isolated.

Isolating the writing transaction is easy. If it runs at isolation level 1, it will be two-phase with respect to writes. Because the writing transaction does not read dirty reads, unrepeatable reads, or phantoms are not problems. RMs that use versioning to implement isolation do not support isolation level 1. In this case, the writing transaction should run at isolation level 2.

Isolating the reading transaction is more difficult. The conventional wisdom is that reading transactions can run at lower levels of isolation than writing transactions. However, this is not the case. In fact, in this example, the reading transaction has to run at a *higher* level of isolation than the writing transaction. Let me explain why.

Assume that the order system is deployed in an RM that uses read locks to implement isolation. If the two transactions' statements happened to execute in the following order and the reading transaction ran at isolation level 2, it would see line items without an order—a violation of the consistency of the system.

1. Read transaction starts.
2. [r1] acquires well-formed read locks, reads order's line items, releases locks.
3. Write transaction starts.
4. [w1] acquires two-phase write locks, deletes order's line items, holds locks.
5. [w2] acquires two-phase write lock, deletes order, holds lock.
6. Write transaction commits, releases locks.
7. [r2] attempts to read order, but it is gone.
8. Read transaction ends.

The foreign key constraint encoded in the order system schema cannot prevent this violation of consistency. Line items never exist without an associated order; it just appears that way from the reading transaction's point of view. The problem is that level 2 transactions are only well formed with respect to reads. The solution is to run the reading transaction at an isolation level that is two-phase with respect to reads so that it holds onto its read locks until it ends. Running the reading transaction at isolation level 2.99 or higher would change the order of operations, as follows.

1. Read transaction starts.
2. [r1] acquires two-phase read locks, reads order's line items, holds locks.
3. Write transaction starts.
4. [w1] attempts to acquire two-phase write locks to delete order's line items, blocks.
5. [r2] acquires two-phase read lock, reads order, holds lock.
6. Read transaction commits, releases locks.
7. [w1] resumes, acquires two-phase write locks, deletes order's line items, holds locks.

8. [w2] acquires two-phase write lock, deletes order, holds lock.
9. Write transaction commits, releases locks.

In this case, the first read operation, r1, acquires locks that cause the first write operation, w1, to block. The writing transaction will wait until the reading transaction completes before deleting the order and its line items. If the writing transaction started first, the reading transaction would wait, and when it finally ran, it would not see either an order or its line items. Either way, consistency is guaranteed. You may think that it would be simpler to solve this problem by rewriting the reading transaction to read an order and then its line items. In that case, however, the order of the preceding operations would cause a deadlock, and one of the transactions would have to be aborted (more about deadlock shortly). It is preferable to resolve the problem by using the appropriate isolation level.

The same problem arises (for a different reason) if the order system is deployed in an RM that uses versioning to implement isolation. Once again, if the two transactions' statements happen to execute in the following order and the reading transaction ran at isolation level 2, it would see line items without an associated order—a violation of the consistency of the system.

1. Read transaction starts.
2. [r1] reads latest visible versions of order's line items.
3. Write transaction starts.
4. [w1] acquires two-phase write locks, deletes order's line items, holds locks.
5. [w2] acquires two-phase write lock, deletes order, holds lock.
6. Write transaction commits, releases locks; new versions become visible.
7. [r2] reads latest visible version of order; it is gone.
8. Read transaction ends.

The problem is that level 2 transactions read the latest visible version of a piece of data. One solution is to run the reading transaction at an isolation level that reads the version of a piece of data that was visible when it started. Running the reading transaction at isolation level 3 would change the order of operations as follows.

1. Read transaction starts.
2. [r1] reads versions of order's line items that were visible when transaction started.

3. Write transaction starts.
4. [w1] acquires two-phase write locks, deletes order's line items, holds locks.
5. [w2] acquires two-phase write lock, deletes order, holds lock.
6. Write transaction commits, releases locks.
7. [r2] reads version of order that was visible when transaction started.
8. Read transaction ends.

In this case, the second read operation, r2, doesn't see the changes made by the second writing, w2. Instead, the reading transaction sees the order and its line items as they were at the time it started, before the writing transaction deleted them. This resolves the issue; consistency is guaranteed.

Another way to solve the problem is to run the reading transaction at isolation level 2 and force it to acquire two-phase write locks using an RM-specific technique (e.g., Oracle's SELECT... FOR UPDATE syntax). Rewriting the reading transaction that way would change the order of operations as follows.

1. Read transaction starts.
2. [r1] acquires two-phase write locks, reads latest visible version of order's line items *for update,* holds locks.
3. Write transaction starts.
4. [w1] attempts to acquire two-phase write locks to delete order's line items, blocks.
5. [r2] reads latest visible version of order.
6. Read transaction commits, releases lock.
7. [w1] resumes, acquires two-phase write locks, deletes order's line items, holds locks.
8. [w2] acquires two-phase write lock, deletes order, holds lock.
9. Write transaction commits, releases locks.

This is simply a variation on the solution used with a locking RM. The first read operation, r1, acquires a lock that causes the first write operation, w1, to block so that the two transactions do not execute at the same time. Again, consistency is guaranteed. The disadvantage of this approach is that the read operation r1 now acquires an exclusive lock and a key benefit of version-based isolation (i.e., that reads do not acquire locks) is lost.

It is worth noting that there is an entirely different approach to isolating the order system's reading transaction that works on *both* locking and versioning

RMs. If the reading transaction were rewritten to execute only a single statement that joined an order and its line items, it could run safely at isolation level 2 (without acquiring write locks in the versioning case). Because individual SQL statements always execute atomically (this is part of the SQL-92 specification), this approach guarantees consistency as well. Here is an example.

```
select * from orders full outer join lineitems on orders.orderid =
lineitems.orderid where orders.orderid = n
```

The downside is that the join will return a rectangular set of results with one copy of the order record for each line item.

### Isolation-Level Guidelines

At this point, it should be fairly obvious that choosing the appropriate isolation level for a transaction is complicated, especially for transactions that read data. The answer varies depending on what the transaction does, what the other transactions in the system do, and whether the underlying RM implements isolation by locking or versioning data. Selecting appropriate isolation levels promotes efficient use of resource usage and, therefore, scalability. Unfortunately, there are no specific rules for choosing isolation levels. You must analyze how concurrent transactions are going to use the data in your system. With this analysis, and knowledge of the locking and versioning behaviors described in this section, you must come up with a set of guidelines that is specific to the RM(s) you are using and the application you are building. Table 7-7 summarizes the general guidelines that I follow for selecting a transaction's isolation level. Bear in mind that they cannot account for all possible situations. The first column describes the transaction. The second and third columns list the isolation levels for locking RMs and versioning RMs, respectively, that I apply by default.

Selecting an isolation level for a transaction that reads or writes but does not do both is fairly straightforward. Selecting an isolation level for a transaction that reads and writes is quite difficult and depends entirely on the transaction's logic. If you aren't sure what isolation level to use for a given transaction, you should favor consistency and protect it completely. This is easy on an RM that uses read locks because isolation level 3 ensures that none of the four possible isolation problems ever occur. This is harder on a versioning RM because isola-

**Table 7-7   Isolation-level guidelines**

| Transaction . . . | RM Locks Data (e.g., SQL Server) | RM Versions Data (e.g., Oracle) |
|---|---|---|
| Only writes | 1, read uncommitted, or higher | 2, read committed |
| Reads once or reads multiple times but does not require consistency | 2, read committed | 2, read committed |
| Reads multiple times and does require consistency | 2.99, repeatable read; or 3, serializable | 2, read committed, with exclusive locks; or 3, serializable |
| Reads and writes data | Depends on logic | Depends on logic |

tion level 3 suffers from the race condition just described, and isolation level 2 suffers from unrepeatable reads and phantoms. A combination of isolation level 2 and exclusive locks is usually the best bet in this case.

Some people might argue that you should always protect all transactions completely simply because selecting more appropriate isolation levels is too difficult. This approach guarantees consistency, but depending on what your transactions do, it may be much slower than necessary. Given the impact of locking on scalability (remember Rule 1.2), I can't condone this point of view.

## Specifying Isolation Levels

From an RM's perspective, isolation level is actually a property of a connection, not a transaction. The initial isolation level of a brand new connection is RM-dependent, but most databases (including both SQL Server and Oracle) use isolation level 2, read committed, as the default.[4] In general, the lowest-level API for specifying a connection's isolation level is the SET TRANSACTION ISOLATION LEVEL statement defined by SQL-92. For example, the following TSQL statement sets the isolation level of a connection to SQL Server to 2.99, repeatable read.

```
set transaction isolation level repeatable read
```

---

[4] The SQL-92 specification defines isolation level 3, serializable, as the setting for new connections. This is a better default because it guarantees consistency in all cases.

According to the SQL-92 specification, the SET TRANSACTION ISOLATION LEVEL statement changes a connection's isolation level for the *next* transaction. Under SQL Server, however, the SET TRANSACTION ISOLATION LEVEL statement changes a connection's isolation level immediately, even if a transaction is in progress. SQL Server also allows you to change the isolation level for a single select statement by using a TSQL-specific "table hint." Here is an example.

```
select au_fname, au_lname from authors (repeatable read)
```

This SELECT statement runs at isolation level repeatable read, independent of the connection's isolation level. Under Oracle, the SET TRANSACTION ISOLATION LEVEL statement changes a connection's isolation level immediately, even if a transaction is in progress, but it will fail if it is not the first statement in the transaction. Under other RMs, the SET TRANSACTION ISOLATION LEVEL statement may behave differently.

### Isolation Levels and OLE DB

You must specify an initial isolation level when you start a local transaction with OLE DB. The ITransactionLocal::StartTransaction method takes an isolation level flag as its first parameter. It is up to a provider's session object to execute the appropriate SQL statements to set the underlying connection's isolation level to the requested value. The flag is of type ISOLEVEL, an alias for long, but OLE DB providers actually expect a value from the ISOLATIONLEVEL enumerated type.

```
typedef enum ISOLATIONLEVEL
{
  ISOLATIONLEVEL_UNSPECIFIED = 0xffffffff,
  ISOLATIONLEVEL_CHAOS = 0x10,
  ISOLATIONLEVEL_READUNCOMMITTED = 0x100,
  ISOLATIONLEVEL_BROWSE = 0x100,              // same as READUNCOMMITTED
  ISOLATIONLEVEL_READCOMMITTED = 0x1000,
  ISOLATIONLEVEL_CURSORSTABILITY = 0x1000,  // same as READCOMMITTED
  ISOLATIONLEVEL_REPEATABLEREAD = 0x10000,
  ISOLATIONLEVEL_SERIALIZABLE = 0x100000,
  ISOLATIONLEVEL_ISOLATED = 0x100000        // same as SERIALIZABLE
} ISOLATIONLEVEL;
```

Here is an example.

```
CComPtr<ITransactionLocal> spLocalTx = GetSessionSomehow();
hr = spLocalTx->StartTransaction(ISOLATIONLEVEL_REPEATABLEREAD,
                                 0, 0, 0);
if (FAILED(hr)) return hr;
```

Needless to say, a given OLE DB provider may not accept all of the ISOLATION LEVEL values. For instance, SQL Server supports only isolation levels 1 and higher, so SQLOLEDB does not accept ISOLATIONLEVEL_UNSPECIFIED, and it treats ISOLATIONLEVEL_CHAOS as ISOLATIONLEVEL_READUNCOMMITTED. The ISOLEVEL parameter is typed as a long to allow you to pass 0 (as you can with the grfTC parameter to ITransaction::Commit) to indicate that you want to use the parameter's default value. Some OLE DB providers may support this option for local transactions. SQLOLEDB does not.

The ATL OLE DB consumer templates and ADO both provide support for specifying a local transaction's isolation level. In ATL, isolation level is passed as an argument to CSession::StartTransaction.

```
CSession sess;
hr = GetSessionSomehow(&sess);
hr = sess.StartTransaction(ISOLATIONLEVEL_REPEATABLEREAD)
```

In ADO, isolation level is passed using the Connection class's Isolation Level property.

```
Dim conn As Connection;
Set conn = GetSessionSomehow()
conn.IsolationLevel = asXactRepeatableRead
conn.BeginTrans
```

### Isolation Levels and the DTC

You must also specify an initial isolation level when you start a distributed transaction with the DTC. The ITransactionDispenser::BeginTransaction method takes an ISOLEVEL flag as its second parameter. The DTC accepts all values of ISOLATIONLEVEL and 0 for this parameter. It isn't picky because it simply stores the requested isolation level as part of the metadata for a newly created distributed transaction. However, when you enlist a connection against a distributed transaction using ITransactionJoin, an OLE DB provider may be picky and refuse to join if the distributed transaction is running at an isolation level the underlying database does not support. For example, SQLOLEDB will refuse to enlist against a distributed transaction that was created with an `ISOLEVEL` of `ISOLATIONLEVEL_UNSPECIFIED` or 0. It will enlist against a distributed transaction created with `ISOLATIONLEVEL_CHAOS`, but it treats it as `ISOLATIONLEVEL_READUNCOMMITTED`. Alternatively, an OLE DB provider may simply ignore a distributed transaction's isolation level and choose a different level for a connection that is being enlisted. OLE DB providers for Oracle take this approach. Newly enlisted Oracle connections always join a distributed transaction at `ISOLATIONLEVEL_READCOMMITTED`, independent of the isolation level that was specified when the distributed transaction was started.

The `ITransactionJoin::JoinTransaction` method also takes an `ISOLEVEL` as its second parameter. In theory, this flag allows you to override a provider's default enlistment behavior and explicitly set the isolation level for a newly enlisted connection. However, OLE DB providers are not required to implement this functionality. SQLOLEDB, for instance, ignores the flag you pass and sets the connection's isolation level based on the value specified by the distributed transaction.[5] In general, you should not expect the isolation-level flag you pass to `JoinTransaction` to have any effect at all on a connection's isolation level. You should always pass the distributed transaction's isolation level, whatever it is. You can retrieve a distributed transaction's isolation level by calling `ITransaction::GetTransactionInfo`. Here is an example.

```
// get a distributed transaction from DTC
CComPtr<ITransaction> spDistTx = GetDistributedTransactionSomehow();
// extract transaction information
XACTTRANSINFO info;
hr = spDistTx->GetTransactionInfo(&info);
// get an OLE DB session
CComPtr<ITransactionJoin> spJoinTx = GetSessionSomehow();
// enlist using transaction's isolation level for 2nd isolevel
hr = spJoinTx->JoinTransaction(spDistTx, info.isoLevel, 0, 0);
```

This code calls `ITransaction::GetTransactionInfo` to retrieve an `XACTTRANSINFO` structure that describes the distributed transaction. It passes

---

[5] Oddly enough, the flag you pass has to be one that SQLOLEDB considers valid (i.e., not `ISOLATIONLEVEL_UNSPECIFIED` or 0), or `JoinTransaction` fails.

the distributed transaction's isolation level, which is stored in the `info` struc-ture's `isoLevel` field, to `ITransactionJoin::JoinTransaction` when it enlists a new connection.

## Isolation Levels and COM+

The declarative transaction service is designed to hide the details, including isolation level, of distributed transaction management. When the runtime creates a new distributed transaction for a transaction stream, it favors correct-ness over performance and always passes `ISOLATIONLEVEL_SERIALIZABLE` to `ITransactionDispenser::BeginTransaction`. When you autoenlist a SQL Server connection against a declarative transaction, the connection's isola-tion level is set to match the distributed transaction's isolation level. When you autoenlist an Oracle connection against a declarative transaction, the connec-tion's isolation level is always set to `ISOLATIONLEVEL_READCOMMITTED`, independent of the distributed transaction's isolation level. These isolation lev-els are reasonable defaults given that the declarative transaction service does not know what the objects in a transaction stream are going to do.

## Bring Your Own Transaction

The next version of the COM+ declarative transaction service will allow you to tailor isolation levels on a per-class basis. You can approximate this functional-ity today by leveraging a little-known COM+ mechanism called *bring your own transaction* (BYOT). BYOT allows you to attach an existing distributed trans-action to a new transaction stream. The heart of BYOT is a simple, nonconfig-ured factory class. The BYOT factory implements an interface called `ICreate WithTransactionEx`:

```
interface ICreateWithTransactionEx : IUnknown
{
  HRESULT CreateInstance([in] ITransaction *pTransaction,
                         [in] REFCLSID rclsid,
                         [in] REFIID riid,
                         [iid_is(riid), out] void **pObject);
}
```

The `CreateInstance` method creates a new object of the requested type. If the object is transactional, its transaction stream is seeded with the

DTC-managed distributed transaction passed as the first parameter.[6] Here is an example of its use.

```
HRESULT CSomeNonTxCfgClass::DoWorkWithOwnDeclarativeTx(void)
{
  // acquire reference to DTC proxy core object (PCO)
  CComPtr<ITransactionDispenser> spTxDisp = GetPCOSomehow();
  // start a distributed transaction at the desired isolation
     level
  CComPtr<ITransaction> sptDistTx;
  HRESULT hr = spTxDisp->BeginTransaction(0,
                        ISOLATIONLEVEL_REPEATABLEREAD, 0, 0,
                        &sptDistTx);
  if (FAILED(hr)) return hr;
  // create an instance of the BYOT factory class
  CComPtr<ICreateWithTransactionEx> spBYOTFactory;
  hr = spBYOTFactory.CoCreateInstance("BYOTServerEx.BYOT");
  if (FAILED(hr)) return hr;
  // use the BYOT factory object to create a transactional object
  CComPtr<ISomeTxClass> spTxObj;
  hr = spBYOTFactory->CreateInstance(sptDistTx,
                           __uuidof(SomeTxClass),
                           __uuidof(spTxObj),
                           (void**)&spTxObj);
  if (FAILED(hr)) return hr;
  ... // do some work with the transactional object
  // commit the distributed transaction
  hr = sptDistTx->Commit(FALSE, XACTTC_SYNC_PHASEONE, 0);
  if (FAILED(hr)) return hr;
  return S_OK;
}
```

The DoWorkWithOwnDeclarativeTx method wants to work with a transactional object, but it wants that object to work at isolation level 2.99, repeatable read. It acquires a reference to a PCO and uses it to start its own distributed transaction running, setting ISOLATIONLEVEL_REPEATABLEREAD as the isolation level. Then it creates an instance of the BYOT factory class, using its ProgID instead of its CLSID because, although the BYOT factory class's interfaces are defined in a header file, the factory class itself is not. When it is

---

[6] The BYOT factory object also implements an interface called ICreateWithTip TransactionEx with a single method CreateInstance that takes a TIP URL in place of a reference to a distribute transaction object as its first parameter.

done using the transactional object, `DoWorkWithOwnDeclarativeTx` calls `Commit` to end the distributed transaction.

When you use BYOT, the object that creates the distributed transaction and the BYOT factory object become, in essence, the root of a new transaction stream. The objects the BYOT factory creates are nonroot objects in the transaction stream. This architecture is shown in Figure 7-1. Object A in context A used a BYOT factory object to create object B. Object B created object C using `CoCreateInstance[Ex]`. Objects B and C both live in nonroot contexts in transaction stream P. Object A is the "root" of the stream.

Note that BYOT fully integrates with the transaction stream mechanism. In fact, nonroot objects cannot tell that they are in a BYOT-initiated transaction stream. When you attempt to `Commit` a BYOT-initiated transaction stream's distributed transaction, all of the appropriate processing takes place. If one of the stream's remaining objects is unhappy or the stream's doomed bit has been set, the transaction will abort, and Commit will return the well-known error code `CONTEXT_E_ABORTED`.

Remember that the declarative transaction service has to acquire an activity lock in order to examine the happy bits of a transaction stream's contexts. That work is done asynchronously on a separate thread and, therefore, a separate

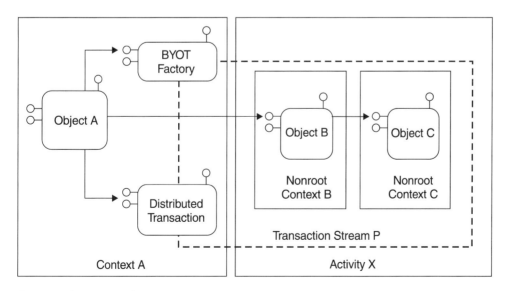

**Figure 7-1  The BYOT architecture**

causality. The BYOT factory class is nonconfigured, so new instances always live in their creator's context. If you create a BYOT factory object in a context within an activity, the transactional objects the BYOT factory creates will live in a transaction stream in that activity. If you call `ITransaction::Commit` from the thread whose causality owns the activity's lock, the declarative transaction service's thread will not be able to enter the activity to see if the objects in the transaction stream's contexts are happy. However, the call to `Commit` cannot complete until the happy bits are checked, so the system deadlocks.[7] You can solve this problem by using BYOT only from contexts that are not in activities. In fact, this provides an admittedly esoteric but compelling reason to mark a configured class something other than `COMAdminSynchronization Required` or `COMAdminSynchronizationIgnored`, that is, `COMAdmin SynchronizationNone`. This is the technique depicted in Figure 7-1—transaction stream P is not fully scoped by activity X. You can also solve this problem by deploying the BYOT factory class in a library application and marking it `COMAdminSynchronizationRequiresNew` so that the transactional objects it creates share its activity but not the activity of its creator.

The BYOT architecture violates Rule 6.3 by exposing nonroot objects to a client, that is, the object that is using BYOT. BYOT gets a special dispensation from Rule 6.3 specifically because, in this one case, the object that is using BYOT knows exactly what is going on. Note that BYOT-created objects are associated with not just a transaction stream, but also a particular distributed transaction. The relationship is established when the objects are created, and it cannot be changed over time. Because there is no way to reassociate an existing object with another distributed transaction, a "root" object that uses BYOT should release the nonroot objects it creates when its distributed transaction ends. They are useless after that point.

It is debatable whether using BYOT is a good idea. It is an obscure feature that is not part of the main COM+ toolkit. (The fact that the Platform SDK documentation does not include a header file with the BYOT factory class's CLSID is quite telling.) It is very powerful, but it is also quite dangerous because, among other things, you can use it to introduce parallelism in a single declara-

---

[7] This is a great example of the second activity-related deadlock scenario described in Chapter 4.

tive transaction. For example, in Figure 7-1, transaction stream P is not fully scoped by activity X. If you do introduce parallelism, you're on your own. The declarative transaction service can no longer protect you. I include BYOT here for completeness. The next version of the declarative transaction service may make adjusting a distributed transaction's isolation level easier. Until it does, unless you are completely comfortable with contexts, activities, and transaction streams, it is best to avoid BYOT and use SQL statements to adjust a declarative transaction's isolation levels on a per-connection basis.

### ISOFLAGs

There is one more thing that I need to mention about isolation levels. All three of the methods that take an `ISOLEVEL` as an input parameter (that is, `ITransactionLocal::StartTransaction`, `ITransactionDispenser ::BeginTransaction`, and `ITransactionJoin::JoinTransaction`) take an additional input parameter of type `ISOFLAG`. In theory, an `ISOFLAG` lets you tell RMs to extend isolation beyond a transaction's lifetime, so locks are held even *after* a transaction commits or aborts. This feature is not supported. You should always pass 0 for this argument.

## Deadlocks

Both techniques for implementing isolation rely on locks. If two transactions each lock a different resource and each want, but cannot acquire, a lock against the other's resource, neither transaction can progress, and the result is deadlock. This is simply a form of the notorious "deadly embrace" that arises in any concurrent system that uses multiple locks. The longer a transaction holds onto locks, the greater the chance of a deadlock. This is one of the reasons transactions need to hold locks as briefly as possible. However, even transactions that hold locks only briefly must have a strategy for dealing with deadlocks.

### Avoiding Deadlocks

The best strategy for dealing with deadlocks is to avoid them. This is possible in simple scenarios if you implement your transactions correctly. Some deadlocks can be avoided if all transactions acquire locks in the same order. The writing transaction presented in the previous section deletes an order's line items and then an order so that it does not violate the line items' foreign key constraint. The reading transaction reads an order's line items and then an order simply to avoid deadlocking with a writing transaction that happens to run concurrently. This is important if the reading transaction is isolated using locks, which, as explained earlier in this chapter, may be the case even on a versioning RM.

Some deadlocks in locking RMs can also be avoided if all transactions that read and then write the same piece of data acquire write locks before they begin. If multiple transactions share a read lock against the same data, none of them can escalate to a write lock. If multiple transactions try, they'll deadlock. Transactions can avoid this problem by forcibly acquiring an exclusive lock when they first read the data they plan to update. SQL Server uses update locks to support this "intent to write" locking semantic. Update locks block write locks and other update locks, but not read locks. As long as each transaction that is going to read and then write the same data uses an update lock, lock escalation deadlocks do not occur. Update locks are acquired using another TSQL-specific table hint. Here is an example.

```
select * from orders (updlock) where orderid = 'n'
```

SQL Server update locks are morally equivalent to the exclusive update locks acquired in Oracle using the SELECT ... FOR UPDATE statement mentioned earlier, although here the concern is with efficiency not correctness.

Unfortunately, although both these techniques work in simple cases, avoiding deadlocks by coordinating the order and type of lock acquisition across all the transactions in a complex system would be extremely difficult. Realistically, deadlock avoidance is impossible in a large distributed system.

### Detecting Deadlocks

If transactions cannot avoid deadlocks, they must have a way to *detect* deadlocks. Deadlocks can be detected by a *wait-for graph* that tracks which transactions are waiting for which locks. A cycle in a wait-for graph indicates a deadlock that must be broken. Wait-for graphs are often used to detect deadlocks *inside* individual RMs. In general, if two transactions (it doesn't matter whether they are local or distributed) deadlock in a single RM, the RM will notice the problem and abort one of them.

Wait-for graphs cannot reasonably be used to detect deadlocks *across* multiple RMs. Maintaining a wait-for graph across either machine or RM vendor boundaries is simply unmanageable. The only reasonable way to detect deadlocks across RMs is to use a *timeout*. In other words, a transaction is given a finite amount of time in which to complete. Any transaction that does not commit within its allotted time is assumed to be deadlocked and is aborted, whether it is really deadlocked or not. It is tempting to push the timeout period up to accommodate long-running transactions. The problem with high timeouts is that, if a transaction does deadlock, it takes a long time to resolve the problem. For example, if a transaction with a 5-minute timeout deadlocks after only 5 seconds of execution, you have to wait 4 minutes and 55 seconds for it to abort.

### Timeouts and the DTC

Timeouts are the only reasonable way to detect deadlocks involving distributed transactions. When you ask the DTC to start a new distributed transaction, you have the option of specifying a timeout. If you do, the timer starts running as soon as the distributed transaction is created. It stops running when you call `ITransaction::Commit` (or, trivially, `ITransaction::Abort`). If time runs out before you call `Commit`, the distributed transaction expires and is automatically aborted by the DTC. If a distributed transaction times out and is aborted while the object that is using it is waiting for a call into a database to complete, the call is interrupted and immediately returns. If an object calls into a database through a connection that is enlisted against a distributed transaction that has timed out, the database rejects it. SQLOLEDB returns `DB_E_ERRORSINCOMMAND` in this case. If an object attempts to commit a timed-out distributed transaction `ITransaction::Commit` fails with the well-known error code `XACT_E_TIMEOUT`. It is important to note that if you do not specify a timeout and your distributed transaction deadlocks, you will have to find the problem yourself and resolve it by hand by restarting one or more parts of your system. Timeouts should be considered nonoptional for distributed transactions.

You specify the timeout for a new distributed transaction by passing a reference to a transaction option's object as the fourth parameter to `ITransaction`

`Dispenser::BeginTransaction`. A transaction options object is just a thin wrapper around an XACTOPT structure.

```
typedef struct XACTOPT
{
  ULONG ulTimeout;
  char szDescription[40];
} XACTOPT;
```

The ulTimeout field specifies a transaction's timeout in milliseconds. A ulTimeout value of 0 means that there is no timeout at all. The szDescription field specifies a transaction's name, which is displayed in the Component Services Explorer's Distributed Transaction Coordinator Transaction List. You can acquire a transaction options object from the DTC by calling ITransactionDispenser::GetOptionsObject. It returns a reference of type ITransactionOptions, defined as follows.

```
interface ITransactionOptions : IUnknown
{
  HRESULT SetOptions(XACTOPT *pOptions);
  HRESULT GetOptions(XACTOPT *pOptions);
};
```

The two methods of ITransactionOptions simply provide access to the structure the object wraps. Here is an example that shows how to use an options object to set a distributed transaction's timeout.

```
// given a pointer to a PCO
CComPtr<ITransactionDispenser> spTxDisp = GetPCOSomehow();
// get a transaction options object
CComPtr<ITransactionOptions> spTxOpts;
hr = spTxDisp->GetOptionsObject(&spTxOpts);
if (FAILED(hr)) return hr;
// set up XACTOPT structure
XACTOPT opts = { 0 };
opts.ulTimeout = 10000;
// put structure into options object
hr = spTxOpts->SetOptions(&opts);
if (FAILED(hr)) return hr;
// start a distributed transaction
CComPtr<ITransaction> spDistTx;
hr = spTxDisp->BeginTransaction(0, ISOLATIONLEVEL_SERIALIZABLE, 0,
                                spTxOpts, &spDistTx);
```

This code acquires a reference to a PCO and retrieves a transaction options object by calling `ITransactionDispenser::GetOptionsObject`. It fills in an XACTOPT structure, specifying a timeout of 10,000 milliseconds (10 seconds). It pushes the XACTOPT structure into the options object by calling `ITransactionOptions::SetOptions`. Then it passes a reference to the transaction options object as the fourth parameter to `ITransaction Dispenser::BeginTransaction` when it creates a new distributed transaction and the DTC sets the new transaction's timeout.

**Timeouts and COM+**

When you start a distributed transaction with the COM+ declarative transaction service, the plumbing sets the transaction's timeout automatically. The service uses three declarative attributes to control transaction timeouts. They are listed in Table 7-8. The first attribute, `TransactionTimeout`, specifies the default timeout for all declarative transactions started on a machine. Its value can range from 0 (no timeout) to 3,600 seconds (one hour). The default value for `TransactionTimeout` is 60 seconds. Individual classes can specify their own timeout values by setting their `ComponentTransactionTimeoutEnabled` and `ComponentTransactionTimeout` attribute. `ComponentTransaction TimeoutEnabled` is a flag that tells the declarative transaction service that a class wants to use its own timeout. `ComponentTransactionTimeout` is a value between 0 (no timeout) and 3,600 seconds (one hour). A declarative transaction's timeout is always based on the default timeout for the machine where it starts or the class-specific timeout for the initial object created in the transaction stream, that is, the stream's root object. The class-specific timeout values for nonroot objects and the machinewide default timeout values for the machines where nonroot objects run are ignored. If you use BYOT, you can specify a timeout when you create your distributed transaction using the technique described in the previous section. In this case, the class-specific timeout values for nonroot objects and the machine-specific timeout values for the servers where they run are still ignored.

The `ITransactionJoin::JoinTransaction` method gives you the option of specifying a timeout when you enlist a connection against a distributed transaction. In theory, this allows you to override a distributed transaction's

**Table 7-8   Transaction timeout attributes**

| Attribute | Type | Default | Notes |
|---|---|---|---|
| TransactionTimeout | Long, 0–3,600 | 60 | Per-machine default timeout in seconds |
| ComponentTransaction TimeoutEnabled | Boolean | False | Enables per-class timeout |
| ComponentTransaction Timeout | Long, 0–3,600 | None | Per-class timeout in seconds |

timeout and give a particular database less time to finish its work, but this feature is not supported. If you pass an `ITransactionOptions` reference to SQLOLEDB's implementation of `JoinTransaction`, for instance, it will fail with the well-known error code, `XACT_E_NOTIMEOUT`. You should always pass 0 for this argument.

**Timeouts and OLE DB**

Timeouts are not the only reasonable way to detect deadlocks involving local transactions. RMs typically detect deadlocks between local transactions using wait-for graphs, which are practical in a single process. As a result, although OLE DB's `ITransactionLocal::StartTransaction` method accepts a reference to a transaction options object as its third parameter, providers generally don't support specifying a timeout for a local transaction. If you pass a reference to a transaction options object that specifies a timeout to SQLOLEDB's implementation of `ITransactionLocal::Start Transaction`, for instance, it will fail with the well-known error code `XACT_E_NOTIMEOUT`. If you are using an RM that does not support timeouts for local transactions, you should always pass 0 for this argument.

If your RM doesn't support timeouts for local transactions, you should also be very careful to avoid deadlocks. The RM can detect and resolve deadlocks that arise entirely in its process, but it cannot detect deadlocks that involve other processes. For example, imagine an MTA-based object that starts a local transaction and executes some SQL statements that acquire two-phase locks. Then, between calls to the database and while its local transaction is running, the MTA-based object calls to a subordinate object that happens to run in an STA. Unfortunately, another object in that STA is calling into the database and waiting to acquire the locks the MTA-based object's local transaction holds. In this case, the MTA-based object cannot complete its call and then end its local transaction until the STA thread is free. But the STA thread will not be free until the MTA-based object completes its call and ends its local transaction. The result is deadlock. Unfortunately, in this case there is nothing the database can do because it does not know about all of the locks. Specifically, it does not know about the implicit lock an STA thread represents. The simplest solution to this problem is to insist that local transactions complete in a single roundtrip to the database so that an object never holds locks while it is doing nondatabase work. Another solution is to make sure that a COM+ object that uses a local transaction does not attempt to acquire resources—including STA threads—that might cause it to block until after its transaction completes.

## Application-Level Isolation

To minimize locking, transactions should be designed to execute quickly. However, many systems need to lock data for extended periods of time. For example, interactive systems that allow users to check out records, edit them, and then update them need some way to lock those records across "user think time." You might be tempted to solve this problem by creating long-running transactions, but this is not a good idea. If you protect the data with an RM lock, you must accept the policies of the RM's lock manager, and they are designed with short-lived transactions in mind. For instance, in an RM that uses locking to implement isolation, a write lock blocks read requests that are executed at isolation level 2 or higher. This is okay for transactions that are brief, but should checking out a record for an extended period block other reads? If you rely on the RM's lock manager to protect the checked out record, you have little control over this policy. You could work around it by mandating that reading transactions run at isolation level 1, dirty read, but that has other broad repercussions. Beyond lock management policies, using a long-running transaction to protect data for extended periods has another major downside. A database connection can be participating only in a single local or distributed transaction at any given time. As long as a transaction is running, its connection can't be used for anything else. Database connections are notoriously precious resources. Binding them to objects, which are in turn bound to clients, in order to keep their transactions running creates a major bottleneck in a system. For both these reasons, you should not use a long-running transaction and RM locks to protect data for an extended time.

The best way to protect data over time is to use application-level locks. Application-level locks are a combination of logic and durable state that provides whatever locking semantics you desire. For example, if you create an application-level lock to protect a record that's been checked out for editing, you get to decide whether that lock should block reads, let them see the record, or force them to skip the record and continue. Once you move to application-level locks, you can use two transactions to read and write the data you are locking, thereby minimizing restrictive RM locking and freeing database connections for others to use. While creating application-level locks requires work on your part, the increased flexibility and better resource sharing they offer are well worth the effort.

### Optimistic Application-Level Locking

There are two kinds of application-level locking, optimistic and pessimistic. Optimistic application-level locking isn't really locking at all. You implement optimistic application-level locks simply by closing your eyes really tight, crossing your fingers, and thinking, "Boy, I hope the data I'm reading in this transaction doesn't change before I update it in that transaction!" Of course, if the data you're hoping won't change does change, you have to have some way to detect and deal with that.

If a database table includes a timestamp column, detecting a change is easy. A timestamp is just a counter that is automatically incremented whenever a record is changed. For example, the `customers` table defined with the following T-SQL statement includes a timestamp column called `modified`.

```
create table customers (
  id integer not null,
  name varchar (32) not null,
  address varchar(32) not null,
  modified timestamp not null,
  primary key (id)
)
```

When a transaction reads a `customer` record, it selects the timestamp column and returns the result, as follows.

```
select name, address, modified as oldtime from customers
       where id = n
```

When a second transaction updates the record, it compares the original timestamp value to the current timestamp value. If the timestamps are different, the second transaction knows the record has changed since the first transaction read it. If the record *hasn't* changed, the second transaction can update it. However, if the record *has* changed, the second transaction has to figure out what to do. It could overwrite the modified record with its own changes, or it could discard its own changes. Here is an update statement that takes the latter approach.

```
update customers set name = '...', address = '...' where id = n
       and modified = oldtime
```

The UPDATE statement's WHERE clause ensures that the statement will not modify a record that has been changed since it was read. Other strategies for reconciling changes to optimistically "locked" records are possible, but increasingly complex. You can apply this technique to tables that do not have timestamps as long as they have a field that every transaction is guaranteed to set to a unique value.

### Pessimistic Application-Level Locking

Optimistic application-level locking is a form of gambling. As long as the risk that another transaction will change the data you are "protecting" is low, being optimistic pays off. For example, the optimistic approach is perfect in the classic online shopping cart scenario where each user's cart is isolated implicitly. As the risk that another transaction will change "protected" data rises, however, optimistic application-level locking becomes less useful because more and more transactions have to spend time reconciling their changes with changes made by other transactions. If "reconciling changes" means discarding them and starting over—as it did in the previous example—users will not be happy. In short, when contention for data is high, optimistic locking is a bad bet. You need to do more than hope data won't change between the time it is read and the time it is updated. You need to use pessimistic application-level locking instead.

You implement pessimistic application-level locking by marking records as owned by particular users. The lock state is stored durably in the database itself and at a minimum it includes an owner ID and expiration time. The owner ID— a username, an IP address, or some other identifier—uniquely identifies the client that owns the lock. The expiration time indicates when the client's lock should time out if the client does not come back to release it. Transactions that modify records must be implemented to explicitly check lock state before proceeding.

The preceding `customers` example can be extended to support pessimistic locking by adding a new table to track customer locks. The T-SQL statement that defines the `customerlocks` table follows.

```
create table customerlocks (
  customerid integer not null,
  owner varchar (32) not null,
  expires datetime not null,
  primary key (customerid),
  foreign key (customerid) references customers
)
```

Each `customerlock` record represents a lock against a particular customer record, as identified by the record's `customerid`. The `customerid` field is used as both a primary and a foreign key to ensure that there is no more than one lock per customer and that the customer actually exists. The locks are stored in a separate table in order to save space. If they were added to the `customers` table, there would have to be space allocated for a lock for each row, whether the row was locked or not.

Access to the `customers` table is encapsulated using a pair of stored procedures that use the `customerlocks` table to manage application-level pessimistic locks. The `sp_readcustomerforupdate` stored procedure attempts to check out a customer record by locking it and then reading it. Here is the definition.

```
create procedure sp_readcustomerforupdate
  @customerid integer,
  @caller varchar(32)
```

```
as
  set nocount on
  declare @owner as varchar(32)
  declare @expires as datetime
  -- start a local transaction (unless using dist tx)
  begin transaction
    -- check lock owner id and expiration time
    select @owner = owner, @expires = expires from
          customerlocks (updlock, serializable)
          where customerid = @customerid
    if (@owner is null) begin
      -- if no owner, make caller owner
      insert into customerlocks (customerid, owner, expires)
            values (@customerid, @caller, DATEADD(mi, 5,
            GETDATE()))
      if (@@rowcount = 1)
        select @owner = @caller
      else
        raiserror('cannot insert lock record', 1, 1)
    end else if (DATEDIFF(mi, @expires, GETDATE()) > 0) begin
      -- else if lock expired, make caller owner
      update customerlocks set owner = @caller, expires =
            DATEADD(mi,5,GETDATE()) where customerid =
            @customerid
      if (@@rowcount = 1)
        select @owner = @caller
      else
        raiserror('cannot update lock record', 1, 1)
    end
    if (@owner = @caller) begin
      -- if caller is now owner, read info
      select name, address from customers where id = @customerid
      if (@@rowcount = 1) begin
        -- if everything works, commit (unless using dist tx)
        commit
        return 0
      end
    end else
      raiserror('someone else has customer record locked', 1, 1)
  -- if something failed, rollback (even if using dist tx)
  rollback
  return -1
```

Before sp_readcustomerforupdate reads a customer record, it checks the customerlocks table to see if someone is holding a pessimistic lock. If the customer record has no current owner, @owner, the procedure inserts a new record into customerlocks to indicate that its caller, @caller, has taken a pessimistic lock against it that will expire in 5 minutes. If the customer record has a current owner whose lock has expired, sp_readcustomerforupdate updates the record in customerlocks to indicate that its caller, @caller, has taken over the pessimistic lock against it, and the lock is reset to expire in 5 minutes. Then, if and only if the caller has acquired the necessary pessimistic lock, the procedure selects the requested customer record.

The sp_writecustomer stored procedure attempts to check in a customer record by updating and unlocking it. Here is the definition.

```
create procedure sp_writecustomer
  @customerid integer,
  @caller varchar(32),
  @new_name varchar(32),
  @new_address varchar(32)
as
  set nocount on
  declare @owner as varchar(32)
  declare @expires as datetime
  -- begin local transaction (unless using dist tx)
  begin transaction
    -- check lock owner id and expiration time
    select @owner = owner from customerlocks
           (updlock, serializable)
           where customerid = @customerid
    -- if caller is owner
    if (@owner = @caller) begin
      -- remove lock
      delete from customerlocks
             where customerid = @customerid
      if (@@rowcount = 1) begin
        -- update information
        update customers set name = @new_name,
               address = @new_address
               where customerid = @customerid
        if (@@rowcount = 1) begin
          commit
          return 0
        end else
          raiserror('could not update customer', 1, 1)
```

```
        end else
          raiserror('could not delete lock', 1, 1)
      end else
        raiserror('caller does not own customer lock', 1, 1)
    rollback
    return -1
```

Before `sp_writecustomer` writes a customer record, it checks the `customer locks` table to see if someone is holding a pessimistic lock against it. If and only if the caller, `@caller`, owns the lock, the procedure releases it and updates the customer record.

The `sp_readcustomerforupdate` and `sp_writecustomer` stored procedures need to be isolated to work correctly. The key is to make sure that only one stored procedure is able to select and possibly insert or update a given customer lock record at any given time. To that end, both stored procedures use local transactions to acquire and hold database locks while they do their work. To guarantee the correct semantics, both stored procedures use two TSQL-specific table hints when they attempt to select a customer's lock record. The `updlock` hint forces the acquisition of an exclusive update lock against the customer's lock record. If multiple instances of the stored procedures are executed in parallel with the same customer ID, the `updlock` hint will cause all but one of them to block. A stored procedure's transaction cannot acquire an update lock against a customer lock record if one does not exist. To ensure proper isolation in this case, the stored procedures must protect against phantoms. To that end, they also use the `serializable` table hint. Selecting from the `customerlocks` table at isolation level 3 forces each transaction to acquire an update lock against the `customerlocks` table's metadata (a range in either its index or its size). If the stored procedures execute concurrently with the same customer ID, the `serializable` hint will cause all but one of them to block even when a customer does not have a lock record.

This approach to protecting a checked out customer record for an extended time is certainly more complex than relying on a long-running transaction that uses write locks. However, despite the additional complexity, it is preferable because it realizes the two advantages of application-level locking described earlier: It allows you to define locking policies independent of an RM and to reuse database connections while users are interactively editing records.

# Summary

COM+ objects use transactions to extend the object-per-client model from middle-tier processes to back-end databases, that is, they are transactional clients. If you are implementing a COM+ class that uses local, distributed, or declarative transactions, it is up to you to ensure that its instances always leave your system in a consistent state. Consistency cannot be maintained if transactions are not properly isolated. It is up to RMs to implement isolation efficiently. By default, RMs ensure that transactions are completely isolated so that no problems arise. This is safe, but it is also slow and often unnecessary. A transactional client can, at its discretion, give an RM a categorical hint indicating that a transaction will not encounter certain problems simply because of its logic. An RM can use this information to tune its isolation behavior to increase concurrency and throughput. These hints are represented by a transaction's isolation level. Choosing an appropriate isolation level for a transaction is a difficult task. Some databases, like SQL Server 7, implement isolation using a combination of read locks and write locks. Some databases, like Oracle 8i, implement isolation using a combination of versioned histories of data and write locks. You cannot choose a transaction's isolation level without knowing how your RMs implement isolation and how the data in your system is going to be used.

Both techniques for implementing isolation rely on locks, so transactions must have a strategy for dealing with deadlocks. Some deadlocks can be avoided if all transactions acquire the right kinds of locks in the right order. However, in complex systems it is essentially impossible to avoid deadlocks; transactions have to rely on deadlock detection instead. Deadlocks that occur entirely in a single RM can be detected by a wait-for graph. Deadlocks that occur across processes can be detected using timeouts.

Systems that need to lock data for extended periods of time (e.g., across "user think time") should use application-level locks. Application-level locks are a combination of logic and durable state that provides whatever locking semantics you desire. Application-level locks are more flexible than normal database locks because they do not have to abide by an RM's stringent locking policies. They are more efficient than RM locks because they are not bound to a particular database connection that has to remain open over time. There are two types of application-level locking, optimistic and pessimistic. Optimistic application-level locking isn't really locking at all; it is simply gambling that the data being "protected" won't change. Pessimistic application-level locking actually protects data by marking records as owned by particular users for particular periods of time.

# Chapter 8

# Protocols

DCOM is the standard protocol for invoking methods on COM+ objects in remote contexts, but it is not the only communication protocol that COM+ applications rely on. Most COM+-based systems also use the Hypertext Transfer Protocol (HTTP) because it is Internet-friendly, easy to load-balance, and can be integrated with clients on many platforms. HTTP has traditionally been used to create browser-based user interfaces, but some clients use it as a lightweight RPC protocol. Increasingly, those clients adopt the Simple Object Access Protocol (SOAP), which formalizes the use of HTTP and the Extensible Markup Language (XML) as a way to encode and transmit a function's call stack from one process to another.

Internet Information Server (IIS) is the standard HTTP server for Windows 2000. It is layered directly on top of the COM+ runtime and provides two APIs that allow you to implement your own HTTP (or SOAP) request handlers: the low-level Internet Server API (ISAPI) and the high-level Active Server Pages (ASP). These two mechanisms integrate HTTP (and SOAP) processing with contexts and causalities in different but related ways. In addition to DCOM and HTTP, some COM+ applications use Microsoft Message Queue (MSMQ) to build custom communication protocols. MSMQ is also integrated with COM+, albeit in a much different manner from that of either DCOM or HTTP. This chapter explores these alternative protocols.

## HTTP

HTTP is a message-based request/response protocol. HTTP clients, called User-Agents, send request messages to HTTP servers over TCP connections, asking to invoke specific methods on specific endpoints called resources. Resources are uniquely identified by Uniform Resource Locators (URLs). A URL is a Uniform

Resource Identifier (URI) that includes information about how to access a resource. (Uniform Resource Names, URNs, are URIs that do not specify location or retrieval information. URNs are not used in HTTP.) An HTTP URL contains a DNS name (or an IP address), an optional IP port number (80 is the default), and an absolute path; together they identify a resource managed by a server process on a specific machine. Here is the syntax of an HTTP URL.

```
http://host:port/absolute-path
```

Here is an example of an HTTP URL.

```
http://store.company.com:8080/ordersystem/buy
```

In this case, `store.company.com:8080` identifies the target server and `/ordersystem/buy` identifies the desired resource. An HTTP server waits for a client request message to arrive, invokes the specified method on the specified resource, and returns a response message that describes the method's outcome.

### HTTP Messages

HTTP request and response messages include a plain-text request or a status line, respectively, a set of plain-text headers, and an optional message body represented as a stream of bytes. Message headers are newline delimited name/value pairs. They are separated from a message's body by a double newline. The size of a message's body can be indicated explicitly by using the `Content-Length` header or implicitly by closing a TCP connection. A message body's type is indicated explicitly by using the `Content-Type` header. The `Content-Type` header's value is a MIME-type identifier (e.g., `text/xml`). Here is an example.

```
<request or status line>
Content-Type: text/xml
Content-Length: 68

<PlaceOrder><Item>Ketchup</Item><Quantity>20</Quantity></PlaceOrder>
```

This message body's type is `text/xml`, and its size is 68 bytes. A request message can include an `Accept` header that indicates which MIME types the sending User-Agent is willing to accept in the body of a response message (e.g., `Accept: text/xml`).

HTTP request messages always start with a request line that includes a method to perform, a URI to perform the method on, and the version of the HTTP protocol being used. Here is the general syntax.

```
METHOD Request-URI HTTP-Version
```

HTTP 1.1 defines seven well-known methods that can be invoked on resources. The two most common methods are `GET` and `POST`. The `GET` method retrieves information identified by the `Request-URI`. A `GET` request message cannot include a body, and server processing of `GET` requests must be idempotent, that is, repeatable without side effects. The `POST` method sends information to the `Request-URI` to be processed. A `POST` request message can include a body, and server processing of `POST` requests does not have to be idempotent.

A `Request-URI` is either a complete URL (e.g., `http://store.company.com:8080/ordersystem/buy`) or the absolute path from the end of a URL (e.g., `/ordersystem/buy`). Under HTTP 1.1, request messages that use the latter format must include a `Host` header that identifies the destination machine's name and optional port number (e.g., `Host: store.company.com:8080`). Together, an absolute path `Request-URI` and a `Host` header provide the same information as a complete URL.

Here is a sample request message that uses a complete URL as a `Request-URI`.

```
POST http://store.company.com:8080/ordersystem/buy HTTP/1.1
Accept: text/xml
Content-Type: text/xml
Content-Length: 68

<PlaceOrder><Item>Ketchup</Item><Quantity>20</Quantity></PlaceOrder>
```

Here is a version of the same request message with an absolute path as a `Request-URI`. Note the use of the `Host` header in this case.

```
POST /ordersystem/buy HTTP/1.1
Host: store.company.com:8080
```

```
Accept: text/xml
Content-Type: text/xml
Content-Length: 68

<PlaceOrder><Item>Ketchup</Item><Quantity>20</Quantity></PlaceOrder>
```

The `Accept` header in both request messages indicates that the sending User-Agent is only willing to accept responses encoded in XML.

HTTP response messages always start with a status line that includes the version of the HTTP protocol being used and a number and phrase indicating the status of the request. Here is the general syntax.

```
HTTP-Version Status-Code Reason-Phrase
```

A `Status-Code` is a three-digit number. The first digit indicates the category of the response; the next two digits indicate the exact outcome. HTTP 1.1 defines five well-known response categories, which are listed in Table 8-1.

HTTP 1.1 also defines quite a few well-known `Status-Codes` and corresponding `Reason-Phrases`. The most common ones are listed in Table 8-2. Here is a sample response message.

```
HTTP/1.1 200 OK
Content-Type: text/xml
Content-Length: 68

<PlaceOrderResponse><OrderId>1049</OrderId></PlaceOrderResponse>
```

The `Status-Code` and `Reason-Phrase` (200 OK) indicate that the User-Agent's request was successfully processed.

**Table 8-1  HTTP Status-Code categories**

| Status-Code | Category | Meaning |
|---|---|---|
| 1xx | Informational | Request is still being processed. |
| 2xx | Success | Request was successfully processed. |
| 3xx | Redirection | Further action must be taken to complete request. |
| 4xx | Client error | Request was invalid and cannot be processed. |
| 5xx | Server error | Request was valid but cannot be processed. |

**Table 8-2   Common HTTP Status-Codes**

| Status-Code | Reason-Phrase | Meaning |
| --- | --- | --- |
| 200 | OK | Request was successfully processed |
| 400 | Bad request | Request was malformed |
| 401 | Unauthorized | Access denied |
| 403 | Forbidden | Illegal method request |
| 404 | Not found | Unknown resource |
| 500 | Internal server error | Server failure |
| 501 | Not implemented | Server doesn't implement HTTP feature |

## HTTP Connection Management

HTTP is often referred to as a connectionless protocol, but that is a little misleading. A User-Agent has to establish a TCP connection with a server in order to send a request and receive a response, so a connection does exist. Further, under HTTP 1.1, once a connection is established it stays open by default (under HTTP 1.0, a User-Agent and a server had to negotiate to keep a connection alive using `Keep-Alive` headers). A connection is closed when a User-Agent or a server sends a request or response message that includes a `Connection: close` header. For example, the presence of the `Connection` header in the following request message tells the server that the TCP connection should be closed after its response message is sent.

```
POST /ordersystem/buy.dll HTTP/1.1
Host: store.company.com:8080
Connection: close
Accept: text/xml
Content-Type: text/xml
Content-Length: 58

<PlaceOrder><Item>Ketchup</Item><Quantity>20</Quantity></PlaceOrder>
```

Most HTTP User-Agents and servers do not hold connections open for extended periods of time. Instead, they close connections after a burst of communication. Because of this usage style, HTTP is generally considered a connectionless protocol.

# Internet Information Server

Internet Information Server (IIS) is the HTTP server built into Windows 2000. IIS integrates the HTTP protocol with COM+. The heart of IIS is a service called `inetinfo.exe` that spends its time waiting for an HTTP request to arrive, invoking the specified method on the specified resource, and sending a response back to the client. HTTP is widely used in COM+-based applications, so the mechanics of IIS must be well understood.

### Mapping Requests to Files

Each HTTP request message operates on a particular resource that is uniquely identified by a URL. When a request arrives, IIS translates the message's target URL (possibly reconstituted from an absolute path and a `Host` header) into a path identifying a (possibly executable) file on disk. The scheme it uses to map URLs to files is based on a logical tree that organizes the HTTP-accessible resources on a machine. The structure of the tree is defined in the IIS *metabase.* The metabase stores IIS configuration information; it is the moral equivalent of the COM+ catalog. The metabase can be managed programmatically through a hierarchical object model with `IISComputer` at its root. The metabase can also be managed interactively via the Internet Services Manager (ISM), a Microsoft Management Console snap-in built on top of the metabase's object model.

Figure 8-1 shows the basic structure of IIS's logical tree. The root of the tree is the IIS service itself, `inetinfo.exe`. Each instance of the service has one or more *sites*. Each site corresponds to one or more unique combinations of IP address, IP port number, and optional DNS name. (A site may have two port numbers for a given IP address/DNS name pair, one for normal HTTP traffic, and one for secure HTTPS traffic sent over a Secure Sockets Layer (SSL) connection.) Each site is the root of a virtual directory hierarchy. Each virtual directory corresponds to a specific physical directory hierarchy somewhere on disk, as shown in Figure 8-2. The physical directories, shown in rectangles, are grafted onto the logical tree structure and form its outermost branches and leaves.

IIS interprets each URL as a path through its logical tree that locates a specific resource. A URL's address and port identify a site. A URL's absolute path identifies at least a virtual directory, which maps to a physical directory. The

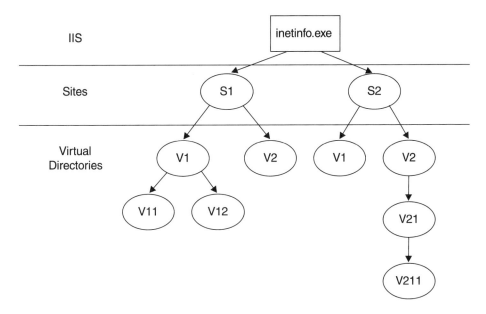

**Figure 8-1    The basic structure of IIS's logical tree**

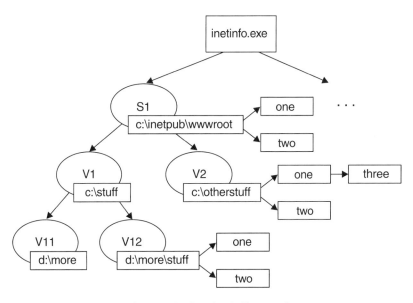

**Figure 8-2    Virtual directories and physical directories**

end of a URL's absolute path may also identify a physical subdirectory, a specific file, or both. If an absolute path identifies a directory but not a file, IIS maps the URL to a default file. You can configure a priority-ordered list of default files on a per-directory basis. Table 8-3 lists several sample absolute paths and the directories and files they map to. The mapping is based on site S1 in the logical tree depicted in Figure 8-2.

Once IIS has identified the file a request message applies to, it has to invoke the specified method against it. The target file type determines the way this is done. If the target file is static (e.g., an XML file), `inetinfo.exe` invokes the method against the file itself. The most common method applied to a static resource is GET, which IIS implements by returning a response message that includes the contents of the target file as its body. If the target file is dynamic (i.e., a DLL or an executable), `inetinfo.exe` loads and executes it, asking it to process the request message and generate a response message to send back to the calling User-Agent. File extensions are mapped to executable code using the `ScriptMaps` property in the metabase. If a DLL or executable is asked to process a request message that targets a static file, it can retrieve the name of that file if desired. (Note that an HTTP request message's URL can identify an arbitrary nonexecutable file that does not actually exist on disk as long as that file's extension is associated with either a DLL or an executable that can process the message.)

If clients are using HTTP to invoke operations on COM+ objects on middle-tier servers, request messages that apply to static files are useless. Each request message needs to target a dynamic file that knows how to translate the mes-

Table 8-3  Sample absolute path mappings for site S1

| URL | Path to File |
| --- | --- |
| / | c:\inetpub\wwwroot\<default file> |
| /one/data.xml | c:\inetpub\wwwroot\one\data.xml |
| /v1 | c:\stuff\<default file> |
| /v1/v11/info.xml | d:\more\info.xml |
| /v1/v12/two/org.xml | d:\more\stuff\two\org.xml |
| /v2/one/three | c:\otherstuff\one\three\<default file> |

**Table 8-4   The four EXTENSION_CONTROL_BLOCK functions**

| Function | Purpose |
|---|---|
| GetServerVariables | Reads HTTP request message headers (and pseudoheaders added by server) |
| ReadClient | Reads HTTP request message body |
| ServerSupportFunction | Writes HTTP response message headers (and performs miscellaneous ISAPI operations) |
| WriteClient | Writes HTTP response message body |

sage's body into one or more method calls against one or more objects. DLLs are the preferred way to do this because they are significantly more efficient than executables. Once a DLL is loaded, it can be used to service any number of requests. IIS defines the ISAPI as the standard interface for DLLs that process HTTP request messages and generate response messages.

An *ISAPI extension* is simply a DLL that exports three well-known C functions.[1] One of the functions, HttpExtensionProc, is used to process HTTP requests. It is called whenever a request message that applies a method to the ISAPI extension arrives. Here is the signature.

```
DWORD WINAPI HttpExtensionProc(EXTENSION_CONTROL_BLOCK *pECB)
```

The single parameter is a pointer to an EXTENSION_CONTROL_BLOCK (ECB), a structure that encapsulates the contents of a request message and the corresponding response message. Each ECB includes pointers to four functions, listed in Table 8-4, that can be used to access the entire contents of an HTTP request message and to generate a corresponding HTTP response message.

The following is a sample implementation of HttpExtensionProc that processes all requests by generating response messages containing the current time encoded in XML.

```
DWORD WINAPI HttpExtensionProc(EXTENSION_CONTROL_BLOCK *pECB)
{
  // get time
```

---

[1] There are also ISAPI filters. For more information on filters see *ASP Internals* by Jon Flanders or the Platform SDK documentation.

```
time_t t = time(0);
struct tm* ptm = localtime(&t);
if (!ptm) return HSE_STATUS_ERROR;
// convert to XML
char szXML[256];
DWORD nXML = strftime(szXML, sizeof(szXML),
                    "<time>%a %b %d %X %Z %Y</time>", ptm);
// generate response headers
char szHeader[256];
DWORD nHeader = sprintf(szHeader, "Content-Type: text/xml\r\n"
                    "Content-Length: %d\r\n\r\n", nXML);
// send response message headers
HSE_SEND_HEADER_EX_INFO info = { 0 };
info.pszStatus = "200 OK";
info.cchStatus = strlen(info.pszStatus);
info.pszHeader = szHeader;
info.cchHeader = nHeader;
info.fKeepConn = false;
if (!pECB->ServerSupportFunction(pECB->ConnID,
                                HSE_REQ_SEND_RESPONSE_HEADER_EX,
                                &info, 0,0))
    return HSE_STATUS_ERROR;
// send response message body
if (!(pECB->WriteClient(pECB->ConnID, szXML, &nXML, HSE_IO_SYNC)))
    return HSE_STATUS_ERROR;
return HSE_STATUS_SUCCESS;
}
```

This implementation of `HttpExtensionProc` processes all request messages the same way. It calls `time` to get the current time, `localtime` to adjust it to the current time zone, and `strftime` to convert it to a string. The string is formatted as a serialized XML document. Once the XML output is produced, the function emits response message headers by calling the ECB's `ServerSupportFunction` method and passing `HSE_REQ_SEND_HEADERS_EX`. It also passes an `HSE_SEND_HEADERS_EX_INFO` structure containing a `Status-Code` and corresponding `Reason-Phrase` for an HTTP response message status line, a string containing additional headers, and a flag indicating that the TCP connection should be closed upon completion. Finally, the function emits the response message body by calling the ECB's `WriteClient` method and passing the generated XML string containing the current time. Note that headers must be sent before a response message's body is written because

ISAPI sends HTTP response message data to the calling User-Agent immediately when `ServerSupportFunction` or `WriteClient` is called.

Here is a sample HTTP response message generated by this extension.

```
HTTP/1.1 200 OK
Server: Microsoft-IIS/5.0
Date: Mon, 23 Oct 2000 18:22:20 GMT
Connection: close
Content-Type: text/xml
Content-Length: 59

<time>Mon Oct 23 14:22:20 Eastern Daylight Time 2000</time>
```

The status line, the `Connection`, `Content-Type`, and `Content-Length` headers, and the message body were all emitted by the ISAPI extension itself. IIS added the `Server` and `Date` headers.

### Mapping Requests to Processes

Before `inetinfo.exe` can call an ISAPI extension's implementation of `HttpExtensionProc`, it has to load the DLL into a process. Loading and executing arbitrary code inside `inetinfo.exe` is risky. If the IIS service on a machine crashes, User-Agents will not be able to establish connections and send HTTP requests to that server. So for safety's sake, `inetinfo.exe` typically loads DLLs into surrogate processes and then forwards requests to them there. This increases the overhead involved in processing each request, but it reduces the risk that buggy code will render a server unreachable.

So how does `inetinfo.exe` decide which process an ISAPI extension should be loaded into? The decision is based on which *IIS application* the target DLL belongs to (don't confuse IIS applications with COM+ applications; the two are closely related, but they are not the same). Every virtual directory (and site) in the logical tree that IIS uses to map URLs to files is part of either its own or its parent's IIS application.[2] Figure 8-3 illustrates this relationship.

Every IIS application is configured to run at a particular level of protection: low, medium (the default), or high. An IIS application's level of protection

---

[2] It is technically possible to have a virtual directory that is not in an IIS application by creating a parent site that is not in an IIS application. However, if a virtual directory is not in an application, requests that target dynamic target files in that virtual directory will fail.

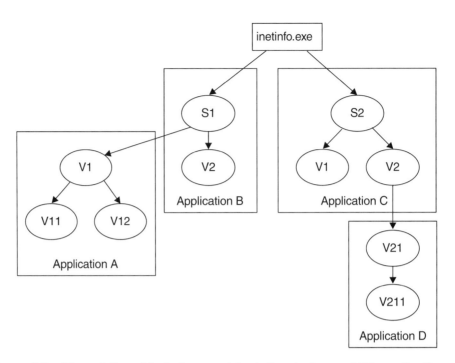

**Figure 8-3  The relationship between virtual directories and IIS applications**

determines which process the ISAPI extensions in its virtual directory or sub-directories are loaded into. If an IIS application has low protection, its ISAPI extensions are loaded into `inetinfo.exe`. If an IIS application has medium protection, its ISAPI extensions are loaded into a surrogate process that it shares with all other IIS applications with medium protection. If an IIS application has high protection, its ISAPI extensions are loaded into a surrogate process of their own.

This scheme for mapping DLLs to processes is built on top of COM+. The surrogate processes into which ISAPI extensions are loaded are instances of `dllhost.exe`. Every IIS application is associated with a particular COM+ application that is created and managed by IIS. All IIS applications with low protection are associated with a single COM+ *library* application called IIS In-process Applications. All IIS applications with medium protection are associated with a single COM+ *server* application called IIS Out-of-process Pooled Applications. Each IIS application with high protection is associated with its own COM+ *server* application. The name of the dedicated COM+ application is derived from the names of IIS application's virtual directory and site, according to the following pattern.

```
IIS-{<site-name>//Root/<virtual-dir-name>}
```

For example, if a virtual directory called OrderSystem in a site called Store were mapped to its own IIS application with high protection, the corresponding COM+ server application would be named `IIS-{Store//Root/OrderSystem}`. If the Store site's root virtual directory were mapped to its own IIS application with high protection, the corresponding COM+ server application would be named `IIS-{Store//Root}`. Table 8-5 summarizes the relationship between IIS applications and COM+ applications.

All of the COM+ applications associated with IIS applications have something in common: They all contain a Web Application Manager (WAM) raw-configured class. `inetinfo.exe` uses instances of WAM classes to route request messages that target ISAPI extensions to the processes where the DLLs are to be loaded. It's the WAM's job to actually load the target DLL (unless it has been loaded already) and to call its implementation of `Http ExtensionProc`, passing in an `EXTENSION_CONTROL_BLOCK` that encapsulates the request and a corresponding response message. `inetinfo.exe` creates a single instance of a WAM class for each IIS application. It delays creation until a request for an ISAPI extension in a particular IIS application arrives. Once `inetinfo.exe` has a reference to a WAM object for a given IIS application, it does not release it. Instead, it holds on to the object and uses it to service all requests that target ISAPI extensions in that same IIS application. Figure 8-4 illustrates this caching architecture.

HTTP request messages arrive in the `inetinfo.exe` process, shown in the middle of Figure 8.4. If the request message's URL resolves to an ISAPI

Table 8-5   IIS applications and COM+ applications

| IIS Application Protection Level | COM+ Application Name | COM+ Application Type |
|---|---|---|
| Low | IIS In-process Applications | Library |
| Medium | IIS Out-of-process Pooled Applications | Server |
| High | IIS-{<site-name>//Root/<virtual-dir-name>} | Server |

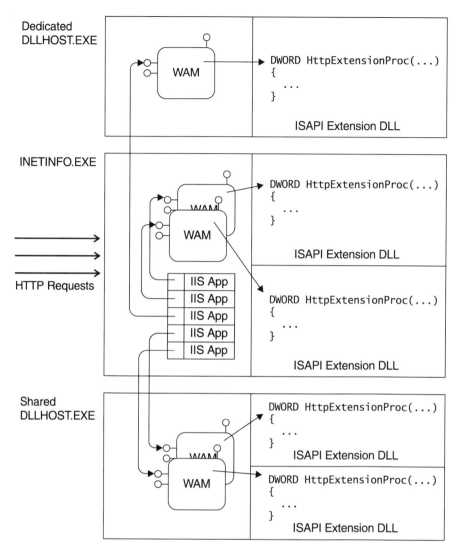

**Figure 8-4　How inetinfo.exe uses WAM objects**

extension, `inetinfo.exe` determines which IIS application the DLL resides in. Then it forwards the request to the appropriate WAM object, which calls the target DLL's implementation of `HttpExtensionProc`. WAM objects are created and ISAPI extensions are loaded as necessary and remain in memory over time.

To create a WAM object for a particular IIS application, `inetinfo.exe` needs to figure out which WAM class it should use. After the service maps a URL to an ISAPI extension in a particular IIS application, it consults the metabase to determine the IIS application's level of protection. Based on that, it derives the text-based programmatic ID (ProgID) of the WAM class in the COM+ application associated with the IIS application. The ProgID of the WAM class in the IIS In-process Applications library application is `IISWAM.W3SVC`. The ProgID of the WAM class in the IIS Out-of-process Pooled Applications server application is `IISWAM.OutOfProcessPool`. The ProgID of a WAM class in a dedicated COM+ server application associated with an IIS application with high protection is derived from the name of the IIS application's virtual directory and the number of its parent site according to the following pattern.

```
IISWAM.<site-number>__Root__<virtual-dir-name>
```

For example, if a virtual directory called OrderSystem in the fourth site created on a system were mapped to its own IIS application with high protection, the WAM class in the corresponding COM+ server application would have the ProgID `IISWAM.4__Root__OrderSystem`. If the fourth site's root virtual directory were mapped to its own IIS application with high protection, the WAM class in the corresponding COM+ server application would have the ProgID `IISWAM.4__Root`. Table 8-6 summarizes the relationship between IIS applications and WAM class ProgIDs.

Once `inetinfo.exe` has the ProgID of the WAM class associated with a particular IIS application, it can convert it to a CLSID and create a WAM object that can be used to process requests.

There is one important caveat to all this. If an ISAPI extension is listed under the `InprocessIsapiApps` key in the metabase, request messages that apply methods to that DLL are always processed via a WAM object in `inetinfo.exe`,

**Table 8-6  IIS applications and WAM class ProgIDs**

| IIS Application Protection Level | WAM Class ProgID |
| --- | --- |
| Low | IISWAM.W3SVC |
| Medium | IISWAM.OutOfProcessPool |
| High | IISWAM.<site-number>__Root__<virtual-dir-name> |

regardless of the protection level of the IIS application the DLL belongs to. This loophole allows you to configure particular DLLs to process requests as quickly as possible, without having to install them in a virtual directory that is part of an IIS application with low protection.[3]

### Mapping Requests to Contexts and Apartments

All WAM classes are registered as raw-configured and use threading model Free. That means that WAM objects always live in contexts in their processes' MTAs, as shown in Figure 8-5.

WAM objects are created from threads running in the default context of the `inetinfo.exe`'s MTA. In-process WAM objects that represent IIS applications with low protection are created in that same context. Out-of-process WAM objects that represent IIS applications with medium or high protection are always created in new nondefault contexts in the MTAs of their surrogate processes (this reflects the behavior summarized in Table 4-4). These nondefault contexts are not configured to support any services. They are not in an activity or a transaction stream, and they do not support JITA.

An ISAPI extension's implementation of `HttpExtensionProc` always executes within the calling WAM object's context. Like a nonconfigured or raw-configured class, an ISAPI extension can access object context simply by calling `CoGetObjectContext`. Unlike instances of nonconfigured and raw-configured classes, which can't predict where they will be created and must be prepared to behave correctly in *any* context, ISAPI extensions know the characteristics of the context they are called from—either the default context of `inetinfo.exe`'s MTA or a nondefault context in a surrogate process's MTA. Here is some sample code that demonstrates the relationship between WAM objects and contexts.

```
DWORD WINAPI HttpExtensionProc(EXTENSION_CONTROL_BLOCK *pECB)
{
  // get context id, if available
  GUID ctxId = GUID_NULL;
  CComPtr<IObjectContextInfo> spCtxInfo;
```

---

[3] For more information, see the Platform SDK documentation on the `InprocessIsapiApps` metabase entry.

TRANSACTIONAL COM+: BUILDING SCALABLE APPLICATIONS

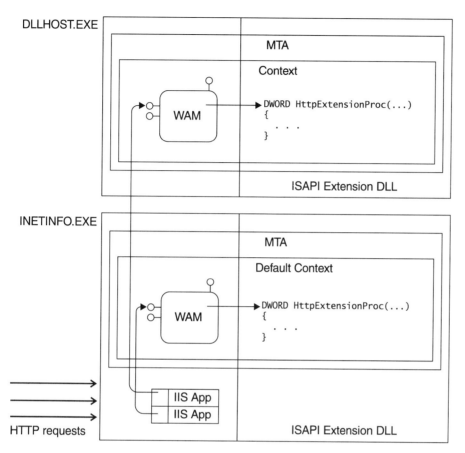

**Figure 8-5  WAMs, contexts, and apartments**

```
HRESULT hr = CoGetObjectContext(__uuidof(spCtxInfo),
                                (void**)&spCtxInfo);
if (SUCCEEDED(hr))
{
  hr = spCtxInfo->GetContextId(&ctxId);
  if (FAILED(hr)) return HSE_STATUS_ERROR;
}
// convert to XML
char szXML[256];
DWORD nXML = sprintf(szXML, "<context>%S</context>",
                     ctxId != GUID_NULL ?
                     CComBSTR(ctxId) : L"default");
// generate response headers
char szHeader[256];
```

```
            DWORD nHeader = sprintf(szHeader, "Content-Type: text/xml\r\n"
                                "Content-Length: %d\r\n\r\n", nXML);
      // send response message headers
      HSE_SEND_HEADER_EX_INFO info = { 0 };
      info.pszStatus = "200 OK";
      info.cchStatus = strlen(info.pszStatus);
      info.pszHeader = szHeader;
      info.cchHeader = nHeader;
      info.fKeepConn = false;
      if (!pECB->ServerSupportFunction(pECB->ConnID,
                                       HSE_REQ_SEND_RESPONSE_HEADER_EX,
                                       &info, 0,0))
          return HSE_STATUS_ERROR;
      // send response message body
      if (!(pECB->WriteClient(pECB->ConnID, szXML, &nXML, HSE_IO_SYNC)))
          return HSE_STATUS_ERROR;
      return HSE_STATUS_SUCCESS;
   }
```

This implementation of `HttpExtensionProc` processes all request messages
the same way. It calls `CoGetObjectContext` to retrieve an `IObject
ContextInfo` reference to object context. If it succeeds, it retrieves the current
context's ID. Then it builds an XML string that contains either the current context ID or the word *default,* indicating that the function was called from the
default context of the MTA and no context ID was available. Once the XML output is produced, the function emits the headers and the body for a response
message by calling the ECB's `ServerSupportFunction` and `WriteClient`
methods.

Here is the body of an HTTP response message generated by this extension
when it was deployed in a virtual directory that is part of an IIS application with
medium or high protection. The DLL was loaded into a surrogate process, and
`HttpExtensionProc` was called from a nondefault context in the MTA.

```
   <context>{51A5BEFC-F035-4746-A787-ECFC28B25E56}</context>
```

Here is the body of an HTTP response message generated by this extension when it was redeployed in a virtual directory that is part of an IIS application with low protection. The DLL was loaded into `inetinfo.exe`, and
`HttpExtensionProc` was called from the default context of the MTA.

```
   <context>default</context>
```

Of course, since an ISAPI extension's `HttpExtensionProc` is always called in a context, it can use instances of nonconfigured, raw-configured, or configured classes as needed to help generate HTTP response messages.

**Processing Requests in Parallel**

`inetinfo.exe` is an HTTP server and a COM client. It creates a pool of MTA threads to receive and process incoming HTTP request messages, forwarding them to WAM objects if necessary. These HTTP receive threads run in the MTA's default context, right next to the pool of RPC receive threads the COM+ runtime uses to process incoming DCOM requests. The size of the HTTP receive pool is adjusted dynamically based on the current number of inbound HTTP requests, up to a maximum number of threads calculated based on the number of CPUs installed in the machine IIS is running on, as defined by the following formula.

$$n_{HTTP} \leq n_{CPU} \times 20$$

In other words, the number of HTTP receive threads available in `inetinfo.exe`, $n_{HTTP}$, cannot exceed the number of CPUs in the machine, $n_{CPU}$, times 20. (This multiplier can be adjusted by setting the `MaxPoolThreads` named value of the `HKEY_LOCAL_MACHINE\System\CurrentControlSet\Services\InetInfo\Parameters` Registry key.)

It is important to note that HTTP receive threads that are currently calling WAM objects to forward request messages to ISAPI extensions do not count against this total. `inetinfo.exe` has no idea what a given DLL does when `HttpExtensionProc` is called, and it is possible that a poorly implemented ISAPI extension might block the calling HTTP receive thread for an extended time, perhaps indefinitely. To ensure that it does not run out of HTTP receive threads, `inetinfo.exe` does not count threads that are calling WAM objects when it adjusts the size of its thread pool. However, while `inetinfo.exe` does not want to run out of HTTP receive threads, it does not want to create an endless number of threads either.

To constrain concurrency and avoid contention for hardware resources, `inetinfo.exe` limits the number of threads it will use to 256. (This value can be adjusted by setting the `PoolThreadLimit` named value of the `HKEY_LOCAL_MACHINE\System\CurrentControlSet\Services\InetInfo\Parameters`

Registry key.) Well-written ISAPI extensions use their own thread pools to handle requests, thereby freeing up the calling HTTP receive thread as quickly as possible and keeping the number of threads in `inetinfo.exe` low. The ISAPI infrastructure is designed specifically to support this style of asynchronous processing.[4]

## Active Server Pages

ISAPI provides a very flexible way to invoke arbitrary code to generate responses to HTTP requests, which is exactly what is needed to bridge HTTP requests to operations on COM+ objects in middle-tier servers. However, building ISAPI extensions requires significant effort, especially when you consider that extensions should have their own thread pools. To simplify HTTP-based development, IIS defines a higher-level API called Active Server Pages (ASP). ASP offers a simpler programming model centered on the notion of a *page* that acts as an exemplar (or template) for an HTTP response message.

An ASP page is simply a text file with an `.asp` extension that contains an arbitrary combination of executable scripts and static content. When an HTTP request message that targets an ASP page arrives, it is routed to a well-known ISAPI extension called `asp.dll` (as determined by the virtual directory's `ScriptMap` property in the metabase). The ASP ISAPI extension retrieves the name of the target `.asp` file from IIS by calling the ECB `GetServerVariable` function, passing in `SCRIPT_NAME`. Then it uses an Active Script engine to parse and execute the page's scripts and to generate an HTTP response message.[5] The page's static content is embedded directly in the response message's body. ASP provides a set of intrinsic objects for scripts to program against. In particular, the `Request` and `Response` objects encapsulate access to the underlying `EXTENSION_CONTROL_BLOCK` passed to `asp.dll`'s implementation of `Http ExtensionProc`—and to the HTTP request and response messages it represents.

Here is a sample ASP page that processes all requests by generating response messages containing the current time encoded in XML. It is equivalent

---

[4] See the Platform SDK documentation on `HttpExtensionProc` and `HSE_STATUS_ PENDING` for more information.

[5] `asp.dll` uses multiple Active Script engines if a page includes scripts in more than one language. See the Platform SDK documentation for more information on Active Scripting.

to the first `HttpExtensionProc` implementation presented earlier, but it is obviously much simpler.

```
<%@ language=jscript %>
<%
  Response.ContentType = "text/xml";
  Response.AddHeader("Connection", "close");
%>
<time><%= new Date() %></time>
```

This page generates the following HTTP response message.

```
HTTP/1.1 200 OK
Server: Microsoft-IIS/5.0
Date: Thu, 26 Oct 2000 19:27:41 GMT
Connection: close
Content-Length: 45
Content-Type: text/xml
Set-Cookie: ASPSESSIONIDQGQGQLTQ=IJLNNFGCAGLDDHDJKOJBCEJO; path=/
Cache-control: private

<time>Thu Oct 26 15:27:41 EDT 2000</time>
```

The ASP page emitted the `Connection` and `Content-Type` headers and the message body. `asp.dll` added the status line and `Content-Length`, `Set-Cookie`, and `Cache-control` headers. IIS added `Server` and `Data` headers.

### Processing ASP Requests

As with all ISAPI extensions, HTTP requests are delivered to `asp.dll` via a WAM object in the appropriate process, which calls the extension's implementation of `HttpExtensionProc` from within a context in the process's MTA. Although `asp.dll` receives requests in that environment, it does not process them there. Instead, it forwards each request for a page to a nondefault context in one of the STAs in the process's COM+-managed STA pool. This architecture, shown in Figure 8-6, provides two benefits.

First, it defers work to a separate thread pool and returns the HTTP receive thread that called the WAM object to `inetinfo.exe`'s control as quickly as possible. This reduces contention in the IIS service. Second, it ensures that a page's scripts can call instances of classes that use threading model Apartment—such as those implemented in (or for) Visual Basic 6—without

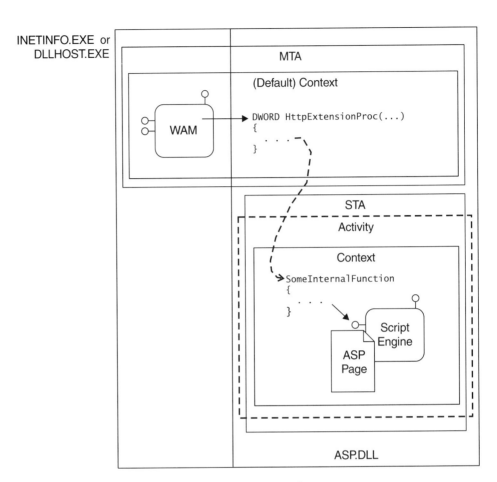

INETINFO.EXE or
DLLHOST.EXE

MTA

(Default) Context

WAM

```
DWORD HttpExtensionProc(...)
{
    . . .
}
```

STA

Activity

Context

```
SomeInternalFunction
{
    . . .
}
```

ASP
Page

Script
Engine

ASP.DLL

**Figure 8-6   How ASP requests are processed**

having to switch threads. In short, ASP trades a single mandatory thread switch for every page request in order to avoid multiple thread switches when executing scripts that access STA-based objects.

As Chapter 4 explains, the SCM will not put an instance of a configured class into a pooled STA unless it also uses an activity. Similarly, the context `asp.dll` uses to process a page request in an STA must be in an activity. The presence of an activity also ensures that instances of configured classes that require synchronization can inherit the page's activity and reside in contexts in the same STA. If a page were processed in a context that was not in an activity, instances of classes marked `COMAdminSynchronizationRequired` would be forced into other STAs in the pool, and calls to them would require a thread switch (see Table 4-5). For both these reasons, each ASP-generated context is created in a new activity of its own.

The mechanism `asp.dll` uses to dispatch a request into a context in an STA and an activity is not documented (it is depicted in Figure 8-6 as a call to `SomeInternalFunction`).[6] It does not involve an instance of a configured or a raw-configured class. `asp.dll` also uses an undocumented hook to adjust the constant used to calculate the upper bound on the size of a process's STA pool from 10 to 25, as the following statement shows.

$$7 + n_{CPU} \leq n_{STA} \leq n_{CPU} \times 25.$$

In other words, the number of STAs available in `inetinfo.exe` and the instances of `dllhost.exe` that house WAM objects range from 7 plus the number of CPUs in the machine to 25 times the number of CPUs in the machine, inclusive. You can adjust this constant by setting the value of the `ASPProcessor ThreadMax` property in the IIS metabase. This option adjusts the size of the STA pool in the processes used by IIS only. It does not affect the size of the STA pool in other processes, which are bound to a maximum of 10 STAs per CPU.

## Transactional Pages

Clearly, the ASP infrastructure has a much more complex relationship with COM+ than the ISAPI infrastructure does. While HTTP requests that target ISAPI extensions are processed in nondescript contexts in the MTA, HTTP requests that target ASP pages are processed in new contexts in pooled STAs and activities. ASP also supports processing requests in contexts in transaction streams. A page that uses a COM+-managed declarative transaction is called a *transactional page*.

The use of declarative transactions is controlled on a page-by-page basis by the `@Transaction` directive. An ASP page indicates its disposition toward declarative transactions by including an `@Transaction` directive in its initial script block.

```
<%@ Transaction = declarative transaction option %>
```

---

[6] For more information on how this works, see *ASP Internals* by Jon Flanders.

asp.dll treats a page that has an @Transaction directive differently from a page that does not. Instead of executing the page's scripts directly in a new context in an STA and an activity, the ASP extension creates a new object and asks it to process the page in its own context, possibly inside a transaction stream. The object ASP uses for this task is an instance of one of four configured classes deployed in the IIS Utilities library application. It selects a class based on the value of a page's @Transaction directive. The four possible values for the @Transaction directive and the corresponding configured classes are listed in the first two columns of Table 8-7. The third column lists the values of the configured classes' transaction attributes.

All four of the ObjectContextTx... classes are implemented the same way, and they all expose the IASPObjectContextCustom interface that follows. (This interface is undocumented, but is described by the type library embedded in the component that implements these classes, asptxn.dll.)

```
typedef long LONG_PTR;
interface IASPObjectContextCustom : IUnknown
{
    HRESULT SetComplete();
    HRESULT SetAbort();
    HRESULT Call([in] LONG_PTR pvScriptEngine,
                 [in] LPWSTR strEntryPoint,
                 [in, out] char* pfAborted);
    HRESULT ResetScript([in] LONG_PTR pvScriptEngine);
};
```

asp.dll processes a page with an @Transaction directive by instantiating the appropriate ObjectContextTx... class and calling its implementation of the IASPObjectContextCustom::Call method. It passes the method a

Table 8-7   @Transaction options

| @Transaction Value | Configured Class | Transaction Attribute |
|---|---|---|
| Not_Supported | ASP.ObjectContextTxNotSupported | COMAdminTransactionNone |
| Supported | ASP.ObjectContextTxSupported | COMAdminTransactionSupported |
| Required | ASP.ObjectContextTxRequired | COMAdminTransactionRequired |
| Requires_New | ASP.ObjectContextTxRequiresNew | COMAdminTransactionRequiresNew |

reference to an object that encapsulates a page's parsed scripts as the first parameter, `pvScriptEngine`. The object reference is typed as a LONG_PTR, which is just an alias for long. This stops the object reference from being marshaled, which is good because the reference being passed refers to a C++ object, not to a COM object. The implementation of the `Call` method casts the long back into a pointer of the appropriate C++ type and executes the scripts it refers to. This is done in the context created for the instance of whichever `ObjectContextTx…` class was used. If a page is marked `@Transaction = Required`, `asp.dll` will use the `ObjectContextTxRequired` class, and the page's scripts will be executed inside the root context of a new transaction stream, as Figure 8-7 shows.

Calls from the `ObjectContextTxRequired` object to the C++ object wrapping the scripts, and ultimately to the underlying Active Script engine(s), are not intercepted. As a result, although the page's scripts were parsed in context A, they are executed in the transaction stream's root context B, and the stream's distributed transaction is implicitly available for them to use. The transaction will end when the distinguished object in the root context (i.e., the instance of `ObjectContextTxRequired`) deactivates.

If a page is going to use a declarative transaction, it needs a way to affect the transaction's outcome. In short, a page's scripts must be able to adjust the state of the happy and done bits of the context they run in. To that end, ASP seeds the Active Scripting engine for any page with an `@Transaction` directive with a reference to the `ObjectContextTx…` object that is going to execute that page's scripts. The reference is named `ObjectContext`, and the scripts can use it to interact with the `ObjectContextTx…` object, which is, by definition, the distinguished object in the context. All four of the `Object ContextTx…` classes implement the same scripting interface, `IASPObject Context`, the same way.

```
interface IASPObjectContext : IDispatch
{
    HRESULT SetComplete();
    HRESULT SetAbort();
};
```

These two methods simply call `CoGetObjectContext` to retrieve a reference to object context and then use it to turn the done bit on and the happy bit

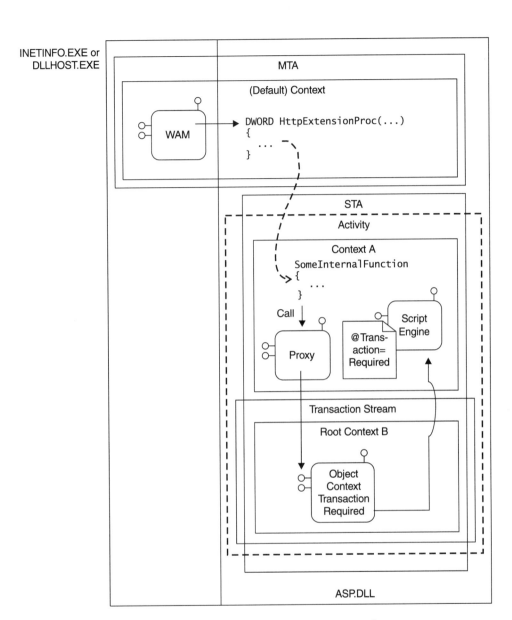

**Figure 8-7    How @Transaction=Required affects processing**

on or off, respectively. In other words, the methods determine whether the
`Object-ContextTx…` object that is processing a page's scripts completes
the invocation of its `IASPObjectContextCustom::Call` method in the
`SetComplete` or `SetAbort` state. Figure 8-8 illustrates this architecture.

Here is an example of a transactional ASP page.

TRANSACTIONAL COM+: BUILDING SCALABLE APPLICATIONS

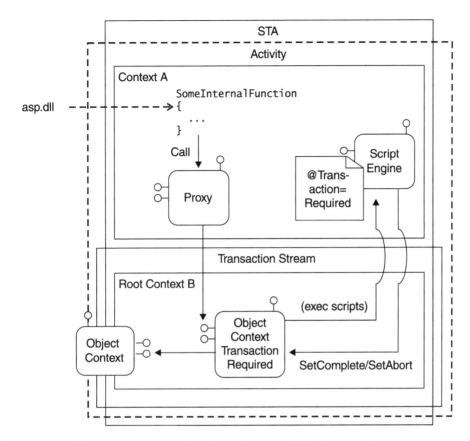

**Figure 8-8   How a page controls the outcome of its transaction**

```
<%@ transaction=required language=jscript %>
<%
  // ask ObjectContextTxRequired object to
  // turn done bit on and happy bit off
  ObjectContext.SetAbort();
  // use declarative transaction implicitly
  var conn = Server.CreateObject("ADODB.Connection");
  conn.Open("Provider=SQLOLEDB.1;...");
  conn.Execute("insert into...");
  // ask ObjectContextTxRequired object to
  // turn done bit and happy bit on
  ObjectContext.SetComplete();
%>
```

Because this page is marked with the `@Transaction = Required` directive, `asp.dll` executes its scripts using an instance of the `ObjectContext`

`TxRequired` that lives in the root context of a transaction stream. The call to `ObjectContext.SetAbort` turns the context's done bit on and its happy bit off. The call to open an ADO connection to a database causes the OLE DB Service Components to autoenlist the underlying OLE DB session against the stream's distributed transaction (which is created by the declarative transaction service on demand). The distributed transaction then protects the work submitted to the database through the connection. Finally, if no exceptions have been thrown, the call to `ObjectContext.SetComplete` turns the context's done and happy bits on so the declarative transaction can commit. The transaction's outcome is determined when the COM+ interception plumbing post-processes `asp.dll`'s call to the `ObjectContextTxRequired` object's implementation of `IASPObjectContextCustom::Call`.

It is important to note that an `ObjectContextTx…` object cannot return from `IASPObjectContextCustom::Call` in either the `EnableCommit` or `DisableCommit` state. If a page's scripts do not explicitly call `IASPObject Context::SetAbort`, the `ObjectContextTx…` object's implementation of `IASPObjectContextCustom::Call` will call the `IASPObjectContext:: SetComplete` method *after the page's scripts are done executing*. In practice this means that if a page's scripts do not explicitly vote to abort the page's declarative transaction, the ASP infrastructure will explicitly vote to commit it. This ensures that a page's `ObjectContextTx…` object is not left in the default `EnableCommit` state (happy but not done) simply because the page's scripts did not call either `IASPObjectContext::SetComplete` or `IASPObject Context::SetAbort`.

If a transactional ASP page creates a transactional object, that object is created in a new nonroot context in the page's transaction stream. The object can influence the page's distributed transaction's outcome using its own context's happy and done bits. In this case, the normal rules for determining the outcome of a declarative transaction described in Chapter 6 apply.

### Transaction Outcome Notifications

An ASP page is an exemplar for an HTTP response message. It is easy to imagine that a transactional ASP page would want to tailor the response message it generates based on the outcome of its declarative transaction. Unfortunately, a transactional page does not know its transaction's outcome when its scripts finish executing. The transaction's outcome is not known until `asp.dll` receives a response from the `ObjectContextTx...` object that processed the page. When its call to `IASPObjectContextCustom::Call` returns, the ASP extension examines the single out parameter, `pfAborted`, and the HRESULT. The out parameter indicates whether the `ObjectContextTx...` object was in the `SetComplete` or `SetAbort` state when `IASPObjectContextCustom ::Call` returned (it is really returning the final state of the happy bit). If the object was in the `SetComplete` state, the HRESULT tells `asp.dll` whether the transaction committed—if the value is not `CONTEXT_E_ABORTED`, the two-phase commit process succeeded (remember that the declarative transaction service always returns this HRESULT when a root object attempts to commit its distributed transaction but the two-phase commit protocol fails).

Once `asp.dll` knows the outcome of a page's declarative transaction, it notifies a page by calling an optional event handler function. The functions are named `OnTransactionCommit` and `OnTransactionAbort`, as the following shows.

```
<%@ transaction=required language=jscript %>
<%
   // main script
   ObjectContext.SetAbort();
   var conn = Server.CreateObject("ADODB.Connection");
   conn.Open("Provider=SQLOLEDB.1;...");
   conn.Execute("insert into...");
   ObjectContext.SetComplete();

   // function will be called if page's
   // declarative transaction commits
   function OnTransactionCommit()
   {
     Response.ContentType = "text/xml";
     Response.Write("<outcome>committed</outcome>");
   }

   // function will be called if page's
   // declarative transaction aborts
   function OnTransactionAbort()
   {
     Response.ContentType = "text/xml";
     Response.Write("<outcome>aborted</outcome>");
   }
%>
```

If this page's declarative transaction commits, the response message body will contain the following XML.

```
<outcome>committed</outcome>
```

If its declarative transaction aborts, the response message body will contain this XML instead.

```
<outcome>aborted</outcome>
```

Note that `OnTransactionCommit` and `OnTransactionAbort` are always called after a page's main scripts have been executed and after any static content that is not embedded in a function has been added to the generated HTTP response message. This can cause problems, as demonstrated by this new and naïve version of the previous page.

```
<%@ transaction=required language=jscript %>
<% Response.ContentType = "text/xml"; %>
<outcome>
<%
  // main script
  ObjectContext.SetAbort();
  var conn = Server.CreateObject("ADODB.Connection");
  conn.Open("Provider=SQLOLEDB.1;...");
  conn.Execute("insert into...");
  ObjectContext.SetComplete();

  // functions will be called after
  // static content has been embedded
  // in response message body
  function OnTransactionCommit()
  {
    Response.Write("committed");
  }
  function OnTransactionAbort()
  {
    Response.Write("aborted");
  }
%>
</outcome>
```

This page always produces an HTTP response message containing invalid XML because neither transaction event handler will be called until after the page's static content—the `<outcome>` and `</outcome>` tags—has been processed. For instance, if this page's declarative transaction commits, the response message body contains the following text.

```
<outcome></outcome>committed
```

One way to solve this problem is to embed any static content of the HTTP response message in a function that is not called until the outcome of the page's transaction is known, as demonstrated by the following page.

```
<%@ transaction=required language=jscript %>
<% Response.ContentType = "text/xml"; %>
<%
  // main script
  ObjectContext.SetAbort();
  var conn = Server.CreateObject("ADODB.Connection");
  conn.Open("Provider=SQLOLEDB.1;...");
  conn.Execute("insert into...");
  ObjectContext.SetComplete();

  // functions will be called after
  // static content has been embedded
  // in response message body
  function OnTransactionCommit()
  {
%>
<outcome>committed</outcome>
<%
  }
  function OnTransactionAbort()
  {
%>
<outcome>aborted</outcome>
<%
  }
%>
```

Another way to solve the problem is to rely on buffering. The ASP extension buffers an HTTP response message until a page is completely processed. This includes execution of the appropriate transaction outcome event handler. If a page's transaction aborts, you can erase the current HTTP response message by clearing the buffer. Here is a page that takes this approach.

```
<%@ transaction=required language=jscript %>
<% Response.ContentType = "text/xml"; %>
```

```
<outcome>committed</outcome>
<%
  // main script
  ObjectContext.SetAbort();
  var conn = Server.CreateObject("ADODB.Connection");
  conn.Open("Provider=SQLOLEDB.1;...");
  conn.Execute("insert into...");
  ObjectContext.SetComplete();

  // functions will be called after
  // static content has been embedded
  // in response message body
  function OnTransactionCommit()
  {
    // everything is fine, flush buffer and
    // send response message
    Response.Flush();
  }
  function OnTransactionAbort()
  {
    // everything is not fine, clear buffer
    // and generate new response message
    Response.Clear();
%>
<outcome>aborted</outcome>
<%
  }
%>
```

Be sure to note that `OnTransactionCommit` and `OnTransactionAbort` are not called in the same context as the rest of a page's scripts. Remember that a page's main scripts are executed in the context created for an `ObjectContextTx…` object. However, the outcome of a page's transaction is not known until after the call to that object completes.

As Figure 8-9 shows, `asp.dll` invokes the appropriate transaction outcome event handler from within the current context and not the context where the `ObjectContextTx…` object lived. Among other things, that means that a context relative interface pointer acquired while a page's scripts were executing is not safe to use in a transaction outcome event handler. Consider the following page.

```
<%@ transaction=required language=jscript %>
```

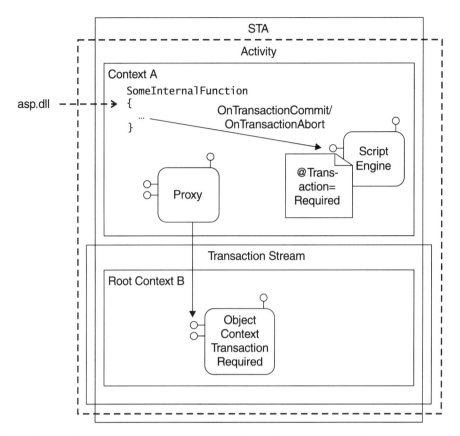

**Figure 8-9  Transaction outcome event handlers and context**

```
<%
  // main script called in one context
  var obj = Server.CreateObject("SomeSrv.SomeObj");
  ObjectContext.SetComplete();

  // handler function called in another context
  function OnTransactionCommit()
  {
    // use of object reference may cause error
    obj.DoSomething();
  }
%>
```

The interface pointer stored in `obj` is acquired in the context where the page's scripts execute. It may or may not be safe to use the interface pointer in the `OnTransactionCommit` handler. If it refers to a proxy, the proxy will reject the call and return `RPC_E_WRONGTHREAD` (remember that that really means `RPC_E_WRONGCONTEXT`). If the interface pointer refers directly to an object, it may or may not be safe to use, depending on the object's implementation. In general, you must assume that an object acquired by a page's main scripts cannot be safely used from the page's transaction outcome event handlers.

### Server.Execute and Server.Transfer

A page without an `@Transaction` directive is processed in a context in a pooled STA and an activity but not in a transaction stream. A page that is marked `@Transaction=Required` is processed in a context in a pooled STA and an activity and a transaction stream. That seems to cover all the options, so what are the other three `@Transaction` values for? The answer is declarative transaction propagation.

The ASP intrinsic `Server` object has two methods that allow one ASP page to invoke another. Like a normal method call, the `Server.Execute` method invokes another ASP page and then finishes processing the current page. The `Server.Transfer` method invokes another ASP page and does not finish processing the current page (this is sometimes called a "tail call"). Both methods process pages in the same overall ASP environment, that is, with the same set of intrinsic objects (`Request`, `Response`, etc.). Both methods work only with ASP pages in the same virtual directory.

Here is a simple example that shows how `Server.Execute` works with nontransactional ASP pages. Here is `page1.asp`.

```
<%@ language=jscript %>
<% Response.ContentType = "text/xml"; %>
<one><% Server.Execute("page2.asp"); %></one>
```

As shown below, `page1.asp` uses `Server.Execute` to call `page2.asp`.

```
<%@ language=jscript %>
<two><%= new Date() %></two>
```

When `page1.asp`'s scripts are executed, they produce an HTTP response message with the following body.

```
<one><two>Sat Oct 28 12:34:56 EST 2000</two></one>
```

The `Server.Execute` and `Server.Transfer` methods both execute a page's scripts using these techniques. If the target page does not have an

@Transaction directive, its scripts are executed directly in the calling page's current context. If the target page does have an @Transaction directive, an instance of the corresponding ObjectContextTx… class is created and asked to execute the target page's scripts in its new context. Figure 8-10 provides an example.

All of the pages that are shown in Figure 8-10 were processed in response to a single HTTP request message that targeted page A. Each page used Server.Execute to call the page to its right, that is, page A in context A called page A', and so on. Page A is marked @Transaction = Required or @Transaction = Requires_New. Either one would cause the creation of a new transaction stream X. Page A' does not have an @Transaction directive, so its scripts are executed in its caller's context A and therefore transaction stream X. Pages B and C are marked @Transaction = Supported or @Transaction = Required. Either directive would cause the two pages to execute in new contexts in transaction stream X. Page D is marked @Transaction = Not_Supported. That forced it to execute in a new context outside its caller's transaction stream. Page E is like page A; it is marked @Transaction = Required or @Transaction = Requires_New. Either one would cause the creation of a new transaction stream Y.

As with normal transactional objects (which is what transactional pages map to under the covers), if a page's scripts are executed in a nonroot context in a transaction stream, they can still influence the outcome of the stream's distributed transaction by setting that context's happy bit. If the Object ContextTx… object that is executing a page's scripts completes its work in the SetAbort state, the stream's distributed transaction is doomed. It will be aborted

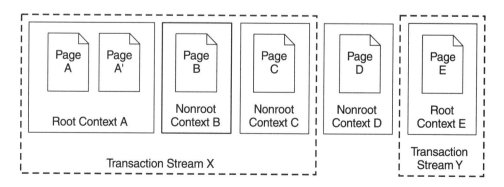

**Figure 8-10   Server.Execute contexts and transaction streams**

when the scripts on the page in the root context finish executing (when the call to the root `ObjectContextTx…` object's `IASPObjectContextCustom::Call` method completes).

If a called page includes an `@Transaction` directive and has transaction outcome event handlers, the `Server.Execute` and `Server.Transfer` methods will call one of them when the page's scripts complete. Remember that these handlers are always invoked from the current context. When a page is called via `Server.Execute` or `Server.Transfer`, the current context is the one in which the *calling* page's scripts are executing. In Figure 8-10, page B's handlers would be invoked from root context A, page C's handlers would be invoked from context B, and so on. Note that the context in which a handler is called may or may not be in a transaction stream, depending on the `@Transaction` setting of the calling page.

Also, for pages whose scripts are not executed in the root context of a transaction stream, the decision about which handler to call is based solely on whether the page called `ObjectContext.SetComplete` or `ObjectContext.SetAbort` (remember that if a page does not call either method, `SetComplete` is called automatically). This is true even for pages that are marked `@Transaction = Not_Supported`. Only when a page's scripts are executed in the root context of a transaction stream does the decision about which handler to call accurately reflect the outcome of the stream's distributed transaction.

I include `Server.Execute` and `Server.Transfer` here for completeness. You should avoid using these mechanisms to propagate a declarative transaction from one page to another for two reasons. First, neither method returns a value indicating whether the page you just called doomed your transaction (this makes it very difficult to comply with Rule 6.1). Second, there is no way a page's transaction outcome event handlers can know whether they are being told the real outcome of the page's declarative transaction or just what the page's scripts wanted the outcome to be (it depends on whether the page was invoked directly or via `Server.Execute` or `Server.Transfer`).

### ASP Pages and Raw-Configured Classes

The scripts in an ASP page can create instances of nonconfigured, configured, and raw-configured classes to help generate an HTTP response message. However, an instance of a raw-configured class may or may not be able to live in the context in which an ASP page's scripts are being executed. If an ASP page does not have an `@Transaction` directive, its scripts are executed in a new context in a pooled STA and an activity (see Figure 8-6). The ASP extension creates the context using an internal mechanism that is not documented. Unfortunately, the context `asp.dll` cobbles together for this purpose is subtly different from a context created to house a new object—and instances of raw-configured classes cannot live there *even if all of the COM+ services that require interception are turned off*. If you try to create an instance of a raw-configured class from a script in a page, the SCM will either put the new object in a separate context or, if the class's `MustRunInClientContext` attribute is enabled, fail the creation request. If an ASP page has an `@Transaction` directive, its scripts are executed in a new context created for an instance of the appropriate `ObjectContextTx...` class (see Figure 8-7). This context is created to house a new object and can house instances of raw-configured classes as well.

If you want to create objects in the context in which a page's scripts are being executed in order to minimize context overhead, there are two things you can do. First, you can use nonconfigured classes. Although the SCM will not put instances of raw-configured classes in the contexts `asp.dll` uses for pages without `@Transaction` directives, it will put instances of nonconfigured classes there. This works, but you lose the benefits that raw-configured classes offer over nonconfigured classes—easier deployment, construct strings, and support for object pooling. Second, you can make sure that all your ASP pages had an `@Transaction` directive—`@Transaction = Not_Supported` for pages that do not require a declarative transaction. This increases the overhead of processing a request, but it makes raw-configured classes work the way you expect and regains the benefits they offer.

### ASP Pages and Object Context

An ASP page's scripts are always executed in a context. Like an ISAPI extension, an ASP page can access its context's object context if it wants to. However, while an ISAPI extension can retrieve a reference to object context simply by calling `CoGetObjectContext`, an ASP page's scripts have to do something a little trickier. An ASP page's scripts can acquire a reference to object context using the COM+-provided object that implements the script-friendly `GetObjectContext` method provided for classes written in Visual Basic. You can create an instance of this helper class using its ProgID, `MTxAs.AppServer.1`, as shown.

```
<%@ language=jscript %>
<%
  Response.ContentType = "text/xml";
  var appSrv = new ActiveXObject("MTxAs.AppServer.1");
  var ctx = appSrv.GetObjectContext(); // the function VB calls
%>
<context><%= ctx.ContextInfo.GetContextId() %></context>
```

This ASP page is equivalent to the second `HttpExtensionProc` implementation presented above. It retrieves a reference to object context and then extracts and emits the ID of the context in which the page's scripts were executed.

The relationship between ASP pages and object context goes further. `asp.dll` stores references to its intrinsic objects as extended properties of object context using an undocumented API. The references can be retrieved from the context in which a page's scripts execute. The references also flow to—and can be retrieved from—any new nondefault contexts that the SCM creates for new objects created from a script in an ASP page. These references can be retrieved from object context using the `IGetContextProperties` interface.

```
interface IGetContextProperties : IUnknown
{
  HRESULT Count([out, retval] long *plCount);
  HRESULT GetProperty([in] BSTR name,
                      [out, retval] VARIANT *pProperty);
  HRESULT EnumNames([out, retval] IEnumNames **ppenum);
};
```

Here is an example that demonstrates how this interface is used.

```
HRESULT CSomeClass::UseASPObjects(void)
{
  // get reference to object context
  CComPtr<IGetContextProperties> spCtxProp;
  HRESULT hr = CoGetObjectContext(__uuidof(spCtxProp),
                                  (void**)&spCtxProp);
  if (FAILED(hr)) return hr;
  // retrieve "Response" property
```

```
    CComVariant vProp;
    hr = spCtxProp->GetProperty(CComBSTR("Response"), &vProp);
    if (FAILED(hr)) return hr;
    if (vProp.vt != VT_UNKNOWN || vProp.vt != VT_DISPATCH)
      return E_FAIL;
    // convert to correct type
    CComPtr<IResponse> spResp;
    hr = vProp.punkVal->QueryInterface(__uuidof(spResp),
                                       (void**)&spResp);
    if (FAILED(hr)) return hr;
    // write text to response message body
    hr = spResp->Write(CComVariant(CComBSTR("bathysphere")));
    if (FAILED(hr)) return hr;
    return S_OK;
};
```

The `UseASPObjects` method retrieves an `IGetContextProperties` reference to object context. It calls `GetProperty` to retrieve a reference to the ASP Response object. It casts the reference to an `IResponse` pointer and then calls the `Write` method to emit the word *bathysphere* into the HTTP response message being generated by the calling ASP page. Here is a page that calls the `UseASPObjects` method.

```
<%@ language = jscript %>
<% Response.ContentType = "text/xml"; %>
<device>
<%
  var obj = Server.CreateObject("SomeSrv.SomeClass");
  obj.UseASPObjects();
%>
</device>
```

When this page's scripts are executed, it generates an HTTP response message with the following body.

```
<device>bathysphere</device>
```

Classes implemented in Visual Basic can also retrieve references to the ASP intrinsic objects from object context. However, instead of using `IGetContextProperties` directly, VB classes use the `Item` property exposed by the `ObjectContext` interface. Here is the `UseASPObjects` method implemented in VB.

```
Public Sub ISomeClass_UseASPObjects()
  Dim resp As Response
  Set resp = GetObjectContext("Response")
  resp.Write "bathysphere"
End Sub
```

Obviously, using the ASP intrinsic objects from classes implemented in Visual Basic is much easier! (A VB project must reference the Microsoft Active Server Pages Object Library, `asp.dll`, to use strongly typed references to the ASP intrinsic objects.)

All of the ASP intrinsic objects aggregate the Free-Threaded Marshaler (FTM) and bypass the standard cross-context and cross-apartment marshaling infrastructure inside a process. As a result, you do not have to worry about the overhead of calls to the ASP intrinsic objects from any context in the process (either `inetinfo.exe` or a surrogate `dllhost.exe`) in which an ASP page's scripts are executed. You *do* have to worry about the overhead of calls to the ASP intrinsic objects from contexts in *other* processes because each call requires a roundtrip back into the process in which the ASP objects reside.

## HTTP + XML = RPC

ISAPI and ASP enable programmatic processing of HTTP requests. Both APIs can be used to convert HTTP invocations to calls to COM+ objects. Remember that the body of an HTTP request or response message is simply a MIME-typed stream of bytes, and it is up to the User-Agent and corresponding server code processing a particular pair of messages to interpret the payloads in a meaningful way. If you are going to use HTTP to invoke methods on COM+ objects, you have to figure out what type of payload the HTTP request and response messages are going to carry.

Traditionally, HTTP has been used to support browser-based "thin" user interfaces, with GET request messages conveying information about user actions (such as selecting a hyperlink or submitting a form) encoded in their Request-URIs and response messages containing descriptions of "pages" encoded in HTML (and other binary resources, such as images). Increasingly, however, other types of applications are using HTTP to make programmatic RPC calls to remote servers. Some are "thick" user interfaces written in C++,

Visual Basic, Java, or even Dynamic HTML (DHTML). Some are server processes sending requests to other servers. These User-Agents are not interested in retrieving HTML (well, a DHTML client might be). Programs that want to use HTTP to make RPC calls need a way to encode function call stacks in HTTP messages. A number of encoding schemes are possible, but the modern solution is to use the Extensible Markup Language (XML). The Simple Object Access Protocol (SOAP) is a standard specification that formalizes the use of XML for message-based communication in general. It also defines rules for using SOAP messages to make RPC calls over HTTP.

### SOAP Messages
SOAP messages contain a mandatory body and optional headers wrapped in an envelope. Here is the basic structure of a SOAP message.

```
<soap-env:Envelope
   xmlns:soap-env="http://schemas.xmlsoap.org/soap/envelope/"
   soap-env:encodingStyle="http://schemas.xmlsoap.org/soap/encoding/">
  <soap-env:Header>
    ... <!-- optional headers go here -->
  </soap-env:Header>
  <soap-env:Body>
    ... <!-- mandatory body goes here -->
  </soap-env:Body>
</soap-env:Envelope>
```

SOAP message headers convey information about how messages should be processed. SOAP includes headers for future extensibility; there are no standard headers today. SOAP message bodies contain serialized data being sent to message recipients. Section 5 of the SOAP specification defines an encoding scheme for serializing standard programming language data types to XML data types. Section 5 essentially adopts the XML schema specification for defining types and then mandates the use of "element normal form," meaning that data should be represented by XML elements, not attributes. Attributes are reserved for SOAP-specific metadata. For instance, the `encodingStyle` attribute on the `soap-env:Envelope` element in the preceding example indicates the use of the section 5 encoding rules.

A pair of SOAP messages can be used to make an RPC call. The request message's body contains the input parameters, and the response message's body contains the output parameters (including the return value if there is one). XML schema types define the formats of both messages' bodies. For example, consider the following function declaration.

```
HRESULT PlaceOrder(BSTR Item, long Quantity, long *pOrderId);
```

It maps to the following pair of schema types.

```
<schema xmlns="http://www.w3c.org/2000/10/XMLSchema"
        targetNamespace="urn:txcom:soap-methods"
        xmlns:target="urn:txcom:soap-methods">
  <complexType name="PlaceOrder">
    <sequence>
      <element name="Item" type="string" />
      <element name="Quantity" type="long" />
    </sequence>
  </complexType>
  <element name="PlaceOrder" type="target:PlaceOrder" />
  <complexType name="PlaceOrderResponse">
    <sequence>
      <element name="OrderId" type="long" />
    </sequence>
  </complexType>
  <element name="PlaceOrderResponse"
           type="target:PlaceOrderResponse" />
</schema>
```

The `PlaceOrder` and `PlaceOrderResponse` types represent the two halves of a call to the `PlaceOrder` function. The `PlaceOrder` type contains an element corresponding to each input parameter (`Item` is a string, and `Quantity` is a long). The `PlaceOrderResponse` type contains an element corresponding to the single output parameter (`OrderId` is a long). Note that the HRESULT return value is not represented in the response type because the SOAP specification defines a standard Fault element that can be embedded in a response message body to provide information about a processing failure.

Here is an instance of the `PlaceOrder` request type and a corresponding instance of the `PlaceOrderResponse` type, both sealed in SOAP envelopes.

```
<soap-env:Envelope
   xmlns:soap-env="http://schemas.xmlsoap.org/soap/envelope/"
   soap-env:encodingStyle="http://schemas.xmlsoap.org/soap/encoding/">
```

TRANSACTIONAL COM+: BUILDING SCALABLE APPLICATIONS

```
    <soap-env:Body>
      <methods:PlaceOrder xmlns:methods="urn:txcom:soap-methods">
        <Item>Ketchup</Item>
        <Quantity>20</Quantity>
      </methods:PlaceOrder>
    </soap-env:Body>
  </soap-env:Envelope>

<soap-env:Envelope
    xmlns:soap-env="http://schemas.xmlsoap.org/soap/envelope/"
    soap-env:encodingStyle="http://schemas.xmlsoap.org/soap/encoding/">
    <soap-env:Body>
      <methods:PlaceOrderResponse xmlns:methods="urn:txcom:soap-methods">
        <OrderId>1049</OrderId>
      </methods:PlaceOrderResponse>
    </soap-env:Body>
  </soap-env:Envelope>
```

Together, these two instances represent an invocation of the `PlaceOrder` function, passing `"Ketchup"` and 20 as input and receiving 1049 as output.

## SOAP and HTTP

In addition to defining the structure of an envelope and the section 5 encoding scheme, the SOAP specification includes rules for sending SOAP messages using HTTP. A SOAP message can be sent to an HTTP server as the body of an HTTP `POST` request message. The HTTP request message must contain a `SOAPAction` header whose value is a URI that specifies the logical intent of the request. The `SOAPAction` header allows routing plumbing to identify a SOAP message and decide how it should be processed—should it be allowed through?—without examining the body of the HTTP request (the SOAP envelope itself). The `SOAPAction` URI does not have to have a direct relationship to either the HTTP request message's `Request-URI` or the namespace URI of the type encoded in the SOAP message body. Here is an example.

```
POST http://store.company.com:8080/ordersystem/buy HTTP/1.1
SOAPAction: urn:txcom:soap-sample
Accept: text/xml
Content-Type: text/xml
Content-Length: nnn
<soap-env:Envelope...
```

A SOAP message can also be returned from an HTTP server as the body of an HTTP response message. The HTTP response message's `Status-Code` and `Reason-Phrase` indicate if a corresponding SOAP request message was processed successfully. In the case of a SOAP processing failure, the HTTP response message's `Status-Code` and `Reason-Phrase` must be 500 and "Internal Server Error," respectively, and the response message's body must be a SOAP message whose body contains a standard SOAP Fault element. Of course, in the case of a network failure, it is also possible that a client will not receive a response message. This is a standard problem with RPC protocols of all types, and the way clients deal with it varies across applications.

Here is a JavaScript function that uses the MSXML library to construct the first complete SOAP message discussed previously and to send it to an HTTP endpoint.

```
function placeorder(item, quantity)
{
  // build XML DOM for SOAP request message
  var domReq = new ActiveXObject("MSXML2.DOMDocument");
  // create envelope
  var elemEnv = domReq.createNode(1, "soap-env:Envelope",
                        "http://schemas.xmlsoap.org/soap/envelope/");
  elemEnv.setAttribute("soap-env:encodingStyle",
                        "http://schemas.xmlsoap.org/soap/encoding/");
  domReq.appendChild(elemEnv);
  // create body
  var elemBody = domReq.createElement("soap-env:Body");
  elemEnv.appendChild(elemBody);
  // create method
  var elemMethod = domReq.createNode(1, "tns:PlaceOrder",
                                  "urn:txcom:soap-methods");
  elemBody.appendChild(elemMethod);
  // add item argument
  var elemArg = domReq.createElement("Item");
  elemArg.text = item;
  elemMethod.appendChild(elemArg);
  // add quantity argument
  elemArg = domReq.createElement("Quantity");
  elemArg.text = quantity;
  elemMethod.appendChild(elemArg);
  // create HTTP "channel"
  var httpReq = new ActiveXObject("MSXML2.XMLHTTP");
  httpReq.open("POST", "http://localhost/test/soap_placeorder.asp",
            false);
```

```
// add SOAPAction header
httpReq.setRequestHeader("SOAPAction", "urn:txcom:soap-sample");
// send HTTP request message with SOAP request message as body
httpReq.send(domReq);
// if unexpected status code, throw exception
if (httpReq.status != 200 && httpReq.status != 500)
  throw "Unexpected response";
// retrieve XML DOM containing SOAP response message
var domResp = httpReq.responseXML;
// find SOAP response message body
var elemBody = domResp.
        selectSingleNode("/soap-env:Envelope/soap-env:Body");
// if SOAP fault, throw exception
if (httpReq.status == 500)
{
  var nodeFaultString = elemBody.
          selectSingleNode("soap-env:Fault/faultstring");
  var nodeNumber = elemBody.
          selectSingleNode("soap-env:Fault/detail/tns:Error/number");
  throw nodeFaultString.text + ", " + nodeNumber.text;
}
// if normal SOAP response, return OrderId
var nodeOrderId = elemBody.
        selectSingleNode("tns:PlaceOrderResponse/OrderId");
return parseInt(nodeOrderId.text);
}
```

The `placeorder` function constructs an XML Document Object Model (DOM) representing the SOAP message that it wants to send via HTTP. It adds a SOAP envelope and body and then a serialized instance of the `urn:txcom:soap-methods#PlaceOrder` type with the Item and Quantity elements set to the `item` and `quantity` input parameters, respectively. At that point, the function creates an `XMLHttpRequest` object that can be used to send an HTTP request message and receive an HTTP response message. It sets the request's method to `POST` and its endpoint to an ASP page called `soap_placeorder.asp`. It also adds the `SOAPAction` header, as mandated by the SOAP specification. Finally, it sends the HTTP request message, passing the SOAP message as the body. When the HTTP invocation completes, `placeorder` checks its status. If an unexpected problem occurs, the function throws an exception. Otherwise, it parses the SOAP message contained in the HTTP response message's body. If the SOAP message contains a standard

Fault element, the function extracts the relevant information and throws an exception. If the SOAP message contains a serialized instance of the `urn:txcom:soapmethods#PlaceOrderResponse` type, the function extracts the OrderId output element, converts it to a number, and returns it.

Here is a simple JavaScript client that calls the `placeorder` function. It is oblivious to the fact that the function makes an RPC call using SOAP.

```
try
{
  var orderId = placeorder("Ketchup", 20);
  WScript.Echo("Your order number is: " + orderId);
}
catch (e)
{
  WScript.Echo("An exception was thrown: " + e);
}
```

The implementation of the `soap_placeorder.asp` page that processes `placeorder`'s SOAP request message and generates a SOAP response message follows.

```
<%@ transaction=required language=jscript %>
<%
    Response.ContentType = "text/xml";
%>
<soap-env:Envelope
   xmlns:soap-env="http://schemas.xmlsoap.org/soap/envelope/"
    soap-env:encodingStyle="http://schemas.xmlsoap.org/soap/encoding/">
<soap-env:Body>
<tns:PlaceOrderResponse xmlns:tns="urn:txcom:soap-methods">
<OrderId>
<%
  // turn off page's happy bit
  ObjectContext.SetAbort();
  // create XML document to hold SOAP request message
  var domReq = Server.CreateObject("MSXML2.DOMDocument");
  domReq.async = false;
  domReq.load(Request);
  // validate SOAP envelope
  var elemEnv = domReq.documentElement;
  if (elemEnv.nodeName != "soap-env:Envelope" ||
      elemEnv.namespaceURI !=
                      "http://schemas.xmlsoap.org/soap/envelope/")
```

```
        throw "bad envelope";
      // validate SOAP encoding scheme
      var enc = elemEnv.getAttribute("soap-env:encodingStyle");
      if (enc != "http://schemas.xmlsoap.org/soap/encoding/")
        throw "bad encoding scheme";
      // validate SOAP body
      var elemBody = elemEnv.firstChild;
      if (elemBody.nodeName != "soap-env:Body")
        throw "bad body";
      // validate method
      var elemMethod = elemBody.firstChild;
      if (elemMethod.nodeName != "tns:PlaceOrder" ||
          elemMethod.namespaceURI != "urn:txcom:soap-methods")
        throw "bad method";
      // retrieve input parameters
      var elemItem = elemMethod.firstChild;
      var elemQuantity = elemMethod.lastChild;
      if (elemItem.nodeName != "Item" ||
          elemQuantity.nodeName != "Quantity")
        throw "bad parameter";
      // create an object and process request
      var obj = Server.CreateObject("OrderSystem.OrderProcessor");
      var orderId =
          obj.PlaceOrder(elemItem.text, parseInt(elemQuantity.text));
      // embed out parameter in HTTP/SOAP response message
      Response.Write(orderId);
      // turn page's happy bit on again
      ObjectContext.SetComplete();

      // map transaction abort to an exception
      function OnTransactionAbort()
      {
        throw "transaction aborted";
      }
  %>
  </OrderId>
  </tns:PlaceOrderResponse>
  </soap-env:Body>
  </soap-env:Envelope>
```

This page parses the SOAP request message that is embedded in the HTTP request message body into an XML DOM. It walks through the DOM looking for the elements and attributes defined by the SOAP specification (e.g., the envelope, the encoding style, and the body). If any of these is missing, the page throws an exception. Then the page looks for a PlaceOrder element containing an Item and a Quantity element. If any of these is missing, the page throws an exception. If the input SOAP message is valid, the page creates an instance of the `OrderSystem.OrderProcessor` class and calls its `PlaceOrder` method, passing both item and quantity as input. The `PlaceOrder` method returns an ID for the order that the page writes directly into the body of the HTTP response message. The rest of the HTTP response message's body is generated using static content that defines a valid SOAP message.

If the `soap_placeorder.asp` page encounters a problem, it throws an exception that is caught by the ASP extension. When `asp.dll` catches an exception, it automatically translates it into an HTTP response message. You can override this translation by creating a custom error page for a virtual directory (this option is configured in the metabase). Here is a sample error page that translates exceptions thrown by the preceding ASP page into SOAP messages containing standard Fault elements.

```
<%@ language=jscript %>
<%
    var err = Server.GetLastError();
    Response.Clear();
    Response.ContentType = "text/xml";
    Response.Status = "500 Internal Server Error";
%>
<soap-env:Envelope
    xmlns:soap-env="http://schemas.xmlsoap.org/soap/envelope/"
    soap-env:encodingStyle="http://schemas.xmlsoap.org/soap/encoding/">
<soap-env:Body>
<soap-env:Fault>
<faultcode>soap-enc:Server</faultcode>
<faultstring>
<%= err.Description %>
</faultstring>
<detail>
<tns:Error xmlns:tns="urn:txcom:soap-methods">
<number><%= err.Number</number>
</tns:Error>
</detail>
</soap-env:Fault>
</soap-env:Body>
</soap-env:Envelope>
```

This page retrieves the exception information from the ASP intrinsic `Server` object using the `GetLastError` method and resets the HTTP response message. The majority of the SOAP message is defined using static content, with relevant pieces of error information embedded where appropriate.

### Applying SOAP

At the time of this writing, SOAP is still a young protocol. The SOAP 1.1 specification has been published, and there is a lot of excitement about it, but there are not a lot of SOAP-enabled tools or frameworks shipping yet (although many are planned).[7] Some early adopters are already building SOAP-based distributed systems. In general, they are rolling their own serializers to map between their component technologies' type systems and the XML schema type system as restricted by SOAP's section 5. They are also defining their own mappings of SOAP requests to method invocations against objects. If you want to use SOAP today you will have to do the same thing. If you want to add SOAP support to IIS, an ISAPI extension that uses the Simple API for XML (SAX) provides the best performance (the previous example used ASP and the DOM for simplicity's sake). Note that you do not have to implement the SOAP specification in its entirety if your system does not have to interoperate with applications built by other groups. You can leave some features out and add them only when you need them (and chances are good that you will replace your hand-rolled SOAP code with a vendor's implementation before then).

In the short-term, SOAP will be used primarily by clients that want to make function calls to servers across the Internet (a problem desperately in need of a standard lightweight solution). Implementations will be layered on top of traditional HTTP servers such as IIS. Over time, SOAP will also be used as a foundation for more sophisticated distributed object frameworks in which any process can receive requests directly. It is easy to envision a future implementation of the COM+ runtime infrastructure layered on this type of plumbing. In fact, the canonical example of a SOAP extension header encodes a transaction identifier, perhaps, a TIP URL, as the following shows.

---

[7] IBM has given a Java-based implementation to the Apache open source project. Microsoft has shipped the COM-based SOAP Toolkit as an unsupported sample.

```
<soap-env:Envelope
    xmlns:soap-env="http://schemas.xmlsoap.org/soap/envelope/"
    soap-env:encodingStyle="http://schemas.xmlsoap.org/soap/encoding/">
  <soap-env:Header>
    <hdrs:TIPTxURL xmlns:hdrs="urn:txcom:headers"
                   soap-env:mustUnderstand=1>
    tip://source.xyz.com/?OleTx-687E90B0-E0DC-4658-956D-21D3BD493DBC
    </hdrs:TIPTxURL>
  </soap-env:Header>
  <soap-env:Body>
    ... <!-- mandatory body goes here -->
  </soap-env:Body>
</soap-env:Envelope>
```

There is one very common question about SOAP that I cannot leave unanswered. If a client can use SOAP and HTTP to call a function in a server, can a server use SOAP and HTTP to call back to a client? The answer is yes. As SOAP becomes more prevalent, client processes will start listening for HTTP request messages representing callbacks. However, RPC-style callbacks are unlikely to work across the Internet. This is not because of SOAP or HTTP, but because of the structure of the Internet itself. The proxy servers, bridges, routers, and firewalls that form the Internet's backbone are generally configured to allow clients to establish connections and send messages to servers, but not the other way around. These obstacles restrict the flow of messages, and that's the way security-conscious users like it. Schemes for sending SOAP messages via the standard Internet mail protocols, SMTP and POP3, will be developed to address this problem. (The Apache open source SOAP kit from IBM already supports these protocols.)

## Message Queuing

DCOM and HTTP are both request/response protocols. To use either of them, you have to establish a connection to a server, send a request message, and then wait for a response message. Both protocols support sending request messages without blocking clients' threads and deferring the generation of response messages without blocking server threads. (Unfortunately, DCOM's support for these semantics is incompatible with COM+.) Neither protocol supports sending request messages that do not generate response messages, or sending a request and receiving a response without holding a connection open for the entire duration of the exchange. If you want either of these semantics, you need to use *message queueing*.

The idea behind message queuing is simple: Programs asynchronously communicate with one another by sending messages to and receiving messages from queues. A message is an opaque array of bytes with certain well-known header fields that control how it gets delivered. The body of a message can contain raw XML, a SOAP message, a serialized COM object, or anything else an application requires. A queue is a named, ordered repository of messages on a particular machine. Queues act as buffers that allow processes to exchange messages without connecting directly to one another, even when the processes' lifetimes do not overlap. A message queuing infrastructure handles all the details of message delivery and queue management. Windows 2000's built-in queuing infrastructure is called Microsoft Message Queue (MSMQ). You can use it to create custom application-level protocols that are not restricted to the simple request/response model of DCOM and HTTP.

The heart of MSMQ is the queue manager service, `mqsvc.exe`, which runs on MSMQ-enabled servers and independent clients (dependent clients rely on an instance of the service running on a local server). Message queuing applications use their machines' queue managers to send and receive messages to and from queues, as illustrated in Figure 8-11.

Queue managers can be accessed via a set of Visual Basic and script-friendly nonconfigured COM classes or a low-level C API. Queue managers are responsible for the temporary storage of outgoing messages destined for queues on other machines, the delivery of messages to queue managers on other machines, and the reception and storage of incoming messages being sent to queues on their own machines. Information about all queue managers in a given MSMQ installation is stored in the Windows 2000 Active Directory.

MSMQ has a special place in COM+-based systems because queue managers are transaction-aware RMs. Messaging operations (i.e., sends and receives) can be protected using local MSMQ transactions or DTC-dispensed distributed transactions, including declarative transactions managed by COM+. The outcome of the messaging operations depends on whether the transaction commits or aborts.

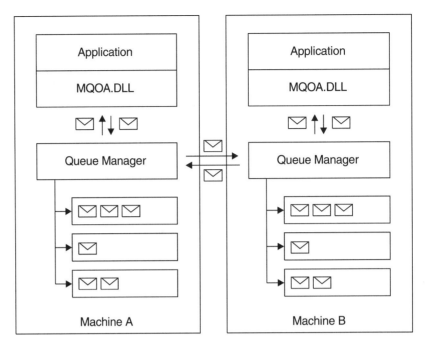

**Figure 8-11   The role of queue managers**

### Transactional Messaging

Messages can be sent to local or remote queues within the scope of a transaction. If messages are sent in a transaction, the local queue manager holds them until the transaction ends. If the transaction commits, the queue manager sends the messages to their destination queues. If the transaction aborts, the messages are discarded. Messages can be received from local queues within the scope of a transaction. The local queue manager removes the messages from their destination queues. If the transaction commits, the messages are gone. If the transaction aborts, the messages are returned to their queues. It is important to note that transactions are the only way to ensure that messages are delivered to their destination queues *exactly once* and, if multiple messages are sent to the same queue, that they arrive *in order* (although other messages may be interleaved). It is equally important to note that, by definition, a message that is sent in a transaction cannot arrive in its destination queue until after the transaction commits. As a result, a single transaction cannot protect the sending and receiving of the same message.

The MSMQ COM application program interface provides the `IMSMQMessage::Send` and `IMSMQQueue::Receive` methods for sending and receiving messages, respectively. Both methods take a transaction argument, encoded in a VARIANT. Either argument can be a numeric constant or a pointer to an object representing a local or distributed transaction.

Here is an example that shows how a local transaction is used.

```
HRESULT CSomeClass::SendMessages(BSTR bstrMsg1,
                                 BSTR bstrMsg2,
                                 BSTR bstrDestQ)
{
  // open destination queue for sending
  CComPtr<IMSMQQueueInfo> spDestQInfo;
  HRESULT hr = spDestQInfo.CoCreateInstance(__uuidof(MSMQQueueInfo));
  if (FAILED(hr)) return hr;
  hr = spDestQInfo->put_PathName(bstrDestQ);
  if (FAILED(hr)) return hr;
  CComPtr<IMSMQQueue> spDestQ;
  hr = spDestQInfo->Open(MQ_SEND_ACCESS, MQ_DENY_NONE);
  if (FAILED(hr)) return hr;
  // figure out if queue is transactional
  bool bTxQ = false;
  hr = pQInfo->get_IsTransactional(&bTx);
  if (FAILED(hr)) return hr;
  // initialize VARIANT parameter to pass to IMSMQMessage::Send
    CComVariant vTx;
  if (!bTxQ)
    vTx = MQ_NO_TRANSACTION;
  else
  {
    // create object representing local transaction manager
    CComPtr<IMSMQTransactionDispenser> spLocalTM;
    hr = spLocalTM.
           CoCreateInstance(__uuidof(MSMQTransactionDispenser));
    if (FAILED(hr)) return hr;
    // begin local transaction
    CComPtr<IMSMQTransaction> spLocalTx;
    hr = spLocalTM->BeginTransaction(&spLocalTx);
    if (FAILED(hr)) return hr;
    vTx = spLocalTx.p;
  }
  // send messages using appropriate transaction option
  CComPtr<IMSMQMessage spMsg;
  hr = spMsg.CoCreateInstance(__uuidof(MSMQMessage));
```

```
    if (FAILED(hr)) return hr;
    hr = spMsg->put_Label(bstrMsg1);
    if (FAILED(hr)) return hr;
    hr = spMsg->Send(spDestQ, &vTx);
    if (FAILED(hr)) return hr;
    hr = spMsg->put_Label(bstrMsg2);
    if (FAILED(hr)) return hr;
    hr = spMsg->Send(spDestQ, &vTx);
    if (FAILED(hr)) return hr;
    // commit local transaction if necessary
    if (bTxQ)
    {
      hr = spLocalTx->Commit(&CComVariant(false),
                             &CComVariant(XACTTC_SYNC_PHASETWO),
                             &CComVariant(0));
      if (FAILED(hr)) return hr;
    }
    return S_OK;
}
```

The `CSomeClass::SendMessages` method takes three input parameters:
`bstrMsg1` and `bstrMsg2` are messages that need to be sent to the destination queue identified by `bstrDestQ`. The method opens the queue for send access and then examines the queue's metadata to see whether it is transactional. A transactional queue is simply a queue that was marked as supporting transactions when it was created. Queue managers enforce a strict set of rules for mixing transactions and queues. Specifically, all sends to transactional queues *must* be protected by transactions, receives from transactional queues *may or may not* be protected by transactions, and all sends to and receives from nontransactional queues *must not* be protected by transactions. If you violate these rules, a queue manager will reject your request with a well-known error code, `MQ_ERROR_TRANSACTION_USAGE`.

Once `SendMessages` knows whether the destination queue is transactional, it initializes a VARIANT called `vTx` to pass to `IMSMQMessage::Send`. If the destination queue is not transactional, `vTx` is set to the constant `MQ_NO_TRANSACTION`, indicating that a transaction should not be used. If the destination queue is transactional, `vTx` is set to a reference to an object representing a local MSMQ transaction acquired from MSMQ's internal transaction manager. Once `vTx` is initialized, `SendMessages` sends the two messages it is passed as input to the local queue manager using a new message object. The VARIANT is passed as the second parameter to both calls to `IMSMQ Message::Send`. Finally, if the destination queue is transactional, `Send Messages` commits the transaction (the `IMSMQTransaction::Commit` method takes the same parameters as the `ITransaction::Commit` method discussed in Chapter 6, "Transactions"). If the destination queue is not transactional (`vTx` contains `MQ_NO_TRANSACTION`), the local queue manager will immediately forward each message when `Send` is called. If the destination queue is transactional (`vTx` contains a reference to a local MSMQ transaction), the queue manager will cache the two messages until it knows the transaction's outcome and will forward them only if the transaction commits.

MSMQ defines the constant `MQ_SINGLE_MESSAGE` to tell the implementation of `IMSMQMessage::Send` to implicitly create a local transaction to protect the operation and then to commit it immediately. This is simply a convenience so that you do not have to write a lot of extra code when you want to send a single message with transactional semantics, that is, guaranteed-exactly-once delivery, or to a transactional queue. This simplified version of the previous example demonstrates.

```
HRESULT CSomeClass::SendMessage(BSTR bstrMsg,
                                BSTR bstrDestQ)
{
  // open destination queue for sending
  CComPtr<IMSMQQueueInfo> spDestQInfo;
  HRESULT hr = spDestQInfo.CoCreateInstance(__uuidof(MSMQQueueInfo));
  if (FAILED(hr)) return hr;
  hr = spDestQInfo->put_PathName(bstrDestQ);
  if (FAILED(hr)) return hr;
  CComPtr<IMSMQQueue> spDestQ;
  hr = spDestQInfo->Open(MQ_SEND_ACCESS, MQ_DENY_NONE);
  if (FAILED(hr)) return hr;
  // figure out if queue is transactional
  bool bTxQ = false;
  hr = pQInfo->get_IsTransactional(&bTx);
  if (FAILED(hr)) return hr;
  // initialize VARIANT parameter to pass to IMSMQMessage::Send
  CComVariant vTx;
  if (!bTxQ)
    vTx = MQ_NO_TRANSACTION;
  else
```

```
        vTx = MQ_SINGLE_MESSAGE;
    // send messages using appropriate transaction option
    hr = pMsg->Send(pDestQ, &vTx);
    if (FAILED(hr)) return hr;
    return S_OK;
}
```

The `CSomeClass::SendMessage` method works the same way the previous `CSomeClass::SendMessages` method does. However, in this case, the local queue manager will forward the message immediately even if the destination queue is transactional because the implicit local transaction's outcome is known by the time the call to `IMSMQMessage::Send` completes.

The discussion of raw configured classes in Chapter 3, "Mechanics," uses as an example a class that encapsulates sending event notifications using MSMQ. Specifically, it says that the class could be implemented as a raw-configured class that uses a context's declarative transaction if there is one or an internal MSMQ transaction if there is not. Here is a new version of the previous example that illustrates this idea.

```
HRESULT CRawCfgNotifierClass::SendMessage(BSTR bstrMsg,
                                          BSTR bstrDestQ)
{
    // open destination queue for sending
    CComPtr<IMSMQQueueInfo> spDestQInfo;
    HRESULT hr = spDestQInfo.CoCreateInstance(__uuidof(MSMQQueueInfo));
    if (FAILED(hr)) return hr;
    hr = spDestQInfo->put_PathName(bstrDestQ);
    if (FAILED(hr)) return hr;
    CComPtr<IMSMQQueue> spDestQ;
    hr = spDestQInfo->Open(MQ_SEND_ACCESS, MQ_DENY_NONE);
    if (FAILED(hr)) return hr;
    // figure out if queue is transactional
    bool bTxQ = false;
    hr = pQInfo->get_IsTransactional(&bTx);
    if (FAILED(hr)) return hr;
    // get info about context
    CComPtr<IObjectContextInfo> spCtxInfo;
    hr = CoGetObjectContext(__uuidof(spCtxInfo), (void**)&spCtxInfo);
    if (FAILED(hr)) return hr;
    bool bTxCtx = spCtxInfo->IsInTransaction();
    // initialize VARIANT parameter to pass to IMSMQMessage::Send
    CComVariant vTx;
```

```
    if (!bTxQ)
      vTx = MQ_NO_TRANSACTION;
    else if (!bTxCtx)
      vTx = MQ_SINGLE_MESSAGE;
    else
      vTx = MQ_MTS_TRANSACTION;
    // send messages using appropriate transaction option
    hr = pMsg->Send(pDestQ, &vTx);
    return S_OK;
}
```

The `CRawCfgNotifierClass::SendMessage` method examines information about the destination queue to see if it is transactional. It also examines information about the current context to see if it is transactional, that is, if it is in a transaction stream. If the destination queue is not transactional, the method does not use a transaction; that is, it passes `MQ_NO_TRANSACTION` to `IMSMQMessage::Send`. If the destination queue is transactional, but the context is not, the method uses a local MSMQ transaction; that is, it passes `MQ_SINGLE_MESSAGE` to `IMSMQMessage::Send`. If both the destination queue and the current context are transactional, the method tells the queue manager to use the context's declarative transaction by passing `MQ_MTS_TRANSACTION` to `IMSMQMessage::Send`. The implementation of `Send` extracts a reference to the transaction stream's distributed transaction and asks the local queue manager to enlist against it. The local queue manager will cache the message until the declarative transaction ends. Then it will send or discard the message, depending on the transaction's outcome.

Here is an example that shows how this raw-configured event notification class is used.

```
HRESULT CSomeTxClass::DoWorkAndSendMessage(void)
{
  CComPtr<IContextState> spCtxState;
  HRESULT hr = CoGetObjectContext(__uuidof(spCtxState),
                                  (void**)&spCtxState);
  if (FAILED(hr)) return hr;
  hr = spCtxState->SetDeactivateOnReturn(VARIANT_TRUE);
  if (FAILED(hr)) return hr;
  hr = spCtxState->SetMyTransactionVote(TxAbort);
  if (FAILED(hr)) return hr;
  CComPtr<IMessageSender> spMsgSender;
```

```
hr = spMsgSender.CoCreateInstance(__uuidof(CRawCfgNotifierClass));
if (FAILED(hr)) return hr;
hr = spMsgSender->SendMessage(CComBSTR("Doing work"),
                              CComBSTR("adminbox\\events"));
if (FAILED(hr)) return hr;
... // use decl. transaction to protect database work
hr = spCtxState->SetMyTransactionVote(TxCommit);
if (FAILED(hr)) return hr;
return S_OK;
}
```

The `CSomeTxClass::DoWorkAndSendMessage` uses a declarative transaction to protect the work it does with a back-end database. It also creates an instance of `CRawCfgNotifierClass` and calls `SendMessage` to send a "`Doing work`" message to the `adminbox\events` queue. The `CRawCfg NotifierClass` object is created in the `CSomeTxClass` object's context and will use its declarative transaction. The local queue manager will send the message only if the `CSomeTxClass` object's declarative transaction commits.

## Applying Message Queuing

MSMQ provides an asynchronous, disconnected, message-based communication model that can be integrated with transactions. It is a great way to send event notifications without having to connect to receivers and wait while they process the messages (the receivers do not even have to be running). MSMQ is also a great way to defer crucial but not time-critical work in order to reduce client response time. For example, imagine a server that wants to record auditing information when it responds to a client request. Instead of making the client wait while it writes to the auditing database, the server does whatever work is required to respond to the client's request and simply leaves a message about what happened in a queue. The auditing system receives the message and records the information in the auditing database. This latter step is crucial, but not time critical. Using MSMQ to defer this work decreases client response time. It also adds a buffer—the queue—that can help the auditing system handle different load levels more gracefully.

Although MSMQ provides benefits that DCOM and HTTP do not, it is not nearly as widely used as either of those traditional RPC technologies. I attribute this to two factors. First, MSMQ is not installed by default and many system administrators do not want to install, configure, and maintain it. Second, MSMQ is extremely flexible, so it leaves a lot of things up to you. You have to define the contents of messages and how they flow. Simple request/response exchanges are possible, but are not required and are often not desired. Complex publish-subscribe message flows are possible, but MSMQ provides no intrinsic support for them (today). You have to explicitly create and destroy endpoints, that is, queues. You have to deal not just with logical errors in message processing (e.g., the message's contents were unexpected), but also with physical errors in message delivery (e.g., the message didn't reach the queue in time, the sender does not have the right to send the message to the queue, etc.). In short, along with MSMQ's power comes a lot of responsibility.

The most telling example of this extra responsibility is the requirement that you build a message receiver. While the operating system provides support for receiving DCOM and HTTP request messages and automatically executing code to generate response messages, it does not provide support for receiving MSMQ messages. If you want to receive MSMQ messages in a given process, it is up to you to write the code that retrieves those messages from their destination queue, processes them, and generates the required output messages, if any. This would be simply a threading problem if it weren't for transactions. If you receive a message from a queue using a transaction, the message will be returned to the queue if the transaction aborts. If the message's content is causing the transaction to abort (as opposed to some mechanical problem such as being unable to acquire a database connection), the message will continually return to the queue and be reprocessed *ad infinitum*. This is known as the *poison message* problem. The typical solution is to implement a receiver that keeps track of the number of times it has seen a given message and, after some number of retries, decides that the message must be poisonous, receives it without using a transaction, and then discards it. This approach is very similar to the timeout solution used by distributed transactions to detect and resolve deadlocks. It is not difficult to implement, but it is an additional burden that you have to carry.

The MSMQ team is aware of these issues and working on fixing them. There is already an add-on service that lets you define triggers to execute programs or call COM objects when messages that meet defined criteria arrive in a specific queue. This simplifies implementing a receiver, but it does not deal with the poison message problem.[8] The next version of MSMQ is likely to provide a more sophisticated solution. It is also expected to provide intrinsic support for publish-subscribe message flows and for transferring messages between queue managers using SOAP messages over HTTP (messages are transferred using RPC and TCP protocols today).

MSMQ's integration with transactions sets it apart from other protocols. Despite all the tasks it leaves to you, it is well worth considering MSMQ as an option for communication in your COM+ applications.[9]

## Summary

Most COM+ applications use HTTP in some capacity. HTTP is a simple message-based request/response protocol. HTTP messages contain headers and optional bodies encoded using MIME types. HTTP servers like IIS listen for request messages, apply their methods to target resources identified by URLs, and generate response messages capturing the method's output. You can extend IIS's default behavior using low-level ISAPI extensions or high-level ASP pages. Both mechanisms allow you to process HTTP request messages and generate HTTP response messages programmatically. IIS is tightly integrated with COM+ and uses it to control what processes ISAPI extensions and ASP pages are executed in. A side effect of this relationship is that both ISAPI and ASP requests are processed in COM+ contexts with predictable configurations. Specifically, an ISAPI extension's `HttpExtensionProc` is invoked in a context in a process's MTA, and an ASP page's scripts are executed in a context in an STA, an activity, and, if a page is transactional, in a transaction stream. An increasing number of systems are using HTTP as a way to make RPC calls across the Internet. SOAP formalizes this idea by defining a standard scheme for encoding function calls as instances of XML schema types. SOAP is still very young and is not widely adopted today. You should expect SOAP to become increasingly important in the future.

---

[8] The infrastructure for Queued Components provides a listener too, but as I mentioned in the preface, it is bound to `dllhost.exe` and cannot be used to send messages to other processes, that is, clients.

[9] This is a very brief introduction to MSMQ. For more information, see *Designing MSMQ Applications* by Alan Dickman and the Microsoft Platform SDK documentation on MSMQ.

Finally, some COM+-based systems use MSMQ to define their own message-based communication protocols. MSMQ is unique among COM+ protocols because it extends transactional protection to the sending and receiving of messages. MSMQ is a great way to send event notifications without having to establish a connection with an interested party or wait for it to process an event. MSMQ is also a great way to defer crucial work from the critical path in order to reduce client response times.

# Chapter 9

# Design

The first chapter of this book summarizes the basic architectural model for COM+-based systems using three simple rules: Embrace the object-per-client model, minimize locking in both time and space, and model client tasks using processor objects that execute on middle-tier servers. Chapters 2 through 8 describe the mechanical details of the core COM+ runtime services and provide rules about the best ways to use them. Building on the blocks of contexts, causalities, threads, objects, transactions, and communication protocols in hand, this final chapter returns to the topic of architecture and prescribes a simple, flexible, and scalable model for COM+ applications.

## Machines, Processes, and Protocols

The COM+ runtime environment serves as a foundation for the development of distributed systems. The first step in building a COM+-based system is designing its distributed architecture, that is, deciding how machines will be used, what processes will run on them, and what protocols those processes will use to communicate. It makes sense to start with these physical aspects of a system because they influence the basic structure of the code you have to write.

### Machine Architecture

A COM+-based system can use machines in any number of ways, but two architectures are very common. Many COM+-based systems opt for a simple model, shown in Figure 9-1, that uses a single middle tier of Web servers to process client requests. The tight integration between COM+ and IIS makes it easy to leverage any necessary runtime services from a combination of ASP pages and objects.

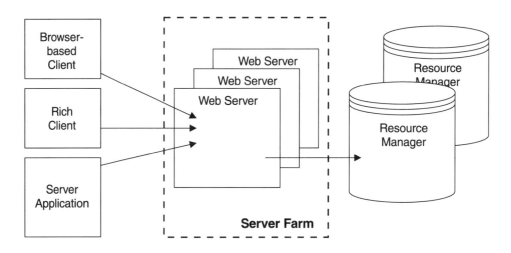

**Figure 9-1    A simple machine architecture**

Some COM+-based systems use more complex machine architecture, such as the one shown in Figure 9-2, that backs an outer middle tier of Web servers with an inner middle tier of application servers, which may also be accessed by other server applications. Some systems use this approach in order to place a firewall in front of the application server code that accesses their back-end databases. Some systems use this approach in order to offload complex logic processing from the Web servers, leaving more resources free to generate HTTP response messages. This makes sense when the Web servers can respond to a significant percentage of client requests without relying on the application servers, a common occurrence in many systems that return lots of static resources such as HTML and images to browser-based thin clients. If you design a COM+-based system with this latter architecture, you must be careful about how you divide work between the two sets of middle-tier machines. Specifically, there must be a clean separation so that a Web server can respond to a client request with a minimal number of calls (preferably no more than one) to an application server.

### Process Architecture

Once you have decided on an overall machine architecture, you must design a process architecture for each machine. For best performance, a COM+-based system should use as few processes on each machine as possible, optimally

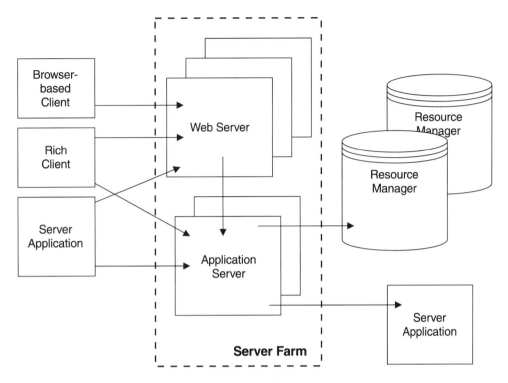

**Figure 9-2  A more complex machine architecture**

one. Processes consume operating system resources, and interprocess communication is expensive, so if a system uses a single process on each machine, overhead will be minimized. In some cases, however, multiple processes are necessary. You might want an additional process to isolate potentially buggy code so that if that process crashes it won't harm the rest of your system. For instance, as Chapter 8 explains, `inetinfo.exe` achieves fault isolation by loading ISAPI extensions into instances of `dllhost.exe`.

You also might want to create an additional process in order to take complete control of its threading and its lifecycle. For example, if you were creating an MSMQ "listener" to process messages when they arrive in a queue, it might make sense to create a dedicated process with a thread pool custom-designed for that task. The process could still leverage COM+ runtime services either by loading library applications or calling out to server applications. As Chapter 8 explains, IIS takes this approach with `inetinfo.exe`.

Finally, you might want an additional process in order to execute code under a different security principal.[1]

**Protocols**

In the previous section, both of the examples that motivate the use of multiple processes on a single machine (i.e., fault isolation and a custom thread pool) are tied to the integration of communication protocols and the COM+ runtime. The use of a particular protocol can have a significant impact on how processes are used. You cannot define a complete process architecture without specifying the protocols that processes will use to communicate. It is important to get protocol choices right early in the design process because changing them later is typically difficult and time-consuming.

The vast majority of COM+ systems use at least one of the three mainstream protocols discussed in the previous chapter: HTTP (carrying some combination of HTML, XML, and SOAP messages), DCOM, and MSMQ. Some COM+ systems also have to use RPC, MQ Series (IBM's message queuing infrastructure), SMTP (the Internet e-mail protocol), custom socket-based APIs, and other protocols to integrate with non-COM+ and non-Windows systems.

Although COM+-based systems have a wide choice of communication protocols in general, two factors are likely to limit your options in practice. First, if processes need to communicate across the Internet, they need to use an Internet-friendly protocol such as HTTP (or SMTP). Second, if two processes need to be tightly integrated with regard to COM+ services, they need to communicate with DCOM. If two processes communicate using a protocol other than DCOM, neither context properties (i.e., an activity or a transaction stream) nor causality properties (i.e., a CID or call chain security information) can propagate between them.

Another important factor that affects protocol selection is support for load balancing. Load balancing helps minimize response time and maximize the use of available resources by dynamically assigning client connection requests to servers based on some algorithm (e.g., round-robin or server load). HTTP's

---

[1] In some cases this can also be achieved by impersonation. See *Programming Windows Security* by Keith Brown for more information.

connectionless usage style makes it easy to load balance because clients are continually closing and reopening connections. Windows 2000 supports HTTP load balancing using the Network Load Balancing (NLB) service. Lots of other third-party products support HTTP load balancing too (e.g., Cisco's Local Director). DCOM's connection-oriented style makes it harder to load balance. DCOM clients typically create and hold connections to objects over time. Since client requests sent through a proxy always go to the same destination context, the only way to dynamically rebalance server-side load is for clients to continually release their proxies and create new objects to force the creation of new connections. As Chapter 5 explains, just-in-time activation (JITA) does not change this. This is not an issue if your DCOM clients are ASP pages that release their proxies when their scripts are done executing. It is an issue if your DCOM clients are traditional Windows programs that hold onto objects for extended periods. Application Center 2000, a Windows 2000 extension, supports DCOM load balancing using the Component Load Balancing (CLB) service. Of course HTTP and DCOM are not the only protocols that support load balancing, lots of protocols can be balanced using the NLB service or other products.

For many systems, the choice of protocols is obvious. Simple COM+-based systems with the basic machine architecture shown in Figure 9-1 use HTTP for all client-server access, as shown in Figure 9-3. The `inetinfo.exe` process uses DCOM to dispatch work to the surrogate `dllhost.exe` process, but this is hidden from view.

More complex COM+-based systems use a wider range of protocols in a wider range of ways. For example, a system with the machine architecture shown in Figure 9-2 might use both HTTP and DCOM for client-server communication and DCOM, MSMQ, and even HTTP for server-server communication, as shown in Figure 9-4.

It is worth noting that a small (but increasing) number of COM+-based systems use HTTP and XML for lightweight cross-machine RPC calls from Web servers to application servers within their middle-tier server farms. This limits what you can do with the COM+ runtime services, but it gains the simplicity and flexibility of the HTTP programming model, without sacrificing scalability.

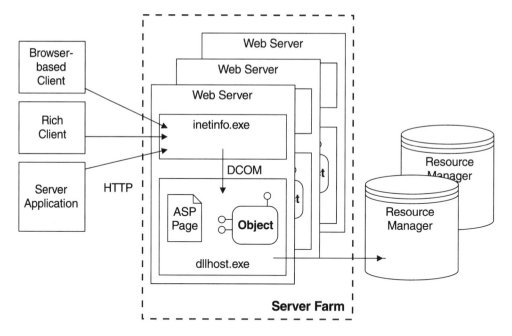

**Figure 9-3   A simple process and protocol model**

## Processors and Helpers

Once you have decided on a physical architecture for the middle tier (i.e., you know the machines, processes, and protocols you are going to use), you need to define the set of classes each process can use to respond to client requests. You must consider the classes' logical and physical models, both of which are shaped by the Rules defined in earlier chapters.

### A Simple Logical Model

The logical model for any COM+ process is based on the notion of processor objects introduced in Chapter 1 (Rule 1.3). A processor object is in essence a part of a client that executes in a middle-tier server process for mechanical reasons, that is, efficiency with regard to network roundtrips and access to a transaction manager. Processors model the world from a client's perspective, using that broader knowledge to implement tasks both correctly and efficiently, using a transaction when necessary. Each client creates its own processor objects and invokes their methods to accomplish tasks; processor objects are never shared (Rule 1.1).

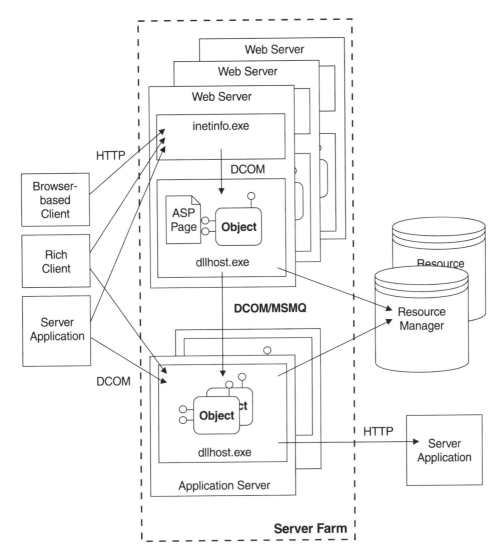

**Figure 9-4  A more complex process and protocol model**

Processor classes use helper classes (or utility classes) to accomplish tasks. Helper classes encapsulate useful pieces of code and make them reusable. For instance, a piece of code that creates a database connection, invokes a SQL statement, and checks for errors could be implemented as a reusable helper class. Similarly, code that sends an event notification via MSMQ might be implemented as a reusable helper class. A helper class could also be used to encapsulate a particular security policy by testing for the presence of a particular digital certificate when a request arrives from an HTTP client, for instance. Figure 9-5 shows how clients use processors to accomplish tasks and processors use helpers to implement tasks.

Processors may communicate with databases and other RMs directly or indirectly through helpers. They use transactions to protect their data access work. Clients and processors pass data back and forth by value. This is the simple logical model that COM+ is designed to support (Rule 6.4).

## A Simple Physical Model

A logical class model is necessary for the design of a COM+-based system, but it is not sufficient. You also need a physical model for classes to define the various aspects of their relationship to context, that is, what declarative attribute settings they use, how they use object context and call context, how they marshal, and how they are deployed. The basic goal in defining this model is to ensure that contexts are used efficiently. In short, that means ensuring that new contexts are created only when they are absolutely required to provide a useful runtime service.

Defining a standard and efficient physical model for classes is easy. The basic concept is simple: Processor classes are solely responsible for defining the runtime services a context needs to provide to accomplish a given client

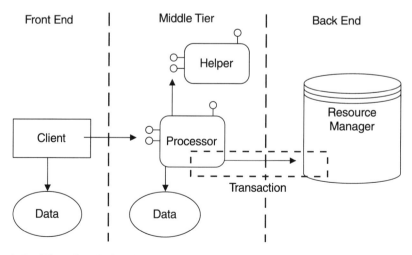

**Figure 9-5   The simple logical model that COM+ is designed to support**

task. Processors are configured classes. Helper classes define minimal context requirements, and their instances reside in the contexts of the processors that created them. Helpers can be raw-configured like the database connection pooling classes described in Appendix B, "Building a Better Connection Pool"; non-configured, like the COM classes implemented by OLE DB providers and ADO; or language-level classes, like the ATL OLE DB consumer templates. Defining helper classes that can be instantiated in their processors' contexts reduces resource consumption in both time and space (Rule 3.2).

Table 9-1 lists the appropriate default values for a configured processor class's declarative attributes. Processor classes are responsible for establishing appropriately configured contexts of their own, so they should never require activation in their clients' contexts (though, if possible, the SCM will put them there). Processor classes can use the object construction service if they implement `IObjectConstruct`. They should disable the statistics service unless they are being instantiated via the CLB service, which uses the aggregate data

**Table 9-1  Default declarative attributes for processor classes**

| Declarative Attribute | Value |
| --- | --- |
| MustRunInClientContext | False |
| ConstructionEnabled, et al. | True, if useful (must implement IObjectConstruct) |
| EventTrackingEnabled | False, unless DCOM load balancing is required |
| COMAdminThreadingModel | COMAdminThreadingModelBoth or COMAdminThreadingModelApartment |
| COMAdminSynchronization | COMAdminSynchronizationRequired |
| COMAdminTransaction | COMAdminTransactionNone, unless a declarative transaction is required |
| ComponentTransaction TimeoutEnabled, et al. | False, unless a declarative transaction with a specific timeout is required |
| ObjectPoolingEnabled, et al. | True, if useful (should implement IObjectControl) |
| JustInTimeActivation | False, unless a declarative transaction is required |

it generates to measure server load. In general, processor classes should be marked `COMAdminThreadingModelBoth` or `COMAdminThreadingModel Apartment`, depending on implementation language and whether they rely on STA-based objects (Rule 4.1). They should also be marked `COMAdmin SynchronizationRequired` so that calls to instances are serialized based on causality, and data members do not have to be explicitly protected from concurrent access (Rule 4.2). Processor classes should be marked `COMAdmin TransactionNone` (Not Supported)—and should not support a custom timeout—unless a distributed transaction is needed to protect work against more than one RM (Rule 6.5). Processor classes should use the object pooling service if the benefits are worthwhile (Rule 5.4). Remember that pooled classes should implement `IObjectControl` and must manage context-relative resources correctly (Rules 5.1, 5.2, and 5.3). Finally, processor classes should manage resources efficiently without relying on JITA (Rule 5.5). You should not deviate from these defaults unless you have a compelling reason to do so (e.g., one of the caveats regarding thread affinity or synchronization defined by Rules 4.1 or 4.2, respectively, applies). Also, as noted in Chapter 2, once a processor class's declarative settings are defined, they should not be changed without the express permission of the author, the only person who knows which attribute values are safe (Rule 2.1).

Table 9-2 lists the appropriate default values for a raw-configured helper class's declarative attributes. If a helper class is nonconfigured, only the threading model attribute applies. None of the attributes apply to language-level helper classes, whose instances are always instantiated in the current context.

Most of the default settings for raw-configured helper classes are identical to the options for processors. However, there are a few key differences. Helper classes should require activation in their clients' contexts because they are designed to work in the environment the processor that creates them provides. Helper classes should never use either the statistics service or JITA; both these services force new objects into contexts of their own. Finally, helper classes should be marked `COMAdminTransactionIgnored` (Disabled), indicating that instances should be placed in the creating processor's context independent of its relationship to a transaction stream. Again, you should not

**Table 9-2 Default declarative attributes for helper classes**

| Declarative Attribute | Value |
| --- | --- |
| MustRunInClientContext | True |
| ConstructionEnabled, et al. | True, if useful (must implement IObjectConstruct) |
| EventTrackingEnabled | False |
| COMAdminThreadingModel | COMAdminThreadingModelBoth or COMAdminThreadingModelApartment |
| COMAdminSynchronization | COMAdminSynchonizationRequired |
| COMAdminTransaction | COMAdminTransactionIgnored |
| ComponentTransaction TimeoutEnabled, et al. | False |
| ObjectPoolingEnabled, et al. | True, if useful (should implement IObjectControl) |
| JustInTimeActivation | False |

deviate from these defaults unless you have a compelling reason to do so, and, once a helper class's attributes have been defined, you should not change them without the permission of the author.

Instances of helper classes must be able to work in any context that provides the level of thread affinity and synchronization they require (Rule 3.2). In practice, that means being prepared to execute logic conditionally based on the configuration of a processor's context. Configuration information can be retrieved from object context using the `IObjectContextInfo` interface or from call context using the `ISecurityCallContext` interface. For instance, the last MSMQ example in Chapter 8 includes the code for a raw-configured helper class that tested for the presence of a transaction stream by calling `IObjectContextInfo::IsInTransaction`.

A helper object can examine object context in its language-level constructor (or in `FinalConstruct` in ATL)—or if it is an instance of a pooled class, its implementation of `IObjectControl::Activate`—and fail to instantiate if the environment it is being created in does not meet its needs. This technique is useful because it allows helper classes to insist that runtime services be present without declaring their need for them, which requires deployment in the COM+ catalog and may cause the SCM to create a new context. For instance, a nonconfigured helper class can still require activity-based synchronization by testing for the presence of an activity in its `FinalConstruct` method, as the following example shows.

```
HRESULT FinalConstruct(void)
{
  // get reference to object context
  CComPtr<IObjectContextInfo> spCtxInfo;
  HRESULT hr = CoGetObjectContext(__uuidof(spCtxInfo),
                                  (void**)&spCtxInfo);
  if (FAILED(hr)) return hr;
  // retrieve activity id
  GUID actId;
  hr = spCtxInfo->GetActivityId(&actId);
  if (FAILED(hr)) return hr;
  // fail call and stop object construction if not in an activity
  return actId != GUID_NULL ? S_OK : E_FAIL;
}
```

Although a helper object can interrogate object context to see how the context it is being used in is configured, it should not modify object context by setting the state of either the happy or done bits, if present. The happy and done bits should be set only by a context's distinguished object, that is, a transactional processor object. In short, control of a declarative transaction's outcome should be left to the object explicitly configured to use one.

There are two mechanical issues to consider when implementing helper classes. First, as Chapter 3 explains, you have to be aware of the subtle complexities of creating multiple objects in a single context. Remember that COM+ configures a context to meet the needs of an initial object—the context's distinguished object—but then applies the context's runtime services to all the objects that live there. This can lead to unpredictable results, so you must avoid handing out to callers any references to nondistinguished objects in a context unless they custom marshal (Rules 3.3 and 3.4). In practical terms, that means that while processor classes use standard marshaling to get required runtime services, raw-configured and nonconfigured helper classes should, strictly speaking, implement `IMarshal` and either prevent marshaling by failing every method call, rely on the Free-Threaded Marshaler (FTM) to bypass standard marshaling and interception or implement marshal-by-value semantics. Many raw-configured and nonconfigured helper classes do not implement custom marshaling. Instead, they simply expect their processors not to return references to them to callers. This is the only option for helper classes written in Visual Basic, which cannot implement `IMarshal`. Marshaling is obviously not an issue for instances of language-level helper classes, whose references cannot be marshaled anyway.

Second, instances of raw-configured helper classes cannot be instantiated in a processor object's context unless they are deployed in an application that does not support role-based security. Remember that the SCM always puts new instances of classes deployed in an application that supports role-based security into new contexts of their own, whether access checks are enabled or not. If you want instances of raw-configured helper classes to share their creators' contexts, you must deploy them in applications marked `AccessChecksLevel = AccessChecksApplicationLevel` (the default value for an application is `AccessChecksApplicationComponentLevel`).

## Accessing Processors via HTTP

Clients use processor classes to accomplish tasks. Although processor objects can be accessed directly via DCOM, most COM+-based systems use HTTP for client-server communication, and some use it for server-server communication as well. Fortunately, the processor model's function-oriented nature makes it easy to integrate with HTTP. All you need is some code to receive HTTP request messages, invoke operations on processor objects, and generate response messages. You can do this with a custom ISAPI extension, which offers significantly better performance, or with ASP pages, which are significantly easier to implement. As Figure 9-6 illustrates, most COM+ applications take the latter approach.

Note, however, that Figure 9-6 does not show how pages and objects relate to contexts. Whether an instance of a class executes in the same context as a page's scripts depends on both the class's declarative attributes and the page's `@Transaction` directive, if present. Remember that instances of configured or raw-configured classes cannot share a page's context if the page does not have an `@Transaction` attribute. If the page has an `@Transaction` attribute, even if it is `@Transaction = Not_Supported,` instances of configured or raw-

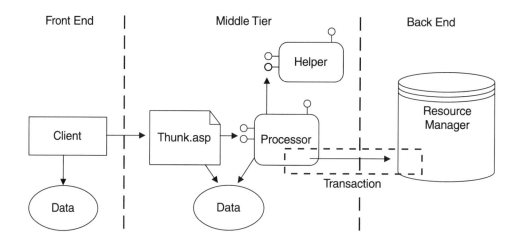

**Figure 9-6 Using ASP pages to integrate processors with HTTP**

configured classes can share the page's context. Processor and helper classes that use the default declarative attributes listed in Tables 9-1 and 9-2, respectively, will share the page's context. If an ASP page makes multiple calls to instances of configured or raw-configured classes that could share its context, it is worth adding an `@Transaction` directive (i.e., `@Transaction = Not_Supported`) simply to force the page's scripts to be processed in a context that can house those objects as well. This avoids multiple cross-context calls at the price of one (`asp.dll`'s invocation of `IASPObjectContext Custom::Call`). Of course, instances of processor classes that use declarative transactions and therefore JITA would still require contexts of their own.

If you compare the environment an ASP page's scripts execute in and the environment established by the SCM to house an instance of a processor class marked `COMAdminThreadingModelApartment`, you will see that their basic characteristics (e.g., STA, activity, and optional transaction stream) are the same. In other words, in addition to being exemplars for HTTP response messages, ASP pages are also equivalent to processor classes. The server-side scripts that pages use to help accomplish their tasks are similar to helper classes. They encapsulate reusable pieces of code that are always executed in their callers' contexts. In short, as Figure 9-7 illustrates, you can implement the

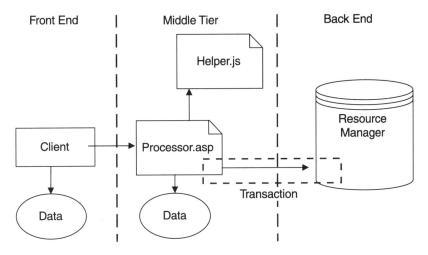

**Figure 9-7 Using ASP pages as processors**

model shown in Figure 9-6 using only pages and scripts, without any compiled code at all.

This simplified approach to the development of COM+-based systems is quite popular because it facilitates rapid development and easy deployment. However, there are downsides, including performance, which isn't as high as compiled C++ code, more difficult debugging, and the inability to take advantage of some useful COM+ runtime services such as object pooling. These problems are easily overcome by adding compiled classes as needed. Implementing processor logic using ASP pages and scripts creates inherently tight coupling to HTTP, and some would argue that this is a disadvantage as well because code cannot be easily reused in other contexts. Frankly, given the importance of HTTP today, and the increased role it is likely to play tomorrow, this is not much of an issue because many COM+-based systems are bound to HTTP anyway. It does make sense, however, to structure scripts so that processor logic can be invoked from multiple ASP pages. This makes it easier to support HTTP-based clients of different types, that is, some requesting HTML and some requesting raw XML or SOAP messages.

## Transactions and Data Access

Much of the work processor classes or pages do on their clients' behalf involves accessing information maintained by back-end databases. They protect their work using transactions, which maintain the integrity of distributed system state in the face of highly concurrent access and complex failure modes. For each client task a processor implements, you must decide whether a transaction is necessary and, if so, whether it should be a local or a declarative transaction, what isolation level it should run at, and how to deal with deadlocks. In addressing these issues, you must always remember that to maximize through-put, and therefore scalability, transactions must lock as little data as possible for as short a time as possible (Rule 1.2). The processor model helps by focus-ing attention on a single code path that can be validated for correctness and also tuned for performance.

If you are designing a processor, the key question is, Does it need a trans-action? As Chapter 7 observes, the conventional wisdom that database writes need transactions but that database reads do not need transactions is incorrect. In fact, if a task requires the execution of more than a single simple SQL state-ment, a transaction is almost certainly required. It is also important to remem-ber that you cannot determine transaction requirements by evaluating the work done by tasks individually. You must consider all tasks executing in parallel to understand how they might affect each other and how their work needs to be protected. If you are not sure whether a transaction is required in a particular situation, you should use one (it is better to be safe than sorry).

If a processor requires a transaction, you have to decide what sort of trans-action is required. Performance dictates that processors should use local trans-actions when they are working with individual RMs and declarative transactions when they are working with multiple RMs (Rule 6.5). If a processor class uses a declarative transaction, it must raise an error if it dooms its stream's distrib-uted transaction, it must manage RM locks efficiently but does not necessarily have to be stateless in the strict JITA sense, and it must not return references to nonroot objects to callers (Rules 6.1, 6.2, and 6.3).

If a processor class or page uses a transaction, you must decide what iso-lation level to use. Remember that there are no concrete rules for selecting a transaction's isolation level; the answer varies depending on the RM you are using and functionality of the application you are building (there are some gen-eral guidelines, summarized in Table 7-6). If a processor uses a local transac-tion, it can specify an isolation level explicitly. If a processor uses a declarative transaction, the COM+ runtime starts the underlying distributed transaction at isolation level 3, serializable. Most databases use this isolation level for connections that the OLE DB Service Components autoenlist against declarative transactions. Oracle, however, ignores it and uses isolation level 2, read committed. Processors can alter the isolation level of their declarative transactions using RM-specific techniques, which includes the standard `SET TRANSACTION ISOLATION LEVEL` statement and, in the case of SQL Server, `SELECT` statement table hints, that is, `SELECT * FROM TABLE (READ COMMITTED)`.

If a processor class or page uses a transaction, you also have to decide how to deal with deadlocks. The COM+ declarative transaction service can start distributed transactions with timeouts specified on a per-machine or per-class basis. In general, you should always configure declarative transactions to use as short a timeout as possible. OLE DB providers do not typically support timeouts for local transactions because RMs can detect internal deadlocks using wait-for graphs. As a result, processors must be very careful not to cause a deadlock involving RM locks held by a local transaction and some other blocking resource in a middle-tier process (e.g., an STA thread). One way to avoid this is to complete local transactions in a single roundtrip to the database so that no RM locks are held while a processor is doing work outside the database. Another way is to ensure that processors do not attempt to acquire resources that might cause them to block while a local transaction is still in progress.

### Accessing Data Efficiently

In addition to using the correct isolation levels and timeouts, if any, correctly, transactional processors can minimize locking in time and space by accessing data as efficiently as possible. First and foremost, this means avoiding unnecessary database work. Whenever possible, a processor should perform security checks, validate and preprocess input, post event messages via MSMQ, create other objects it needs to complete its task, and perform any other operations it can before starting its database work. Then, after all those operations succeed, it should manipulate RM-managed state. This approach ensures that connection acquisition is deferred for as long as possible and that distributed transactions are not started until they are needed. Once a processor starts to access data, it should complete its work as quickly as possible so its transaction can end and the RM locks it holds can be released.

One significant source of data access overhead in COM+-based systems is the expense of calling from a middle-tier process to a back-end database process in order to execute a SQL statement. As is always the case, network roundtrips adversely affect performance and must be kept to a minimum. A processor should not use a "data object" model derived from a database schema because, as Chapter 1 explains, they tend to introduce many more database calls than are actually necessary, greatly reducing performance. Instead, a processor should, whenever possible, use a stored procedure to execute all its data access operations in a single roundtrip to an RM. In some circumstances, a single stored procedure invocation cannot do everything a processor requires. When multiple stored procedure calls are necessary, a processor should execute them in a batch if possible. Not all databases and OLE DB providers support the use of batch statements. For instance, Oracle can process batch requests, but neither of the standard Oracle OLE DB providers handles output from batch statements correctly. In short, how well the batch processing technique works depends entirely on which database and provider you are using. SQL Server and SQLOLEDB process batch statements exceptionally well.

Processors should avoid extracting data from databases unless they are going to return it to their clients or cache it in their middle-tier server processes for future use. If a processor wants to update data, it should execute the appropriate SQL statements to update in place. Specifically, processors should use only OLE DB rowset objects and ADO `Recordset` objects to read the results of a query. They should never use them to modify data within a single transaction. Processors should access data in read-only, forward-only "fire hose" mode or using a client-side cursor. Processors should avoid server-side cursors because they consume too many database resources and introduce additional network roundtrips. This is a significant departure from the cursor-heavy data access style prevalent in stand-alone and two-tier client-server systems, which is too inefficient to scale well.

## Middle-Tier State

Processors use transactions to manipulate RM-managed state. While a processor's transaction is in progress, it holds RM locks against the data being accessed in order to maintain the illusion that there is only one transaction running at a time. However, this protection is only temporary. When the locks are released at the end of a processor's transaction—if not before, depending on isolation level—other processors can access and modify the data as they see fit. In short, processors deal with snapshots of data that are synchronized only periodically with original RM-managed state.

In most cases, processors exchange these snapshots of data with their clients, copying them back and forth as the input to and output from individual requests. How this is done varies by communication protocol, such as XML over HTTP, a marshal-by-value object over DCOM, or a persistent object over MSMQ. There are also times when it is useful to cache snapshots of data in a middle-tier process for use in responding to further requests. If you choose to do this, you have to keep several things in mind. First, memory is limited, and you have to use it efficiently. Second, memory is volatile, and you have to be prepared to lose information held in memory if a process crashes. Third, if state is stored in memory in a particular process on a particular machine, you have to come back to that process and machine to access it. Fourth, if, in order to avoid being bound to a particular machine, you cache the same state in multiple processes on multiple machines, you *may* need to keep all the copies synchronized. COM+ does not provide a standard infrastructure for keeping cached data synchronized across middle-tier servers; therefore, if you cache read-write data in multiple processes, you have to implement synchronization by hand (and in such a way that it does not introduce too much additional network traffic, sometimes known as "cache coherency cross-talk"). If you cache read-only reference data, such as a list of valid product IDs, this is not an issue.

COM+ offers the Shared Property Manager (SPM) and ASP offers its intrinsic `Application` object as standard ways to store state in a middle-tier process over time. Both of these mechanisms store named properties with arbitrary values: the SPM stores them on a per-process basis, and the `Application` stores them on a per-IIS application (that is, a per-WAM) basis. Unfortunately, neither the SPM nor the `Application` makes a very good cache because they both implement overly restrictive locking policies. The SPM stores properties in different groups, and each group has an exclusive, causality-based lock. An `Application` object stores properties together and protects them with a single, exclusive thread-based lock. At a minimum, each request to read or write a property's value requires the acquisition of the appropriate lock. If a processor class or page wants to perform multiple reads and writes on one or more properties, it can acquire and hold the appropriate lock over time (either by accessing the SPM group in `LockMethod` mode or by calling an ASP `Application` object's `Lock` method). Because both SPM groups and `Application` objects always use exclusive locks, processors cannot read from them concurrently, significantly reducing throughput.

In order to use SPM groups or `Application` objects, you need to know how they relate to contexts. Like most ASP intrinsic objects, `Application` objects custom marshal using the Free-Threaded Marshaler so they can be accessed from any context without interception. Processors access the SPM by instantiating a nonconfigured class called `SharedPropertyGroupManager`. Instances of `SharedPropertyGroupManager` do not custom marshal, but each processor is expected to create its own instance in its own context.[2] The end result in both cases is the same: Cached data can be accessed without the cost of interception, as Figure 9-8 shows. This is efficient, but it means that object references do not get marshaled when they are stored in or retrieved from either repository. Since SPM groups and `Application` objects can be accessed from different contexts, this violates the principle of interface pointer context relativity (Rule 3.1). In practice this means that processors should only put references to instances of raw-configured or nonconfigured classes that use the FTM (or a similar custom marshaling scheme) into SPM groups or `Application` objects.

ADO `Recordset` objects and MSXML `FreeThreadedDOMDocument` objects use the FTM and can be stored safely in either a SPM group or an `Application` object. By caching data using instances of these classes, proces-

---

[2] For esoteric mechanical reasons related to locking, instances of `SharedPropertyGroup Manager` and its subordinate objects do not work correctly in an apartment's default context. Nor do they work in the initial context ASP creates to execute a page's scripts. However, they do work correctly in the additional context ASP creates to execute the scripts of pages with an `@Transaction` attribute, including `@Transaction = Not_Supported`.

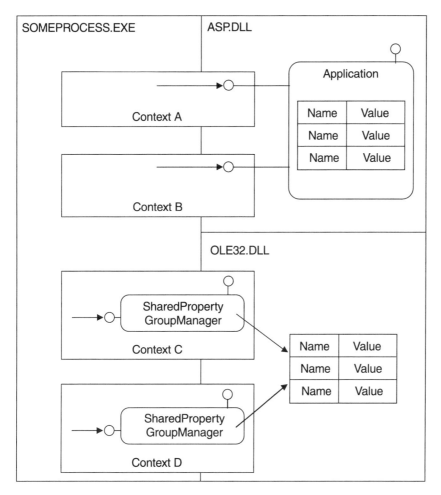

**Figure 9-8 The SPM application objects and contexts**

sors can reduce SPM or `Application` locking because an exclusive lock has to be held only long enough to extract a reference to the object encapsulating the desired data. Unfortunately, the `FreeThreadedDOMDocument` class also uses an exclusive lock to protect its internal state, so parallel access to it is impossible. The `Recordset` class does not use a lock to protect its internal state; parallel access is possible, but dangerous. Processors could ensure exclusive access by holding a lock against the SPM group or `Application` object they extract the `Recordset` reference from, but, again, this significantly reduces the usefulness of this infrastructure for caching.

Keeping snapshots of data cached in middle-tier processes for use in responding to further requests can improve performance by eliminating unnecessary roundtrips to back-end databases. It works particularly well when the data being cached is generic (i.e., it can be used by multiple clients) and read-only, so cache synchronization is not an issue. There is one situation, however, in which caching data in a middle-tier process is *not* a good idea. A middle-tier process is not the right place to maintain per-client "conversation state," information pertaining to a client task that is in progress. For instance, a middle-tier process is not the right place to keep track of the contents of a Web shopping cart before the client checks out and purchases whatever the cart contains.

The main problem with this approach is that per-client conversation state is not generic. If conversation state is stored in a process on a middle-tier machine, all of a client's requests have to be delivered to that process on that machine. Binding a client to a machine not only limits load balancing, but also creates additional work for a system's communication layer, which has to figure out to which process to deliver a given client request. Also, if a middle-tier process that is storing per-client conversation state crashes, the information is lost, which may or may not be a problem, depending on how important it was. In short, this approach hinders both scalability and reliability.

In practice, that means that processors should never use ASP `Session` objects or any other mechanism that stores conversation state in memory on a middle-tier machine. Instead, they should maintain conversation state in a client process or in a back-end database. If conversation state is kept in a client process, it must be sent up to a middle-tier server process with each request. This works as long as there is not too much data and the client knows what it is supposed to do with it. HTTP cookies provide an excellent example of client-managed conversation state. A server can send an HTTP response message back to a client containing a `Set-Cookie` header, indicating that the client should create a cookie with the specified value. HTTP clients know that they are supposed to use Cookie headers to send cookie values back to servers when they construct HTTP request messages that target resources in the namespace to which a cookie applies. This approach allows client requests to be routed to a different middle-tier server, but if the client process crashes, the conversation state is lost. In short, it solves the scalability but not the reliability problem. If there is a lot of conversation state or it has to be durable, it needs to be stored in a back-end database. In this case, clients propagate a small amount of conversation state—a key embedded in an HTTP cookie or passed some other way—that identifies their conversations' records. Processors executing in middle-tier server processes use these keys to access conversation state only when necessary, using transactions and the efficient data access techniques described. Although this approach may increase the number of roundtrips to databases, it provides both scalability and reliability, making it the preferred model for maintaining conversation state in COM+-based systems.

## Some Final Advice

This last chapter summarizes the lessons in this book and presents the archetypal model for COM+-based system architectures. It is important to note, however, that COM+ provides only a foundation for scalable distributed applications, nothing more. It simplifies many basic programming chores, but it leaves you with the real task: designing a distributed system that uses transactions. This is hard. So, beyond the ideas in this chapter, I want to give you some final advice. Keep your designs as simple as possible. Use as few machines and processes as you can and do not use COM+ services you do not need. It is hard to predict where bottlenecks will arise. In the early stages of a system's design, you should optimize based on broad structural limitations, such as roundtrips and memory footprint. During development, you should apply the guidelines prescribed in this chapter. You should also use profilers and stress testing tools to continually assess throughput and scalability, optimally as part of a nightly build process. (This work must be done on a set of machines configured to mirror the production environment in which a system will be deployed.) Some developers respond to this advice by saying, "I suppose you think I should write my code in assembly too?" The answer is no, but they are missing the point. Modern compilers can generate better assembly code than most people can write by hand, but there is no equivalent tool for distributed systems. It is hard to find and remove bottlenecks after a system is built, so you have to eliminate as many as possible during initial development. If you do these things, you can build COM+ applications that scale.

# Appendix A

# Toward .NET

Microsoft formally announced its .NET initiative at their Professional Developers Conference (PDC) in Orlando in July of 2000. .NET is the next step in the evolution of Microsoft's Windows DNA platform, the primary advance being the move from Web-enabled distributed systems to Web-centric distributed systems. This is a very subtle shift and may seem like so much marketing fluff, but it is very important because Microsoft has fully embraced XML as a core integration technology in order to facilitate the change.

In practical terms, the move toward .NET means two things. First, there will be new versions of operating systems and add-on servers intended to better integrate with the Web (in fact, many familiar software products have already been rebranded as .NET Servers, and COM+ is likely to be renamed .NET Component Services). Second, and of more immediate importance to developers, is the introduction of a next-generation component technology that is the heir apparent to—and completely backward compatible with—COM. The foundation of this new technology is the Common Language Runtime (CLR), which ships with the .NET Framework SDK (a beta version is available at the time of this writing). When most developers talk about .NET, they are really talking about the CLR and the languages that use it (e.g., C#, Visual Basic 7, and Managed C++).

The motivation for moving to the CLR is type information. Although COM does a reasonable job merging language type systems with its own component-technology type system, it doesn't go far enough, and many well-known type deficiencies have hindered COM developers for years. Specifically, not all languages can use all COM data types, so component designers have to target particular languages when they write code. The information in a COM typelib is not complete and does not accurately reflect everything that can be expressed in COM IDL. Also, the information in a component's typelib reflects only the types that component exposes, not the types it relies on. That fact makes it difficult to track dependencies between components. Finally, the information in a component's typelib reflects only the external details of that component's exposed types, that is, the signatures of its interfaces' methods and the names of its concrete classes, not the internal implementation details. Many might argue that this last point is not a weakness, because exposing a component's implementation details violates the principles of encapsulation. However, the lack of binary type information about a class's data members makes it impossible to implement many very useful services, such as automatic persistence of object graphs to a database or to XML. The CLR fixes all of these problems by making type information ubiquitous. CLR components include metadata that describes everything about them. The metadata is accessible via reflection and extensible via custom attributes.

The CLR is a replacement for COM, but not for COM+. CLR classes can be configured to use COM+ runtime services the same way that COM classes do. In fact, you can mix both classes using both component technologies in the same COM+-based system. This works because the CLR is backward-compatible with COM. The .NET Framework SDK simplifies COM+ programming by allowing you to define a class's declarative attributes inline using custom metadata attributes. There are tools that use reflection to support automatic Catalog registration based on the values of these attributes, either during installation time or the first time a class is instantiated. There is also a class called `Microsoft.ComServices.ContextUtil` that uses static methods and properties to simplify access to object context. Here is an example written in C# (the details may change before the .NET Framework SDK is released).

```
namespace DOTNET
{
  using System;
  using Microsoft.ComServices;
  [ Transaction(TransactionOption.Required) ]
  public class SomeTxClass : ServicedComponent
  {
    public SomeTxClass() {}
    public SomeMethod()
```

```
    {
        // turn done bit on and happy bit off
        ContextUtil.DeactivateOnReturn = true;
        ContextUtil.TransactionVote = TransactionVote.Abort;
        ... // do work that requires declarative transaction
        // turn happy bit back on
        ContextUtil.TransactionVote = TransactionVote.Commit;
    }
  }
}
```

The DOTNET.SomeTxClass class extends ServicedComponent, indicating to the CLR that it relies on COM+. It is marked with the Transaction attribute, so that its instances will be put into contexts in transaction streams. The SomeMethod method makes use of the distributed transaction and controls its outcome using the ContextUtil.Transaction and ContextUtil.DeactivateOnReturn properties, which set the state of the happy and done bits, respectively.

Although the .NET Framework SDK makes using declarative attributes easier, it does not simplify other aspects of COM+ programming. Specifically, you still have to be aware of contexts and causalities, threads, objects and transactions and how they relate to one another. Things will get simpler in some cases, but not in others. For instance, CLR classes use threading model Both implicitly, which means STAs—and all their inherent complexity—can be ignored; but if you mix CLR classes with COM classes written in Visual Basic, all of the STA issues return. There will be some new twists too. For example, while a CLR class's methods execute within an object's context, its static methods execute within the caller's context. This makes sense when you consider that static methods express class-level, not object-level, functionality; but it means you will have to be very careful when you use static methods or static data members. Also, it will be interesting to see how nondeterministic destruction (i.e., garbage collection) affects the management of resources such as database connections.

In addition to integrating with the COM+ context model, the .NET Framework SDK ships with classes that support a new context architecture based on intercepting calls made using SOAP. This new infrastructure, defined primarily in the System.Runtime.Remoting namespace, does not provide all the services that COM+ offers; for instance, it does not support declarative transactions. COM+ is likely to use this new framework someday, but it will not be ported for the initial .NET Framework release. That does not mean, however, that CLR-based classes cannot use COM+ services and new features too. For instance, the `ServicedComponent` base type that configured CLR classes extend is itself an extension of the `System.MarshalByRefObject` type, which allows it to integrate with the new SOAP-based remoting layer. (COM+ context properties such as activities and transaction streams will not flow via SOAP calls.)

Finally, in addition to the fundamental changes to programming style inherent in the adoption of the CLR, the new version of COM+ included with Windows.NET (Whistler) offers several new features, including the ability to mark configured classes as private so that they cannot be instantiated from outside an application and to specify declarative transaction isolation level on a per-class basis. It also includes some new tools for simplifying configuration management for clusters of systems.

The .NET Framework SDK and Windows.NET are both expected to ship sometime in the second half of 2001.

# Appendix B

# Building a Better Connection Pool

Chapter 5, "Objects," mentions that you can use the COM+ object pooling service to manage database connections more flexibly and with better performance than the connection pooling infrastructure provided by the OLE DB Service Components (and used by ADO). However, this approach to connection management relies on implementing pooled classes that violate the rules of pooled object resource management. It works only with OLE DB providers whose objects are context neutral, including the current implementation of the SQLOLEDB provider.

There are three problems with the standard OLE DB connection pooling mechanism. First, if a connection is not used for a period of time, it is considered stale and closed. There is no way to keep some small number of connections alive in a process. Second, there is no way to limit the number of connections a process can use. You cannot stop a single process from consuming all of the connections to a particular database, and thereby leaving other processes unable to read it. Third, acquiring a connection from the pool requires comparing requested initialization properties against each pooled connection's properties until a match is found.

Object pooling can solve all three of these problems. Instead of relying on the OLE DB Service Components to provide connection pooling, you create a pooled class whose instances hold OLE DB session objects that encapsulate database connections. Simply constraining the class's pool size using the `MinPoolSize` and `MaxPoolSize` attributes solves the first two problems. If you create one pooled class for each unique combination of database connection properties, you solve the third problem. When an object or an ASP page needs a database connection, it instantiates the corresponding pooled class. There is no need to search for a connection with the appropriate properties because all pooled instances of a class are, by definition, equivalent. For flexibility's sake, pooled connection classes can store their initialization properties as constructor strings that system administrators can modify as needed. Finally, for efficiency's sake, each pooled class should be raw-configured so that instances always live in their creators' contexts.

This object-based approach to connection pooling presents one significant technical challenge. A pooled connection object holds onto an OLE DB session object and uses it to execute SQL statements over time. For safety's sake, a reference to that session should never be handed out to a caller because if the caller held onto it, the pooled connection object would not know when to return to the pool. But if a pooled object does not expose its session reference to callers, it has to provide some way to indirectly execute SQL statements and to process their results. Unfortunately, a pooled object cannot simply execute a SQL statement and give back a reference to an OLE DB rowset because rowsets maintain internal references to the sessions that produced them. In short, handing out a reference to a rowset is equivalent to handing out a reference to a session.

The best long-term solution to this problem is for connection objects to use the object pooling service themselves because they know how they are being used and when it is safe to return to the pool. This is coming—the .NET SDK Framework's managed SQL provider's connection class, `System.Data.SQL.SQLConnection`, implements `IObjectControl`—but in the meantime, you have to solve this problem some other way.

The easiest solution is for the pooled connection object to use its internal session object to execute SQL statements on its client's behalf and to return a reference to an object that blindly aggregates the rowset and holds a reference to the pooled connection object itself, as shown in Figure B-1.

The beauty of this approach is that the client is unaware of the details and can use the rowset normally. The pooled connection object will be released when the rowset is released and can then return to its class's pool. This approach can be extended to handle OLE DB multiple result objects too.

## An Example

What follows is the definition of a pooled class that manages OLE DB sessions. It uses raw OLE DB instead of the ATL OLE DB consumer templates so that it can aggregate rowsets.

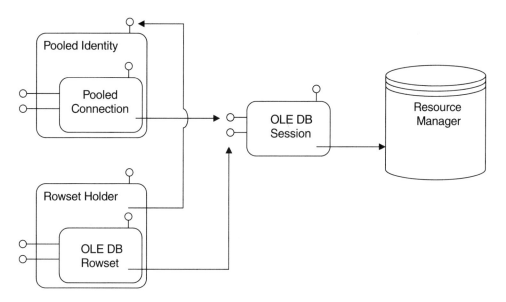

**Figure B-1    Pooled connection objects and aggregated rowsets**

```cpp
class CConn : public IObjectConstruct,
              public IObjectControl,
              public IConn,
              ... // other details removed for clarity
{
  CComPtr<IDBInitialize>      m_spSrc;
  CComPtr<IDBCreateCommand>   m_spSess;
  CComPtr<ITransactionJoin>   m_spTxJoin;
  GUID                        m_txId;
public:
  CConn() : m_txId(GUID_NULL) {}
  void FinalRelease()
  {
    m_spTxJoin.Release();
    m_spSess.Release();
    m_spSrc->Uninitialize();
    m_spSrc.Release();
  }
// IObjectConstruct
  STDMETHODIMP Construct(IDispatch *pCtorObj);
// IObjectControl
  STDMETHODIMP Activate(void);
  STDMETHODIMP_(BOOL) CanBePooled(void);
```

```
      STDMETHODIMP_(void) Deactivate(void);
   // IConn
      STDMETHODIMP ExecSQL(BSTR bstrSQL, long *pnRows,
                           REFIID riid, void **ppResults);
      ... // other details removed for clarity
   };
```

The `CConn` class implements three interfaces: `IObjectConstruct`, `IObjectControl`, and `IConn`. The first two interfaces are for integration with the COM+ object construct string mechanism and the object pooling service, respectively. Clients use the latter interface to submit SQL requests and retrieve their results. The class relies on four data members. The first one, `m_spSrc`, is a reference to an OLE DB data source object. The second two, `m_spSess` and `m_spTxJoin`, are references to the same OLE DB session object. The last data member, `m_txId`, is for managing distributed transaction enlistment when instances of the class are used from contexts in transaction streams.

### IObjectConstruct

Let's examine the `CConn` class's implementation of each of its three interfaces in detail, starting with `IObjectConstruct`. Here is the definition of the `Construct` method. It is called once for each object when the object is created.

```
STDMETHODIMP CConn::Construct(IDispatch *pCtorObj)
{
  // retrieve strongly-typed constructor object interface
  CComPtr<IObjectConstructString> spCtorStr;
  HRESULT hr = pCtorObj->QueryInterface(__uuidof(spCtorStr),
                                        (void**)&spCtorStr);
  if (FAILED(hr)) return hr;
  // retrieve constructor string
  CComBSTR bstr;
  hr = spCtorStr->get_ConstructString(&bstr);
  if (FAILED(hr)) return hr;
  // append property to disable OLE DB Service Components
  bstr += L";OLE DB Services=0";
  // create OLE DB provider factory
  CComPtr<IDataInitialize> spDataInit;
  hr = spDataInit.CoCreateInstance(CLSID_MSDAINITIALIZE);
  if (FAILED(hr)) return hr;
```

```
    // ask factory to load desired provider
    CComPtr<IDBInitialize> spDBInit;
    hr = spDataInit->GetDataSource(0, CLSCTX_ALL, bstr,
                                   uuidof(spDBInit),
                                   (IUnknown**)&spDBInit);
    if (FAILED(hr)) return hr;
    // initialize provider
    hr = spDBInit->Initialize();
    if (FAILED(hr)) return hr;
    // create session
    CComPtr<IDBCreateSession> spDBCreateSess;
    hr = spDBInit->QueryInterface(__uuidof(spDBCreateSess),
                                  (void**)&spDBCreateSess);
    if (FAILED(hr)) return hr;
    hr = spDBCreateSess->CreateSession(0, __uuidof(m_spSess),
                                       (IUnknown**)&m_spSess);
    if (FAILED(hr)) return hr;
    // retrieve ITransactionJoin reference and cache it
    hr = m_spSess->QueryInterface(__uuidof(m_spTxJoin),
                                  (void**)&m_spTxJoin);
    if (FAILED(hr)) return hr;
    return S_OK;
}
```

The implementation of `Construct` sets up a database connection. It retrieves an OLE DB initialization string (the class's constructor string) from the constructor object that COM+ passed in. It appends a property, `OLE DB Services = 0`, which disables the Service Component's intrinsic connection pooling and autoenlistment mechanisms. Then, `Construct` initializes its `m_spSrc`, `m_spSess`, and `m_spTxJoin` data members. This establishes a connection with the data source identified by the constructor string. These interface pointers are released in the class's implementation of `FinalRelease`. By acquiring these interface pointers before activation, instances of the `CConn` class violate Rule 5.2. By holding onto the references across activation cycles, they also violate Rule 5.3. This works only if an OLE DB provider's objects are context neutral, as is the case with SQLOLEDB.[1]

---

[1] Unfortunately, this is not programmatically verifiable, that is, SQLOLEDB's objects do not use the FTM. You simply have to trust that it will work correctly.

## IObjectControl

Here are the definitions for all three `IObjectControl` methods. `Activate` is the only interesting method. It is called each time a pooled connection object begins an activation cycle.

```
STDMETHODIMP CConn::Activate(void)
{
  GUID txId = { 0 };
  // get reference to object context
  CComPtr<IObjectContextInfo> spCtxInfo;
  HRESULT hr = CoGetObjectContext(__uuidof(spCtxInfo),
                                  (void**)&spCtxInfo);
  // test for non-default context in transaction stream
  if (SUCCEEDED(hr) && spCtxInfo->IsInTransaction())
  {
    // if in transaction stream, get transaction ID
    hr = spCtxInfo->GetTransactionId(&txId);
    if (FAILED(hr)) return hr;
    // compare current transaction ID to previous
    // transaction ID, if they do not match connection
    // must be enlisted
    if (txId != m_txId)
    {
      // get current transaction
      CComPtr<IUnknown> spTxUnk;
      hr = spCtxInfo->GetTransaction(&spTxUnk);
      if (FAILED(hr)) return hr;
      CComPtr<ITransaction> spTx;
      hr = spTxUnk->QueryInterface(&spTx);
      if (FAILED(hr)) return hr;
      // enlist connection against transaction
      hr = m_spTxJoin->JoinTransaction(spTx,
                     ISOLATIONLEVEL_SERIALIZABLE, 0, 0);
      if (FAILED(hr)) return hr;
    }
  }
  else if (m_txId != GUID_NULL)
  {
    // if not in transaction stream and old transaction ID is not 0
    // unenlist connection from previous distributed transaction
    hr = m_spTxJoin->JoinTransaction(0, 0, 0, 0);
    if (FAILED(hr)) return hr;
  }
  // store current transaction if (may be 0)
```

```
   // as previous transaction ID
   m_txId = txId;
   return S_OK;
}
STDMETHODIMP_(void) CConn::Deactivate(void) { return; }
STDMETHODIMP_(BOOL) CConn::CanBePooled(void) { return TRUE; }
```

The CConn class uses the Activate method to autoenlist against declarative transactions. It extracts a reference to object context and uses it to determine if a pooled object is being activated in a context in a transaction stream. If it is, the method extracts the stream's distributed transaction's ID. It compares the current transaction ID to the transaction ID from the previous activation cycle, which is stored in m_txId (and may be 0). If the values are different, Activate knows this is the first time the pooled object has been used in the transaction stream, so it extracts a reference to the stream's transaction and uses the ITransactionJoin reference cached in m_spTxJoin to enlist the database connection against it. If the pooled object is being activated in a context that is not in a transaction, Activate examines the transaction ID from the previous activation cycle. If it is not 0, it uses the ITransactionJoin reference cached in m_spTxJoin to unenlist the database connection. Finally, Activate stores the current context's transaction ID in m_txId for use the next time the object is activated. If the current context is not in a transaction stream, m_txId is set to 0.

Remember that connections that are enlisted against a DTC-dispensed distributed transaction must remain open and enlisted until the transaction ends. If they do not, the distributed transaction cannot commit. The OLE DB Service Components connection pooling infrastructure ensures that this will always be the case by keeping enlisted connections in special transaction-specific reservoirs until their transactions end and then returning them to the general pool. The pooled object technique must exhibit the same behavior. Fortunately, this is built into the object pooling service. If a pooled object touches its context's transaction, that is, it calls IObjectContextInfo::GetTransaction, the object pooling service will keep it in a special transaction-specific pool. While the object is in that pool, it can be reused in other contexts in the same transaction stream. When the stream's distributed transaction ends, the pooling service returns the object to its class's main pool.

### IConn

Finally, here is the definition of the ExecSQL method exposed by the IConn interface.

```
STDMETHODIMP CConn::ExecSQL(BSTR bstrSQL, long *pnRows,
                            REFIID riid, void **ppResults)
{
  *pnRows = 0;
  *ppResults = 0;
  // create OLE DB command
  CComPtr<ICommand> spCmd;
  HRESULT hr = m_spSess->CreateCommand(0, __uuidof(spCmd),
                                       (IUnknown**)&spCmd);
  if (FAILED(hr)) return hr;
  // set command text
  CComPtr<ICommandText> spCmdText;
  hr = spCmd->QueryInterface(__uuidof(spCmdText),
                             (void**)&spCmdText);
  if (FAILED(hr)) return hr;
  hr = spCmdText->SetCommandText(DBGUID_DBSQL, bstrSQL);
  if (FAILED(hr)) return hr;
  // create outer object to aggregate rowset
  CComPtr<IRowsetHolder> spHolder;
  hr = CRowsetHolder::CreateInstance(&spHolder);
  if (FAILED(hr)) return hr;
  // attach self to holder
  hr = spHolder->AttachConnection(GetControllingUnknown());
  if (FAILED(hr)) return hr;
  // execute statement and aggregate generated rowset
  long nRows = 0;
  CComPtr<IUnknown> spRowset;
  hr = spCmd->Execute(spHolder, __uuidof(spRowset), 0,
                      &nRows, (IUnknown**)&spRowset);
  if (FAILED(hr)) return hr;
  // if there is a rowset, store reference to its inner
  // IUnknown in outer object and ask for desired pointer
  if (spRowset)
  {
    hr = spHolder->AttachRowset(spRowset);
    if (FAILED(hr)) return hr;
    hr = spHolder->QueryInterface(riid, ppResults);
    if (FAILED(hr)) return hr;
  }
```

```
    // return count of rows
    *pnRows = nRows;
    return S_OK;
}
```

The ExecSQL method creates an OLE DB command object for the state-ment passed in by the client. Then it constructs an instance of a helper class called CRowsetHolder to aggregate the command's output, if any, and attaches itself to the holder by calling IRowsetHolder::Attach Connection. Next, SQLExec executes the client's command, passing a refer-ence to the CRowsetHolder object as first parameter. If the command gener-ates a rowset, the method stores a reference to the rowset's inner IUnknown in the CRowsetHolder object by calling IRowsetHolder::AttachRowset and then querying the holder object for the interface requested by the client. If everything works, ExecSQL returns a reference to the aggregated rowset, if any, and a count of rows affected by the statement.

Here is the implementation of the CRowsetHolder class. Notice that this class uses COM_INTERFACE_ENTRY_AGGREGATE_BLIND macro to blindly for-ward requests for interfaces it does not support to its inner rowset object.

```
class CRowsetHolder : public IRowsetHolder,
                      ... // other details removed for clarity
{
  CComPtr<IUnknown> m_spConn;
  CComPtr<IUnknown> m_spRowset;
public:
  CRowsetHolder() {}
BEGIN_COM_MAP(CRowsetHolder)
  COM_INTERFACE_ENTRY(IRowsetHolder)
  COM_INTERFACE_ENTRY_AGGREGATE_BLIND(m_spRowset.p)
END_COM_MAP()
// IRowsetHolder
  STDMETHODIMP AttachConnection(IUnknown *pConn)
  {
    if (!pConn) return E_INVALIDARG;
    return pConn->QueryInterface(__uuidof(m_spConn),
                                  (void**)&m_spConn);
  }
  STDMETHODIMP AttachRowset(IUnknown *pRowset)
  {
```

```
    if (!pRowset) return E_INVALIDARG;
    return pRowset->QueryInterface(__uuidof(m_spRowset),
                                   (void**)&m_spRowset);
  }
  ... // other details removed for clarity
};
```

## Using a Pooled Connection

Here is a sample client that uses the `CConn` class to execute a SQL statement and the ATL OLE DB consumer templates to process the results.

```
HRESULT CSomeTxClass::SomeMethod(void)
{
  // get reference to object context
  CComPtr<IContextState> spCtxState;
  HRESULT hr = CoGetObjectContext(__uuidof(spCtxState),
                                  (void**)&spCtxState);
  if (FAILED(hr)) return hr;
  // turn done bit on and happy bit off
  hr = spCtxState->SetDeactivateOnReturn(VARIANT_TRUE);
  if (FAILED(hr)) return hr;
  hr = spCtxState->SetMyTransactionVote(TxAbort);
  if (FAILED(hr)) return hr;
  // get connection from pool
  CComPtr<IConn> spConn;
  hr = spConn.CoCreateInstance(__uuidof(Conn));
  if (FAILED(hr)) return hr;
  // execute statement
  long nRows = 0;
  CAccessorRowset<CDynamicAccessor, CRowset> rowset;
  hr = spConn->ExecSQL(CComBSTR("select customerid from orders"),
                       &nRows, __uuidof(rowset.m_spRowset),
                       (void**)&rowset.m_spRowset);
  if (FAILED(hr)) return hr;
  // process results
  while ((hr = rowset.MoveNext()) == S_OK)
  {
    long nCustomerId = *(long*)rowset.GetValue(1);
    ... // do something with customer ID
  }
  // close rowset and release connection so it can be reused
  rowset.Close();
  spConn.Release();
```

```
    // turn happy bit back on
    hr = spCtxState->SetMyTransactionVote(TxCommit);
    if (FAILED(hr)) return hr;
    return S_OK;
}
```

## Source Code

The complete source code for this example is available on the book's Web site, *http://www.develop.com/books/txcom.*

# Appendix C

# Debugging

Debugging is an integral part of developing software, including components that rely on COM+. To debug a COM+ class, you have to be able to attach a debugger to the COM+ process that loads your DLL. The easiest way to do this is to launch the server process from inside Visual C++.[1] You can configure your DLL project's debugging options using the Project Settings property sheet. On the Debug tab, set the executable for the debug session to `c:\winnt\system32\dllhost.exe`, the COM+ surrogate server process. Set the program arguments to `/ProcessId:{applicationid}`, where `{applicationid}` is the GUID that identifies the application your class is used in. You can get an application's ID from the Component Services Explorer. It is on the General tab of both an application's property sheet and a configured class's property sheet.

If you want to, you can also attach a debugger to a COM+ server process that is already running. The status view of the COM+ Applications folder in Component Services Explorer lists the process IDs for all the COM+ server processes that are running. Once you've identified the process you want to debug, you can attach a debugger to it by finding it on the Processes tab in Task Manager, right-clicking, and selecting the Debug option. You have to use this technique to debug code in an IIS application. You cannot launch an IIS application server process from inside Visual C++.

Before you debug a COM+ server application, you should use the Component Services Explorer to adjust a couple of attributes and make the

---

[1] You have to use the Visual C++ debugger even if you are working in Visual Basic 6 because the VB IDE's integrated debugger does not work correctly with code that accesses object context. You can debug VB code in Visual C++ if you compile it with the Create Symbolic Debug Info option turned on.

**Table C-1   HRESULT decoder ring**

| Pattern | Technology | Defined in... |
| --- | --- | --- |
| 0x8004e0xx | Context | winerror.h |
| 0x8004d0xx | Transactions | transact.h |
| 0x0004d0xx | Transactions | transact.h, alternate success codes |
| 0x80040exx | OLE DB | oledberr.h |
| 0x00040exx | OLE DB | oledberr.h, alternate success codes |
| 0x800a0xxx | ADO | adoint.h |
| 0xc00e00xx | MSMQ | mqoai.h |
| 0x400e00xx | MSMQ | mqoai.h, warnings |

debugging process easier. First, you should set the application to execute as Interactive User. This setting is on the Identity tab of an application's property sheet. You may also want to set an application to shut down immediately when the last object is released to make it easier to rapidly rebuild class DLLs without linker errors. This setting is on the Advanced tab of an application's property sheet. Finally, you may want to disable timeouts for transactional objects so that transactions do not expire while you trace through code. The per-class timeout setting is on the Transactions tab of a class's property sheet. The per-machine timeout setting is on the Options tab of a computer's property sheet.

When you debug COM+ code, you're likely to encounter unfamiliar HRESULTs. COM+ systems involve lots of different technologies, and debugging COM+ code is easier if you know which technologies use which error codes. Table C-1 lists some standard patterns for HRESULTS, the technologies that generate them, and the header files where they are defined.

Appendix D

# Catalog Attributes and Component Services Explorer Property Pages

This appendix contains screens showing the attributes used by the COM+ catalog mapped to the property page user-interface elements used by Component Services Explorer (CSE).

# Application Property Pages

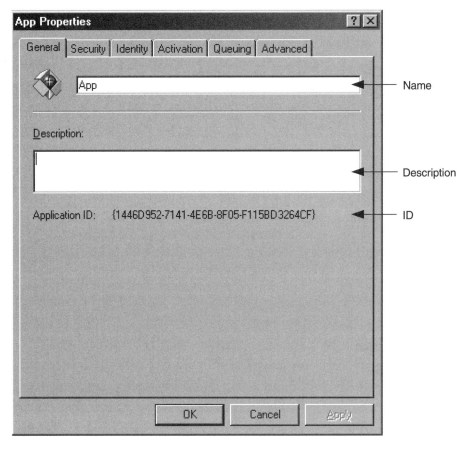

**Figure D-1  Application general properties**

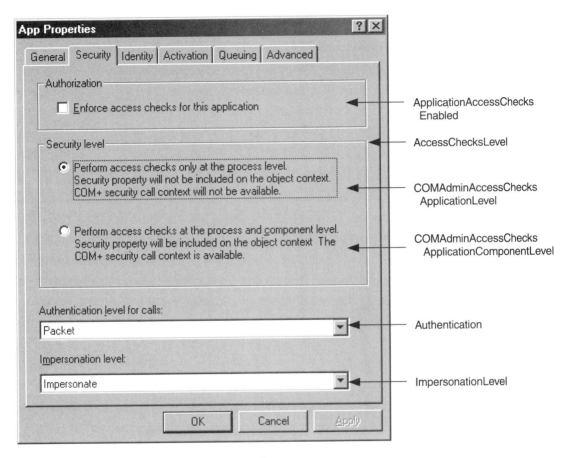

Figure D-2   **Application security properties**

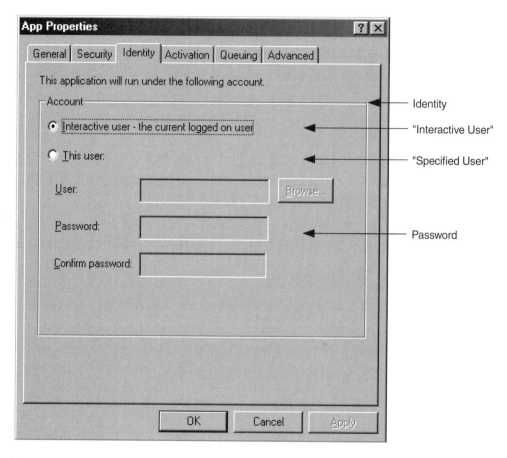

Figure D-3 Application identity properties

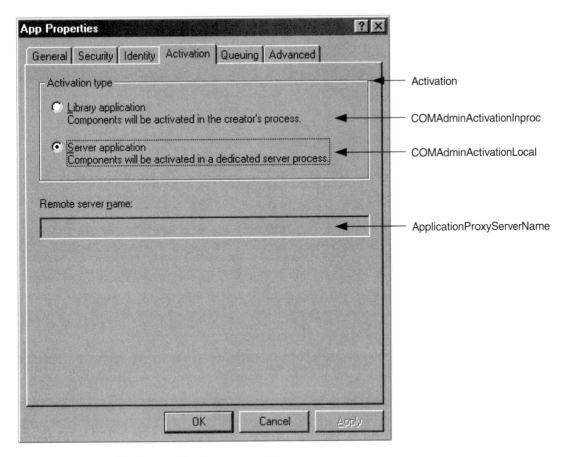

Figure D-4    Application activation properties

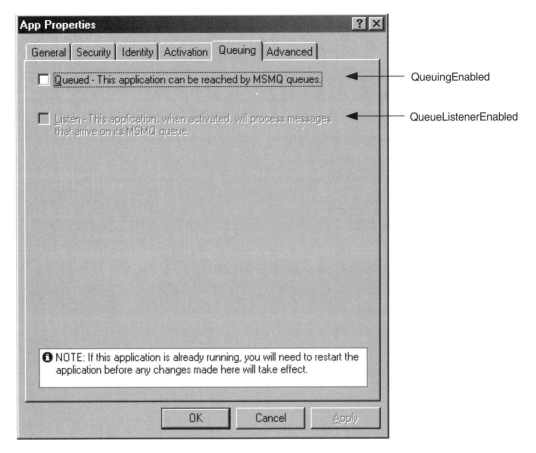

Figure D-5   Application queuing properties

TRANSACTIONAL COM+: BUILDING SCALABLE APPLICATIONS

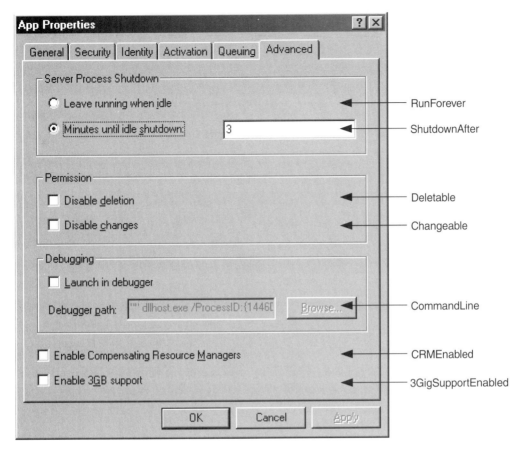

Figure D-6  Application advanced properties

# Class Property Pages

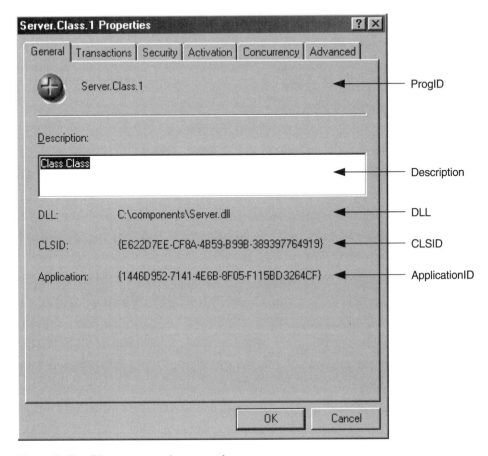

Figure D-7    Class general properties

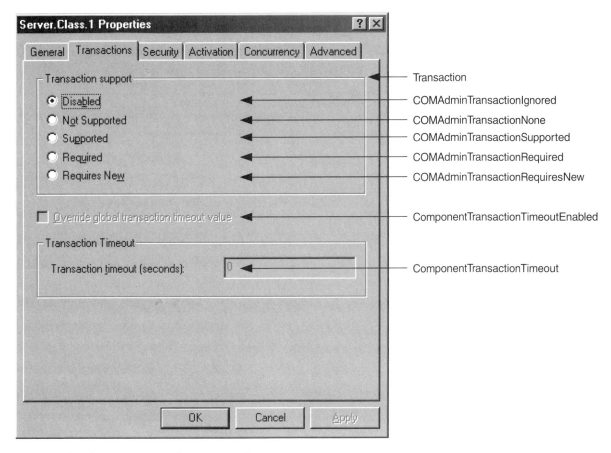

Figure D-8   Class transaction properties

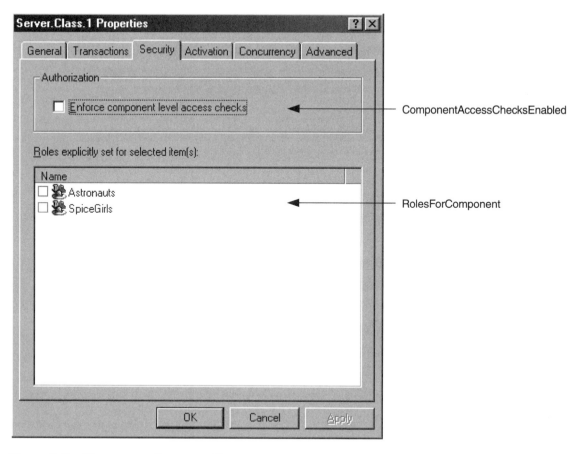

Figure D-9   Class security properties

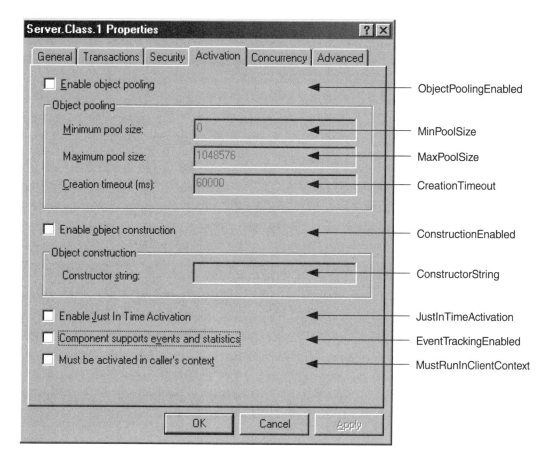

Figure D-10   Class activation properties

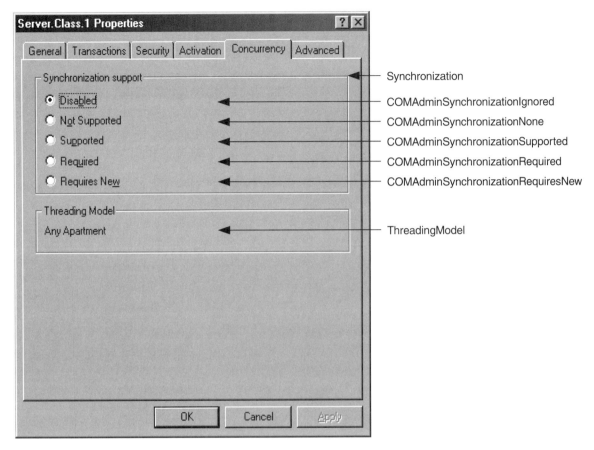

Figure D-11    Class concurrency properties

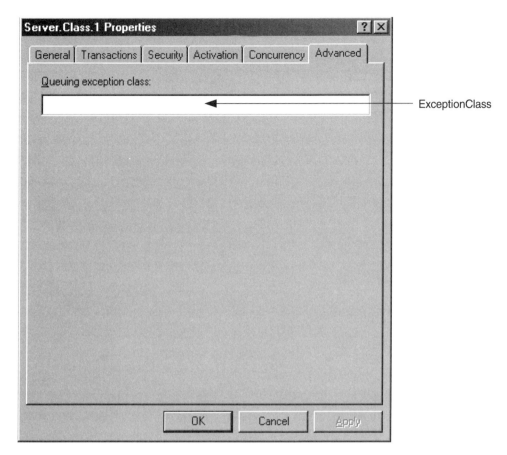

ExceptionClass

**Figure D-12 Class advanced properties**

# Interface Property Pages

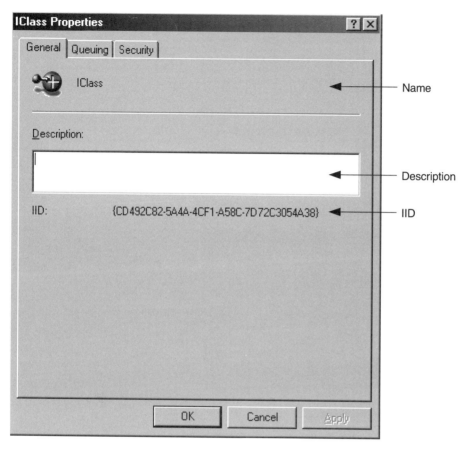

Figure D-13  Interface general properties

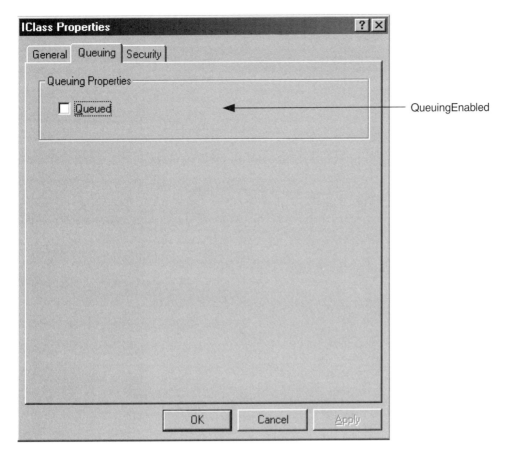

**Figure D-14  Interface queuing properties**

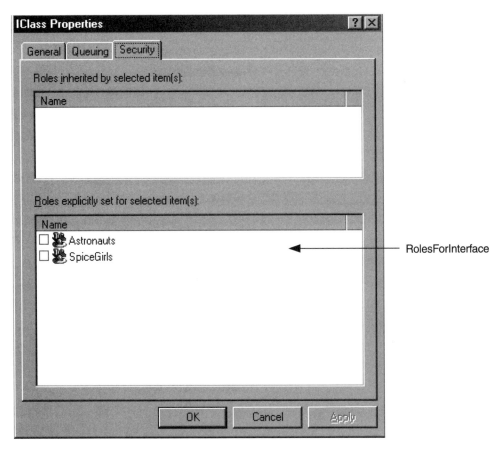

RolesForInterface

Figure D-15   Interface security properties

# Method Property Pages

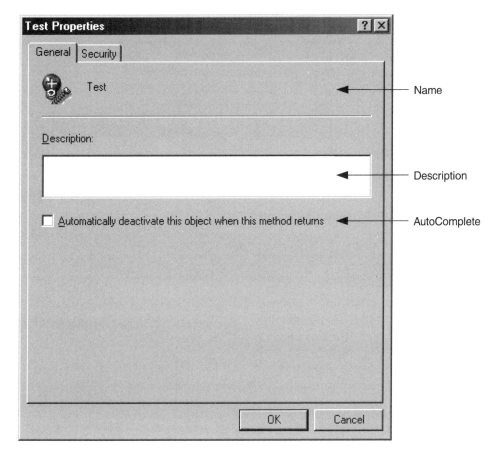

Figure D-16  Method general properties

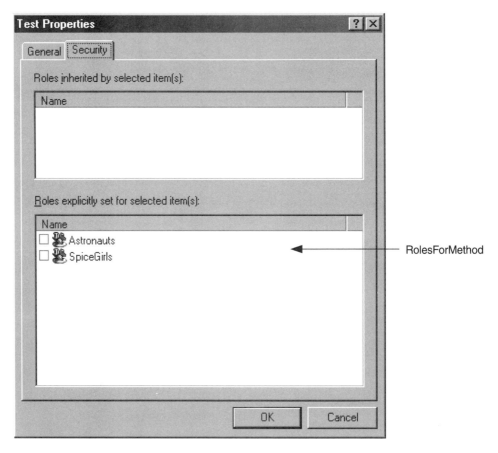

Figure D-17   Method security properties

# Rules Summary

**RULE 1.1**

COM+ clients do not share physical COM objects; they only share state stored in middle-tier processes and back-end databases. This is the object-per-client model.

**RULE 1.2**

To maximize throughput, lock as little data as possible for as short a time as possible.

**RULE 1.3**

Model client tasks using processor objects that execute on middle-tier servers.

**RULE 2.1**

Do not change any configured class's declarative attributes (other than constructor string and security settings) without the express permission of the author, who is the only one who can verify which settings are safe.

**RULE 3.1**

Do not pass interface pointers from one context to another without using a system-provided facility (e.g., system API, COM interface method, the Global Interface Table) to translate the reference to work in the destination context.

**RULE 3.2**

Give raw-configured classes preference over configured classes whenever possible to reduce context and interception overhead. Always use this technique for classes that do not care about context. Consider using this technique for classes that do care about context if you can guarantee that they will behave correctly in any context.

**RULE 3.3**

Use instances of raw-configured (or nonconfigured) classes to help implement the methods of configured classes, but do not return references to them to callers.

**RULE 3.4**

If a configured class does return a reference to an instance of a raw-configured class to a caller, make sure the raw-configured class uses custom marshaling.

**RULE 4.1**

Use threading model Both (Any) whenever possible, with the following caveats:
- Use threading model Apartment when there is no alternative.
- Match a class's threading model to the threading model of the classes it depends on, where appropriate.
- Use threading model Free for classes with methods that block the calling thread indefinitely.
- Use threading model Neutral for classes whose instances are called from multiple apartments in the same process (rare, but may be useful for building plumbing).
- Never use threading model Main.

**RULE 4.2**

Use synchronization Required whenever possible. Use the other synchronization settings only if you are stepping outside the object-per-client model or starting your own threads.

**RULE 5.1**

Classes that use object pooling should implement `IObjectControl`.

**RULE 5.2**

A pooled object should access context only during an activation cycle.

**RULE 5.3**

Classes that use object pooling must not hold context-relative resources across activation cycles.

**RULE** **5.4**

Use object pooling when the following is true:
- The cost of creating and destroying an object is greater than the cost of activating and deactivating an object.
- You want to specify a lower or upper bound on the number of instances of a class that can exist in memory at a time.

**RULE** **5.5**

Do not use JITA unless another service (i.e., declarative transactions) requires it. Implement your classes to manage resources efficiently.

**RULE** **6.1**

A transactional object must raise an error when it completes a method in the SetAbort state (unhappy and done).

**RULE** **6.2**

A transactional object must manage RM locks efficiently (however, this does not imply that it must be stateless.)

**RULE** **6.3**

A transactional object should not expose a transaction stream's nonroot objects to clients.

**RULE** **6.4**

A transactional object must be a processor.

**RULE** **6.5**

COM+ classes should use local transactions to protect work against a single RM and declarative transactions to protect work against multiple RMs.

# Index

# O

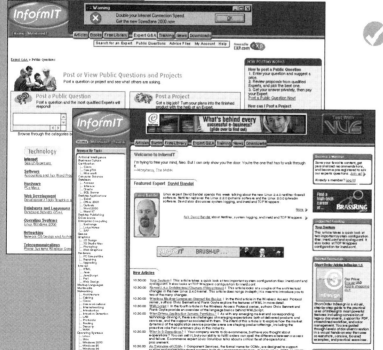